W9-ADZ-572

Commentary *on the* First Epistle *to the* Corinthians

CHARLES HODGE

WILLIAM B. EERDMANS PUBLISHING COMPANY
GRAND RAPIDS, MICHIGAN

Published by Wm. B. Eerdmans Publishing Co.
255 Jefferson Ave. S.E., Grand Rapids, Michigan 49503

First printing 1950
Paperback edition published 1980

Reprinted 1994

ISBN 0-8028-8031-2

INTRODUCTION

§ 1. Corinth.

The Grecian Peloponnesus is connected with the continent by an isthmus from four to six miles wide. On this isthmus stood the city of Corinth. A rocky eminence, called the Acrocorinthus, rises from the plain almost perpendicularly, to the height of two thousand feet above the level of the sea, and is sufficiently broad at the summit for a town of considerable size. From the top of this abrupt hill the eye reaches towards the east over the expanse of the Ægean sea, with its numerous islands; and westward, towards the Ionian sea, a prospect scarcely less inviting was presented. Looking towards the north, the eye rests on the mountains of Attica on the one hand, and north-eastern Greece on the other. The Acropolis of Athens was clearly visible at a distance of forty-five miles. As early as the days of Homer, Corinth was an important city. Its position made it, in a military point of view, the key of the Peloponnesus; and its command of a port on two seas, made it the centre of commerce between Asia and Europe. The supremacy enjoyed by one Grecian State after another, had at last fallen to the lot of Corinth. It became the chief city of Greece, not only in authority but in wealth, magnificence, literature, the arts, and in luxury. It was characteristic of the place, that while the temple of Minerva crowned the Acropolis of Athens, the Acrocorinthus was the site of the temple of Venus. Of all the cities of the ancient world it was most notorious for licentiousness. It was entirely destroyed by the Roman consul Mummius, 120 years B. C., its inhabitants were dispersed, and the conqueror carried with him to Rome the richest spoils that ever graced the triumph of a Roman General. For a century after this event it lay in ruins, serving only as a quarry whence the Roman patricians gathered marble for their palaces. Julius Cæsar, recognizing the military and commercial importance of the position, determined to rebuild it, and for that purpose sent thither a colony consisting principally of freed men. This accounts for the predominance of Latin names which we meet with in connection with the Christians of this city. Erastus, Phoebe and Sosthenes are Greek names; but Gaius, Quintus, Fortunatus, Crispus, Justus, Achaicus are of Roman origin. This colony, however, was little more than the nucleus of the new city. Merchants flocked thither from all parts of Greece; Jews also were attracted by the facilities of commerce; wealth, art, literature and luxury revived. The Isthmian games were again celebrated under the presidency of the city. It was made the capital of Achaia, which, as a Roman province, included the greater part of Greece. Under the fostering care of Augustus, Corinth regained much of its ancient splendour, and during the century which had nearly elapsed since its restoration, before it was visited by the apostle Paul, it had reached a preëminence which made it the glory of Greece. It was at this time under the rule of the Proconsul Gallio, the brother of Seneca;—a man distinguished for integrity and mildness. His brother says of him: *Nemo enim mortalium uni tam dulcis est, quam hic omnibus.* His refusal to entertain the frivolous charges brought by the Jews against Paul (Acts 18, 14–16), is in keeping with the character given of him by his contemporaries. He was one of the victims of the cruelty of Nero.*

§ 2. Paul's Labours in Corinth.

As Corinth was not only the political capital of Greece, but the seat of its commercial and intellectual life; the place of concourse for the people not only of the neighbouring cities but of nations; a source whence influences of all kinds emanated in every direction, it was specially important for the diffusion of the gospel. Paul therefore, leaving Athens, which he had visited in his second missionary journey, went alone to Corinth, where he was soon after joined by Silas and Timotheus, who came from Macedonia. (Acts 18, 5.) A stranger in this great city, and without the means of support, he associated himself with Aquila, a Jew lately come from Italy in consequence of the edict of Claudius banishing the Jews from Rome. While living in the house of Aquila, and working with him at his trade of tent making, Paul attended the synagogue every Sabbath, and "persuaded the Jews and Greeks." But "when they opposed themselves and blasphemed, he shook his raiment and said unto them, Your blood be upon your own heads. I am clean: henceforth I will go unto the Gentiles. And he departed thence and went into a certain man's house named Justus, one who worshipped God, and whose house joined hard to the synagogue. And Crispus, the chief ruler of the synagogue, believed on the Lord, with all his house; and many of the Corinthians hearing it believed and were baptized. Then spake the Lord to Paul by night, by a vision,

* Several monographs, proceeding from German scholars, are devoted to the description and history of Corinth. Wilchen's "Rerum Corinthiarum specimen ad illustrationem utriusque Epistolæ Paulinæ." 1747. Barth's "Corinthiorum Commercia et Mercaturae particula." Berlin, 1844. A very interesting chapter in Conybeare and Howson's Life and Epistles of Paul is devoted to this subject. Vol. 1: ch. 12. See also Winer's Real Wörterbuch and Arnold's Epistles of Paul to the Corinthians.

Be not afraid, but speak, and hold not thy peace: for I am with thee, and no man shall set on thee to hurt thee; for I have much people in this city. And he continued there a year and six months, teaching the word of God among them." (Acts 18, 1–11.) The success of Paul aroused the enmity of the Jews, who determined to arraign him before the Roman Governor. As soon as the governor ascertained the nature of the charge he refused to listen to it, and dismissed the accusers from the judgment seat with evident displeasure, which encouraged the bystanders to beat the Jews. Thus the opposers of the apostle were ignominiously defeated. After remaining some time longer in Corinth he sailed from Cenchrea, the eastern port of the city, to Ephesus, with Aquila and Priscilla. Leaving his friends in that city he sailed to Cæsarea, and thence went up to Jerusalem. After remaining a short time in the Holy City he went to Antioch, and thence through Phrygia and Galatia again to Ephesus. Shortly after Paul left Ephesus the first time, Apollos, an Alexandrian Jew, having been more fully instructed in the doctrine of Christ by Aquila and Priscilla, went to Corinth, and there "mightily convinced the Jews, and that publicly, shewing by the Scripture that Jesus was the Christ." (Acts 18, 24–28.) It is altogether probable, considering the constant commercial intercourse between Corinth and Ephesus, that the apostle had frequent opportunities of hearing of the state of the Corinthian church during his three years' residence in the latter city. The information which he received led him, as is generally supposed, to write a letter no longer extant, exhorting them "not to keep company with fornicators." (See 1 Cor. 5, 9.) Not satisfied with this effort to correct an alarming evil, he seems himself to have made them a brief visit. No record is indeed found in the Acts of his having been to Corinth more than once before the date of this epistle; but there are several passages in his second epistle which can hardly be understood otherwise than as implying an intermediate visit. In 2 Cor. 12, 14 he says, "Behold the third time I am ready to come to you." This may indeed mean that for the third time he had prepared to go to Corinth, but this the context does not suggest, and would really amount to nothing. It was not how often he had purposed to visit them, but how often he had actually made the journey, which was the point on which stress is laid. In ch. 13, 1 he says, "This is the third time I am coming to you," which is still more explicit. In ch. 2, 1 he says, "I determined I would not come again to you in heaviness." This supposes that he had already made them one sorrowful visit, i. e. one in which he had been obliged to cause sorrow, as well as to experience it. See also ch. 12, 21, and 13, 2, where further allusion seems to be made to a second visit. Notwithstanding his frequent injunctions, the state of things in Corinth seemed to be getting worse. The apostle therefore determined to send Timothy and Erastus to them (1 Cor. 4, 17. Acts 19, 22.) Whether Timothy reached Corinth at this time is doubtful; and it would seem from 1 Cor. 16, 10, that the apostle himself feared that he might not be able to accomplish all that had been appointed him in Macedonia, and yet get to Corinth before the arrival of this letter. After the departure of Timothy, Paul received such intelligence from the household of Chloe, and from a letter addressed to him by the Corinthians themselves (1 Cor. 7, 1), that he determined at once to write to them.

§ 3. State of the Church in Corinth.

The state of the church in Corinth may be partially inferred from the character and circumstances of the people, but with certainty only from the contents of this and the following epistles. As remarked above, the population of the city was more than ordinarily heterogeneous. The descendants of the colonists sent by Julius Cæsar, the Greeks who were attracted to the principal city of their own country, Jews and strangers from all parts of the Roman Empire, were here congregated. The predominant character of the people was doubtless Grecian.

The majority of the converts to Christianity were probably Greeks, as distinguished from Jews. (See ch. 12, 1.) In all ages the Greeks were distinguished by their fondness for speculation, their vanity and love of pleasure, and their party spirit. A church composed of people of these characteristics, with a large infusion of Jewish converts, educated in the midst of refined heathenism, surrounded by all the incentives to indulgence, taught to consider pleasure, if not the chief good, yet in any form a good, plied on every hand by philosophers and false teachers, might be expected to exhibit the very characteristics which in this epistle are brought so clearly into view.

Their party spirit. "One said I am of Paul, another I am of Apollos; another I of Cephas, another I of Christ." Much ingenuity and learning have been expended in determining the nature of these party divisions. What may be considered as more or less satisfactorily determined is, 1. That there were factions in the church of Corinth which called themselves by the names above mentioned, and therefore that the names themselves give a clew to the character of the parties. The idea that the names of Paul, Apollos and Cephas are used figuratively, when other teachers were really intended, is so unnatural and has so little to sustain it, that it is now almost universally repudiated. 2. There can be little doubt that those who called themselves by the name of Paul, or made themselves his partisans, were in the main the Gentile converts; men brought up free from the bondage of the Mosaic law, and free from the influence of Jewish ideas and usages. They were disposed to press to extremes the liberty of the gospel, to regard as indifferent things in themselves sinful, and to treat without respect the scruples of the weak. 3. The intimate relations which subsisted between Paul and Apollos, as indicated in these epistles, authorizes the inference that it was not on doctrinal grounds that the followers of the latter differed from those of the former. It is probable that those who objected to Paul that he did not preach with the "wisdom of words" were those attracted by the eloquence of Apollos 4. It is scarcely less certain that those who said "We are of Peter" were the Judaizers, as Peter was specially the apostle of the circumcision. There is no evidence, however, from this epistle, that the leaders of this party had attempted to introduce into Corinth the observance of the Jewish law. But they were determined opponents of the apostle Paul. They had come to Corinth with letters of commendation (2 Cor. 2, 1.) They were Hebrews (2 Cor. 11, 22); they professed to be ministers of Christ (ch. 11, 23); they were false apostles (ch. 11, 13); the ministers of Satan, holding the word of God deceitfully. These men, as is evident from the defence which the apostle makes of his divine commission (1 Cor. 9, 1–3. 2 Cor. 12, 11. 12), called in question his apostleship, probably on the ground that he was not of the original twelve. On this ground also, to give themselves the greater authority, they claimed to be disciples of Peter, who was the first of the apostles. They also accused Paul of inconstancy and insincerity (2 Cor. 1, 17–24). In short they stirred up against him all the elements of discord which they could find in a congregation composed of such incongruous materials. 5. With regard to those who said We are of Christ, only two things are certain. First, that they were as much to blame as the other parties. It was in no Christian spirit that they set up their claim to be of Christ. And secondly, that they assumed to have some relation to Christ, which they denied to others. Whether it was because they had seen and heard him; or because they claimed connection with "James, the brother of the Lord;" or because they were the only genuine Christians, inasmuch as through some other channel than the apostles, they had derived, as they pretended, their knowledge of the gospel, is a matter of conjecture. Billroth and Baur regard this class as identical with the followers of Peter, who claimed to be of Christ because Paul was no apostle, and therefore his disciples were not "of Christ." According to this view there were only two, instead of four, parties in Corinth, the followers of

Paul and Apollos belonging to one class. This, however, does violence to the plain meaning of the passage in 1 Cor. 1, 12. These neutrals were probably the worst class in the congregation, as is commonly the case with those who claim to be Christians to the exclusion of all others.

Another great evil in the Corinthian church was the violation of the seventh commandment in various forms. Educated as we are under the light of the gospel, in which the turpitude of such sins is clearly revealed, it is impossible for us to appreciate correctly the state of feeling in Corinth on this subject. Even by heathen philosophers offences of this kind were regarded as scarcely deserving of censure, and by the public sentiment of the community they were considered altogether indifferent. They were in fact so associated with their religious rites and festivals as to lose their character as immoralities. With such previous training, and under the influence of such a public sentiment, and surrounded by all incitements and facilities to evil, it is surely not a matter of surprise that many of the Corinthians should take the ground that things of this class belonged to the same category with questions of food (1 Cor. 6, 12.) It is certain from numerous passages in these epistles that the church of Corinth was not only very remiss in the exercise of discipline for such matters, but also that the evil was widely extended.

Another indication of the latitudinarian spirit of one portion of the church was their conduct in reference to the sacrificial offerings and feasts of the heathen. They had been accustomed not only freely to eat meat which had been offered in sacrifice to idols, but to attend the feasts held in the temples. As they were told as Christians that the distinction between clean and unclean meats was abolished, and that the gods of the heathen were nothing, they insisted on their right to continue in their accustomed habits. This gave rise to great scandal. The stricter portion of the church, whether Jews or Gentiles, regarded all use of sacrificial meat as involving in some form connection with idolatry. This, therefore, was one of the questions of conscience which was answered differently by different parties, and no doubt contributed to promote the divisions existing among them.

The turbulent and independent spirit of the people also was conspicuously manifested in their public assemblies. Instead of following the instructions of the apostles and the usages of the church, they converted the Lord's Supper into a disorderly common meal; in violation of the public sentiment and the custom of all the churches, they allowed women to appear unveiled in their congregations and to speak in public; and in the spirit of emulation and ostentation they exercised their gifts of prophecy and speaking with tongues, without regard to order or edification. Besides all this, under the influence probably of the heathen philosophy, some among them denied the doctrine of the resurrection, and thus subverted the very foundation of the gospel.

Such is the picture presented in this epistle of one of the most flourishing churches of the apostolic age, drawn not by an enemy but by the apostle himself. With all this, however, there were not only many pure and exemplary members of the church, but much faith and piety even in those who were more or less chargeable with these disorders. Paul therefore addressed them as sanctified in Christ Jesus, thanks God for the grace which he had bestowed upon them, and expresses his confidence that God would preserve them blameless until the day of the Lord Jesus. This shows us how the gospel works in heathen lands. It is like leaven hid in a measure of meal. It is long before the whole mass is leavened. It does not transform the character of men or the state of society in a moment; but it keeps up a continual conflict with evil until it is finally overcome.

§ 4. Date. Contents of the Epistle.

The date of this epistle is determined by its contents. It was evidently written from Ephesus towards the close of

Paul's protracted sojourn in that city. He tells the Corinthians that he was to visit Macedonia, and would then come to Corinth, but that he must tarry in Ephesus till Pentecost (ch. 16, 5–8.) Comp. also v. 19, which agrees with the account given in Acts 19, 20. 20, 1. 2. After the uproar excited by Demetrius, Paul, as we learn from these passages, did go to Macedonia and then to Greece; and thence, with the contributions of the saints, to Jerusalem. Accordingly, in his epistle to the Romans, written from Corinth, he says, "Now I go unto Jerusalem to minister to the saints. For it hath pleased them of Macedonia and of Achaia to make a certain contribution for the poor saints which are in Jerusalem." (Rom. 15, 25. 26.) These and other data seem to fix the date of the epistle about the year 57, or five years after his first visit to Corinth. There are no indications of a later date, unless any one should find it hard to believe that Paul had already suffered all that is recorded in 2 Cor. 11, 23–28. Five times he had received of the Jews forty stripes save one, thrice he had been beaten with rods, once he was stoned, thrice he had suffered shipwreck, a day and a night he had been in the deep. These and the other dangers there enumerated seem enough to fill a lifetime. But this only shows how small a part of the labours and sufferings of the apostles is recorded in the Acts. It furnishes no sufficient reason for referring this epistle to a later period of the apostle's career.

As this epistle was written to correct the various disorders which had arisen in the Corinthian church after the apostle's departure, and to meet the calumnies and objections of the false teachers by whom the peace of the church had been disturbed and his own authority called in question, its contents are to a corresponding degree diversified. The apostle begins with the assertion of his divine commission, and with the usual salutation, ch. 1, 1–3. Then follows the general introduction to the epistle, commendatory and conciliatory in its tone and intention, 1, 4–9. He then introduces the subject of the party divisions by which the church was disturbed, and showed how inconsistent they were with the relation which believers bear to Christ and to each other; and how careful he had been to avoid all appearance of desiring to be a party leader among them. He had even abstained from baptizing lest any should say he baptized in his own name, ch. 1, 10–16. He had baptized only a few among them, for his business was to preach rather than to baptize.

As one class of his opponents directed their attacks against his want of philosophy and rhetorical refinement as a preacher, he for a time leaves the subject of their party contentions, and addresses himself to these objections. He tells them that he did not preach the wisdom of this world, because God had pronounced it to be folly, because all experience proved it to be inefficacious to bring men to the knowledge of God, because God had determined to save men by the preaching of Christ as crucified, because their history showed that it was not the wise who embraced the gospel, but God so administered his grace as to force all men to acknowledge that it was of him, and not of themselves, that they became united to Christ, and thereby partakers of the true wisdom, as well as of righteousness, holiness and redemption, 1, 17–31. Such being the case, he had come among them, not with the self-confidence of a philosopher, but as a simple witness to bear testimony to the fact that the Son of God had died for our redemption. Under a deep sense of his insufficiency, he spoke to them with fear and trembling, relying for success not on his own powers of persuasion, but wholly on the power with which the Holy Spirit accompanied the truth; knowing that the true foundation of faith was not argument, but the witness of the Spirit with and by the truth, 2, 1–5. Howbeit, although he repudiated human wisdom, the gospel which he preached was the true wisdom, a system of truth which God had made known, which was far above the power of man to discover, but which the Spirit of God had revealed. This divine wisdom he preached not in the words which the rhetorician prescribed, but which the Holy Ghost dictated. Both the truths which he taught, and the words which he used in communicating that truth were taught by the Holy Ghost. If any man neglected what was thus presented, the fault was neither in the doctrines taught nor in the mode in which they were exhibited, but in the objector. The things of the Spirit must be spiritually discerned, 2, 6–16.

After this defence of his mode of preaching the apostle resumes the subject of their divisions. He had preached to them in as high a strain as they were able to bear. They were but babes in Christ and had to be fed with milk. That they were in this low stage of the Christian life was manifest from their contentions, 3, 1–4. As these contentions had reference to their religious teachers, Paul endeavours to correct the evil by showing what ministers really are. First, he says, they are mere instruments,—servants; men sent to deliver a message or perform a given work; not the authors of the system of truth which they taught. All authority and efficiency are in God. Secondly, ministers are one. They teach the same doctrine, they have the same object, and stand in the same relation to God. Thirdly, every one will have to answer for his work. If he attempt to lay any other foundation than Christ, he is not a Christian minister. If on that foundation he builds with sound doctrine, he shall receive a reward; if with false doctrine, he shall be punished. Fourthly, human wisdom in this matter must be renounced. A man must become a fool in order to be truly wise. Fifthly, such being the relation of ministers to the church, the people should not place their confidence in them, or regard themselves as belonging to their ministers, since all things were subordinate to the people of God, ministers as well as other things, 3, 5–20. Sixthly, ministers being stewards, whose office it is to dispense the truth of God, fidelity on their part is the great thing to be demanded. So far as he was himself concerned it was a small matter what they thought of his fidelity, as the only final judge was the Lord. The true character of the ministerial office he had illustrated by a reference to himself and Apollos, that they might learn to estimate ministers aright, and not contend about them. He then contrasts himself as suffering, labouring and despised, with the false teachers and their followers, and exhorts the Corinthians to be followers of him, and intimates his apprehension that he would have to come to them with a rod, 4, 1–21. This is the end of that portion of the epistle which relates to the divisions existing in the church.

The second evil which it was the design of this epistle to correct, was the remissness of the Corinthians in the exercise of church discipline. Fornication was not only tolerated, but they allowed a man who had married his father's wife to retain his standing in the church. Paul here interferes, and in the exercise of his apostolical authority, not only pronounces on this incestuous person a sentence of excommunication, but delivers him to Satan, 5,1–5. He enforces on the church the general duty to exclude immoral members from their communion, 5, 6–13.

Thirdly, the practice which some of them had introduced of going to law before heathen magistrates, he severely condemns, 6, 1–11. Fourthly, the principle that all things are lawful, which the apostle had often uttered in reference to the ceremonial distinction between clean and unclean meats, some of the Corinthians had perverted as an argument to prove that fornication is a matter of indifference. The apostle shows the fallacy of this argument, and assures them that no sin is so great a desecration of the body, or more fatal to its union with Christ, and participation of the benefits of redemption, 6, 12–20.

Fifthly, marriage was another subject about which the minds of the Corinthians were disturbed, and on which they sought the advice of the apostle. They wished him to tell them whether marriage was obligatory, or lawful, or expedient; whether divorce or separation was allowable; and especially whether a Christian could consistently remain in the conjugal relation with a heathen. All these questions are answered in the seventh chapter, in which the apostle lays down the principles which are applicable to all cases of conscience in reference to that subject, 7, 1–40.

Sixthly: Surrounded as the Corinthians were by idolatry, whose institutions pervaded all the relations of society, it became a question how far Christians might conform to the usages connected with heathen worship. The most important question was, whether it was lawful to eat meat which had been offered in sacrifice to idols. On this point Paul agreed in principle with those who took the affirmative side in this controversy. He admitted that the idols were nothing, and that what was offered them was nothing, i. e. received no new character from its having been a sacrifice, and that the use of it involved no communion with idolatry. A regard, however, to the spiritual welfare of others, should lead them to abstain from the use of such meat under circumstances which might encourage others to act against their own convictions, 8, 1–13.

In exhorting them to exercise self-denial for the benefit of others, Paul urged them to nothing which he was not himself willing to do. Although he enjoyed all the liberty which belongs to other Christians, and had all the rights belonging to ministers or apostles, he had abstained from claiming them whenever the good of the church required. For example, although entitled on all the grounds of justice, usage, and of divine appointment, to be supported by those to whom he preached, he had sustained himself by the labour of his own hands; and so far as the Corinthians were concerned, he was determined still to do so. He was determined that his enemies in Corinth should not have the slightest pretext for accusing him of preaching the gospel from mercenary motives, 9, 1–18. This, however, was not a solitary instance. In all things indifferent he had accommodated himself to Jews and Gentiles, to the strong and to the weak. He had exercised the self-denial and self-control which every combatant in the ancient games was obliged to submit to who hoped to win the prize, 9, 19–27. What he did, other Christians must do. The history of the church shows that the want of such self-denial was fatal even to those who were the most highly favoured. The ancient Israelites had been delivered out of Egypt by the direct and manifest intervention of God; they had been miraculously guided and miraculously fed in the wilderness, and yet the great majority perished. Their experience should be a warning to the Corinthians not to be overcome by similar temptations, and especially to be on their guard against idolatry, 10, 1–13. Their danger in this respect was very great. They knew that the Grecian deities were imaginary beings; they knew that things offered to those deities had no contaminating power; they knew that it was, under some circumstances, lawful to eat meat which had been thus offered; they were, therefore, in danger of being led to eat it under circumstances which would render them guilty of idolatry. As they were constantly exposed to have such meat set before them, it became a matter of the highest importance to know when it might, and when it might not be eaten with impunity. The general principle which the apostle lays down on this subject is, that all participation in the religious services of a people, brings us into communion with them as worshippers, and therefore with the objects of their worship. Consequently, to eat of heathen sacrifices under circumstances which gave a religious character to the act, was idolatry. It is not necessary that they themselves should view the matter in this light. They might worship idols, and incur the guilt and penalty of idolatry, without knowing or suspecting that they did so. To prove this he appealed to their own convictions. They knew that all who came to the Lord's table did thereby join in the worship of Christ; and that all who attended the altars of the Jews, and eat of the sacrifices, did thereby unite in the worship of Jehovah. By parity of reasoning, those who took part in the religious festivals of the heathen, joined in the worship of idols. And although the idols were nothing, still the worship of them was apostacy from God, and the worship of devils, 10, 14–22. On the other hand, to eat of these sacrifices under circumstances which precluded the idea of a religious service, was a matter of indifference. Therefore, if meat offered to idols was exposed for sale in the market, or met with at private tables, it might be eaten with impunity, 10, 23–33.

Seventhly: grave abuses had been introduced into the celebration of public worship at Corinth. The women spoke in public unveiled; the Lord's supper was degraded into a common meal, and the use of spiritual gifts gave rise to great disorder. With regard to the first of these abuses, the apostle teaches that, as by the divine constitution the woman is subordinate to the man, and as the veil was the conventional symbol of that subordination, for a woman to appear in public unveiled, was to renounce her position, and to forfeit the respect due to her sex, 8, 1–16. As to the Lord's supper, it seems probable that it was, in Corinth at least, connected with an ordinary meal in which all the Christians met at a common table. For this meal each one brought what provisions he was able to contribute. Instead, however, of its being a feast of brotherly love, the rich ate by themselves, and left their poorer brethren no part in the feast. To correct this abuse, destructive of the whole intent of the sacrament, the apostle reminds his readers that he had communicated to them the account of the original institution of the ordinance, as he himself had received it of the Lord. According to that institution, it was designed not to satisfy hunger, but to commemorate the death of Christ. It was therefore a religious service of a peculiarly solemn character. The bread and wine being the appointed symbols of his body and blood, to eat and drink in a careless, irreverent manner, making no distinctions between the consecrated elements and ordinary food, was to be guilty of the body and blood of the Lord, 11, 17–34.

With regard to spiritual gifts, the apostle, after reminding the Corinthians that the possession of these gifts was one of the distinctive marks of their Christian as distinguished from their heathen state, teaches that all these extraordinary manifestations of the Holy Ghost have a common origin; that they were all given, not for the exaltation of those who received them, but for the edification of the church, and that they were distributed according to the good pleasure of God.

called out from the world. Sometimes it means the whole number of God's people, as when it is said, Christ loved the church and gave himself for it, Eph. 5, 25. Sometimes it means the people of God as a class, as when Paul said, he persecuted the church of God, Gal. 1, 13. Sometimes it means the professing Christians of any one place, as when mention is made of the church in Jerusalem, Antioch, or Corinth. Any number, however small, of professing Christians collectively considered may be called a church. Hence we hear of the church in the house of Philemon, and in the house of Aquila and Priscilla, Rom. 16, 5. It is called the church *of God*, because it belongs to him. He selects and calls its members, and, according to Acts, 20, 28, it is his, because he has bought it with his blood.

To them that are sanctified in Christ Jesus. This is explanatory of the preceding clauses, and teaches us the nature of the church. It consists of the sanctified. The word (ἁγιάζω) translated *to sanctify*, means *to cleanse.* And as sin is presented under the twofold aspect of guilt and pollution, to sanctify, or to cleanse from sin, may mean either to expiate guilt by an atonement, or to renew by the Holy Ghost. It is used for expiation by sacrifice in Heb. 2, 11. 10, 14. 13, 12, and elsewhere. The word also means to render sacred by consecrating any person or thing to the service of God. In the present case all these ideas may be united. The church consists of those whose guilt is expiated, who are inwardly holy, and who are consecrated to God as his peculiar people.

In Christ Jesus, that is, in virtue of union with him. It is only in him that we are partakers of these inestimable blessings. It is because we are in him as our head and representative, that we are justified by his righteousness; and it is because we are in him as a branch is in the vine, that we are purified by his Spirit.

Called (*to be*) *saints*, that is, by the effectual call of the Holy Spirit constituted saints. "The called" always mean the effectually called as distinguished from the merely externally invited. *Saints.* The original word (ἅγιος) sometimes signifies *sacred*, set apart to a holy use. In this sense the temple, the altar, the priests, the prophets, and the whole theocratic people, are called holy. In the New Testament the word is commonly expressive of inward purity, or consecration of the soul to God. Believers are saints in both senses of the word; they are inwardly renewed, and outwardly consecrated. It is not to be inferred from the fact that the apostle addresses all the nominal Christians in Corinth as saints and as sanctified in Christ Jesus, that they were all true believers, or that those terms express nothing more than external consecration. Men are uniformly addressed in Scripture according to their profession. If they profess to be saints, they are called saints; if they profess to be believers, they are called believers; and if they profess to be members of the church, they are addressed as really belonging to it. This passage teaches also, as Calvin remarks, the useful lesson that a body may be very corrupt both as to doctrine and practice, as such corruptions undoubtedly prevailed even in Corinth, and yet it may be properly recognized as a church of God. Locus diligenter observandus, ne requiramus in hoc mundo ecclesiam omni ruga et macula carentem: aut protinus abdicemus hoc titulo quemvis coetum in quo non omnia votis nostris respondeant.

With all that in every place call on the name of Jesus Christ our Lord. To call upon the name of any one is to invoke his aid. It is properly used for religious invocation. Compare Acts 9, 14, 21, and 22, 16. Rom. 10, 12, 13. 2 Tim. 2, 22. To call upon the name of Jesus Christ our Lord, is to invoke his aid as Christ, the Messiah predicted by the prophets, and as our almighty and sovereign possessor and ruler. It is in that sense Jesus is LORD. All power in heaven and earth has been committed unto him; and he died and rose again that he might be the Lord of the dead and of the living; that is, that he might acquire that peculiar right of possession in his people which arises from his having purchased them with his blood. To call upon the name of Jesus as Lord is therefore to worship him. It is to look to him for that help which God only can give. All Christians, therefore, are the worshippers of Christ. And every sincere worshipper of Christ is a true Christian. The phrase expresses not so much an individual act of invocation, as an habitual state of mind and its appropriate expression.

It might at first view appear from this clause that this epistle was addressed not only to the church in Corinth, but to all the worshippers of Christ. This would make it a catholic, or general epistle, which it is not. To get over this difficulty some explain the connection thus: 'Called to be saints together with all who call upon the name of Christ:' that is, the Corinthians as well as all other worshippers of Christ were called to be saints. A reference to 2 Cor. 1, 1 suggests a better explanation. It is there said, "To the church of God which is at Corinth with all the saints which are in all Achaia." The same limitation must be supplied here. This epistle was addressed not only to the Christians in Corinth, but also to all their brethren in the province of which Corinth was the capital.

Theirs and ours. These words admit of two connections. They may be connected with the word Lord, 'Their Lord and ours.' There were certain persons in Corinth who claimed a peculiar relation to Christ, and said, "We are of Christ;" to whom Paul said, "If any trust to himself that he is Christ's, let him of himself think this again, as he is Christ's, so are we Christ's," 2 Cor. 10, 7. It is possible that he may have intended at the very opening of his epistle, to rebuke this exclusive spirit, and to remind his readers that Christ is the common Lord of all who call upon him. The position of the words however renders it more natural to understand the apostle to mean, "in every place, theirs and ours." If this be the true construction, then the sense may be, 'In every place of worship theirs and ours.' This interpretation supposes that the divisions known to exist in Corinth had led to the separation of the people into different worshipping assemblies. There is, however, not only no evidence that such external separation had occurred, but clear evidence in ch. 11, 18 to the contrary. Others understand the sense to be, 'In every place, theirs and ours,' i. e. 'where they are, and where I am.' This supposes the epistle to be general. A third interpretation has been proposed. The epistle is addressed to all Christians in Corinth and Achaia, wherever they might be. Every place is at once theirs and ours. Their place of abode, and my place of labour.

3. Grace (be) unto you, and peace from God our Father, and (from) the Lord Jesus Christ.

Grace is favour, and *peace* its fruits. The former includes all that is comprehended in the love of God as exercised towards sinners; and the latter all the benefits which flow from that love. All good, therefore, whether providential or spiritual, whether temporal or eternal, is comprehended in these terms: justification, adoption and sanctification, with all the benefits which either accompany or flow from them.

These infinite blessings suppose an infinite source; and as they are sought no less from Christ than from God the Father, Christ must be a divine person. It is to be remarked that God is called our *Father*, and Christ our *Lord*. God as God has not only created us, but renewed and adopted us. God in Christ has redeemed us. He is our owner and sovereign, to whom our allegiance is immediately due; who reigns in and rules over us, defending us from all his and our enemies. This is the peculiar form which piety assumes under the gospel. All Christians regard God as their Father and Christ as their Lord. His person they love, his voice they obey, and in his protection they trust.

4. I thank my God always on your behalf, for the grace of God which is given you by Jesus Christ.

Paul expresses his gratitude for *the grace of God* given to the Corinthians. The word *grace*, as just remarked, means favour, and then the blessings of which that favour is the source; just as we use the word *favour* sometimes for a disposition of the mind, and sometimes for gifts; as when we speak of receiving favours. The latter is the sense of the word in this place.

By Christ Jesus, or rather, *in* Christ Jesus. This limits and explains the kind of favours to which the apostle refers. He renders thanks for those gifts which God had bestowed upon them in virtue of their union with Christ. The fruits of the Spirit are the blessings referred to. These inward spiritual benefits are as much gifts as health or prosperity, and are, therefore, as properly the grounds of gratitude. All virtues are graces, gifts of the grace of God.

5. That in every thing ye are enriched by him, in all utterance, and (in) all knowledge.

This verse is explanatory of the preceding. Paul gives thanks for the grace which they had received, i. e. that in every thing they were enriched. *In every thing* (ἐν παντί), in every respect they were richly endowed with the gifts of the Spirit. *In all utterance and in all knowledge;* that is, with all the gifts of utterance and knowledge. Some were prophets, some were teachers, some had the gift of tongues. These were different forms of the gift of utterance. *In all know-*

ledge, that is, in every kind and degree of religious knowledge. This interpretation gives a good sense, and is the one very generally adopted. The word (λόγος) translated *utterance*, may however be taken in the sense of *doctrine*, and the word (γνῶσις) translated *knowledge*, in the sense of *insight*. The meaning would then be, that the church in Corinth was richly endowed with divine truth, and with clear apprehension or understanding of the doctrines which they had been taught. They were second to no other church either as to doctrinal knowledge or spiritual discernment. Λόγος, according to this view, is the truth preached; γνῶσις, the truth apprehended.—MEYER.

6. Even as the testimony of Christ was confirmed in you.

Even as, i. e. because, inasmuch as. They were thus enriched, because the testimony of Christ, that is, the gospel, was confirmed among them. The gospel is called the 'testimony of Christ,' either because it is the testimony concerning God and divine things, which Christ bore; or because it is the testimony which the apostles bore concerning Christ. Either explanation is agreeable to the analogy of the Scripture. Christ is called the true witness; and is said to have borne witness of the truth. Compare John 3, 11. 32. 33. 8, 13. 14. On the other hand, the apostles are frequently called the witnesses of Christ, and are said to have borne testimony concerning him. The gospel, therefore, is, in one view, the testimony which Christ bore; and, in another, the testimony which the apostles bore concerning him. The former is the higher, and therefore, the better sense. It is good to contemplate the gospel as that system of truth which the eternal Logos, or Revealer, has made known.

Was confirmed in you. This may mean either, was firmly established among you; or was firmly established in your faith. The gospel was demonstrated by the Holy Spirit to be true, and was firmly settled in their conviction. This firm faith was then, as it is now, the necessary condition of the enjoyment of the blessings by which the gospel is attended. Therefore the apostle adds,

7. So that ye come behind in no gift; waiting for the coming of our Lord Jesus Christ.

Such was their strength of faith that the gifts of the Spirit were bestowed upon them as abundantly as upon any other church. This connection of faith with the divine blessing is often presented in Scripture. Our Lord said to the father who sought his aid in behalf of his demoniac child, "If thou canst believe, all things are possible to him that believeth," Mark 9, 23. And on another occasion, "According to thy faith be it unto thee," Matt. 9, 29. In his own country, it is said, he did not many mighty works "because of their unbelief," Matt. 13, 58. The Holy Ghost, therefore, confers on men his gifts in proportion to their faith. The word (χάρισμα) *gift*, is used both for the ordinary and extraordinary gifts of the Spirit; most frequently for the latter. Here it includes both classes. The Corinthians had not only the inward gifts of repentance, faith and knowledge, but also those of miracles, of healing, of speaking with tongues, of prophecy, in rich abundance. No church was superior to them in these respects. The extraordinary gifts, however, seem to be principally intended. Paul's commendation has reference to their wisdom, knowledge and miraculous gifts, rather than to their spiritual graces. Much as he found to censure in their state and conduct, he freely acknowledged their flourishing condition in many points of view.

Waiting the coming of our Lord Jesus Christ. Waiting (ἀπεκδεχομένους) *patiently* expecting, comp. 1 Pet. 3, 20, or expecting with desire, i. e. longing for. Comp. Rom. 8, 19. 20. 23. The object of this patient and earnest expectation of believers is the *coming* (ἀποκάλυψιν) i. e. *the revelation of our Lord Jesus Christ.* The second advent of Christ, so clearly predicted by himself and by his apostles, connected as it is with the promise of the resurrection of his people and the consummation of his kingdom, was the object of longing expectation to all the early Christians. So great is the glory connected with that event that Paul, in Rom. 8, 18–23, not only represents all present afflictions as trifling in comparison, but describes the whole creation as looking forward to it with earnest expectation. Comp. Phil. 3, 20. Tit. 2, 13. So general was this expectation that Christians were characterized as those "who love his appearing," 2 Tim. 4, 8, and as those "who wait for him," Heb. 9, 28. Why is it that this longing for the coming of Christ is awakened in the hearts of his people? The apostle answers this question by saying that the "first fruits of the Spirit" enjoyed by believers in this life

tion, as in 10, 16, "participation of the blood of Christ," 2 Cor. 13, 13, "participation of the Holy Ghost." We are called to be partakers of Christ; partakers of his life, as members of his body; and therefore, partakers of his character, of his sufferings here and of his glory hereafter. This last idea is made specially prominent. Believers are called to be partakers of the glory of Christ, Rom. 8, 17. 23. 2 Thess. 2, 14. It is because believers are thus partakers of Christ, that the apostle was assured they could never perish. The person with whom believers are thus intimately united, is *the Son of God*, of the same nature, being the same in substance and equal in power and glory. He is also *Jesus*, a man; consequently he is both God and man, in two distinct natures, and one person. This incarnate God, the Saviour, is *the Christ*, of whom the Old Testament says and promises so much. He is also *our Lord*, we belong to him; he is our possessor, our sovereign, our protector. How can they apostatize and perish who stand in this relation to the eternal Son of God?

Of the Divisions in the Church of Corinth. Vs. 10–16.

As one of the principal objects of this epistle was to correct the evils which had arisen in the church of Corinth, the apostle adverts, first, to the divisions which there existed. He exhorts the members of that church to unity, v. 10. The reason of that exhortation was the information which he had received concerning their dissensions. v. 11. These divisions arose from their ranging themselves under different religious teachers as party leaders, v. 12. The sin and folly of such divisions are manifest, in the first place, because Christ is incapable of division. As there is one head, there can be but one body. As there is but one Christ, there can be but one church. And in the second place, because religious teachers are not centres of unity to the church. They had not redeemed it, nor did its members profess allegiance to them in baptism, v. 13. These divisions, therefore, arose, on the one hand, from a forgetfulness of the common relation which all Christians bear to Christ; and, on the other, from a misapprehension of the relation in which believers stand to their religious teachers. Paul expresses his gratitude that he had not given any occasion for such misapprehension. He had baptized so few among them, that no man could suspect him of a desire to make himself the head of the church or the leader of a party, vs. 14–16.

10. Now I beseech you, brethren, by the name of our Lord Jesus Christ, that ye all speak the same thing, and that there be no divisions among you, but (that) ye be perfectly joined together in the same mind and in the same judgment.

There is but one exhortation in this verse, which is expressed first in general terms, "that ye all say the same thing;" and is then explained in the negative form, "that there be no divisions among you;" and then positively, "that ye be perfectly joined together."

By the name of our Lord Jesus Christ, i. e. out of regard to Christ, Rom. 12, 1. 15, 30. 2 Thess. 4, 12. Their reverence and love of Christ, and regard for his authority as their Lord, should induce them to yield obedience to the apostle's exhortation. It was not out of respect to him, but out of regard to Christ they should obey. This renders obedience easy and elevating. *To say the same thing* (τὸ αὐτὸ λέγειν) is a phrase of frequent occurrence to express agreement. It may be so understood here, and then the following clauses are explanatory. Or, it may be understood in reference to v. 12, of outward profession. 'Do not say I am of Paul, and I of Apollos, but all say the same thing.' The former explanation appears the more natural.

And that there be no divisions among you, literally, *schisms*. The word (σχίσμα) means, 1. *A rent*, as in a garment, Matt. 9, 16. 2. Difference of opinion, John 7, 43. 3. Alienation of feeling, or inward separation. 4. In its ecclesiastical sense, it is an unauthorized separation from the church. The schisms which existed in Corinth were not of the nature of hostile sects refusing communion with each other, but such as may exist in the bosom of the same church, consisting in alienation of feeling and party strifes.

But (that) ye be perfectly joined together. The original word (καταρτίζω) means *to repair*, or *to mend*, Matt. 4, 21, *to reduce to place*, as a dislocated limb; *to render complete*, or *perfect* (ἄρτιος); then figuratively, *to restore* or *set right* those in error; *to prepare, to render perfect.* Hence in this place the sense may be, 'That ye be perfect,' as the Vulgate renders it; or, 'that ye be united,' as in our translation; or, 'that ye be reduced to order.' The context shows that the idea of union is what the apostle intended. They were not to

Christians cannot be divided without violating the bond which binds them to Christ and to one another.

Is Christ divided? Of course the answer must be in the negative. As Christ is incapable of division, as there can be but one Christ, the church cannot be divided. It is contrary to its nature to be split into hostile parties, just as it is contrary to the nature of a family to be thus divided. As the head is one, so are the members.

Was Paul crucified for you? Did Paul redeem you? Were you purchased by his blood, so as to belong to him? If not, then you are not his, and it is wrong to say, We are Paul's. Believers bear no such relation even to inspired teachers, as to justify their being called by their names. They are called Christians, because they are the worshippers of Christ, because they belong to him, and because they are consecrated to him.

Or were ye baptized in the name of Paul? (εἰς τὸ ὄνομα), literally, *unto the name*, i. e. in reference to Paul, so that he should be the object of your faith and the one whose name you were to confess. By baptism we are brought into the number of the disciples and followers of him into whose name, or in reference to whom, we are baptized. As, therefore, all Christians are baptized unto Christ, and not unto the apostles, much less any uninspired teacher, it is Christ whom they should confess, and by his name they should be called.

14. 15. I thank God that I baptized none of you, but Crispus and Gaius; lest any should say that I had baptized in mine own name.

Although it was the duty of the apostles to baptize, Matt. 28, 19, yet Paul rejoiced that it had so happened that he had administered that ordinance to only a few persons in Corinth, as thus all pretext that he was making disciples to himself, was taken away. Paul did not consider this a matter of chance, but of providential direction, and, therefore, a cause of gratitude. Crispus was the chief ruler of the synagogue in Corinth, whose conversion is recorded in Acts 18, 8. Gaius is mentioned in Rom. 16, 23, as the host of the apostle.

16. And I baptized also the household of Stephanas; besides I know not whether I baptized any other.

Stephanas was one of the three messengers sent to inform the apostle of the state of the church in Corinth, and to deliver the letter to which reference is made, ch. 7, 1, comp. 16, 15. 17. Paul says he baptized the *household* or family of Stephanas. Under the old dispensation, whenever any one professed Judaism or entered into covenant with God as one of his people, all his children and dependents, that is, all to whom he stood in a representative relation, were included in the covenant and received circumcision as its sign. In like manner under the gospel, when a Jew or Gentile joined the Christian church, his children received baptism and were recognized as members of the Christian church. Compare Acts 16, 15 and 33.

Besides I know not whether I baptized any other. The nature of inspiration is to be learnt from the declarations of the Scriptures and from the facts therein recorded. From these sources we learn that it was an influence which rendered its recipients infallible, but it did not render them omniscient. They were preserved from asserting error, but they were not enabled either to know or to remember all things.

Paul's defence of his manner of preaching. Vs. 17–31.

The apostle having been led to mention incidentally that he had baptized very few persons in Corinth, assigns as the reason of that fact that his great official duty was to preach the gospel. This naturally led him to speak of the manner of preaching. It was one of the objections urged against him that he did not preach "with the wisdom of words," that is, that he did not preach the doctrines taught by human reason, which he calls the wisdom of the world. Through the remainder of this, and the whole of the following chapter, he assigns his reasons for thus renouncing the wisdom of the world,—and resumes the subject of the divisions existing in the church of Corinth at the beginning of the third chapter. 1. His first reason for not teaching human wisdom is that God had pronounced all such wisdom to be folly, vs. 19. 20. 2. Experience had proved the insufficiency of human wisdom to lead men to a saving knowledge of God, v. 21. 3. God had ordained the gospel to be the great means of salvation, vs. 21–25. 4. The experience of the Corinthians themselves showed that it was not wisdom nor any other human distinction that secured the salvation of men. Human wisdom could neither discover the method of salvation, nor secure compliance with its terms when revealed. They were in Christ (i. e. converted), not because they were wiser, better, or more distinguished than others, but simply because God had chosen or called them, vs. 26–30. The design of God in all this was to humble men so that he who glories should glory in the Lord. v. 31.

17. For Christ sent me not to baptize, but to preach the gospel: not with wisdom of words, lest the cross of Christ should be made of none effect.

For indicates the connection. 'I baptized few, *for* I was not sent to baptize, but to preach.' The commission was, "Go ye into all the world, and preach the gospel to every creature." This does not mean that baptism was not included, but it does mean that baptizing was very inferior to preaching. It is subordinated in the very form of the commission, "Go ye therefore, *make disciples* of all nations, baptizing them," &c. The main thing was to make disciples; recognizing them as such by baptism was subordinate, though commanded. Baptism was a work which the apostles seem to have generally left to others, Acts 10, 48. During the apostolic age, and in the apostolic form of religion, truth stood immeasurably above external rites. The apostasy of the church consisted in making rites more important than truth. The apostle's manner of speaking of baptism in this connection as subordinate to preaching is, therefore, a wonder to those who are disposed unduly to exalt the sacraments, as may be seen in Olshausen's remarks on vs. 13–16. We must not infer from this that baptism is of little importance, or that it may be safely neglected. Although Paul controverted the Jewish doctrine that circumcision secured salvation and was necessary to its attainment, he nevertheless admitted that its advantages were great every way, Rom. 3, 2. And in the Old Testament it is expressly said that the uncircumcised man-child should be cut off from the people, i. e. deprived of the benefits of the theocracy. While therefore it is unscriptural to make baptism essential to salvation or a certain means of regeneration, it is nevertheless a dangerous act of disobedience to undervalue or neglect it.

His preaching Paul describes by saying it was "not with the wisdom of words," (*οὐκ ἐν σοφίᾳ λόγου*). So far as the signification of these words is concerned, the meaning may be, 1. Not with skilful discourse, that is, eloquence. 2. Or, not with philosophical discourse, that is, not in an abstract or speculative manner, so that the truth taught should be presented in a philosophical form. According to this view the doctrine taught would still be the gospel, but the thing rejected and condemned would be merely the philosophical mode of exhibiting it. 3. The meaning may be, not with a discourse characterized by wisdom; that is, the contents of which was human wisdom, instead of truths revealed by God. The context is in favour of the interpretation last mentioned. In this whole connection the apostle contrasts two kinds of wisdom. The one he describes as the wisdom of the world, the wisdom of men, or of the rulers of the world. By this he means human wisdom, that which has a human origin. This he pronounces to be folly, and declares it to be entirely inefficacious in the salvation of men. The other kind of wisdom, he calls the wisdom of God, i. e. derived from God; the hidden wisdom, consisting in truths which human reason never could discover. The former he repudiates. He says, he did not come to preach the teachings of human reason, but the testimony of God. He was among them in the character, not of a philosopher, but of a witness. As in what follows the apostle argues to prove that human wisdom is folly and cannot save men, and gives that as the reason why he came preaching the doctrine of the cross, it seems plain that this is the meaning of the passage before us. 'Christ sent me to preach, not with wise discourse, that is, not with human wisdom—not as a philosopher, but as a witness.' His preaching therefore was the simple exhibition of the truth which God had revealed.

Lest the cross of Christ should be made of none effect, i. e. rendered powerless and inoperative. If Paul in preaching had either substituted human wisdom for the doctrine of the cross, or had so presented that doctrine as to turn it into a philosophy, his preaching would have been powerless. It would lose its divine element and become nothing more than human wisdom. Whatever obscures the cross deprives the gospel of its power.

18. For the preaching of the cross is to them that perish, foolishness; but unto us which are saved, it is the power of God.

The preaching of the cross, or, *the doctrine* (ὁ λόγος) of the cross, that is, the doctrine of salvation through the crucifixion of the Son of God as a sacrifice for the sins of men. This doctrine, though to one class, viz., *those who are lost*, i. e. those certainly to perish, *foolishness;* yet to another class, viz., *those certainly to be saved*, it is the power of God. That is, it is that through which *the power of God* is manifested and exercised, and therefore it is divinely efficacious. All the hearers of the gospel are divided into two classes. To the one, the doctrine of salvation through a crucified Redeemer appears absurd. They are called "the lost," not only because they are certainly to perish, but also because they are in a lost state while out of Christ, John 3, 18. To the other, this doctrine is divinely efficacious in producing peace and holiness. These are called "the saved," not only because they are certainly to be saved, but also because they are now in a state of salvation. Compare 2 Cor. 2, 15.

This verse contains the reason why Christ sent the apostle to preach, and why he preached the doctrine of the cross, and not human wisdom. That reason is, because the doctrine of the cross alone is effectual to salvation. This proposition he proceeds to establish by a series of arguments designed to prove that the wisdom of the world cannot save men. His first argument is derived from the express declaration of the word of God to this effect.

19. For it is written, I will destroy the wisdom of the wise, and will bring to nothing the understanding of the prudent.

This is not to be considered as the citation of any one particular passage of the Old Testament, so much as an appeal to a doctrine therein clearly revealed. In a multitude of passages, and in various forms, God had taught by his prophets the insufficiency of human reason to lead men to the knowledge of the way of salvation. In Isaiah 29, 14. nearly the same words are used, but with a more limited application. "The wisdom of the wise," and "the understanding of the prudent," are parallel expressions for the same thing.

20. Where (is) the wise? where (is) the scribe? where (is) the disputer of this world? hath not God made foolish the wisdom of this world?

This is a challenge to the wise of every class and of every

nation to disprove what he had said. It was too plain to be denied that God had made foolish the wisdom of this world, i. e. he had showed it to be foolish, and dealt with it as such. Among the Jews there were three classes of learned men, distinguished by terms corresponding to those which the apostle here uses. It is not probable, however, that Paul refers to that classification, because he is not speaking specially of the Jews. The first term (σοφός), *wise man*, is probably to be taken in a general sense including that of the two following words. 'Where is the wise, whether Jewish scribe or Grecian sophist?' The word *scribe* is the common designation of the learned class among the Jews. It was originally applied to the secretaries whose business it was to prepare and issue decrees in the name of the king (2 Sam. 8, 17. 20, 25. 2 Kings 12, 10. 19, 2). Afterwards, and especially in the New Testament, it was used as the designation of those learned in the law, who were charged not only with its transcription, but also with its exposition, and at times with its administration. The same title was given in many of the Asiatic states to the magistrate who presided over the senate, took charge of the laws, and who read them when necessary to the people, Acts 19, 35.

Where is the disputer? (συζητητής) *inquirer, questioner, sophist;* the appropriate designation of the Grecian philosopher. *Of this world*, or *age*. This qualification belongs to all the preceding terms. 'Where is the wise of this world, whether *scribe* or *sophist?*'

21. For after that in the wisdom of God the world by wisdom knew not God, it pleased God by the foolishness of preaching to save them that believe.

This and the following verses contain the apostle's second argument in proof of the insufficiency of human wisdom. The argument is this: experience having shown the insufficiency of human wisdom, God set it aside, and declared it to be worthless, by adopting the foolishness of preaching as the means of salvation. This argument therefore includes two distinct proofs. First, that derived from experience; and secondly, that derived from God's having appointed the gospel, as distinguished from human wisdom, to be the means of saving men.

For after that. It is to be remarked that the word *for* in

Paul's writings very often refers to something implied but not expressed in the context; most commonly it refers to the answer to a preceding question. It is so here. 'Hath not God made foolish the wisdom of this world? *He has*, for, &c.' *After that* (ἐπειδή) properly, *since*. This particle, though in the Greek writers generally used of time, in the New Testament is almost uniformly used in a causal sense. This is its meaning here. 'For, *inasmuch as*, or *because*.'

In the wisdom of God. This means either, in the wise ordination of God, or, in the midst of the manifestation of the wisdom of God. If the former interpretation be adopted, the meaning is, that it was a manifestation of divine wisdom to leave the world for four thousand years to test the power of human wisdom, that thus its insufficiency might be clearly demonstrated. The latter interpretation is generally adopted, and gives a better sense. 'In the wisdom of God, that is, although surrounded by the manifestations of the divine wisdom in creation and providence, man failed to attain any saving knowledge of God.' *The world by* (*its* τῆς) *wisdom knew not God.* This is not inconsistent with Rom. 1, 20, where the apostle says, God's eternal power and Godhead are clearly seen, being understood by the things that are made. In this latter passage Paul speaks of the revelation which God had made of himself; in the former, of the use which men had made of that revelation. The revelation was clear, but men, through their imbecility and perverseness, did not comprehend it. In the midst of light they continued blind. The fault was in them, and not in the revelation. They did not like to retain God in their knowledge, Rom. 1, 28. Besides, sometimes the knowledge of God, in Scripture, means that speculative knowledge which human reason is adequate to derive from the works of God, and which renders their idolatry inexcusable; at other times, it means saving knowledge. Hence it is perfectly consistent to say in the former sense, that men by wisdom may attain the knowledge of God; and, in the latter sense, that they cannot attain that knowledge. Paul is here speaking of the knowledge which is connected with salvation. Such knowledge the world by wisdom had failed to secure. Therefore, *it pleased God by the foolishness of preaching to save them that believe.* "The foolishness of preaching" means the preaching of foolishness, that is, the cross. The doctrine of the cross was foolishness in the estimation of men. God thus put to shame all human wisdom by making a doctrine which the wise of this world regarded as absurd the means of salvation. This passage in its connection clearly teaches two great truths; first, that the cross, or the doctrine of Christ crucified, is the substance of the gospel, that in which its vitality and power consist; and secondly, that it is the preaching, or public proclamation (κήρυγμα) of that doctrine which is the great means of salvation. To this all other means, however important, are either preparatory or subordinate. It is to be remembered, however, that *preaching*, in the Scriptural sense of the term, includes the inculcation of the truth, whether to an individual or to a multitude—whether by the road side, or in the school, or lecture-room, or the pulpit. Philip, as he rode in the chariot with the eunuch, "preached to him Jesus," Acts 8, 35.

22. 23. For the Jews require a sign, and the Greeks seek after wisdom; but we preach Christ crucified, unto the Jews a stumbling-block, and unto the Greeks foolishness.

This passage is parallel to the preceding. '*Since* the world by wisdom knew not God, it pleased God by the foolishness of preaching to save them that believe—and *since* the Jews ask a sign and the Greeks seek wisdom, we preach, &c.' That is, since human reason in all its developments, Jewish or Grecian, had failed, we preach Christ.

The Jews require, or, *ask* (αἰτοῦσι) *a sign.** This was characteristic of the Jews. They required external supernatural evidence as the ground of their faith. Their constant demand was, "What sign showest thou?" Matt. 12, 39. Mark 8, 11. John 6, 30. To this disposition our Saviour referred when he said, "A wicked and adulterous generation seeketh after a sign, and there shall no sign be given to it, but the sign of the prophet Jonas," Matt. 16, 4. *The Greeks*, on the other hand, *seek after wisdom*. They required rational evidence. They would receive nothing as true which they could not understand, and see the rational grounds of. These are types of permanent classes of men.

But we preach Christ crucified. This doctrine met the

* Instead of σημεῖον, *a sign*, the MSS., A. B. C. D. E. F. G., besides many others of later date, read σημεῖα, *signs*, which almost all the modern editors adopt.

demands of neither class. It satisfied neither the expectations of the Jews, nor the requirements of the Greeks. On the contrary, it was to the Jews *a stumbling-block.* They had anticipated in the Messiah a glorious temporal prince, who should deliver and exalt their nation. To present to them one crucified as a malefactor as their Messiah, was the greatest possible insult. He was to them, therefore, a stone of stumbling and a rock of offence, Rom. 9, 33. 1 Pet. 2, 8. To the Greeks this doctrine was foolishness. Nothing in the apprehension of rationalists can be more absurd than that the blood of the cross can remove sin, promote virtue, and secure salvation; or that the preaching of that doctrine is to convert the world.

24. But unto them which are called, both Jews and Greeks, Christ the power of God and the wisdom of God.

The called (κλητοί) always mean the effectually called, as distinguished from those who are merely externally invited. There is a twofold call of the gospel; the one external by the word; the other internal by the Spirit. The subjects of the latter are designated "the called," Rom. 1, 7. 8, 28. Jude 1. Rev. 17, 14. compare Isaiah 48, 12. The Jews desired an exhibition of power; the Greeks sought wisdom: both are found in Christ, and in the highest degree. He is the power of God and the wisdom of God. In his person and work there is the highest possible manifestation both of the divine power and of the divine wisdom. And those who are called not only see, but experience this. The doctrine of Christ crucified produces effects on them which nothing short of divine power can accomplish. And it reveals and imparts to them the true wisdom. It makes them divinely wise; it makes them holy; it makes them righteous; and it makes them blessed. It does infinitely more than human wisdom could ever conceive, much less accomplish. It has already changed the state of the intelligent universe, and is to be the central point of influence throughout eternity. This is the doctrine which the wise of this world wish to see ignored or obscured in behalf of their speculations. Just as the heathen exchange the true God for birds and beasts and creeping things, and think themselves profound.

25. Because the foolishness of God is wiser than men, and the weakness of God is stronger than men.

This is a confirmation of what precedes. The gospel is thus efficacious, *because* the lowest manifestation of divine wisdom exceeds the highest results of the wisdom of men; and the lowest exercise of God's power is more effectual than all human strength. Or, instead of taking the verse in this general sense, *the foolishness of God*, may mean the gospel. The meaning then is, 'The doctrine of the cross, though regarded as absurd and powerless, has more of power and wisdom than any thing which ever proceeded from man.'

26. For ye see your calling, brethren, how that not many wise men after the flesh, not many mighty, not many noble (are called).

The connection is not with the preceding verse but with the whole preceding context. The apostle introduces a new argument in proof of the uselessness of human wisdom. The argument is derived from their religious experience. 'You see, brethren, it is not the wise who are called.'

Your calling (κλῆσις) does not mean mode of life, profession, or station, as the word *vocation* often does with us. The Greek word is never used in this sense in the New Testament, unless 1 Cor. 7, 20 be an exception. It always refers to the call of God by his word and Spirit. It is to be so understood here. 'You see, brethren, your conversion, that not many wise are converted.' In this sense we speak of "effectual *calling*."

Wise after the flesh, i. e. wise with human wisdom. *Flesh* in Scripture often means human nature. There are two kinds of wisdom, the one human, the other divine. There are, therefore, two classes of wise men; those possessing the wisdom which is from men, and those who have the wisdom which comes from God. Few of the former class become Christians; therefore it is not by wisdom that men find out God, which is what the apostle designs to prove.

Not many mighty, i. e. *the great* (οἱ δυνατοί, those having δύναμις, in the sense of power and authority). The opposite class is designated as the weak or uninfluential, see Acts 25, 5. *Not many noble*, i. e. well-born. The converts to Christianity were not in general from the higher ranks in society.

The things which elevate man in the world, knowledge, influence, rank, are not the things which lead to God and salvation. As there is no verb in the original to agree with these nominatives, "the wise," "the mighty," "the noble," we may either supply the simple substantive verb *are*: 'You see your calling, not many of you are wise, or mighty, or noble;' or, we may supply, as in our version, the word *called*, 'not many wise are called;' or, the word *chosen*, 'not many wise ar chosen, for God hath chosen, &c.' The sense remains the same. Human distinctions are insignificant and inefficacious in the sight of God, who is sovereign in the distribution of his grace.

27. But God hath chosen the foolish things of the world to confound the wise, and God hath chosen the weak things of the world to confound the things which are mighty.

In this and the following verses the apostle asserts affirmatively what he had just stated negatively, 'God does not choose the wise, but he chooses the foolish.'

The foolish things of the world, (τὰ μωρὰ τοῦ κόσμου) *the foolish portion of mankind.* In this and in the following clauses the neuter is used although persons are intended, because the reference is indefinite. God hath chosen the foolish, the weak, the insignificant, &c. *Hath chosen.* It is implied in this form of expression, which is repeated for the sake of emphasis, that as, on the one hand, the wise and the great were not chosen on account of their wisdom or greatness, so, on the other, the foolish and the weak were not chosen on account of their want of wisdom or greatness. God chose whom he pleased. He chose the ignorant *that he might confound* the wise; and the weak, *that he might confound* the mighty. That is, that he might put them to shame, by convincing them of the little value of the things on which they prided themselves, and by exalting over them those whom they despised.

28. And base things of the world, and things which are despised, hath God chosen, (yea) and things which are not, to bring to nought things that are;

The base things, i. e. the base, the ignoble (τὰ ἀγενῆ), those without family, as opposed to the noble. *Things which are despised*, i. e. men in low condition, whom the rich and noble look upon with contempt. *Things which are not*, (τὰ μὴ ὄντα,) those who are entirely overlooked as though they had no existence. There is a climax here. God has chosen not only plebeians, but of the plebeians those who were objects of contempt, and even those below contempt, too insignificant to be noticed at all. These, and such as these, does God choose to make kings and priests unto himself. *To bring to nought*, (καταργήσῃ), literally, *that he might bring to nought.* This is a stronger term than that used in the preceding verse, and here specially appropriate. God brings to nothing *the things that are* (τὰ ὄντα), i. e. those who make their existence known and felt, as opposed to those who are nothing. It is apparent from the dispensations of grace, that knowledge, rank, and power do not attract the favour of God, or secure for their possessors any pre-eminence or preference before him. This should render the exalted humble, and the humble content.

29. That no flesh should glory in his presence.

The design of God in thus dealing with men, calling the ignorant rather than the wise, the lowly instead of the great, is that no man should boast before him. No one can stand in his sight and attribute his conversion or salvation to his own wisdom, or birth, or station, or to any thing else by which he is favourably distinguished from his fellow-men.

30. But of him are ye in Christ Jesus, who of God is made unto us wisdom, and righteousness, and sanctification and redemption.

To be *in Christ Jesus* is to be united to him, 1. Representatively, as we were in Adam, Rom. 5, 12–21. 1 Cor. 15, 22. 2. Vitally, as a branch is in the vine, or a member in the body, John 15, 1–7. 3. Consciously and voluntarily by faith, Rom. 8, 1, *et passim.* Of this union with Christ, the apostle teaches us here, first, its origin, and secondly, its effects. As to its origin, it is of God. *Of him ye are in Christ Jesus.* It is (ἐξ αὐτοῦ) of him as the efficient cause. It is to be referred to him alone that ye are in Christ. Your conversion or saving union with Christ is not due to yourselves; it is not because you are wiser, or better, or more diligent than others that you are thus distinguished. This which is the turning point in theology, and therefore in religion, is here most explicitly asserted. And it is not only asserted, but it is declared to be the purpose of God to make it apparent, and to force all men to acknowledge it. He so dispenses his grace as to make men see with regard to others, and to acknowledge with regard to themselves, that the fact that they are in Christ, or true Christians, is due to him and not to themselves. The effects of this union, as here stated, are, that Christ is *of God* (ἀπὸ Θεοῦ), as the author, made unto us, 1. Wisdom. Christ is the true wisdom. He is the Logos, the Revealer, in whom dwells all the fulness of the Godhead, and all the treasures of wisdom and knowledge. No man knoweth the Father but the Son, and he to whom the Son shall reveal him, John 1, 18. Union with him, therefore, makes the believer truly wise. It secures the knowledge of God, whose glory is revealed in the face of Christ, and whom to know is eternal life. All true religious knowledge is derived from Christ, and it is only those who submit to his teaching who are wise unto salvation.

2. The second effect of union with Christ, is righteousness and sanctification (δικαιοσύνη τε καὶ ἁγιασμός); these are intimately united (τε καί) as different aspects of the same thing. *Righteousness* is that which satisfies the demands of the law as a rule of justification; *sanctification*, or holiness, is that which satisfies the law as a rule of duty. Christ is both to us. He is our righteousness, because by his obedience and death he has fully satisfied the demands of justice, so that we are "the righteousness of God in him," 2 Cor. 5, 21. When we stand before the judgment-seat of God, Christ is our righteousness. He answers for us; he presents his own infinite merit as the all-sufficient reason for our justification. Rom. 3, 21. 22. 5, 19. Phil. 3, 9. He is also our *sanctification*. His Spirit dwells in all his people as the Spirit of holiness, so that they are transformed into his likeness from glory to glory. Wherever the Spirit dwells there are the fruits of the Spirit. Acts 26, 18. Rom. 8, 9. 10. Gal. 5, 22. Eph. 2, 5. 10.

3. The third effect is *redemption*, i. e. deliverance from evil. This term sometimes includes all the benefits received from Christ. When he is called our Redeemer he is presented as our deliverer from guilt, from hell, from sin, from the power of Satan, from the grave. But when redemption is distinguished from justification and sanctification, it refers to the final deliverance from evil. The "day of redemption" is the day when the work of Christ shall be consummated in the

perfect salvation of his people as to soul and body. Rom. 8, 23. Eph. 1, 14. 4, 30. Heb. 9, 12.

Those, then, who are in Christ have divine wisdom or the saving knowledge of God and of divine things; they have a righteousness which secures their justification. There is no condemnation to those that are in Christ Jesus, Rom. 8, 1. They are renewed after the image of God, and shall finally be presented without spot or blemish before the presence of his glory. And they are partakers of eternal redemption or full deliverance from all the evils of sin, and are introduced into the glorious liberty of the children of God. These infinite blessings can be obtained only through Christ. Union with him is the necessary, and the only necessary, condition of our participation of these blessings. And our union with Christ is of God. It is not of ourselves, by our own wisdom, goodness, or strength, but solely by his grace; and therefore must be sought as an unmerited favour.

31. That, according as it is written, He that glorieth, let him glory in the Lord.

That, i. e. *in order that*. The design of God in making wisdom, righteousness, sanctification, and redemption dependent on union with Christ, and union with Christ dependent, not on our merit, but on his own good pleasure, is that we should glory only in him; that is, that our confidence should be in him and not in ourselves, and that all the glory of our salvation should be ascribed to him and not to us. Such being the design of God in the work of redemption, it is obvious we must conform to it in order to be saved. We must seek wisdom, righteousness, sanctification, and redemption only in Christ; and we must seek union with Christ as an undeserved favour.

The passage quoted is probably Jeremiah 9, 23. 24, the sense of which is condensed. In quoting the Old Testament the apostle frequently cites the words as they stand, without so modifying them as to make them grammatically cohere with the context. As in the Septuagint, which he quotes, the imperative mood is used, the apostle here retains it, and instead of saying, 'In order that he who glories *should glory* in the Lord,' he says 'That, He that glories *let him glory* in the Lord.' Comp. 2, 9. Rom. 15, 3

CHAPTER II

Continues his defence of his mode of preaching. In vs. 1–5 he shows that he acted on the principles set forth in the preceding paragraph. In vs. 6–9 he shows that the gospel is the true wisdom. The source of this knowledge, as externally revealed and as spiritually apprehended, is the Holy Spirit, vs. 10–16.

Continuation of his defence of his mode of preaching. Vs. 1–16.

As God had determined to save men not by human wisdom but by the gospel, Paul, when he appeared in Corinth, came neither as an orator nor as a philosopher, but simply as a witness, vs. 1, 2. He had no confidence in himself, but relied for success exclusively on the demonstration of the Spirit, vs. 3, 4. The true foundation of faith is not reason, but the testimony of God, v. 5.

Though what he preached was not the wisdom of men, it was the wisdom of God, undiscoverable by human reason, vs. 6–9. The revealer of this divine wisdom is the Holy Ghost, he alone being competent to make this revelation, because he only knows the secret purposes of God, vs. 10–12. In communicating the knowledge thus derived from the Spirit, the apostle used words taught by the Spirit, v. 13. Though the knowledge communicated was divine, and although communicated in appropriate language, it was not received by the natural man, because the things of the Spirit can be discerned only by the spiritual, vs. 14–16.

1. And I, brethren, when I came to you, came not with excellency of speech or of wisdom, declaring unto you the testimony of God.

And I, i. e. *accordingly I.* 'In accordance with the clearly revealed purpose of God to reject the wisdom of the world and to make the cross the means of salvation.'

Excellency of speech or of wisdom. As speech and wisdom (λόγος and σοφία) are here distinguished, the former probably refers to the manner or form, and the latter to the matter of his preaching. It was neither as a rhetorician nor as a philosopher that he appeared among them. This clause may be connected either with the word *came*, 'I came not with excellency of speech;' or with the word *declaring*, 'I came not declaring with excellency of speech, &c.' The former mode is generally preferred, not only because of the position of the words in the sentence, but also because of the sense. Paul does not mean to say merely that he did not declare the testimony of God in a rhetorical or philosophical manner; but that what he declared was not the wisdom of men, but the revelation of God.

The testimony of God may mean either the testimony which Paul bore concerning God, or God's own testimony, i. e. what God had revealed and testified to be true. "The testimony of God" is, in this sense, the gospel, as in 2 Tim. 1, 8. The latter interpretation best suits the connection, as throughout these chapters Paul contrasts what reason teaches with what God teaches. He did not appear as a teacher of human wisdom, but as announcing what God had revealed.

2. For I determined not to know any thing* among you, save Jesus Christ, and him crucified.

For is confirmatory. 'I came not with excellency of speech or of wisdom, *for* I determined, &c.' The negative particle in this sentence may be connected either with the word *to know*, 'I determined *not* to know;' or with the word *determined*, 'I did not determine, i. e. I had no intention or purpose.' The position of the words (οὐ γὰρ ἔκρινα) is in favour of the latter interpretation. The meaning in either case is the same.

Jesus Christ, and him crucified. Paul's only design in going to Corinth was to preach Christ; and Christ not as a teacher, or as an example, or as a perfect man, or as a new starting point in the development of the race—all this would be mere philosophy; but Christ *as crucified*, i. e. as dying for our sins. Christ as a propitiation was the burden of Paul's preaching. It has been well remarked that *Jesus Christ* refers to the person of Christ, and *him crucified*, to his work; which constitute the sum of the gospel.

3. And I was with you in weakness, and in fear, and in much trembling.

* The common text here is τοῦ εἰδέναι τὶ. The τοῦ is omitted in the MSS., A, B. C. D. E. F. G. The reading adopted in the recent editions is τὶ εἰδέναι.

I came to you, ἐγενόμην πρὸς ὑμᾶς, I came to you and was with you, see John 1, 2. The weakness of which he here speaks was not bodily weakness; for although he elsewhere speaks of himself as weak in body, 2 Cor. 10, 10, and as suffering under bodily infirmity, Gal. 4, 14, yet here the whole context shows he refers to his state of mind. It was not in the consciousness of strength, self-confident and self-relying, that he appeared among them, but as oppressed with a sense of his weakness and insufficiency. He had a work to do which he felt to be entirely above his powers.

In fear and trembling, i. e. in anxiety, or solicitude of mind arising out of a sense of his insufficiency, and of the infinite importance of his work, 2 Cor. 7, 15. Phil. 2, 12. Eph. 6, 5.

4. And my speech and my preaching (was) not with enticing words of man's wisdom, but in demonstration of the Spirit and of power.

My speech and preaching (λόγος and κήρυγμα). If these terms are to be distinguished, the former may refer to his private, and the latter to his public instructions; or, the former is general, including all modes of address, and the latter specific, limited to public discourse. 'My instructions in general, and my public preaching in particular.' Both terms, however, may designate the same thing under different aspects.

His mode of preaching is described, first, negatively, and then positively. It was *not* with the enticing words of man's wisdom, i. e. the persuasive words which human wisdom would suggest. In his endeavours to bring men to the obedience of the faith, he did not rely upon his own skill in argument or persuasion. This is the negative statement. Positively, his preaching was *in* (or *with*, ἐν; the preposition is the same in both clauses, though rendered by our translators in the former, *with*, and in the latter, *in*) *the demonstration of the Spirit and of power*. This may mean, 'The demonstration of the powerful Spirit;' or, 'The demonstration of the Spirit and of (miraculous) power;' referring to the twofold evidence or proof of the gospel, viz., the internal influence of the Spirit, and the external evidence of miracles. The word (δύναμις), rendered *power*, often means miraculous power, but as such cannot be its meaning in the following verse, it is not probable it was intended to have that sense here. The phrase probably means 'The demonstration of which the Spirit is the author, and which is characterized by power;' so that the sense is. *the powerful demonstration of the Spirit.*

Demonstration (ἀπόδειξις) *setting forth*, exhibition of proof. Paul relied, therefore, for success, not on his skill in argument or persuasion, nor upon any of the resources of human wisdom, but on the testimony which the Spirit bore to the truth. The Holy Ghost demonstrated the gospel to be true.

5. That your faith should not stand in the wisdom of men, but in the power of God.

That, i. e. *in order that*. The design of the apostle in acting as stated in the preceding verse, was that the faith of his hearers might not rest upon human reason, but on the testimony of God. It might have been easy for him to argue the Corinthians into a conviction of the truth of the Gospel, by appealing to its superiority to heathenism and to the evidence of its divine origin afforded by prophecy and miracles. He might have exhibited the folly of idolatry, and the absurdity of pagan rites and ceremonies, and convinced them of the historical truth of Christianity. The conviction thus produced would be rational and important; but it would not be saving faith. Faith founded on such evidence is merely speculative. The true foundation of faith, or rather, the foundation of true faith, is *the power of God.* This is explained by what he had before called "the demonstration of the Spirit." That exercise of divine power, therefore, to which he refers as the ground of faith, is the powerful operation of the Spirit, bearing witness with and by the truth in our hearts. A faith which is founded on the authority of the church, or upon arguments addressed to the understanding, or even on the moral power of the truth as it affects the natural conscience, such as Felix had, is unstable and inoperative. But a faith founded on the demonstration of the Spirit is abiding, infallible, and works by love and purifies the heart.

In these verses, therefore, we are taught, 1. That the proper method to convert men in any community, Christian or Pagan, is to preach or set forth the truth concerning the person and work of Christ. Whatever other means are used must be subordinate and auxiliary, designed to remove obstacles, and to gain access for the truth to the mind, just as the ground is cleared of weeds and brambles in order to prepare it for the precious seed. 2. The proper state of mind in which to preach the gospel is the opposite of self-confidence or carelessness. The gospel should be preached with a sense of weakness and with great anxiety and solicitude. 3. The success of the gospel does not depend on the skill of the preacher, but on the demonstration of the Spirit. 4. The foundation of saving faith is not reason, i. e. not arguments addressed to the understanding, but the power of God as exerted with and by the truth upon the heart.

6. Howbeit we speak wisdom among them that are perfect: yet not the wisdom of this world, nor of the princes of this world, that come to nought.

Paul had in the preceding chapter, vs. 17–31, asserted the insufficiency of human wisdom, and in vs. 1–5 of this chapter, he had said he was not a teacher of human wisdom. Was it to be inferred from this that he despised knowledge, that he was an illiterate contemner of letters, or that he taught nonsense? Far from it; he taught the highest wisdom. It is plain from this whole discussion, that by the wisdom of the world, Paul means that knowledge of God and divine things which men derive from reason. It is also plain that what he says of the worthlessness of that knowledge has reference to it as a means of salvation. The objection urged against him was, that he did not teach philosophy. His answer is, philosophy cannot save men. Whatever may be its value within its own sphere and for its own ends, it is worse than useless as a substitute for the gospel. He was not for banishing philosophy from the schools, but from the pulpit. Let the dead bury the dead; but do not let them pretend to impart life.

Howbeit, *nevertheless*, i. e. 'although we do not teach human wisdom, we teach the true wisdom.' *Among them that are perfect* (ἐν τοῖς τελείοις), i. e. the mature, the full-grown, the competent. The ἐν here is not redundant as though the sense were *to* the perfect; but has its proper force *among*. Among one class of men the doctrine which he preached was regarded as foolishness, but among another it was seen to be divine wisdom. Who are meant by the perfect? There are two answers to this question. Some say they were the advanced or mature Christians as distinguished from the babes in Christ. Others say, they were believers as opposed to unbelievers; those taught by the Spirit and thus enabled to understand the truth, as opposed to the unrenewed. According to this view, Paul means to say that the gospel, although foolishness to the Greek, was the highest wisdom in the estimation of the truly enlightened. In favour of this view of the passage, and in opposition to the other, it may be argued, 1. That those who regarded Paul's doctrine as foolishness were not the babes in Christ, but the unrenewed, "the wise of this world;" consequently those to whom it was wisdom were not advanced Christians, but believers as such. Throughout the whole context, the opposition is between "the called" or converted, and the unconverted, and not between one class of believers and another class. 2. If "the perfect" here means advanced Christians as distinguished from babes in Christ, then the wisdom which Paul preached was not the gospel as such, but its higher doctrines. But this cannot be, because it is the doctrine of the cross, of Christ crucified, which he declares to be the power of God and the wisdom of God, 1, 24. And the description given in the following part of this chapter of the wisdom here intended, refers not to the higher doctrines of the gospel but to the gospel itself. The contrast is between the wisdom of the world and the wisdom of God, and not between the rudimental and the higher doctrines of the gospel. Besides, what are these higher doctrines which Paul preached only to the élite of the church? No one knows. Some say one thing, and some another. But there are no higher doctrines than those taught in this epistle and in those to the Romans and Ephesians, all addressed to the mass of the people. The New Testament makes no distinction between (πίστις and γνῶσις) higher and lower doctrines. It does indeed speak of a distinction between milk and strong meat, but that is a distinction, not between kinds of doctrine, but between one mode of instruction and another. In catechisms designed for children the church pours out all the treasures of her knowledge, but in the form of milk, i. e. in a form adapted to the weakest capacities. For all these reasons we conclude that by "the perfect" the apostle means the competent, the people of God as distinguished from the men of the world; and by wisdom, not any higher doctrines, but the simple gospel, which is the wisdom of God as distinguished from the wisdom of men.

The apostle describes this wisdom, first negatively, by saying it is not *the wisdom of this world*, or, *wisdom not of this world*, i. e. it belongs not to the world, and is not attained by the men of the world. *Nor of the princes of this world.* This designation includes all who take the first rank among men; men of influence, whether for their wisdom, birth, or power. He does not refer exclusively to magistrates, or princes, in the restricted sense of that term. This seems plain from the connection, and from what follows in v. 8. *Who come to nought,* i. e. whom it is God's purpose to confound, as taught above, 1, 28.

7. But we speak the wisdom of God in a mystery, (even) the hidden (wisdom), which God ordained before the world unto our glory.

Having in v. 6 stated what this wisdom is not, he here states what it is. It is, first, the wisdom of God; secondly, it is mysterious, or hidden; thirdly, it is a system of truth which God from eternity had determined to reveal for the salvation of his people. In other words, it is the revelation of the coun sels of eternity in reference to the redemption of man.

The wisdom of God, i. e. the wisdom derived from God; which he has revealed, as distinguished from any form of knowledge of human origin. *In a mystery.* The word mystery always means something into which men must be initiated; something undiscoverable by human reason. Whether its being undiscoverable arises from its lying in the future, or because hid in the unrevealed purposes of God, or from its own nature as beyond our comprehension, is not determined by the signification of the word, but is to be learned from the context. The most natural connection of the words here is with what precedes, "wisdom in a mystery," for mysterious, or hidden wisdom, as is immediately explained by what follows. As there is no connecting article (between σοφίαν and μυστηρίῳ) in the original, some prefer connecting this clause with the verb. 'We speak in a mystery,' i. e. as declaring a mystery or matter of revelation.

Which God *before the world* (πρὸ τῶν αἰώνων), *before the ages,* i. e. before time, or from eternity, *preordained to our glory*—predetermined in reference to our glory. The word *glory* is often used for all the benefits of salvation. It includes all the excellence and blessedness which Christ has secured for his people, Rom. 5, 2. The idea that the scheme of redemption, which the apostle here calls the wisdom of God, was from eternity formed in the divine mind, far out of the reach of human penetration, and has under the gospel been made known for the salvation of men, is one often presented by the apostle, Rom. 16, 25. 26. Eph. 3, 9.

8. Which none of the princes of this world knew for had they known (it), they would not have crucified the Lord of glory.

Which refers to *wisdom*, and not to *glory;* because the former, and not the latter, is the subject of discourse. 'Which wisdom none of the princes, i. e. the great men, of this world knew.' The reference is here principally to the rulers of the Jews, the authors of the crucifixion of Christ, and the representatives of the class to which they belonged. It was the world in its princes who rejected Christ.

Lord of glory is a title of divinity. It means, possessor of divine excellence. "Who is the King of glory? The LORD of hosts, he is the King of glory," Ps. 24, 10. Acts 7, 2. James 2, 1. Eph. 1, 17. The person crucified, therefore, was a divine person. Hence the deed was evidence of inconceivable blindness and wickedness. It was one that could only be done through ignorance. "And now, brethren," said the apostle Peter to the Jews, "I wot that through ignorance ye did it, as *did* also your rulers," Acts 3, 17. The fact that the princes of this world were so blind as not to see that Christ was the Lord of glory, Paul cites as proof of their ignorance of the wisdom of God. Had they known the one, they would have known the other.

This passage illustrates a very important principle or usage of Scripture. We see that the person of Christ may be designated from his divine nature, when what is affirmed of him is true only of his human nature. The Lord of glory was crucified; the Son of God was born of a woman; he who was equal with God humbled himself to be obedient unto death. In like manner we speak of the birth or death of a man without meaning that the soul is born or dies; and the Scriptures speak of the birth and death of the Son of God, without meaning that the divine nature is subject to these changes. It is also plain that to predicate ignorance, subjection, suffering, death, or any other limitation of the Son of God, is no more inconsistent with the divinity of the person so designated, than to predicate birth and death of a man, is inconsistent with the immateriality and immortality of the human soul.

Whatever is true either of the soul or body may be predicated of a man as a person; and whatever is true of either the divine or human nature of Christ may be predicated of Christ as a person. We need not hesitate therefore to say with Paul, the Lord of glory was crucified; or even, in accordance with the received text in Acts 20, 28, "God purchased the church with his blood." The person who died was truly God, although the divine nature no more died than the soul of man does when the breath leaves his body.

9. But as it is written, Eye hath not seen, nor ear heard, neither have entered into the heart of man, the things which God hath prepared for them that love him.

The meaning of this verse is plain, although there are several difficulties connected with it. Paul had said, he preached the hidden wisdom of God, which none of the princes of this world knew; he taught what no eye hath seen, nor ear heard, nor heart conceived. That is, he preached truth undiscoverable by human reason. *To enter into the heart* means to occur to the mind. Compare in the Hebrew, Isaiah 65, 17.

The first difficulty connected with this verse is a grammatical one, which does not appear in our version because of the freedom of the translation. Literally the passage reads, 'What no eye saw, and no ear heard, and no heart conceived, what God has prepared for those who love him—.' The sentence is incomplete. This difficulty may be met either by a reference to the usage referred to in the note on the last verse of the preceding chapter, v. 31, the custom of the apostles to quote passages from the Old Testament without weaving them grammatically into their own discourses. Or, we may supply, as many do, the word (λαλοῦμεν) '*we speak* what God hath prepared for those who love him.' Or this verse may be connected with what follows: 'What eye hath not seen— what (namely) God hath prepared for his people, he hath revealed to us by his Spirit.'—The first of these explanations is generally adopted and is the most satisfactory.

The second difficulty relates to the passage quoted. As the formula, "As it is written," is never used by the apostles except n the citation of the canonical books of the Old Testament, it cannot be admitted that Paul intended to quote either some book now lost, or some apocryphal writing. If it be assumed that he intended to quote Isaiah 64, 4, the difficulty is twofold, first, the language or words are different, and secondly, the sense is different. Isaiah 64, 4, (or 3 in the Hebrew) as literally translated by Dr. J. A. Alexander, is: "And from eternity they have not heard, they have not perceived by the ear, the eye hath not seen, a God beside thee (who) will do for (one) waiting for him." The idea is, that men had never known any other God than Jehovah who did, or could do, what he threatened to do. The Septuagint expresses the same idea. The meaning in Isaiah as connected with what precedes, seems to be that the reason why such fearful things as had been predicted were to be expected from Jehovah is, that he alone had proved himself able to perform them. To get over this difficulty some propose a different interpretation of the passage in the prophet. By connecting it with what follows, and by taking the word *God* in the vocative, the sense may be, 'From eternity they have not heard, nor perceived by the ear, eye hath not seen, O God, without thee, (i. e. without a revelation) what he, (or, by change of person) what thou hast prepared for those that wait for thee.' This is the version given in the Vulgate, and brings the passage into harmony with the apostle's quotation.

Others, assuming the first-mentioned interpretation of the passage in Isaiah to be the true one, consider the apostle as using scriptural language without intending to give the sense of the original. This we often do, and it is not unfrequently done in the New Testament, Rom. 10, 18. *As it is written* is not, in this case, the form of quotation, but is rather equivalent to saying, 'To use the language of Scripture.'

A third explanation of this difficulty is, that the apostle did not intend to quote any one passage of scripture, but to appeal to its authority for a clearly revealed truth. It is certainly taught in the Old Testament that the human mind cannot penetrate into the counsels of God; his purposes can only be known by a supernatural revelation. This is the truth for which the apostle cites the authority of the Old Testament. There is, therefore, not the slightest ground for imputing failure of memory, or an erroneous interpretation to the inspired apostle.

10. But God hath revealed (them) unto us by his Spirit: for the Spirit searcheth all things, yea, the deep things of God.

What was undiscoverable by human reason, God hath revealed by his Spirit. *Unto us*, i. e. unto those to whom this revelation, was made, viz. "the holy apostles and prophets," Eph. 3, 5. This revelation was made by the Spirit, *for* he alone is competent to make it; for he alone searches the deep things of God. *Searches*, i. e. explores, accurately and thoroughly knows. The word does not express the process of investigation, but rather its results, viz., profound knowledge. Thus God is said to search the hearts of the children of men, to intimate that there is nothing in man that escapes his notice, Rom. 8, 27. Rev. 2, 23. So there is nothing in God unknown to the Spirit. *The deep things*, i. e. depths of God, the inmost recesses, as it were, of his being, perfections and purposes. The Spirit, therefore, is fully competent to reveal that wisdom which had for ages been hid in God. This passage proves at once the personality and the divinity of the Holy Ghost. His personality, because intelligent activity is ascribed to him; he *searches;* his divinity, because omniscience is ascribed to him; he knows all that God knows.

11. For what man knoweth the things of a man, save the spirit of man which is in him? even so the things of God knoweth no man, but the Spirit of God.

This verse is designed to illustrate two points: First, as no one knows the thoughts of a man but the man himself, so no one knows the thoughts of God, but God himself. Therefore no one but a divine person is competent to make a revelation of the thoughts and purposes of God. Second, as every man does know his own thoughts, so the Spirit of God knows the thoughts of God. His knowledge of what is in God is analogous to that which we have of the contents of our own consciousness. The analogies of scripture, however, are not to be pressed beyond the point which they are intended to illustrate. The point to be illustrated here is, the knowledge of the Spirit. He knows what is in God, as we know what is in ourselves. It is not to be inferred from this that the Spirit of God bears in other points the same relation to God, that our spirits do to us.

12. Now we have received, not the spirit of the world, but the Spirit which is of God; that we might know the things that are freely given to us of God.

The apostle had set forth two sources of knowledge, the one, human; the other, divine; the one, the informing principle which is in man; the other, the informing principle which is of God. And he asserts that the source of that wisdom or knowledge which he communicated, was not the former, but the latter. It was not human reason, but the Spirit of God. *The spirit of the world* does not here mean a worldly disposition or temper; but *spirit* is that which knows and teaches. The spirit of the world is therefore a periphrase for reason, which is the principle of knowledge in men. When Paul says he had not received that spirit, he means that human reason was not the source of the knowledge which he communicated. *The Spirit which is of God*, is the Holy Spirit as proceeding from him and sent by him as the instructor of men. *To receive* the Spirit is to be the subject of his influence. It, therefore, depends upon the context and on the nature of the influences spoken of, who are intended by those who receive the Spirit. Here the whole connection shows that the apostle is speaking of revelation and inspiration; and therefore *we* must mean *we apostles*, (or Paul himself,) and not we Christians.

That, i. e. in order that, *we might know the things freely given to us of God*, i. e. the things graciously revealed by God. This clause does not refer to inward spiritual blessings now enjoyed by believers, nor to the future blessedness of the saints, except so far as these are included in the general subject of Paul's preaching. The connection is with v. 10. 'What human reason could not discover, God hath revealed to us apostles, in order that we might know what he has thus graciously communicated.' The subject is the wisdom of God, the gospel, as distinguished from the wisdom of the world. This is clear both from what precedes and from what follows.

13. Which things also we speak, not in the words which man's wisdom teacheth, but which the Holy Ghost teacheth; comparing spiritual things with spiritual.

Which things; the things revealed by the Spirit. *We also* speak. We do not only know, we also communicate the things which God has revealed. How is this done? What language did the apostle use in communicating what he had received by divine revelation? He answers, according to his usual method, first, negatively; and then, positively. It was not done "in the words which man's wisdom teacheth." This includes two things. The words used by the apostle were neither such as the skill of the rhetorician would suggest, nor such as his own mind, uninfluenced by the Spirit of God, suggested. The affirmative statement is, that the words used were taught by the Holy Ghost. This is verbal inspiration, or the doctrine that the writers of the Scriptures were controlled by the Spirit of God in the choice of the words which they employed in communicating divine truth. This has been stigmatized as "the mechanical theory of inspiration," degrading the sacred penmen into mere machines. It is objected to this doctrine that it leaves the diversity of style which marks the different portions of the Bible, unaccounted for But, if God can control the thoughts of a man without making him a machine, why cannot he control his language? And why may he not render each writer, whether poetical or prosaic, whether polished or rude, whether aphoristic or logical, infallible in the use of his characteristic style? If the language of the Bible be not inspired, then we have the truth communicated through the discolouring and distorting medium of human imperfection. Paul's direct assertion is that the words which he used, were taught by the Holy Ghost.

Comparing spiritual things with spiritual; or rather, *joining spiritual things to spiritual words*, or, explaining the things of the Spirit in the words of the Spirit. For the use of συγκρίνειν in the sense of *interpreting* or *explaining*, see Gen. 40, 8. 16. 41, 12. 15. Dan. 5, 12. in the LXX. This interpretation is demanded by the connection. The apostle had said that the truths which he taught were revealed by the Spirit; and that the words which he used were taught by the Spirit, which he sums up by saying, he explained spiritual things in spiritual words. This view of the passage is perfectly consistent with the signification of the words. The original word (συγκρίνω) means not only mentally to combine and hence to compare, but also to join together; and also to explain. It is used in the Septuagint to express the act of interpreting dreams or enigmas. The clause in question may, therefore, be translated either, *combining spiritual things with spiritual words;* or, *explaining* the one by the other. Besides, the word *spiritual* (πνευματικοῖς), which has no substantive connected with it, most naturally agrees with *words* (λόγοις) understood, which immediately precedes.

The other interpretation, *comparing spiritual things with spiritual*, whether it means comparing the Old Testament with the New, as some say; or, as others understand it, comparing one portion of the Spirit's teaching with another, is inconsistent with the context. Much less can be said in favour of a third interpretation of this clause adopted by many, who understand the apostle to say, he explains spiritual things to spiritual *persons*. This anticipates what follows.

14. But the natural man receiveth not the things of the Spirit of God; for they are foolishness unto him: neither can he know (them), because they are spiritually discerned.

Although *the things of the Spirit*, that is, the truths of his word, are so clearly revealed; and although they have been communicated in language taught by the Spirit, yet, by a certain class of men, they are rejected. That is, they are not believed, appreciated, and obeyed. This class of men is called *natural*. The meaning of this term cannot be determined by the mere signification of the word (ψυχικός), for it signifies both sensual (i. e. under the influence of the lower animal principles of our nature), and also *natural*, i. e. under the influence of what belongs to the nature of man as it now exists, as distinguished from the Spirit of God. Many commentators say that the (ψυχικοί) *natural* are the sensual, and the opposite class the (πνευματικοί) *spiritual* are the intellectual, the rational, those under the influence of the (πνεῦμα) *spirit* in the sense of the higher, as distinguished from the lower, principles of our nature. According to this view, Paul means to say, that although sensual men do not receive the things of the Spirit, intellectual men do. This interpretation, however, cannot be correct. 1. Because it gives a meaning to the passage not only inconsistent with the direct assertion of the apostle, but opposed to the whole drift and design of his argument. He not only declares that it was not the wise, the refined and cultivated who received the gospel—but his whole object is to prove that the reason of man, or man in the highest development of his nature, can neither discover "the things of the Spirit," nor receive them when revealed. It is of God, and not because of their superior culture or refinement, that men are in Christ, 1, 30. These things are hid from the wise and prudent, and revealed unto babes, Matt. 11, 25. 2. Because the word *spiritual*, when used in the New Testament of persons, never means *intellectual*. It always means one under the influence of the Holy Spirit. It therefore must have that meaning here. 3. The very distinction designed to be expressed here and elsewhere by the terms natural and spiritual, is that between nature and grace, between the natural and supernatural, James 3, 15. Jude 19. 4. The reason assigned why the natural man does not receive the things of the Spirit, viz., because "they are spiritually discerned," does not mean 'because they are rationally discerned,' and therefore it is not the want of due cultivation of the reason that characterizes the natural man, but the want of the Spirit. By *natural man*, therefore, we must understand the unrenewed man; the man under the influence of human nature, as distinguished from those who are under the influence of the Holy Spirit. The natural or unrenewed man does not *receive* the things of the Spirit. As the things which the Holy Ghost has revealed address themselves not only to the intellect as true, but to the conscience as obligatory and to the affections as excellent and lovely, not to receive them, is not to recognize, in our inward experience, their truth, authority, and excellence.

For they are foolishness unto them. The word (μωρός) *foolish*, as an adjective, means in Greek, *dull*, *insipid*, *tasteless;* as a substantive, one that is dull, or stupid; that is, one on whom truth, duty and excellence do not produce their proper effect. *Foolishness* (μωρία) is that which is to us absurd, insipid, powerless. When, therefore, it is said that the things of the Spirit are foolishness to the natural man, it means that they are to him absurd, insipid and distasteful.

And he cannot know them. *To know* is to discern the nature of any thing, whether as true, or good, or beautiful. This is in accordance with the constant usage of scripture. To know God is to discern his truth and excellence; to know the truth is to apprehend it as true and good. The wise are the good, that is, those who discern the truth and excellence of divine things. The fools are the wicked, those who are insensible to truth and goodness. What, therefore, the apostle here affirms of the natural or unrenewed man is, that he cannot discern the truth, excellence, or beauty of divine things. He cannot do it. It is not simply that he does not do it; or that he will not do it, but he cannot. We do not say of a clown that he will not discern the truth, excellence, and beauty of a poem. The difficulty is not merely in his will but in his whole inward state. The thing is foolishness to him. So the scriptures do not say of the natural man merely that he will not discern the things of the Spirit, because the difficulty in his case is not in the will alone, but in his whole inward state. He cannot know them. And the reason is,

Because they are spiritually discerned. That is, because they are discerned through the Spirit. Therefore those who have not the Spirit cannot discern them. If the effect of sin on the human soul is to make it blind to the truth, excellence and beauty of divine things; if, as the apostle asserts, the natural, or unrenewed, man is in such a state that the things of the Spirit are foolishness to him, absurd, insipid and distasteful, then it follows that he can discern them only through the Spirit. His inward state must be changed by the influence of the Spirit before he can apprehend the truth and excellence of the gospel. There must be congeniality between the perceiver and the thing perceived. Only the pure in heart can see God. If our gospel be hid, says the apostle, it is hid to them that are lost. The only hope of the unrenewed, therefore, is in doing as the blind did in the days of Christ. They must go to him for spiritual discernment; and those who go to him he will in no wise cast out.

15. But he that is spiritual judgeth all things, yet he himself is judged of no man.

To judge here means to discern, to appreciate, and thus pass judgment upon. As the original word is the same in this as in the preceding verse, there is no good reason why the translation should vary. The spiritual man discerns the things which are spiritually discerned, though he himself is not discerned or properly appreciated by any natural man. The *all things* here spoken of are limited by the context to the things of the Spirit. It is not of the officers of the church only, nor of the church collectively, but of each and every man in whom the Holy Spirit dwells, that the apostle affirms this ability to discern the truth, excellence and beauty of divine things. It is as impossible that one man should discern for another what is true and good, as that one man should see for another. We must see for ourselves or not at all. The right of private judgment in matters of religion, is inseparable from the indwelling of the Spirit. Those who can see, have the right to see. It is the office of the Holy Spirit to reveal the truth, to open our eyes to discern it in its true nature, and to feel its power. It is on this demonstration of the Spirit, as taught above, that saving faith is founded. And as this demonstration is granted to every one who has the Spirit, the faith of the Christian is founded neither on the wisdom of men nor on the authority of the church, and is subject to neither.

Yet he himself is judged of no man. This again is limited by the context. He is appreciated by no man who has not the Spirit. Paul afterwards says it was to him a small matter to be judged by man's judgment, 4, 3. He is not here speaking of the legitimate subjection of the believer to his brethren; for he elsewhere teaches that those who have the Spirit may sit in judgment on those who profess to be spiritual, and determine how far they are really led by the Spirit. And he gives the rule by which that judgment is to be directed, 5, 9–12. 12, 3. Gal. 1, 8. If any man profess to be spiritual, and yet does what the Spirit in his word forbids, or denies what the Spirit teaches, we know that he deceives himself, and that the truth is not in him. We must try the spirits, whether they be of God. This is true, and is perfectly consistent with what the apostle here says, which only means that the spiritual man cannot be discerned or estimated aright by those who are not spiritual.

16. For who hath known the mind of the Lord, that he may instruct him? But we have the mind of Christ.

This is a confirmation of what precedes. No one can judge a spiritual man, for that would be to judge the Lord. The Lord had revealed certain doctrines. The spiritual discern those doctrines to be true. For any man to pronounce them false, and to judge those who held them, supposes he is able to teach the Lord. As no one can do this, no one can judge those who have the mind of Christ, that is, those whom Christ by his Spirit has taught the truth. Syllogistically stated, the argument would stand thus: No one can instruct the Lord. We have the mind of the Lord. Therefore no one can instruct or judge us. The first member of this syllogism is expressed in the language of Isaiah 40, 15, according to the Septuagint. The philosophers of Greece and the scribes among the Jews had sat in judgment upon Paul, and pronounced his preaching foolishness. He tells them they were not competent judges. The natural man cannot discern the things of the Spirit, and is incompetent to judge those whom the Spirit has taught. As what we teach is the mind of the Lord, to condemn our doctrine, or to judge us as the teachers of those doctrines, is to condemn the Lord.

What in the Old Testament is said of Jehovah is often in the New Testament applied to Christ. This is the case here. Who hath known the mind of the Lord? means, who hath known the mind of Jehovah? *We have the mind of Christ*, therefore, means, we have the mind of Jehovah. What is true of the one is true of the other. The same person who is revealed in the New Testament as the Son of God, was revealed of old as Jehovah. This teaches how firm a foundation the believer has for his faith, and how impossible it is for any one taught by the Spirit to give up his convictions to the authority of men.

CHAPTER III.

Transition from the defence of his mode of preaching to the subject of their divisions, vs. 1–5. The true relation of ministers to the church as servants, and not party leaders, vs. 7–23.

Reproof of the Corinthians for their dissensions about their religious teachers. Vs. 1–23.

The apostle resumes the subject of the contentions in the church of Corinth. He passes to that subject from the defence of his mode of preaching by a natural association. One of the objections against him was, that his preaching was too simple. He answers, he could not make it otherwise, because they were mere babes in Christ. The proof of their being in this infantile or carnal state was that strifes and divisions existed among them; one saying, I am of Paul; and another, I am of Apollos, vs. 1–4.

As their dissensions had reference to their religious teachers, the apostle endeavours to correct the evil by presenting the ministerial office in its true light. 1. Ministers were not heads of schools or rival sects as were the Grecian philosophers, but mere servants, without any authority or power of their own. One may plant, and another water, but the whole increase is of God, vs. 5–7. 2. Ministers are one. They have one master and one work. They may have different departments in that great work, but they are like fellow-labourers on the same farm, or fellow-builders on the same temple, vs. 8. 9. 3. In the discharge of their respective duties they incur a great responsibility. If they attempt to build up the temple of God with the rubbish of their own wisdom, they will be severely punished. If they employ the materials which God has furnished, they will be rewarded, vs. 10–15. 4. It is because the church is the temple of God, that ministers will be held to this strict account for the doctrines which they preach, and for the way in which they execute their office, vs. 16. 17. 5. No minister need deceive himself in this matter. He cannot preach a higher wisdom than the wisdom of God; and to learn that wisdom he must renounce his own, vs. 18–20. 6. Therefore the people should not place their confidence in ministers, who belong to the church, and not the church to them. To the interests and consummation of the church, all things, visible and invisible, are made subservient, vs. 21–23.

1. And I, brethren, could not speak unto you as unto spiritual, but as unto carnal,* (even) as unto babes in Christ.

There were two classes of opponents of the apostle in Corinth. The false teachers, some of whom he denounces as anti-Christian, and others he speaks of as only errorists; and secondly, those members of the church whom these false teachers had seduced. As against the false teachers and the unconverted Jews and Greeks he upheld the simple gospel as higher than the wisdom of the world. His only answer to their objection that he did not preach with "the wisdom of words," was that the wisdom of the world was foolishness with

* Instead of σαρκικοῖς, *unto carnal*, ach, Tischendorf and others read σαρκίνοις, *to those made of flesh*, comp. 2 Cor. 3, 3. The latter term, used in a moral sense, would be stronger than the former, as indicating the very nature as carnal. In all the places in the New Testament where the form σάρκινος appears, except in 2 Cor 3, 3, the reading is doubtful. Rom. 7, 14. Heb. 7, 16, and here.

God. To the objection, as urged by believers, that his preaching was too elementary, he answered, it was adapted to their state. He could only speak to them as to children.

They were *babes in Christ*, that is, children in Christian knowledge and experience. This idea he expresses by saying they were not *spiritual* but *carnal*. Now as all Christians are spiritual, in the sense in which that term is used in the preceding chapter, to say that men are not spiritual in that sense, would be to say they are not Christians. Here, however, the apostle tells those whom he admits to be Christians, and whom he calls brethren, that they are not spiritual. He must use the word therefore in a modified sense. This is a very common usage. When we predicate spirituality of a Christian as compared to other Christians, we mean that he is eminently spiritual. But when the distinction is between Christians and the world, then every Christian is said to be spiritual. In like manner we speak of some Christians as worldly or carnal, without intending to deny that they are Christians. It is obvious that the apostle uses the terms here in the same manner. He is not speaking of Christians as distinguished from the world, but of one class of Christians as distinguished from another.

2. I have fed you with milk and not with meat; for hitherto ye were not able (to bear it), neither yet now are ye able.

As they were children, he had treated them accordingly. He *had fed them with milk*; literally, 'I gave you milk to drink and not meat.' A concise form of expression. What is the distinction which the apostle here makes between milk and meat? It is evidently not the distinction between the wisdom of the world and the wisdom of God. Paul did not preach the wisdom of the world to babes in Christ, and the wisdom of God to advanced Christians. Neither does he sanction any thing of the nature of the *Disciplina Arcani*, or doctrine of the hidden essence of Christianity, which was introduced in later times. For the sake either of conciliating the heathen, or of preventing beginners from forming false notions of the gospel, it became common deliberately to conceal the truth. This is the foundation of the doctrine of reserve, as it is called, which the Romish church has so extensively practised and taught, inculcating a blind faith, and keeping the people in ignorance. Neither is the distinction that which also extensively prevailed in the early church after the age of the apostles, between truth as the object of faith and truth as the object of knowledge. This is a distinction true in itself, but as then understood, it meant nothing less than the difference between the doctrines of the Bible and the speculations of men. Philosophers of our own, and of every other age, have been willing to allow the people the truth as presented in the Scriptures, provided they themselves were allowed to explain them away into philosophical formulas. The true nature of the distinction is to be learnt partly from the import of the figure, and partly from parallel passages. The import of the figure leads to the conclusion that the difference is rather in the mode of instruction, than in the things taught. The same truth in one form is milk, in another form strong meat. "Christ," says Calvin, "is milk for babes, and strong meat for men." Every doctrine which can be taught to theologians, is taught to children. We teach a child that God is a Spirit, every where present and knowing all things; and he understands it. We tell him that Christ is God and man in two distinct natures and one person for ever. This to the child is milk, but it contains food for angels. The truth expressed in these propositions may be expanded indefinitely, and furnish nourishment for the highest intellects to eternity. The difference between milk and strong meat, according to this view, is simply the difference between the more or less perfect development of the things taught. This view is confirmed by those passages in which the same distinction is made. Thus in Hebrews 5, 11–14, the apostle speaks of his readers as having need of milk and not of strong meat. The reference is there to the distinction between the simple doctrine of the priesthood of Christ and the full development of that doctrine. The important truth is that there are not two sets of doctrine, a higher and a lower form of faith, one for the learned and the other for the unlearned; there is no part of the gospel which we are authorized to keep back from the people. Every thing which God has revealed is to be taught to every one just so fast and so far as he has the capacity to receive it.

3. For ye are yet carnal: for whereas (there is)

among you envying, and strife, and divisions, are ye not carnal, and walk as men?

Their unfitness to receive any other nourishment than that adapted to children, is proved by their being carnal; and their being carnal is proved by the divisions existing among them. *Ye are yet carnal*, i. e. under the influence of the flesh, or corrupt nature. They were imperfectly sanctified. Even Paul said of himself, 'I am carnal.' This term therefore may be applied even to the most advanced Christians. Its definite meaning depends on the context.

The existence among them of the evils mentioned was proof of their low religious state. Of these evils the first was *envying* (ζῆλος). The word means zeal, fervid feeling. Whether good or bad, and of what particular kind depends on the connection. Here *party spirit* would seem to be the special evil intended. This gives rise to *strife* (ἔρις), and that again to *divisions* (διχοστασία), literally, *standing apart*; here not sects, but parties. If these things are among you, asks the apostle, are ye not carnal, *and walk as men?* 'To walk as men' is to be guided by principles which belong to men, as distinguished from the Spirit of God. The doctrine that human nature is corrupt, and that all holiness in man is due to the influence of the Spirit, is taken for granted every where in the Bible. Therefore "the world" means the wicked or the unrenewed; to be worldly, or to act after the manner of men, is to act wickedly.

The description here given of the state of the church of Corinth is not inconsistent with the commendations bestowed upon it in the beginning of the first chapter. Viewed in comparison with the heathen around them, or even with other churches, the Corinthians deserved the praise there given them. But judged by the standard of the gospel, or of their privileges, they deserved the censures which the apostle so faithfully administers. Besides, in addressing the same church, the apostle has sometimes one class of its members in view, and sometimes another. He therefore sometimes speaks as if they were all Jews, at other times as though they were all Gentiles; sometimes as though they were weak and narrow-minded, and sometimes as if they were latitudinarian—one time he addresses them as if they were in a high state of piety, and at another, as if they were in a very low state. His language is to be limited in its application to those for whom the context in any case may show it was intended.

4. For while one saith, I am of Paul; and another, I (am) of Apollos; are ye not carnal?

This confirms the fact that there were such divisions among them as proved them to be governed by unholy feelings, and also explains the nature of those divisions. There were in Corinth, as appears from 1, 12, more parties than two; but the apostle confines himself to those here mentioned, because throughout the whole discussion he has had reference to the opposition of the Grecian element in the church; and because from the intimate relation between himself and Apollos, he could speak of him as freely as he did of himself. As the party spirit which disturbed the peace of the Corinthian church arose from wrong views of the relation of ministers to the church, the apostle endeavours to correct the evil by presenting that relation in its true light.

5. Who then is Paul, and who is Apollos, but ministers by whom ye believed, even as the Lord gave to every man?

This passage may read, 'Who then is Paul, and who is Apollos? ministers by whom ye believed,' &c. Ministers are mere instruments in the hands of God. The doctrines which they preach are not their own discoveries, and the power which renders their preaching successful is not in them. They are nothing; and therefore it is an entire perversion of their relation to the church to make them the heads of parties. In the oldest MSS. the name of Apollos stands first; and some of them have τί instead of τίς. '*What* then is Apollos, and *what* is Paul.' Both these emendations are adopted by the later editors.

Paul and Apollos, men of the highest office and of the highest gifts, are *ministers* (διάκονοι) *waiters*, *attendants*, *servants*; so called not from their relation to God merely, as those who serve him, but also because of their relation to the church, whose they are, to whom they belong, and whom they serve.

By whom, i. e. by whose instrumentality, *ye are believers*, or, *became believers*. The design of the ministry is to bring men to "the obedience of faith," Rom. 1, 5. It is appointed for that end by God himself, and therefore it is of the greatest importance and value. This Paul does not deny. He admits, and often urges the necessity of the office for the extension and edification of the church, Eph. 4, 11–16. The people, therefore, are bound to regard the ministry as a divine institution, and to value its services; but preachers are not to be regarded as party leaders, or as lords over God's heritage.

Even as the Lord gave to every man; literally, *to each one*, i. e. to each minister. They are all servants, and each has his appointed work to perform, Rom. 12, 3. *The Lord* here probably refers to God, though elsewhere the appointment of ministers and the distribution of their various gifts are referred to Christ. Here, however, vs. 9. 10, the reference is to God. In scripture the same act is sometimes referred to one, and sometimes to another of the persons in the Trinity, because they are one God.

6. I have planted, Apollos watered: but God gave the increase.

This illustrates two points; first, the diversity of service on the part of ministers, spoken of in v. 5, one plants and another waters; and secondly, the entirely subordinate and instrumental character of their service. As in nature, planting and watering are not the efficient causes of vegetation; so in the church, ministerial acts are not the efficient causes of grace. In both cases all the efficiency is of God. And as in nature, planting and watering by human instrumentality, are not the necessary conditions of vegetation, so neither are ministerial acts the necessary conditions of faith. On the other hand, however, as the work of the husbandman is the ordinary and appointed means of securing a harvest, so the work of the ministry is the ordinary means of conversion.

7. So then, neither is he that planteth any thing, neither he that watereth: but God that giveth the increase.

This is the conclusion. Ministers are nothing. They are the instruments in the hands of God. He only is to be looked up to as the source of truth, of strength, or of success. To him is to be referred all the good ministers may be the instruments of effecting. If this be so, if ministers are thus inefficient, why should any one say, I am of Paul? as though Paul would save him; or, as though a mere instrument could forgive sin or impart grace.

8. Now he that planteth and he that watereth are one: and every man shall receive his own reward, according to his own labour.

Are one. Ministers have the same office; they have the same work, they stand in the same relation to God and to his Church. They are fellow-labourers. To array the one against the other, is, therefore, inconsistent with their relation to each other and to the people whom they serve.

Every man shall receive his own reward. Diversity and unity is the law of all God's works. Ministers are one, yet they have different gifts, different services to perform. One plants and another waters, and they have different rewards.

According to his own labour. The rule of reward is not the talents or gifts, nor the success of ministers, but their labours. This brings the humblest on a level with the most exalted; the least successful with the most highly favoured. The faithful, laborious minister or missionary who labours in obscurity and without apparent fruit, will meet a reward far beyond that of those who, with less self-denial and effort, are made the instruments of great results. Corinth was the field of labour of a multitude of teachers, some faithful, and some unfaithful; some laborious, and others indolent and self-indulgent. Each would have to answer for himself, and would receive a reward proportioned to his fidelity and self-denial.

9. For we are labourers together with God: ye are God's husbandry, (ye are) God's building.

For we are labourers together with God. This is at once the reason why ministers are one, and why they are to be rewarded according to their labours. They are one because they are all co-workers with God in the same great enterprise; and they are to be rewarded according to their labour, because that is the rule according to which labourers are rewarded. The propriety of this representation is apparent, because the church is God's *husbandry*, or farm, which he renders fruitful by the light of truth and the dew of his grace, and on which his servants labour. This is a familiar scriptural illustration, as the church is often called the vineyard of the Lord, in which his ministers are labourers. A labourer who does not labour is a contradiction; and a minister who is not a worker cannot expect a labourer's reward. *Ye are God's building.* A still more frequent figure; as the church is so often compared to a temple which is in the course of erection, and of which ministers are the builders, Eph. 2, 20–22. 1 Pet. 2, 5. Union and fidelity in labour are required of those engaged in tilling the same farm, or in the erection of the same building; and they are no less required in those engaged in cultivating the vineyard of the Lord, or in erecting his temple. The apostle drops the former, and carries out the latter figure.

10. According to the grace of God which is given unto me, as a wise master-builder, I have laid the foundation, and another buildeth thereon. But let every man take heed how he buildeth thereupon.

According to the grace of God given unto me. Paul often speaks of his apostolic office as *a grace* or favour which he had received of God, but here, as in 15, 10, the reference is more general. By *the grace of God* he means all the gifts and influences of the Spirit, which not only qualified him for his work, but rendered him so laborious and faithful. Here, as elsewhere, he attributes to God all he was, and all that he was enabled to accomplish.

As a wise master-builder. Wise (σοφός), i. e. skilful. The word is familiarly used of artificers. Paul was not only a labourer, but an (ἀρχιτέκτων) *architect.* To him was revealed the whole plan of the building, and he was inspired to develope that plan, and to prescribe the way in which it should be carried out. He laid *the foundation.* The same idea as was expressed above by saying, "I have planted, Apollos watered." He began the work in Corinth. Those who came after him were to carry on the edifice which he had commenced. The building must be erected upon the foundation and according to it. And, therefore, he adds, *Let every man* (i. e. every builder) *take heed how he buildeth thereupon.* In the whole context he is speaking of ministers, and therefore this clause must be considered as a warning addressed to them. They are to take heed *how*, i. e. with what materials, they carried on the building of this holy temple. Fidelity as well as diligence is required in a minister. No matter how laborious he may be, unless he employs the proper materials, he will lose his reward. Nothing but truth can be safely used in the development of Christian character, or in building up the

Church. To mix the wisdom of men with the wisdom of God in this work, is, as the apostle afterwards says, like using alternate layers of straw and marble in the erection of a temple. Let no man deceive himself in this matter. He will prove himself a fool, if he attempts to substitute philosophy for the gospel in the work of saving men.

11. For other foundation can no man lay than that is laid, which is Jesus Christ.

For, others can only carry on the work already begun, for the foundation cannot be changed. The foundation of the church is Christ. Is. 28, 16. Acts 4, 11. Eph. 2, 20. 1 Pet. 2, 6. This may be understood either of the person or of the doctrine of Christ. In either way the sense is good. Christ, as the incarnate Son of God, according to one scriptural figure, is the head of the church which is his body, that is, he is the source of its life; according to another figure, he is its foundation or corner-stone, because on him all the members of the church, considered as a temple, rest for salvation. On the other hand, however, it is also true that the doctrine concerning Christ, is the fundamental doctrine of the gospel. We may, therefore, understand the apostle to say, that the work of the ministry is to build up the church on the foundation which *God* has laid in the person and work of Christ. There can be no other ground of confidence for the justification, sanctification, and salvation of men. Or we may understand him to say, that the work of those who followed him in Corinth was simply to build on the foundation which *he* had laid, in preaching the doctrine of Christ and him crucified, for there can be no other foundation of the church than that doctrine. The former interpretation, which is adopted by many distinguished commentators, is more in accordance with the common representations of Scripture which speak of God having constituted Christ the corner-stone of the church. It is also perhaps more in accordance with the form of expression here used. Jesus Christ himself is the foundation, which was already laid. The second interpretation, however, is certainly more consistent with the context. In v. 10 Paul says, *he* had laid the foundation. This can only mean that he had in Corinth taught the doctrine concerning the person and work of Christ. This is the only sense in which he can be said to have laid that foundation *which is Jesus Christ.* Besides, the whole passage has reference to doctrine. Paul had preached the truth; those who came after him must take heed what they preached.

12. 13. Now, if any man build upon this foundation gold, silver, precious stones, wood, hay, stubble; every man's work shall be made manifest: for the day shall declare it, because it shall be revealed by fire; and the fire shall try every man's work, of what sort it is.

In consistency with the context, gold, silver and precious stones, can only mean truth; and wood, hay and stubble, error. If by the foundation which Paul had laid were intended the first converts in Corinth, then the above terms would naturally be understood of good and bad members of the church. The sense would then be, 'I laid the foundation of the church in Corinth by receiving true believers to its communion; let others take heed with what kind of members they build up the church.' But as the foundation which Paul laid is expressly declared to be Jesus Christ, or the truth concerning his person and work, the words above mentioned must refer to true and false doctrines. 'I have laid the foundation of Christ crucified; do you take heed with what kind of doctrine you carry on the work.' Besides, the whole discussion has reference to preachers and their duties. *Precious stones* here mean stones valuable for building, such as granite and marble. Gold and silver were extensively employed in adorning ancient temples, and are therefore appropriately used as the symbols of pure doctrine. Wood, hay, and stubble are the perishable materials out of which ordinary houses were built, but not temples. Wood for the doors and posts; *hay*, (χόρτος,) dried *grass* mixed with mud for the walls; and *straw*, (καλάμη,) for the roof. These materials, unsuitable for the temple of God, are appropriate symbols of false doctrines.

Every man's work shall be made (or, *become*) *manifest.* In this life it may be disputed whether a man's doctrines are true or false. He may have great confidence in their truth, and set himself above his brethren and even above the Bible. But his work hereafter will appear in its true character. *For the day shall declare it. The day* does not mean indefinitely *time*, 'Time shall declare it;' nor the day of tribulation; nor the day of light and knowledge as distinguished from the present ignorance; but the great day, the day of judgment, or, as it is so often called, the day of the Lord. That day shall make manifest the truth or falsehood of the doctrines taught, *because it is* (i. e. is certainly to be) *revealed by fire;* literally, *in* or *with* fire (ἐν πυρί). In 2 Thess. 1, 8, it is said, "The Lord Jesus shall be revealed in flaming fire," i. e. in the midst of flaming fire. Fire is the constant symbol of trial and judgment. The meaning therefore is, that the day of the Lord will be a day of severe trial. Every work will then be subjected to a test which nothing impure can stand. The context shows that the word *day*, and not *work*, is the nominative to *revealed.* 'The day of judgment shall declare every man's work, because that day shall be revealed with fire.'

And the fire shall try every man's work of what sort it is. The figure is that of a building on which many workmen are engaged. Some use proper materials, others wood, hay and stubble. The building is to be subjected to the test of fire. The wood, hay and stubble will be burnt up; only the solid materials will stand. False doctrine can no more stand the test of the day of judgment, than hay or stubble can stand a raging conflagration.

14. 15. If any man's work abide which he hath built thereupon, he shall receive a reward. If any man's work shall be burned, he shall suffer loss: but he himself shall be saved; yet so as by fire.

This is an amplification of what precedes. If the materials employed by a spiritual builder stand the test of the day of judgment, he shall receive the reward of a faithful servant. *Which he hath built thereupon*, i. e. upon the foundation. Comp. v. 12. *If any man's work shall be burned* (κατακαήσεται for κατακαυθήσεται); that is, if the materials used by any builder shall not stand the test of that day, *he shall suffer loss* (σημιωθήσεται, see 2 Cor. 7, 9. Phil. 3, 8). That is, he will lose his reward.

But he himself shall be saved. Just as a man who has built his house of combustible materials, though he may escape when the fire comes, his property is lost, and all his labour comes to nothing. The apostle is here speaking of those teachers who, although they retain the fundamental doctrines of the gospel, yet combine them with error. This is plain from v. 12, "If any man shall build on this foundation." It is not enough, therefore, that a minister hold fast to fundamental truth; he must take heed what he teaches in connection with that truth. If he mingles with it the wood, hay and stubble of his own philosophy, he will find himself a loser on the day of judgment. Many of the Fathers understand σωθήσεται here in the sense of *shall be preserved.* His work shall be consumed, but he himself shall be kept alive in the midst of the fire. It is not then the salvation, but the final perdition of the false teacher that the passage teaches. This, however, is contrary to the uniform meaning of the word in the New Testament. The common interpretation is therefore to be preferred.

Yet so as by fire, i. e. with difficulty. Comp. 1 Pet. 3, 20. Jude 23. Zech. 3, 2. He will just escape with his life, as a man is rescued from a burning building. His salvation will not only be effected with difficulty, but it will be attended with great loss. He will occupy a lower place in the kingdom of heaven than he would have done. Romanists found their doctrine of purgatory on tradition rather than on Scripture. They are glad, however, to avail themselves of any semblance of scriptural support, and therefore appeal to this passage to prove that men are saved through fire. But, 1. Paul is here speaking of ministers and of their doctrines, and not of believers in general. 2. The fire of which he speaks is not a state of trial preceding the judgment, but the judgment itself. 3. The fire is that in the midst of which Jesus Christ is to appear. 4. Paul does not say, the man is to be saved by being purified by fire, but simply 'with difficulty,' as the expression "so as by fire" familiarly means.

16. Know ye not that ye are the temple of God, and (that) the Spirit of God dwelleth in you?

The apostle justifies the representation given above of the responsibility of ministers. The unfaithful builders deserve to be thus punished, because they are engaged in the erection of no ordinary building. They are not raising up a house for themselves, to be constructed of what materials and on whatever plan may suit their taste. They are building the temple of God. This truth the Corinthians seem to have forgotten, for they regarded their teachers as men allowed to preach their own speculations, and valued them according to their proficiency in "the wisdom of words." He, therefore, asks them, "Know ye not that ye are the temple of God?" See 6, 19. 2 Cor. 6,

16. Eph. 2, 21. A temple is a house in which God dwells; and therefore, it is added, *and that the Spirit of God dwelleth in you.* This indwelling of the Spirit constitutes each believer, every separate church, and the Church collectively the temple of God. As in the Jewish temple, in its inmost recess, the Shechinah, or glory of God, was constantly present, and conferred on the building its awe-inspiring power, and rendered any profanation of it a direct offence to God; so does the Holy Spirit dwell in the Church, the profanation of which by false doctrine is therefore sacrilege.

17. If any man defile the temple of God, him shall God destroy: for the temple of God is holy, which (temple) ye are.

The word translated *defile* in the first clause of this verse, is the same as that rendered *destroy* in the second clause. It (φθείρω) has the general meaning *to bring into a worse state.* In the LXX. as well as in the New Testament it means *to mar.* The passage may, therefore, be rendered, 'If any man injure the temple of God, him will God injure.' The temple cannot be injured with impunity. Under the old dispensation the penalty for defiling the sanctuary was either death, Lev. 15, 31, or excision from the people, Num. 19, 20. God is not less jealous of his spiritual temple, than he was of the typical temple, built of wood and stone by the hands of men. Ministers injure the souls of men and injure the church when they preach false doctrine, and therefore they defile the temple of God, and will certainly be punished.

For the temple of God is holy, i. e. sacred; something which cannot be violated with impunity. In this sense every thing consecrated to God is holy, and especially any place or person in which he dwells. *Which (temple) ye are.* As the word for temple is not in the text (which reads οἵτινές ἐστε ὑμεῖς) the reference may be to the word *holy.* 'The temple is holy, which ye also are.' The same reason exists why the church cannot be defiled or injured, that there is that the temple could not be profaned. Both are sacred. The view given in our version is commonly preferred.

18. Let no man deceive himself. If any man

among you seemeth to be wise in this world, let him become a fool, that he may be wise.

Let no man deceive himself. 'Let no man doubt the truth of what I have said of the worthlessness of human wisdom, and of the danger of substituting it for the wisdom of God. If he does, he will find himself mistaken.'

If any man among you seemeth to be wise, (δοκεῖ σοφὸς εἶναι), thinks himself to be wise. *In this world* may be connected with the word *wise*, 'wise with the wisdom of this world.' Or, it may be connected with the whole preceding clause. 'If any imagines he is wise among you, in this world.' The former explanation is more in keeping with the whole context. "Wise in this world" is equivalent to "wise after the flesh," 1, 26.

Let him become a fool, that he may be (or, *become*) *wise.* Let him renounce his own wisdom in order that he may receive the wisdom of God. We must be empty in order to be filled. We must renounce our own righteousness, in order to be clothed in the righteousness of Christ. We must renounce our own strength, in order to be made strong. We must renounce our own wisdom, in order to be truly wise. This is a universal law. And it is perfectly reasonable. We are only required to recognize that to be true, which is true. We would not be required to renounce our own righteousness, strength, or wisdom, if they were really what they assume to be. It is simply because they are in fact worthless, that we are called upon so to regard them.

19. 20. For the wisdom of this world is foolishness with God. For it is written, He taketh the wise in their own craftiness. And again, The Lord knoweth the thoughts of the wise, that they are vain.

We must renounce our own wisdom because it is folly. The infinite mind sees that to be folly which we children think to be wisdom. There are two senses in which this is true, or in which wisdom may be said to be folly. Even truth or true knowledge becomes folly, if employed to accomplish an end for which it is not adapted. If a man attempts to make men holy or happy; if he undertakes to convert the world, by mathematics, or metaphysics, or moral philosophy, he is foolish, and his wisdom, as a means to that end, is folly. He must renounce all dependence on those means if he would accomplish that end. But in the second place, much that passes for wisdom among men is in itself, and not merely as a means to an end, foolishness. Both these ideas are evidently comprehended in the apostle's statement. He means to say that human knowledge is entirely inadequate to save men; because that end can only be accomplished by the gospel. And he means also to brand as folly the speculations of men about "the deep things of God."

In proof of the assertion that the wisdom of men is foolishness with God, he quotes two passages of Scripture. The first is from Job 5, 13, the second is from Ps. 94, 11. The former is a fragment of a sentence containing in the Greek no verb. Our translation renders the participle (ὁ δρασσόμενος) as though it were a verb. Those passages clearly express the same sentiment which the apostle had uttered. They declare the impotency and insufficiency of human wisdom.

21. Therefore let no one glory in men: for all things are yours.

To glory in any person or thing is to trust in him or it as the ground of confidence, or as the source of honour or blessedness. It is to regard ourselves as blessed because of our relation to it. Thus men are said to glory in the Lord, or in the cross; because God, or Christ as crucified, is regarded as the ground of confidence and the source of blessedness. Others are said to glory in the flesh, in the law, or even in themselves. The apostle having shown that ministers are mere servants, nothing in themselves, and that the wisdom of the world is foolishness with God, draws from these premises the inference that they are not the ground of the believer's confidence. The Corinthians did glory in men, when they said, I am of Paul, I of Apollos, and I of Cephas. They forgot their own dignity when they regarded as masters those who were their servants.

For all things are yours. The amplification of these words, given in the next verse, shows that they are to be taken in their widest sense. The universe is yours. How unworthy then is it, that you should glory in men. Paul often appeals to the dignity and destiny of the church as a motive to right action. "Know ye not that the saints shall judge the world?" 6, 2. There are two senses in which the declaration, "All things are yours," may be understood. It means that all things are designed to promote the interests of the church. The consummation of the work of redemption is the great end to which all things are directed, and to which they are to be made subservient. And secondly, the church is the heir of the world, Rom. 4, 13. All things are given to Christ as the head of the chur h, and to the church in him. For his people are to reign with him, Rom. 8, 17, and the glory which the Father gave him, he gives them, John 17, 22. The church, which is to be thus exalted, is not any external society with its hierarchy, nor is it the body of poor, imperfect believers as they now are, who for their own good are despised and down-trodden. But it is the consummated church to be formed out of materials now so unpromising. The people of God, however, should not be unmindful of their high destiny, nor act unworthily of it.

22. Whether Paul, or Apollos, or Cephas, or the world, or life, or death, or things present, or things to come; all are yours;

This is the amplification of the preceding verse. In the "all things" there mentioned are included, 1. The ministry, which belongs to the church and is designed for its edification. The church does not belong to the ministry, as a kingdom belongs to a king, but the reverse. 2. The world (κόσμος) in its widest sense. The present order of things is maintained and directed to the promotion of the great work of redemption. 3. Life and death. This means not merely that the question whether the people of God live or die, is determined with reference to their own good; but also that life and death are dispensed and administered so as best to fulfil the designs of God in reference to the church. The greatest men of the world, kings, statesmen and heroes, ministers, individual believers and unbelievers, live or die just as best subserves the interests of Christ's kingdom. 4. Things present and things to come, i. e. the present and the future. It is no temporary subjection of all things to the church which is intended. The plan of God contemplates the permanent exaltation of the redeemed.

23. And ye are Christ's: and Christ (is) God's.

As all things are subject to the church and belong to it,

the church itself can be subject and belong to none but Christ. In him, therefore, only can it glory.

Christ is God's. As the church is subject only to Christ, so Christ is subject only to God. The Scriptures speak of a threefold subordination of Christ. 1. A subordination as to the mode of subsistence and operation, of the second, to the first person in the Trinity; which is perfectly consistent with their identity of substance, and equality in power and glory. 2. The voluntary subordination of the Son in his humbling himself to be found in fashion as a man, and becoming obedient unto death, and therefore subject to the limitations and infirmities of our nature. 3. The economical or official subjection of the theanthropos. That is, the subordination of the incarnate Son of God, in the work of redemption and as the head of the church. He that is by nature equal with God becomes, as it were, officially subject to him. The passages the most directly parallel with the one before us are 11, 3, and 15, 28, but in Phil. 2, 6–11. Heb. 1, 3, and in many other passages, the same truth is taught.

CHAPTER IV.

Deduction from the preceding discussion, teaching the proper light in which the people should regard the ministry, vs. 1–6. Contrast between the apostles and the false teachers, vs. 6–21.

Ministers, as stewards, should be faithful, as Paul had proved himself to be, vs. 1–21.

It follows, from what was said in the preceding chapter, that the people should regard their ministers as the servants of Christ, and dispensers of the truths which God had revealed, v. 1. The most important qualification of a dispenser is fidelity, v. 2. It is a small matter how men may estimate the fidelity of ministers. The only competent judge is the Lord; and, therefore, to his judgment the decision of that question should be referred, vs. 3–6.

What the apostle had said of himself and of Apollos, in the foregoing exhibition of the true nature of the ministerial office, was intended to apply to all ministers, that the people should not estimate them unduly, and that all emulous contentions might be avoided, vs. 6, 7. The false teachers in Corinth, and the people under their influence, considered themselves to be in a high state of religious prosperity, and were disposed to self-indulgence, v. 8. The apostles were in a very different condition, at least as to their external circumstances. They were despised, afflicted, and persecuted; while their adversaries were honoured, prosperous, and caressed, vs. 9–13. Paul presented this contrast not to mortify, but to admonish his readers, v. 14. He, if any one, had a right to admonish them, for he was their spiritual father, v. 15. They should therefore imitate him; and, to that end, he had sent Timothy to remind them of his instructions and example, vs. 16. 17. He himself intended soon to visit Corinth; and it depended on them whether he should come with a rod, or in the spirit of meekness, vs. 18–21.

1. Let a man so account of us, as of the ministers of Christ, and stewards of the mysteries of God.

This is the conclusion or deduction from the preceding discussion. Ministers are the servants of Christ, and stewards of God. *Let a man*, i. e. every one. *Account of us*, (λογιζέσθω) let him think of us, or regard us as being. *The ministers of Christ.* Literally the word (ὑπηρέτης) means *an under-rower*, or common sailor; and then, subordinate servant of any kind. It is generally and properly used of menials, or of those of the lower class of servants. This is not always the case, but here the idea of entire subjection is to be retained. Ministers are the mere servants of Christ; they have no authority of their own; their whole business is to do what they are commanded.

And stewards of the mysteries of God. Stewards (οἰκονόμοι) were generally slaves appointed as managers or overseers. It was their business to direct the affairs of the household, and dispense the provisions. It is *as dispensers* ministers are here called *stewards.* They are to dispense *the mysteries of God*, that is, the truths which God had revealed, and which, as being undiscoverable by human reason, are called mysteries, into the knowledge of which men must be initiated. *Mysteries* here do not mean the sacraments. The word is never used in reference to either baptism or the Lord's Supper in the New

Testament. And such a reference in this case is forbidden by the whole context. In the second chapter, the mystery which Paul speaks of is declared to be the gospel considered as a revelation of God. In the Romish church, the principal function of ministers is to dispense the sacraments to which they are assumed to have the power, in virtue of the grace of orders, to give supernatural power. In the apostolic church they were regarded as the dispensers of the truth. This verse, therefore, contains two important truths: Ministers have no arbitrary or discretionary authority in the church. Neither have they any supernatural power, such as is attributed to them in the Romish church. Their authority is merely ministerial, limited by the commands of Christ, and, therefore, to be judged by the standard of those commands, which are known to the whole church. And secondly, they are not, like Aristotle or Plato, the originators of their own doctrines, or the teachers of the doctrines of other men, but simply the dispensers of the truths which God has revealed.

2. Moreover, it is required in stewards, that a man be found faithful.

Moreover, (ὃ δὲ λοιπόν) *but what remains is; as to the rest.* Instead of the words just mentioned Lachmann and Tischendorf adopt the reading ὧδε, *here*, i. e. in the earth, or, in this matter. The most ancient MSS. are in favour of this reading, and the sense is good. The great requisite for the discharge of the office of a steward is fidelity. As he is a servant he must be faithful to his master; as he is a dispenser, he must be faithful to those subject to his oversight. He must not neglect to dispense to them their food; neither may he adulterate it, or substitute any thing in the place of that which is given them to distribute. The application of this to the case of ministers is plain. The great thing required of them is fidelity. Fidelity to Christ as servants; not arrogating to themselves any other than ministerial power, or venturing to go beyond his commands. Fidelity also to the people, not failing to dispense to them the truths which God has revealed, nor mixing those truths with their own speculations, much less substituting for those doctrines human knowledge or wisdom.

3. But with me it is a very small thing that I

should be judged of you, or of man's judgment: yea, I judge not mine own self.

Fidelity to duty supposes responsibility to some one. As ministers are required to be faithful, who is to judge of their fidelity? Paul says, so far as he was concerned, it was not the Corinthians, not the world, not himself—but, as he adds in the next verse, the Lord.

But with me, (ἐμοὶ δέ); *to me*, i. e. in my estimation. *It is a very small thing* (εἰς ἐλάχιστόν ἐστι), *it amounts to nothing.* "That I should be judged of you." This does not refer to the judicial judgment of the church, but simply to the opinions which the Corinthians entertained of Paul. It mattered little to him whether they thought him faithful or unfaithful. His responsibility was not to them. They had not sent him; they had not told him what doctrines to preach. He was not their steward, but the steward of God. *Or of man's judgment* (ὑπὸ ανθρωπίνης ἡμέρας) literally, *by human day.* As 'the day of the Lord' means the day of God's judgment, so 'the day of men' means the day of man's judgment. The sense is obvious, though the expression no where else occurs. The apostle, although denying his responsibility to the Corinthians, or to any human tribunal for his fidelity as a minister of Christ, does not mean to assert that he was his own judge. He therefore adds, "I judge not my own self." Many men think themselves faithful, who are most unfaithful. It is not enough that our own conscience does not condemn us. Conscience is a partial, and often an unenlightened judge. We may justify ourselves, and be at last condemned by God. But, if our heart condemn us, how can we stand before him who knows all things?

4. For I know nothing by myself; yet am I not hereby justified: but he that judgeth me is the Lord.

For I know nothing by myself, (οὐδὲν γὰρ ἐμαυτῷ σύνοιδα) *I am conscious of nothing.* That is, my conscience does not accuse me of any thing. Paul is speaking of his fidelity as a steward. He says, he was not his own judge, for though his conscience did not accuse him of want of ministerial fidelity, that did not justify him. *I am not thereby justified.* That is, I am not thereby acquitted. My judgment of myself is not final. The only impartial, competent, and final judge is the

Lord. This interpretation of the verse is suited to the meaning of the words and to the connection, and has the sanction of general approbation. The connection indicated by *for* is between what precedes and the latter part of the verse, 'I judge not myself, *for* he that judgeth me is the Lord.' It need hardly be remarked, that when Paul says, he was conscious of nothing wrong, the declaration is to be limited by the connection. He speaks of himself elsewhere as the chief of sinners, which is perfectly consistent with his saying that his conscience acquitted him of failure in fidelity as a minister.

The clause, *I am not hereby justified*, must also be explained in reference to the connection. He is not speaking of the doctrine of justification; and, therefore, is not to be understood to say, 'My justification is not thereby secured.' That is, he does not mean to say that ministerial fidelity is not the ground of his justification. This would be entirely out of keeping with the context. All he means is, that the question whether he was faithful, was one not to be decided by his conscience, but by the Lord. *Lord* here evidently means Christ, who is therefore a higher judge than conscience. As a moral agent, as a believer, and as a minister, Paul felt himself accountable to Christ. This inward allegiance of the conscience is the highest form of worship. The Lord Jesus was to the apostle the object of all those sentiments and feelings which terminate on God. And he must be so to us, or we are not Christians; because, what makes a man a Christian, is to feel and act towards Christ as God.

5. Therefore judge nothing before the time, until the Lord come, who both will bring to light the hidden things of darkness, and will make manifest the counsels of the hearts: and then shall every man have praise of God.

As the Lord is the only judge, we must wait for his appearance, and neither assume his prerogative, nor anticipate his decision. *Judge nothing before the time* (καιρός), i. e. the appropriate, or appointed time. What time is intended is intimated in the next clause. *Until the Lord come*, (ἕως ἂν ἔλθῃ, shall have come,) i. e. until the second advent of Christ, which in the New Testament is constantly represented as contemporaneous with the resurrection of the dead and the general judgment. He is to come for judgment, Matt. 24, 30. 46. 2 Pet. 3, 4. 12. Jude 14. Rev. 1, 7. The reason why the coming of the Lord is the appropriate time for judgment is, that he will then do what cannot be done before, or by any creature. *He will bring to light* (shed light upon) *the secret things of darkness;* that is, things which are now hidden in darkness. This includes acts which are now unknown, and those principles of action which lie concealed in the recesses of the heart, where no human eye can reach them. This is all the context requires. In other connections the secret things, or the works of darkness, means *wicked works;* works done in the dark to avoid detection; or works which spring from moral darkness, Eph. 5, 11. But the apostle is here speaking of the reason why judgment should be deferred until the coming of Christ. The reason is that he alone can bring to light the secret acts and motives of men. These secret works and motives, and not merely outward acts, are the grounds of judgment. Whether a man is faithful in preaching the gospel depends upon his motives; for some preached Christ of contention, Phil. 1, 16. This view of the passage is confirmed by the explanatory clause which follows, *and will make manifest the counsels of the hearts.* The former expression is general, this is special. The 'counsels of the heart' are included in the 'secret things of darkness.' He who sheds light on the secret things of darkness not only reveals acts done in secret, but makes manifest the counsels of the heart. What a work is here ascribed to the Lord Jesus! He will bring to light the secret acts and hidden motives of every human being. He will exercise the prerogative of judging the heart and conscience; a prerogative which none but an omniscient being can rightfully claim or possibly exercise. It is therefore in Scripture always spoken of as peculiar to God, Ps. 26, 2. Jer. 11, 20. 20, 12. Rev. 2, 23. Paul appealed from the fallible judgment of short-sighted men, to the infallible judgment of his omniscient Lord.

And then; not before, because not until then will the full truth be known. *Shall every man have praise* (ἔπαινος, much praise, applause, a loud and clear acclaim of commendation; Well done, thou good and faithful servant!) The reason why Paul uses the word *praise*, and not the general term *recompense*, probably is, that he is throughout the passage speaking of himself. The Corinthians had sat in judgment on his fidelity. He tells them that neither they nor he could competently decide whether he was faithful, or not. The Lord was the only judge. When he comes, the truth will be known, and then there shall be praise. He knew there was laid up for him a crown of righteousness, which the Lord the righteous judge would give him in that day, 2 Tim. 4, 8. Still, as what is true of him is true of others, he expresses himself in general terms. Then shall *every man* have praise. That is, every faithful servant. Praise *of God*, i. e. from God. He is the ultimate source of all good. He is in Christ; and Christ is in God. The Theanthropos, as final judge, is the representative of the Godhead, so that his decisions and awards are the decisions and awards of God. As remarked above, 2, 15, what the apostle says of his independence of human judgment, and his command not to anticipate the judgment of the Lord, is consistent with his frequent recognition of the right and duty of the church to sit in judgment on the qualifications of her own members. He is here speaking of the heart. The church cannot judge the heart. Whether a man is sincere or insincere in his professions, whether his experience is genuine or spurious, God only can decide. The church can only judge of what is outward. If any man profess to be holy, and yet is immoral, the church is bound to reject him, as Paul clearly teaches in a following chapter. Or if he profess to be a Christian, and yet rejects Christianity, or any of its essential doctrines, he cannot be received, Tit. 3, 10. But "the counsels of the heart" the Searcher of hearts only can judge.

6. And these things, brethren, I have in a figure transferred to myself and (to) Apollos for your sakes; that ye might learn in us not to think (of men) above that which is written, that no one of you be puffed up for one against another.

These things refers to what was said in the preceding chapter of preachers, especially to what is said from 3, 5, and onwards. These things he had *in a figure transferred to himself and Apollos.* That is, instead of teaching in an abstract, general form, that ministers were mere servants, he had presented the truth in a concrete form, saying that he and Apollos were servants, mere instruments in the hand of God. This was the (μετασχηματισμός), the change of form which he had adopted. He did this, he says, that they might learn *in us*, i. e. by what I have said of Apollos and myself, *not to think above that which is written.* That is, not to estimate ministers above the scriptural standard. As Paul had been treating of this subject, *above that which is written*, might seem naturally to refer to what he himself had just written. But as the phrase always elsewhere refers to the Old Testament, which were the *writings* recognized as of divine authority, such is probably the reference here. He does not appeal to any one passage, but to the doctrine taught in the Scriptures concerning ministers of religion. The Corinthians were not to think of their ministers more highly than the Bible authorized them to think. Comp. Jer. 9, 23, 24. The particle (ἵνα), rendered *that*, has its ordinary force, *in order that*, although the following verb (φυσιοῦσθε,) is in the indicative, a combination which occurs nowhere else except in Gal. 4, 17. The connection is with the preceding clause, 'That ye may learn to think correctly, *in order that*,' &c.

That no one be puffed up for one against another; literally, *that ye be not puffed up one for one against another.* This admits of two interpretations. It may mean, 'That ye be not inflated one on account of one teacher, and against another.' The Corinthians were proud of their connection one with one teacher, and another with another. And this led to the strifes and divisions which existed among them. Paul taught them that ministers were servants, in order that they might not thus contend about them. This, although it gives a good sense, is neither consistent with the structure of the passage nor with what follows. The meaning is, 'Be not puffed up one above another,' (εἷς ὑπὲρ τοῦ ἑνός), comp. in the Greek 1 Thess. 5, 11. The followers of Apollos exalted themselves over those of Paul, and those of Paul over those of Cephas. One exalted himself above another and against him. He not only thought himself better than his brother, but assumed a hostile attitude towards him. This view is confirmed by the next verse, which is directed against the self-conceit of the Corinthians and not against their zeal for their teachers.

7. For who maketh thee to differ (from another)? and what hast thou that thou didst not receive? Now if thou didst receive (it), why dost thou glory, as if thou hadst not received (it)?

Who maketh thee to differ? This may mean either, 'Who

thinks you are better than others?' Your superiority over your brethren is mere self-conceit and inflation. The difference between you is only imaginary. Or, it may mean, 'Who is the author of this superiority?' Admitting you to be as superior to others as you imagine, to whom are you indebted for it? According to the latter explanation the verse contains but one argument against their pride, viz., that all distinguishing advantages are derived from God. According to the former, there are two distinct considerations urged: first, that they had no ground for thinking themselves better than others; and second, if they had any superiority it was due not themselves, but to God. So that in either case their inflation was absurd and unchristian. It is here assumed that every thing, whether natural or gracious, by which one man is favourably distinguished from another, is due to God; and being thus due to him and not to the possessor, is a cause of gratitude, but not of self-complacency or of self-applause. This is true even of those things which are acquired by great self-denial and exertion. Paul was as much self-formed as any man ever was, and yet he said, By the grace of God I am what I am.

8. Now ye are full, now ye are rich, ye have reigned as kings without us: and I would to God ye did reign, that we also might reign with you.

Having, says Calvin, repressed their self-conceit, he here derides it. That the passage is ironical, and even sarcastic, cannot be denied. This is not the only instance in which these weapons are used by the inspired writers. The prophets especially employ them freely in their endeavours to convince the people of the folly of trusting to idols. The propriety of the use of weapons so dangerous depends on the occasion and the motive. If the thing assailed be both wicked and foolish, and if the motive be, not the desire to give pain, but to convince and to convert, their use is justified by Scriptural examples. There is an evident climax in the verse. Ye are not only full, but more than full; ye are rich, you have more than enough; and ye are not only rich, ye are as kings. *Now* (ἤδη) *already*. 'You have reached the goal of perfection very quick; and that *without us*. You have left us poor apostles far behind you.' The reference is to the benefits of redemption. Paul represents the Corinthians as thinking that they had already attained the full blessedness of the Messiah's reign; that they had already attained, and were already perfect. He therefore adds, *I would ye did reign.* 'I would that the consummation of Christ's kingdom had really come, for then I would share with you in its glories.' *I would to God* is a translation not authorized, or at least not demanded, by the original, ὄφελον, which in the later Greek, and in the New Testament, is a particle of wishing or an interjection; *would that, O that.* So the Greek phrase (μὴ γένοιτο) so often rendered in our version, "God forbid!" is simply an expression of aversion, "Let it not be." The Scriptures do not countenance such appeals to God as seem to have been common when our version was made.

9. For I think that God hath set forth us the apostles last, as it were appointed to death: for we are made a spectacle unto the world, and to angels, and to men.

For. 'I would that the consummation were really come, *for* we apostles are now very far from being treated as kings.' *God hath set forth*, i. e. publicly exhibited. He has made us conspicuous as the last, the lowest, the most afflicted of men. The original does not admit of the translation proposed by many, *us the last apostles*, i. e. those last appointed—referring to himself, who was, as he says, born out of due time. The emphasis, from the collocation of the words, is thrown on *apostles* and not on *last.* What follows is explanatory. *As appointed unto death.* This does not merely mean that they were exhibited as men daily exposed to death; which indeed was true, 15, 30. 31. 2 Cor. 1, 8. 9. 11, 23; but also that they were treated as men condemned to death, that is, as convicts, men to whom all comforts were denied. '*We have become a spectacle* (θέατρον, literally, *a theatre;* here metonymically, *a show* exhibited in a theatre) to the universe (κόσμῳ), as well to angels, as to men.' Such were the sufferings of the apostles that men and angels gazed on them with wonder, as people gaze on a spectacle in a theatre. The word *angels* when used without qualification always means good angels, and must be so understood here.

10. We (are) fools for Christ's sake, but ye (are) wise in Christ; we (are) weak, but ye (are) strong; ye (are) honourable, but we (are) despised.

In amplification of what he had just said, he contrasts, in this and the following verses, his situation with theirs. There are two things included in these contrasts. The opinion which the Corinthians entertained, and that which was entertained by others. *We are fools on account of Christ;* our devotion to the cause of Christ is such that you and others regard us as fools; *ye are wise in Christ;* your union with Christ is such that you regard yourselves and are regarded by others as wise. *We are weak*, we feel ourselves to be so, and are so considered; *ye are strong*, you so regard yourselves, and are so regarded. *You are honoured*, you are objects of respect, we of contempt. All this doubtless has special, though not exclusive, reference to the false teachers, whose state in Corinth he contrasts with his own.

11. Even unto this present hour we both hunger, and thirst, and are naked, and are buffeted, and have no certain dwelling-place;

That a man should freely subject himself to hunger, thirst, and nakedness, and submit to be buffeted, and homeless, for no selfish purpose, but simply to preach Christ, was indeed, in the eyes of the world, foolishness. The fact that Paul gladly submitted to all these afflictions, presented his case in glaring contrast with that of his opposers in Corinth, who exposed themselves to no such sufferings out of zeal for Christ.

12. 13. And labour, working with our own hands. Being reviled, we bless; being persecuted, we suffer it; being defamed, we entreat: we are made as the filth of the world, (and are) the off-scouring of all things unto this day.

Working with our own hands. The apostle, in a subsequent chapter, proves at length his right, and that of other ministers to an adequate support from the church. But he did not avail himself of that right in Corinth, 9, 15.

Being reviled (λοιδορούμενοι), being railed at, or made the object of scurrility. *We bless*, i. e. we speak well of, or *implore good upon.* We return abuse with kind words, or, with good wishes and prayers. *Being persecuted.* As the former term refers to injurious words, this refers to injurious acts.

We suffer it, i. e. we patiently submit to it without resistance or complaint. *Being defamed*, i. e. having evil deeds or motives ascribed to us. *We entreat* (παρακαλοῦμεν), we exhort. That is, we endeavour to meet with kindness such injurious imputations, instead of repelling them with anger and indignation. In all this the apostle followed the example of his divine master, who when he was reviled, reviled not again; when he suffered, he threatened not, but committed himself to him who judgeth righteously, 1 Peter 2, 23.

We are made as the filth of the earth, or rather of the world (κόσμου). That is, we are regarded as the filthiest of mankind. And *the off-scouring of all things*, or of all men. That is, as the refuse of society. The words (περικάθαρμα and περίψημα) rendered *filth* and *off-scouring*, signify, the former, what is carried off by rinsing, and the latter, what is scraped off. They both express the general idea of refuse. This is all the context demands or suggests. The apostle sums up all he had previously said, by saying, 'We are regarded as the dregs or refuse of the world.' As both of these words, however, and especially the former, are used of victims chosen from the lowest class of the people, who in times of calamity were offered in sacrifice to the gods, it is very generally assumed that Paul here refers to that custom; and means to say that he was regarded as one of those who were considered only fit to be put to death for the good of others. This brings out the same idea in a different form. It is not probable, however, that any such allusion is here intended; because the custom was not so common as to be familiar to his readers generally, and because the word commonly used for such sacrifices was not περικάθαρμα, which Paul uses, but κάθαρμα. In Prov. 21, 18, however, it is said, The wicked is a ransom (περικάθαρμα) for the righteous. Paul certainly did not consider himself or his sufferings as a propitiation for other men. The point of comparison, if there be any allusion to the custom in question, is to the vileness of such victims, which were always chosen from the worthless and despised. This and other passages of Paul's writings (comp. 2 Cor. 11, 23–27) present in a very strong light the indignities and sufferings which he endured in the service of Christ, and may well put us to shame, as well as the self-satisfied and self-indulgent Corinthians. What are we doing for him for whom Paul did and suffered so much?

14. I write not these things to shame you, but as my beloved sons I warn (you).

Not as shaming you (ἐντρέπων) *write I these things.* The word used signifies to invert, to turn round, or back; and then, generally, to move, and especially to move to shame. It may be rendered here, 'I write not these things as moving you,' i. e. to work upon your feelings. The use of the word in 2 Thess. 3, 14, and Tit. 2, 8, is in favour of the common interpretation. Paul's object in drawing such a contrast between their case and his, was not to mortify them; but as his beloved sons, i. e. out of love to them as his sons, he says, *I warn you.* The word (νουθετέω) is that generally used to express parental admonition and instruction. His design was to bring the truth to their minds, and let them see what they really were, as contrasted with what they imagined themselves to be.

15. For though ye have ten thousand instructors in Christ, yet (have ye) not many fathers: for in Christ Jesus I have begotten you through the gospel.

Paul was entitled to admonish them as sons, for he was their spiritual father. The words *in Christ* are not connected with *instructors*, as though the sense were, 'instructors who are in Christ,' i. e. Christian instructors. The position of the words in the original show that they belong to the verb. 'Though ye may have in Christ, i. e. in reference to Christ, or as Christians, many teachers, ye have not many fathers.' The pedagogues (παιδαγωγοί) among the Greeks were usually slaves, who were the constant attendants, rather than the teachers, of the boys of a family. They had, however, the charge of their education, and therefore the word is used in the New Testament for instructors. Paul contrasts his relation to the Corinthians as their spiritual father, with that of their other teachers. The point of the contrast is not that he loved them, and they did not; or that they were disposed to arrogate too much authority, and he was not; but simply, that he was the means of their conversion, and they were not. His relation to them preceded theirs and was more intimate and tender.

He was their father, "*for* in Christ Jesus he had begotten them." That is, in virtue of his union to Christ, as his apostle and minister. In himself he could do nothing. It was only as an instrument in the hand of Christ that he was successful in bringing them to the obedience of faith. Comp. Gal. 2. 8. *By the gospel*, i. e. by means of the gospel. There are three agencies in the conversion of men. The efficiency is in Christ by his Spirit; the administrative agency is in preachers; the instrumental in the word. What God has joined together, let not man put asunder. We cannot do without the first and the third, and ought not to attempt to do without the second. For though multitudes are converted by the Spirit through the word, without any ministerial intervention, just as grain springs up here and there without a husbandman, yet it is the ordinance of God that the harvest of souls should be gathered by workmen appointed for that purpose.

16. Wherefore, I beseech you, be ye followers of me.

Wherefore, i. e. because I am your father. *Be ye followers* (μιμηταί, literally, *imitators*) *of me.* He does not exhort them to become his followers or partisans, instead of being the followers of Apollos or of Cephas. But as he had spoken of himself as being humble, self-denying and self-sacrificing in the cause of Christ, he beseeches them to follow his example. In 11, 1 he says, "Be ye imitators of me, as I am of Christ." Comp. 1 Thess. 1, 6. 2, 14. Eph. 5, 1.

17. For this cause have I sent unto you Timotheus, who is my beloved son, and faithful in the Lord, who shall bring you into remembrance of my ways which be in Christ, as I teach every where in every church.

For this cause, that is, to secure your imitating my example. This end, Timothy, whom he commends as his son, and as faithful, was to accomplish by vindicating the apostle from the aspersions which had been cast upon him, by reminding the Corinthians of his conduct and teaching as a minister of Christ. Nothing more was necessary than to appeal to their own knowledge of what Paul had been among them. *My son;* not only the object of my love, but my child; one whom I have begotten through the gospel. This is implied from the use of the word in v. 14. Comp. 1 Tim. 1, 2, where he speaks of him as "his own son in the faith." The fact that Timothy stood in this endearing relation to Paul, was a reason for his sending him, and also a reason why they should receive him with confidence. He was, however, not only Paul's son, but *faithful in the Lord.* And this was a further reason both for his mission and for their regard and confidence. *Faithful in the Lord* means faithful in the service of Christ, or as a Christian. The words *in the Lord* admit of being connected with the word *son*, so as to give the sense, "My faithful son in the Lord."

The work which Timothy was to do was to remind the Corinthians of what they seem to have forgotten, viz., of Paul's *ways which were in Christ*, *how he taught*, &c. The latter clause limits and explains the former. It was not so muoh his *ways* or deportment in general, as his character and conduct as a teacher, which were to be brought to mind. This, however, included his consistency, his zeal, humility and fidelity. It is evident from 2 Cor. 1, 17–20 that inconsistency and instability both as to his doctrines and plans, was one of the objections urged against Paul in Corinth, as in other places, comp. Gal. 5, 11. *My ways which be in Christ*, means the ways which I follow in the service of Christ. It was his official conduct as an apostle and teacher which Timothy was to bring to their recollection. *As* (καθώς), in the sense of *how*. Acts 15, 14. 3 John 3. He is to remind you *as*, i. e. how, I teach *every where in every church.* Paul's doctrine and mode of teaching were every where the same. And to this fact Timothy was to bear testimony, and thus vindicate him from the aspersions of his enemies.

18. Now some are puffed up, as though I would not come to you.

His sending Timothy was not to be considered as any indication that he himself did not intend to visit Corinth, as some in their pride and self-confidence supposed. It appears from numerous passages in this and the following epistle, that the false teachers in Corinth in various ways endeavoured to undermine Paul's authority. They called in question his apostleship, 9, 1–3. 2 Cor. 12, 12 ; they accused him of lightness, or instability, 2 Cor. 1, 17 ; they represented him as weak in person and contemptible in speech, 2 Cor. 10, 10. These were the persons who *were puffed up*, that is, so conceited as to their own importance, and as to the effect of their injurious representations respecting the apostle, as to give out that he was afraid to come to Corinth, and therefore sent Timothy in his place.

19. But I will come to you shortly, if the Lord will, and will know, not the speech of them which are puffed up, but the power.

In opposition to this boasting of his opponents, Paul declares his purpose soon to visit Corinth, *if the Lord* (i. e. Christ) *will.* Comp. 16, 7, and Acts 16, 7. This is a recognition both of the providential and spiritual government of Christ. It supposes the external circumstances, and the inward state of the apostle, his purposes and convictions of duty, to be determined by the providence and Spirit of Christ. Thus constantly did Paul live in communion with Christ as his God, submitting to him and trusting to him at all times.

And will know not the speech but the power of those who are puffed up. That is, not what they can say, but what they can do. By *power* (δύναμις) some understand miraculous power, which does not suit the context. Others confine it to *spiritual* power, that is, the power derived from the Spirit. The word is sometimes used for the essential power, or true nature and efficacy of a thing. And this sense best suits the antithesis between *speech* and *power.* Paul meant to put to the test, not what these men could say, but what they really were and did; that is, their true character and efficiency Comp. 1 Thess. 1, 5. 2 Tim. 3, 5. "Having the form of godliness, but denying the power (δύναμιν) thereof," i. e. its real nature and efficacy.

20. For the kingdom of God (is) not in word, but in power.

The idea expressed by the phrase "kingdom of God," in the New Testament, is very comprehensive and manifold, and therefore indefinite. The two senses under which most, if not all, its applications may be comprehended are, 1. The royal authority or dominion exercised by God or Christ; and 2. Those over whom that authority extends, or who recognize and submit to it. In the former sense, the word (βασιλεία) *kingdom* is used in such expressions as, Thy kingdom come, Of his kingdom there is no end, The sceptre of his kingdom, &c., &c. In such expressions as, To enter the kingdom of

God; The children, or members of the kingdom, the phrase means the community over which God reigns, whether in this world, or in the world to come. In the former sense the meaning is equivalent to the reign of God. Hence to say, Thy kingdom come, and to say, May God reign, is the same thing. Now as God reigns in the hearts of his people—as well as in the church, and in heaven—so this inward spiritual dominion is called the kingdom of God. In this sense the passage, "the kingdom of God is within you," may be understood; and also Rom. 14, 17, "The kingdom of God is not meat and drink, but righteousness and peace, and joy in the Holy Ghost;" which is equivalent to saying that true religion does not consist in external observances, but in inward graces. This is the form of the idea which seems best suited to the passage before us. 'God's reign, his dominion in the heart, or true religion, does not consist in professions, but in reality.' The word *power* is to be taken in the same sense here as in v. 19. Paul says, 'I will know, not what these men say, but what they really are; *for* the kingdom of God (or religion) does not consist in what is apparent and outward, but in what is inward and real.' It is not a semblance, but a reality.

21. What will ye? shall I come unto you with a rod, or in love, and (in) the spirit of meekness?

Paul, so far from being afraid to go to Corinth, as his enemies imagined, was prepared to go there with authority. He was their spiritual father and ruler. He had the right and the ability to punish them. It depended on themselves in what character he should appear among them; whether as a punisher or as a comforter—whether in the exercise of discipline, or as a kind and tender parent. The preposition (ἐν) rendered *with* in the first clause, is the same as that rendered *in* in those which follow. It has the same force in them all. It means *furnished with, attended by.* That is, it marks the attending circumstances. The expression "spirit of meekness" is commonly understood to mean a meek or gentle spirit or disposition of mind. As, however, the word spirit, when connected with an abstract noun, always refers to the Holy Spirit, as in the phrases Spirit of truth, Spirit of wisdom, Spirit of adoption, Spirit of love, of fear, or of glory, it should be so understood here. Paul asks whether he should come with severity, or filled with the Spirit as the author of meekness. It is plain from this, as from numerous other passages, that the apostles exercised the right of discipline over all the churches; they could receive into the communion of the church, or excommunicate from it, at their discretion. This prerogative was inseparable from their infallibility as the messengers of Christ, sent to establish and to administer his kingdom. The following chapter furnishes a notable instance of the exercise of this authority.

CHAPTER V.

The case of the incestuous member of the church, vs. 1–5. Exhortation to purity, and to fidelity in discipline, vs. 6–13.

Reproof for retaining an unworthy member in the church. Vs. 1–13.

THE second evil in the church of Corinth, to which Paul directs his attention, is allowing a man guilty of incest to remain in its communion. He says it was generally reported that fornication was tolerated among them, and even such fornication as was not heard of among the heathen, v. 1. He reproves them for being inflated, instead of being humbled and penitent, and excommunicating the offender, v. 2. As they had neglected their duty, he determined, in the name of Christ, and as spiritually present in their assembly, to deliver the man guilty of incest to Satan, vs. 3–5. He exhorts to purity, in language borrowed from the Mosaic law respecting the passover. As during the feast of the passover all leaven was to be removed from the habitations of the Hebrews, so the Christian's life should be a perpetual paschal feast, all malice and hypocrisy being banished from the hearts and from the assemblies of believers, vs. 6–8. He corrects or guards against a misapprehension of his command not to associate with the immoral. He shows that the command had reference to church communion, and not to social intercourse; and therefore was limited in its application to members of the church. Those out of the church, it was neither his nor their prerogative to judge. They must be left to the judgment of God. vs. 9–13.

1. It is reported commonly (that there is) fornication among you, and such fornication as is not so much as named among the Gentiles, that one should have his father's wife.

Having dismissed the subject of the divisions in the church of Corinth, he takes up the case of the incestuous member of that church. *It is reported commonly* (ὅλως ἀκούεται). This may mean what our translation expresses, viz., it was a matter of notoriety that fornication existed among them. Ὅλως may have the force of *omnino*, 'nothing is heard of among you except, &c.' Or it may mean, 'In general, fornication is heard of among you.' That is, it was a common thing that fornication was heard of; implying that the offence, in different forms, more or less prevailed. This is the less surprising, considering how little sins of that class were condemned among the heathen, and how notorious Corinth was for its licentiousness. To change the moral sentiments of a community is a difficult and gradual work. The New Testament furnishes sad evidence, that Jewish and Gentile converts brought into the church many of the errors of their former belief and practice. The word *fornication* (πορνεία) is used in a comprehensive sense, including all violations of the seventh commandment. Here a particular case is distinguished as peculiarly atrocious. The offence was that a man had married his step-mother. His *father's wife* is a Scriptural periphrase for step-mother, Lev. 18, 8. That it was a case of marriage is to be inferred from the uniform use of the phrase *to have a woman* in the New Testament, which always means, to marry. Matt. 14, 4. 22, 28. 1 Cor. 7, 2. 29. Besides, although the connection continued, the offence is spoken of as past, vs. 2. 3. Such a marriage Paul says was unheard of among the Gentiles, that is, it was regarded by them with abhorrence. Cicero, *pro Cluent.* 5, 6. speaks of such a connection as an incredible crime, and as, with one exception, unheard of. It is probable from 2 Cor. 7, 12, that the father of the offender was still alive. The crime, however, was not adultery, but incest; for otherwise the apostle would not have spoken of it as an unheard of offence, and made the atrocity of it to arise out of the relation of the woman to the offender's father. We have here therefore a clear recognition of the perpetual obligation of the Levitical law concerning marriage. The Scriptures are a perfect rule of duty; and, therefore, if they do not prohibit marriage between near relatives, such marriages are not sins in the sight of God. To deny, therefore, the permanency of the law recorded in Lev. 18, is not only to go contrary to the authority of the apostle, but also to teach that there is for Christians no such crime as incest.

2. And ye are puffed up, and have not rather mourned, that he that hath done this deed might be taken away from among you.

They were puffed up, i. e. elated with the conceit of their good estate, notwithstanding they were tolerating in their communion a crime which even the heathen abhorred. Some have endeavoured to account for the occurrence of such an offence, and for the remissness of the church in relation to it, by supposing that both the offender and the church acted on the principle taught by many of the Jews, that all bonds of relationship were dissolved by conversion. The proselyte to Judaism became a new creature. He received a new name. His father was no longer his father, or his mother his mother. The Rabbins therefore taught that a proselyte might lawfully marry any of his nearest kindred. It is possible that such a notion may have partially prevailed among the Jewish portion of the church; but not very probable, 1. Because of its absurdity; 2. Because its prevalence among the Jews was only after their reprobation as a people; 3. Because the wiser class of the Jews themselves condemned it. It is more probable, if the crime was defended at all, it was on the principle that the Scriptures and nature condemn intermarriages on the ground only of consanguinity and not also of affinity. A principle opposed to Leviticus 18, and to what the apostle here teaches.

And have not rather mourned (ἐπενθήσατε), i. e. grieved for yourselves. Your condition, instead of filling you with pride, should humble you and make you sad. *That* (ἵνα), not *so that*, but *in order that*, as expressing the design which the apostle contemplated in their humiliation and sorrow. Comp. John 11, 15. 'I would that ye were grieved and sorry for yourselves, *in order that* he who had done this deed might be taken away.' The ἵνα may depend on a word implied. 'Ye have not mourned, *desiring* that, &c.' Chrysostom says the idea is, that they should have acted as they would have done had a pestilence appeared among them which called for mourning and supplication in order that it might be removed. It is a right inherent in every society, and necessary for its existence, to judge of the qualification of its own members; to receive those whom it judges worthy, and to exclude the unworthy. This right is here clearly recognized as belonging to the church. It is also clear from this passage that this right belongs to each particular church or congregation. The power was vested in the church of Corinth, and not in some officer presiding over that church. The bishop or pastor was not reproved for neglect of discipline; but the church itself, in its organized capacity.

3–5. For I verily, as absent in body, but present in spirit, have judged already, as though I were present, (concerning) him that hath so done this deed, in the name of our Lord Jesus Christ; when ye are gathered together, and my spirit, with the power of our Lord Jesus Christ, to deliver such an one unto Satan for the destruction of the flesh, that the spirit may be saved in the day of the Lord Jesus.

These verses constitute one sentence, and must be taken together in order to be understood. The construction of the principal clauses is plain. Paul says, 'I have determined to deliver this man unto Satan.' All the rest is subordinate and circumstantial. The connection of the subordinate clauses is doubtful. Perhaps the best interpretation of the whole passage is the following: 'I, though absent as to the body, yet present as to the spirit, have determined as though present, in the name of the Lord Jesus, ye being gathered together, and my spirit being with you, with the power (i. e. clothed or armed with the power) of our Lord Jesus Christ, to deliver this man to Satan.' There was to be a meeting of the church, where Paul, spiritually present, would, in the name of Christ, and in the exercise of the miraculous power with which he was invested, deliver the offender to the power of Satan. The connection with what precedes is indicated by the particle *for*. 'I would ye were in a state of mind to remove this offender, *for* I have determined to cut him off.' I *verily* (μέν), or I *at least*. 'Whatever you do or leave undone, I *at least* will do my duty.' *Absent in body, but present in spirit.* Neither Paul's capacity nor his authority to judge, nor his power to execute his judgment, depended on his bodily presence. He was present in spirit. This does not mean simply that he was present in mind, as thinking of them and interested in their welfare; but it was a presence of knowledge, authority, and power. *Have judged already.* That is, without waiting either for your decision in the matter, or until I can be personally present with you.

Him that hath so done this deed. This is one of the clauses, the construction of which is doubtful. Our translators insert the word *concerning*, which has nothing to answer to it in the text, unless it be considered a part of the translation of the preceding verb, (κέκρικα,) *I have judged concerning*, i. e. 'I have judged or passed sentence upon him.' This, however, creates embarrassment in the explanation of the fifth verse. The best explanation is to make this clause the object of the verb *to deliver*, in v. 5. 'I have already determined to deliver him who did this deed.' As, however, so much intervenes between the object and the verb, the object (*such an one*) is repeated in v. 5.

In the name of Christ, means by the authority of Christ, acting as his representative. The phrase includes, on the one hand, the denial that the thing done was done in virtue of his own authority; and on the other, the claim of the right to act as the organ and agent of Christ. This clause may be connected with what follows. 'Ye being gathered in the name of Christ.' Against this construction, however, it may be urged, 1. That the words would in that case most naturally have been differently placed. That is, it would be more natural to say; 'Assembled in the name of Christ,' than 'In the name of Christ assembled.' 2. It is a common formula for expressing apostolical authority, to say, 'In the name of Christ.' 3. The sense and parallelism of the clauses are better if these words are connected with the main verb, 'I have determined in the name of Christ to deliver,' &c. Paul was acting in the consciousness of the authority received from Christ. Compare 2 Thess. 3, 6. Acts 16, 18. *When ye are gathered together, and my spirit.* The church was to be convened, and Paul spiritually present. The sentence was not to be passed or executed in secret, but openly. It was to have the solemnity of a judicial proceeding, and, therefore, the people were convened, though they were merely spectators. *With the power of our Lord Jesus Christ.* This may be connected with the immediately preceding words, 'My spirit invested with the power of Christ being present.' Or with what follows, 'I have determined to deliver such an one with the power of Christ to Satan.' The sense is substantially the same. The sentence was to be passed and carried into effect in the name of Christ and by his power.

To deliver such an one unto Satan. There have from the earliest times been two prevalent interpretations of this expression. According to one view, it means simply excommunication; according to the other, it includes a miraculous subjection of the person to the power of Satan. Those who regard it as merely excommunication, say that "to deliver to Satan" answers to "might be taken away from you," in v. 2, and therefore means the same thing. The Corinthians had neglected to excommunicate this offender, and Paul says he had determined to do it. Besides, it is argued that excommunication is properly expressed by the phrase "to deliver to Satan," because, as the world is the kingdom of Satan, to cast a man out of the church, was to cast him from the kingdom of Christ into the kingdom of Satan. Comp. Col. 1, 13. In favour of the idea of something more than excommunication, it may be argued, 1. That it is clearly revealed in scripture, that bodily evils are often inflicted on men by the agency of Satan. 2. That the apostles were invested with the power of miraculously inflicting such evils, Acts 5, 1–11. 13, 9–11. 2 Cor. 10, 8. 13, 10. 3. That in 1 Tim. 1, 20, the same formula occurs probably in the same sense. Paul there says, he had delivered Hymeneus and Alexander unto Satan, that they might learn not to blaspheme. 4. There is no evidence that the Jews of that age ever expressed excommunication by this phrase, and therefore it would not, in all probability, be understood by Paul's readers in that sense. 5. Excommunication would not have the effect of destroying the flesh, in the sense in which that expression is used in the following clause. Most commentators, therefore, agree in understanding the apostle to threaten the infliction of some bodily evil, when he speaks of delivering this offender to Satan. *For the destruction of the flesh.* This is by many understood to mean, for the destruction of his corrupt nature, so that the end contemplated is merely a moral one. But as *flesh* here stands opposed to *spirit*, it most naturally means the body. 'The man was delivered to Satan that his body might be afflicted, in order that his soul might be saved.' *In the day of the Lord Jesus.* That is, the day when the Lord Jesus shall come the second time without sin unto salvation. It appears from 2 Cor. 7, 9–12, that this solemn exercise of the judicial power of the apostle, had its appropriate effect. It led the offender himself, and the whole church, to sincere and deep repentance.

6. Your glorying (is) not good. Know ye not that a little leaven leaveneth the whole lump?

Your boasting, (καύχημα,) ground of boasting. You have no good reason to boast of your religious state; on the contrary, you have abundant reason to be alarmed. *Know ye not;* do ye not consider the obvious and certain danger of this evil spreading? *A little leaven leaveneth the whole lump.* This proverbial expression is not here intended to express the idea that one corrupt member of the church depraves the whole, because, in the following verses, in which the figure is carried out, the leaven is not *a person*, but *sin*. The idea, therefore, is, that it is the nature of evil to diffuse itself. This is true with regard to individuals and communities. A single sin, however secret, when indulged, diffuses its corrupting influence over the whole soul; it depraves the conscience; it alienates from God; it strengthens all other principles of evil, while it destroys the efficacy of the means of grace and the disposition to use them. It is no less true of any community, that any one tolerated evil deteriorates its whole moral sense.

7. Purge out therefore the old leaven, that ye may be a new lump, as ye are unleavened. For even Christ our passover is sacrificed for us:

Purge out the old leaven is an exhortation to purity, as the old leaven is afterwards said to be malice and wickedness. This leaven is said to be *old*, because in the present apostate state of our nature, what is old is evil. Hence, the *old* man is a scriptural designation of our corrupt nature. *That ye may be a new lump. New*, i. e. pure—as the *new* man is the renewed nature. *As ye are unleavened.* Leaven in this connection is a figurative expression for sin. To say, therefore, that they were unleavened, is to say that they were holy. This was their normal state—as Christians. A Christian is a new or holy man. The argument, therefore, is drawn from the acknowledged fact that Christians, as such, are holy. Purge out the leaven of wickedness, that ye may be pure, for believers are holy.' *For even*, (καὶ γάρ,) or, *for also*. This is a second reason why they should be pure; *for Christ our passover is slain for us. Is slain;* rather, *is sacrificed*, as θύω means *to kill and offer in sacrifice*, or, to slay as a victim. When the paschal lamb was slain, the Hebrews were required to purge out all leaven from their houses, Ex. 12, 15. The death of Christ imposes a similar obligation on us to purge out the leaven of sin. Christ is our passover, not because he was slain on the day on which the paschal lamb was offered, but because he does for us what the paschal lamb did for the Hebrews. As the blood of that lamb sprinkled on the door-posts secured exemption from the stroke of the destroying angel, so the blood of Christ secures exemption from the stroke of divine justice. Christ was slain *for us*, in the same sense that the passover was slain for the Hebrews. It was a vicarious death. As Christ died to redeem us from all iniquity, it is not only contrary to the design of his death, but a proof that we are not interested in its benefits, if we live in sin. Our passover, viz., Christ. The words ὑπὲρ ἡμῶν, (*for us*), are omitted in all the older manuscripts, and are not necessary to the sense.

8. Therefore let us keep the feast, not with old leaven, neither with the leaven of malice and wickedness; but with the unleavened (bread) of sincerity and truth.

Let us *therefore* keep the feast. That is, since our passover Christ is slain, let us keep the feast. This is not an exhortation to keep the Jewish passover—because the whole context is figurative, and because the death of Christ is no reason why the Corinthians should keep the Jewish passover. Christians are nowhere exhorted to observe the festivals of the old dispensation. Neither is the feast referred to the Lord's Supper. There is nothing in the connection to suggest a reference to that ordinance. A feast was a portion of time consecrated to God. *To keep the feast* means, 'Let your whole lives be as a sacred festival, i. e. consecrated to God.' As a feast lasting seven days was connected with the slaying of the paschal lamb; so a life of consecration to God should be connected with the death of our passover—Christ. This feast is not to be celebrated with the *old* or corrupt leaven, which is explained to mean *the leaven of malice and wicked-*

ness. Πονηρία, wickedness, is a stronger word than κακία, *badness.* Any one who does wrong is κακός, *bad;* but he who does evil with delight and with persistency, is πονηρός. Hence Satan is called ὁ πονηρός, "The evil one." *But with the unleavened bread of sincerity and truth.* Sincerity and truth are the unleavened bread with which the Christian's life-long feast should be celebrated. *Sincerity,* (εἰλικρίνεια,) is *purity,* transparent clearness; something through which the sun may shine without revealing any flaw. *Truth* is in scripture far more than veracity. In its subjective sense, it means that inward state which answers to the truth; that moral condition which is conformed to the law and character of God.

9. I wrote unto you in an epistle not to company with fornicators:

This may be understood to refer to what he had written above in this epistle. Comp. Rom. 16, 22. 1 Thess. 5, 27. Col. 4, 16, where *the* epistle, ἡ ἐπιστολή, means the epistle he was then writing. Calvin, Beza, and almost all the modern commentators, understand it to refer to an epistle no longer extant. This is obviously the more natural interpretation, first, because the words (ἐν τῇ ἐπιστολῇ), *in the epistle,* would otherwise be altogether unnecessary. And, secondly, because this epistle does not contain the general direction not to company with fornicators; which, it would seem from what follows, the Corinthians had misunderstood. There is, indeed, a natural indisposition in Christians to admit that any of the inspired writings are lost. But nothing is more natural than the assumption that the apostles wrote many short letters, not intended as pastoral epistles designed for the church in all ages, but simply to answer some question, or to give some direction relative to the peculiar circumstances of some individual or congregation. 'I wrote to you in the epistle,' naturally means here as in 2 Cor. 7, 8, the epistle which you have already received, and not the one which he was then writing; and it is not wise to depart from the natural meaning of the words simply to avoid a conclusion we are unwilling to admit. The church has all the inspired writings which God designed for her edification; and we should be therewith content. *Not to company with,* (μὴ συναναμίγνυσθαι), not to be mixed up together with. That is, not to associate with. See 2 Thess. 3, 14. This may have reference either to social intercourse or to church communion. This indefinite command Paul explains, first, by stating that he did not mean to forbid social intercourse; and then saying he did intend to prohibit Christian fellowship with the wicked.

10. Yet not altogether with the fornicators of this world, or with the covetous, or extortioners, or with idolaters; for then must ye needs go out of the world.

Not altogether. This limits the prohibition. The apostle did not intend to prohibit all intercourse with the fornicators of this world. This would be an impossibility; while in the world we must have more or less intercourse with the men of the world. Or, the words (οὐ πάντως), *not altogether*, may be connected with the words *I wrote*, in the sense of *by no means*. Comp. Rom. 3, 9. 'I *by no means* wrote to you not to associate with the wicked.' This, although perhaps the more common explanation, does not give so good a sense. It is not so much a positive denial of having so written, as a limitation of the application of his command, that the apostle designs to give. *The world* means mankind as distinguished from the church, Gal. 4, 3. Eph. 2, 2. Col. 2, 8. The prohibition, such as it was, was not limited to any one class of the immoral; it included all classes. The *covetous;* those who will have more (πλεονέκτης); and especially those who defraud for the sake of gain. In the Scriptures the controlling love of gain is spoken of as a sin specially heinous in the sight of God. It is called idolatry, Eph. 5, 5, because wealth becomes the object supremely loved and sought. The man, therefore, who sacrifices duty to the acquisition of wealth; who makes gain the great object of his pursuit, is a covetous man. He cannot be a Christian, and should not, according to the apostle, be recognized as such.

Or with extortioners, i. e. the ravenous; those who exact what is not justly due to them, or more than is justly due. The sin is not confined to exactions by force or open robbery, but to all undue exactions. The man who takes advantage of another's poverty, or of his necessities, to secure exorbitant gain, is an extortioner. *Or with idolaters*, those who either professedly worship false gods, or who do what, in its own nature, and in the common judgment of men, amounts to such worship. This is said to be the earliest known instance of the use of the word εἰδωλολάτρης; it is never used in the LXX, although εἴδωλον is constantly employed in that version in the sense of *false gods*. *For then ye must needs go out of the world.* This is the reason why the apostle did not prohibit all intercourse with wicked men. We should have to seek another world to live in.

11. But now I have written unto you not to keep company, if any man that is called a brother be a fornicator, or covetous, or an idolater, or a railer, or a drunkard, or an extortioner; with such an one no not to eat.

But now (νυνὶ δέ). If taken in the ordinary sense, these particles refer to time. 'In the former epistle I wrote to you so and so, *but now* I write to you, &c.' They may have an inferential sense—*therefore*. 'Since ye cannot go out of the world, *therefore* I wrote unto you.' The apostle is explaining the meaning of what he had written. 'I did not write this, but I wrote, i. e. I meant, this.' This explanation best suits the context, and agrees better with the force of the tense (ἔγραψα) here used; for although the aorist of this verb is used in the epistolary style in reference to the letter in the process of writing, it is not used to express what is about to be written. The command is not to associate with any one who is *called a brother*, and yet is a fornicator, or covetous, or an idolater, or a railer (slanderer), or a drunkard, or an extortioner. A man in professing to be a Christian professes to renounce all these sins; if he does not act consistently with his profession, he is not to be recognized as a Christian. We are not to do any thing which would sanction the assumption that the offences here referred to are tolerated by the gospel. It may appear strange that Paul should assume that any one calling himself a Christian could be an idolater. By idolatry, however, he understands not merely the intentional and conscious worship of false gods, but doing any thing which, according to the common judgment of men, expresses such worship. Thus eating sacrifices within the precincts of a temple was an act of heathen worship, as much as partaking of the Lord's supper is an act of Christian worship. And yet some of the Corinthians did not hesitate to eat of heathen sacrifices under those circumstances, 10, 14–22. The principle laid down by the apostle is, that to join in the religious rites of any people is to join in their worship, whether we so intend it or not.

With such an one no not to eat. This does not refer to the Lord's supper, which is never designated as a meal. The meaning is, that we are not to recognize such a man in any way as a Christian, even by eating with him. It is not the act of eating with such persons that is forbidden. Our Lord eat with publicans and sinners, but he did not thereby recognize them as his followers. So we may eat with such persons as are here described, provided we do not thereby recognize their Christian character. This is not a command to enforce the sentence of excommunication pronounced by the church, by a denial of all social intercourse with the excommunicated. The command is simply that we are not, in any way, to recognize openly wicked men as Christians. This passage, therefore, affords no plea for the tyranny of Romanists in refusing all the necessaries of life to those whom they cast out of the church.

12. For what have I to do to judge them also that are without? do not ye judge them that are within?

Those without; those out of the church. Mark 4, 11. Col. 4, 5. 1 Thess. 4, 12. The command of the apostle had reference only to those within the church, *for* it was not his prerogative to judge those that are without. The Corinthians acted on the same principle. They confined church discipline to church members, and therefore should not have understood his injunction not to company with the wicked to apply to others than to those within the church.

13. But them that are without God judgeth. Therefore put away from among yourselves that wicked person.

God, and not the church, is the judge of those who are without. The verb may be accented so as to express either the present or the future. God judges (κρίνει); or, God will judge (κρινεῖ). The present gives the better sense, as expressing the divine prerogative, and not merely the assurance of a future judgment. *Therefore put away*, literally, according to the common text (καὶ ἐξαρεῖτε), *and ye shall put away;* which seems to have been borrowed from Deut. 24, 7. The better reading is (ἐξάρατε) *put away.* It is a simple imperative injunction, or necessary application of the principle of Christian communion just laid down. This passage is not inconsistent with the interpretation given to verses 3–5. In consequence of their neglect of duty, Paul determined to deliver the incestuous member of the Corinthian church to Satan. He calls upon them to recognize the validity of that sentence, and to carry it into effect. The sentence was pronounced; they, so far as it involved their communion, were to execute it.

CHAPTER VI.

This chapter consists of two distinct paragraphs. The first, vs. 1–11, relates to lawsuits before heathen magistrates. The second, vs. 12–20, to the abuse which some had made of the principle, "All things are lawful."

On going to law before the heathen. Vs. 1–11.

PAUL expresses surprise that any Christian should prosecute a fellow Christian before a heathen judge, v. 1. If Christians are destined to judge the world, and even angels, they may surely settle among themselves their worldly affairs, vs. 2. 3. If they had such suits, must they appoint those whom the church could not esteem to decide them? Was there not one man among themselves able to act as a judge? vs. 4–6. It was a great evil that they had such lawsuits. It would be better to submit to injustice, v. 7. Instead, however, of submitting to wrong, they committed it, v. 8. He solemnly assures them that the unjust, or rapacious, or corrupt should not inherit the kingdom of God, vs. 9. 10. They had been such, but as Christians they were washed from these defilements, and justified through Christ and by his Spirit, v. 11.

1. Dare any of you, having a matter against another, go to law before the unjust, and not before the saints?

The third evil in the church of Corinth which the apostle endeavours to correct, was the prosecuting legal suits before heathen judges. There was no necessity for this practice. The Roman laws allowed the Jews to settle their disputes about property by arbitration among themselves. And the early Christians, who were not distinguished as a distinct class from the Jews, had no doubt the same privilege. It is not necessary, however, to assume that the apostle has reference here to that privilege. It was enough that these civil suits might be arranged without the disgraceful spectacle of Christian suing Christian before heathen magistrates. The Rabbins say, "It is a statute which binds all Israelites, that if one Israelite has a cause against another, it must not be prosecuted before the Gentiles." *Eisenmenger's* Entdeckt. Judenth. ii. p. 427.

Dare any of you? Is any one so bold as thus to shock the Christian sense of propriety? *Having a matter.* The Greek phrase (πρᾶγμα ἔχειν) means *to have a suit*, which is obviously the sense here intended. *To go to law before the unjust.* It is plain that by the *unjust* are meant the heathen. But why are they so called? As the terms holy and righteous are often used in a technical sense to designate the professed people of God without reference to personal character; so the terms sinners and unjust are used to designate the heathen as distinguished from the people of God. The Jews as a class were holy, and the Gentiles were unholy; though many of the latter were morally much better than many of the former. In Gal. 2, 15, Paul says to Peter, "We are by nature Jews, and not sinners of the Gentiles;" meaning thereby simply that they were not Gentiles. The reason why the heathen as such are called the unjust, or sinners, is that according to the Scriptures the denial of the true God, and the worship of idols, is the greatest unrighteousness; and therefore the heathen, because heathen, are called the unrighteous. The word *unjust* is too limited a word to answer fully to the Greek term (ἄδικος), which in its scriptural sense means *wicked*, not conformed to the law of God. In this verse the opposite term, *saints*, or *the holy*, designates Christians as a class; and, therefore, the *unjust* must mean the heathen as a class. The complaint against the Corinthians was not that they went to law before unjust judges, but that they appealed to heathen judges. It is true their being heathen proved them to be unrighteous in the scriptural sense of the term; but it was not their moral character, so much as their religious status, that was the ground of the complaint. It was indeed not to be expected that men governed by heathen laws and principles of morals, would be as fair and just as those governed by

Christian principles; but what Paul complained of was, not that the Corinthians could not get justice at the hands of heathen magistrates, but that they acted unworthily of their dignity as Christians in seeking justice from such a source. Paul himself appealed to Cesar. It was, therefore, no sin in his eyes to seek justice from a heathen judge, when it could not otherwise be obtained. But it was a sin and a disgrace in his estimation for Christians to appeal to heathen magistrates to settle disputes among themselves.

2. Do ye not know that the saints shall judge the world? and if the world shall be judged by you, are ye unworthy to judge the smallest matters?

Do you not know? a form of expression often used by the apostle when he wishes to bring to mind some important truth, which his readers knew but disregarded. It was a conceded point, one which entered into the common faith of Christians, that the saints are to judge the world. *The saints* (οἱ ἅγιοι), the people of God, who are called saints because separated from the world and consecrated to his service. Those, therefore, who are of the world and devoted to its pursuits, are not saints. *The saints shall judge the world.* This does not mean that the time would come when Christians would become magistrates; nor that the conduct of the saints would condemn the world, as it is said the Queen of the South would condemn those who refused to listen to the words of Christ, Matt. 12, 42. The context and spirit of the passage require that it should be understood of the future and final judgment. Saints are said to sit in judgment on that great day for two reasons; first, because Christ, who is to be the judge, is the head and representative of his people, in whom they reign and judge. The exaltation and dominion of Christ are their exaltation and dominion. This is the constant representation of Scripture, Eph. 2, 6. In Heb. 2, 5–9 the declaration that all things are subject to man, is said to be fulfilled in all things being made subject to Christ. Secondly, because his people are to be associated with Christ in his dominion. They are joint heirs with him, Rom. 8, 17. If we suffer, we shall reign with him, 2 Tim. 2, 12. In Dan. 7, 22 it was predicted that judgment (the right and power to judge) should be given to the saints of the Most High. Comp. Matt. 19, 28. Luke 22,

30. Rev. 2, 26. 27. If then, asks the apostle, such a destiny as this awaits you, are ye unfit to decide the smallest matters? *If the world* (mankind) *shall be judged by you* (ἐν ὑμῖν), i. e. before you as judges. *Are ye unworthy* (ἀνάξιοι), i. e. of too little weight or value, having neither the requisite dignity nor ability. Unworthy *of the smallest matters*. The word (κριτήριον), here rendered *matters*, in the sense of causes, or matters for judgment, means, 1. A criterion or test; a rule of judgment. 2. A tribunal or place of judgment, and then, the court or assembled judges. Ex. 21, 6. Judges 5, 10. Dan. 7, 10, and in the New Testament, James 2, 6. 3. The trial, i. e. the process of judgment. 4. The cause itself, or matters to be tried. This last sense is doubtful, although it is generally adopted here because it suits so well the fourth verse, where the same word occurs. The second sense would suit this verse. 'If ye are to sit with Christ on the seat of universal judgment, are ye unworthy of the lowest judgment seats.' But the fourth verse is in favour of the explanation adopted in our version. 'Are ye unfit for the least causes?'

3. Know ye not that we shall judge angels? how much more things that pertain to this life?

As, according to Scripture, only the fallen angels are to be judged in the last day, most commentators suppose the word must here be restricted to that class. Not only men, but fallen angels are to stand before that tribunal on which Christ and his church shall sit in judgment. If agreeably to the constant usage of the Scriptures, according to which (as remarked above, 4, 9) the word when unqualified means good angels, it be understood of that class here, then the explanation is probably to be sought in the comprehensive sense of the word to judge. As kings were always judges, and as the administration of justice was one of the principal functions of their office, hence to rule and to judge are in Scripture often convertible terms. To judge Israel, and to rule Israel, mean the same thing. And in Matt. 19, 28, "sitting on twelve thrones judging the twelve tribes of Israel," means presiding over the twelve tribes. So in the case before us, "Know ye not that we shall judge angels?" may mean, 'Know ye not that we are to be exalted above the angels, and preside over them; shall we not then preside over earthly things?' This explanation avoids the difficulty of supposing that the good angels are to be called into judgment;

and is consistent with what the Bible teaches of the subordination of angels to Christ, and to the church in him.

4. If then ye have judgments of things pertaining to this life, set them to judge who are least esteemed in the church.

Paul laments that there were litigations among them; but if they could not be avoided, Christians should act in reference to them in a manner consistent with their high destiny. Here the word (κριτήρια), rendered judgments, seems so naturally to mean *causes*, things to be tried, that that sense of the word is almost universally assumed. It may, however, mean *trials, judicial processes;* which is more in accordance with the established use of the words. *Set them to judge who are least esteemed in the church.* The original admits of this translation. If the passage be so rendered, then it has a sarcastic tone. 'Set your least esteemed members to decide such matters.' It may, however, be read interrogatively, 'Do ye set as judges those least esteemed in (i. e. by) the church (that is, the heathen)?' This translation is generally preferred as best in keeping with the context. The sentence is emphatic. 'Those despised (see 1, 28) by the church,—those do you set to judge?' It is an expression of surprise at their acting so unworthily of their high calling.

5. I speak to your shame. Is it so, that there is not a wise man among you? no, not one that shall be able to judge between his brethren?

I speak to your shame. That is, I desire to produce in you a sense of shame. This may refer either to what precedes or to what follows. It was adapted to make them ashamed that they had acted so unworthily of their dignity as Christians; and it was no less disgraceful to them to suppose that there was not in the church a single man fit to act as arbitrator. *Who shall be able.* The future here expresses what should or may happen. *Between his brethren;* literally, *between his brother;* i. e. between his complaining brother and him against whom the complaint was brought.

6. But brother goeth to law with brother, and that before the unbelievers.

Instead of referring the matter to the arbitration of a judicious brother, ye *go to law*, and that before unbelievers. There are here two grounds of complaint. First, that they went to law (κρίνεσθαι) instead of resorting to arbitration (διακρῖναι). Secondly, that they made unbelievers their judges. By *unbelievers* are to be understood the heathen. In this connection the heathen are designated under one aspect, the unjust; under another, the despised; and under a third, the unbelieving, i. e. not Christians—but, as the implication in this particular case is, pagans. *And that* (καὶ τοῦτο), a form of expression often used when particular stress is to be laid on the circumstance indicated.

7. Now therefore there is utterly a fault among you, because ye go to law one with another. Why do ye not rather take wrong? Why do ye not rather (suffer yourselves to) be defrauded?

Now therefore (ἤδη μὲν οὖν), *already indeed therefore.* That is, these lawsuits are already, or in themselves (ὅλως), an evil irrespective of their being conducted before heathen judges. The word ἥττημα does not so properly mean *fault* as loss or evil. It is a loss or evil to you to have these litigations. See Rom. 11, 12, where the rejection of the Jews is called their (ἥττημα) loss. *Why do you not*, &c. That is, why, instead of going to law with your brethren, do you not rather submit to injustice and robbery? This is a clear intimation that, under the circumstances in which the Corinthians were placed, it was wrong to go to law, even to protect themselves from injury. That this is not to be regarded as a general rule of Christian conduct is plain, because, under the old dispensation, God appointed judges for the administration of justice; and because Paul himself did not hesitate to appeal to Cesar to protect himself from the injustice of his countrymen.

8. Nay, ye do wrong, and defraud, and that (your) brethren.

Instead of having reached that state of perfection in which

ye can patiently submit to injustice, ye are yourselves unjust and fraudulent. This must have been the case with some of them, otherwise there would be no occasion for these lawsuits. Their offence was aggravated, because their own brethren were the object of their unjust exactions.

9. 10. Know ye not that the unrighteous shall not inherit the kingdom of God? Be not deceived: neither fornicators, nor idolaters, nor adulterers, nor effeminate, nor abusers of themselves with mankind, nor thieves, nor covetous, nor drunkards, nor revilers, nor extortioners, shall inherit the kingdom of God.

The tendency to divorce religion from morality has manifested itself in all ages of the world, and under all forms of religion. The pagan, the Jew, the Mohammedan, the nominal Christian, have all been exact in the performance of religious services, and zealous in the assertion and defence of what they regarded as religious truth, while unrestrained in the indulgence of every evil passion. This arises from looking upon religion as an outward service, and God as a being to be feared and propitiated, but not to be loved and obeyed. According to the gospel, all moral duties are religious services; and piety is the conformity of the soul to the image and will of God. So that to be religious and yet immoral is, according to the Christian system, as palpable a contradiction as to be good and wicked. It is evident that among the members of the Corinthian church, there were some who retained their pagan notion of religion, and who professed Christianity as a system of doctrine and as a form of worship, but not as a rule of life. All such persons the apostle warned of their fatal mistake. He assures them that no immoral man,—no man who allows himself the indulgence of any known sin, can be saved. This is one of the first principles of the gospel, and therefore the apostle asks, *Know ye not that the unrighteous shall not inherit the kingdom of God?* Are ye Christians at all, and yet ignorant of this first principle of the religion you profess? The *unrighteous* in this immediate connection, means the *unjust;* those who violate the principles of justice in their dealings with their fellow-men. It is not the unjust alone, however, who are to be thus debarred from the Redeemer's kingdom—but also those who break any of the commandments of God, as this and other passages of Scripture distinctly teach.

Believers are, in the Bible, often called heirs. Their inheritance is a kingdom; that kingdom which God has established, and which is to be consummated in heaven, Luke 12, 32. Matt. 24, 34, &c. &c. From this inheritance all the immoral, no matter how zealous they may be in the profession of the truth, or how assiduous in the performance of religious services, shall be excluded. Let it also be remembered that immorality, according to the Bible, does not consist exclusively in outward sins, but also in sins of the heart; as covetousness, malice, envy, pride, and such like, Gal. 5, 21. No wonder that the disciples, on a certain occasion, asked their master, Lord, are there few that be saved? or that the Lord answered them by saying, "Strait is the gate, and narrow is the way that leadeth unto life, and few there be that find it," Luke 13, 24.

11. And such were some of you: but ye are washed, but ye are sanctified, but ye are justified in the name of the Lord Jesus, and by the Spirit of our God.

And such were some of you. This is understood by many as equivalent to *Such were you.* The word (τινές) being redundant, or the idea being, 'Some were impure, some drunkards, some violent, &c., or ταῦτά τινες being taken together as equivalent to τοιοῦτοι. The natural explanation is, that the apostle designedly avoided charging the gross immoralities just referred to upon all the Corinthian Christians in their previous condition. With regard to the three terms which follow, *washed, sanctified, justified,* they may be taken, as by Calvin and others, to express the same idea under different aspects. That idea is, that they had been converted, or completely changed. They had put off the old man, and put on the new man. Their sins, considered as filth, had been washed away; considered as pollution, they had been purged or purified; considered as guilt, they had been covered with the righteousness of God, Rom. 1, 17. The majority of commentators take the several terms separately, each expressing a distinct idea. In what precise sense each of these words is to be understood, becomes, then, somewhat doubtful,

But ye are washed. The word here used (ἀπελούσασθε) is in the middle voice, and therefore may be rendered, *ye have washed yourselves*, or, *permitted yourselves to be washed;* or, as the majority of commentators prefer, on account of the following passives, *ye were washed.* This use of the First Aorist Middle in a passive sense is very unusual, but not unauthorized; see 1 Cor. 10, 2. It does not seem to be of much moment whether the word be taken here as active or as passive, for the same thing may be expressed in either form. Men are called upon to wash away their sins, Acts 22, 16; to put off the old man, etc. and to put on the new man, Eph. 4, 22. 24; although the change expressed by these terms is elsewhere referred to God. The reason of this is, that a human and a divine agency are combined in the effects thus produced. We work our own salvation, while God works in us, Phil. 2, 12. 13. With equal propriety, therefore, Paul might say to the Corinthians, 'Ye washed yourselves;' or, 'Ye were washed.' *To wash* means to purify, and is frequently used in Scripture to express moral or spiritual purification. Is. 1, 16, "Wash ye, make you clean." Ps. 51, 7, "Wash me, and I shall be whiter than snow." Jer. 4, 14. In these and many other passages the word expresses general purification, without exclusive reference to guilt or to pollution. There is no reason why it should not be taken in this general sense here, and the phrase be rendered, either, 'Ye have purified yourselves,' or, 'Ye are purified.' The reference which so many assume to baptism, does not seem to be authorized by any thing in the context.

But ye are sanctified. This clause is either an amplification of the preceding one, expressing one aspect or effect of the washing spoken of, viz., their holiness; or, it is to be understood of their separation and consecration. 'Ye have not only been purified, but also set apart as a peculiar people.' In Scripture, any thing is said to be sanctified that is devoted to the service of God. Thus, God blessed the seventh day and sanctified it, Gen. 2, 3. Moses sanctified the people, Ex. 19, 14, &c. &c.

But ye are justified. As to justify in Scripture always means to pronounce righteous, or to declare just in the sight of the law, it must be so understood here. The Corinthians had not only been purified and consecrated, but also justified, i. e. clothed in the righteousness of Christ, and on that account accepted as righteous in the sight of God. They were therefore under the highest possible obligation not to relapse into their former state of pollution and condemnation.

In the name of the Lord Jesus, and by the Spirit of our God. These clauses are not to be restricted to the preceding word, as though the meaning were, 'Ye have been justified in the name of the Lord Jesus, and by the Spirit of our God.' They belong equally to all three of the preceding terms. The believers were indebted for the great change which they had experienced; for their washing, sanctification, and justification, to Christ and to the Holy Ghost. The Spirit had applied to them the redemption purchased by Christ. *In the name of the Lord Jesus.* "The name of God," or "of Christ," is often a periphrase for God or Christ himself. To call upon the name of God is to call on God. To baptize unto the name of Christ, and to baptize unto Christ, are interchanged as synonymous expressions. So here, to be justified or sanctified in the name of Christ, means simply by Christ; see John 20, 31, "That believing ye might have life through his name." Acts 10, 43, "That through his name whoso believeth in him might have remission of sins." Though these forms of expression are substantially the same as to their import, yet the "name of God" means not strictly God himself, but God as known and worshipped. The Holy Ghost is called *the Spirit of our God;* that is, the Spirit of our reconciled God and Father, by whom that Spirit is sent in fulfilment of the promise of the Father to the Son. Christ hath redeemed us from the curse of the law in order that we might receive the promise of the Spirit, Gal. 3, 13. 14.

Abuse of the principle of Christian liberty. Vs. 12–20.

The principle of Christian liberty, or the doctrine that "all things are lawful," is to be limited in its application to things indifferent; first, by considerations of expediency; and secondly, by regard to our own spiritual freedom, v. 12. From that principle it is legitimate to infer, because of the adaptation of the stomach to food, that all things suited for food are lawful. The one is obviously designed for the other, during the temporary condition of the present life. But no such application of the principle is allowable in the case of fornication; because the body is not designed for that end, but belongs to the Lord, with whom it stands in an indissoluble connection, so that he who raised him up will also raise up our bodies, vs. 13. 14. It is because of this intimate relation of our bodies to Christ as his members, that fornication is so great a crime, inconsistent with our union to him as partakers of his Spirit, vs. 15–17. It is, in a peculiar manner, a sin against the body, destructive of its very nature, v. 18. The body is a temple in which the Spirit dwells, but it ceases to be such if profaned by licentiousness, v. 19. Believers must remember that they, even their bodies, are the objects of redemption, having been purchased by the blood of Christ, and therefore they should be devoted to his glory, v. 20.

12. All things are lawful unto me, but all things are not expedient: all things are lawful for me, but I will not be brought under the power of any.

Having in the preceding paragraph declared that the immoral cannot inherit the kingdom of God, and having given special prominence to sins against the seventh commandment, the Apostle comes in this paragraph to consider the ground on which the violations of that commandment were defended or palliated. That ground was a gross perversion of the principle of Christian liberty. Paul was accustomed to say in reference to the ceremonial or positive enactments of the Jewish law, and especially in reference to the distinction between clean and unclean meats, "All things are lawful to me." As the Greeks and Romans generally regarded fornication as belonging to the class of things indifferent, that is, not immoral in themselves; it is not surprising that some of the Corinthians educated in that belief should retain and act on the principle even after their profession of Christianity. They reasoned from analogy. As it is right to eat all kinds of food which are adapted to the stomach, so it is right to gratify any other natural propensity. Paul's answer to this argument is twofold. He first shows that the principle of Christian liberty in things indifferent is to be restricted in its application; and secondly, that there is no analogy between the cases mentioned. Food is a thing indifferent; whereas fornication is in its own nature a profanation and a crime.

The first limitation to which the principle "all things are lawful" is subject in its application to things indifferent, is expediency. All lawful things are not expedient. It is both absurd and wicked to do any thing which is injurious to ourselves or others, simply because it is not in its own nature sinful. This principle of expediency the Apostle enforces at length in Rom. 14, 15–23, and 1 Cor. 8, 7–13, and 10, 23–33. The second limitation of our liberty in the use of things indifferent, is self-respect. Because it is lawful to eat, that is no reason why I should make myself a slave to my appetite. "I will not," says Paul, "be brought under the power of any thing." I will not make myself its slave. It is of great importance to the moral health of the soul that it should preserve its self-control, and not be in subjection to any appetite or desire, however innocent that desire in itself may be. This is a scriptural rule which Christians often violate. They are slaves to certain forms of indulgence, which they defend on the ground that they are not in themselves wrong; forgetting that it is wrong to be in bondage to any appetite or habit.

13. Meats for the belly, and the belly for meats: but God shall destroy both it and them. Now the body (is) not for fornication, but for the Lord; and the Lord for the body.

Meats for the belly, and the belly for meats. The one is evidently adapted and designed for the other. It is a legitimate inference from this constitution that it is lawful to eat, and to eat every thing adapted for food. But this is a mere temporary arrangement. *God will destroy both it and them.* The time shall come when men shall no more be sustained by food, but shall be as the angels of God. The fact that the present constitution of the body is temporary, is a proof that meats belong to the class of things indifferent. They can have no influence on the eternal destiny of the body. This is not true with regard to fornication. The body was never designed for promiscuous concubinage. And such a use of it is inconsistent with the design of its creation and with its future destiny.

The body is for the Lord; and the Lord for the body. The one stands in an intimate relation to the other. The body is designed to be a member of Christ, and the dwelling-place of his Spirit. And he so regards it; redeeming it with his blood, uniting it to himself as a member of his mystical body, making it an instrument of righteousness unto holiness. With this design of the body the sin in question is absolutely in compatible, and destructive of the relation which the body sustains to the Lord.

14. And God hath both raised up the Lord, and will also raise up us by his own power.

The destiny of the body being what is stated in the preceding verse, it is not to perish, but is to share in the resurrection of Christ. "He who raised Christ from the dead shall also quicken our mortal bodies by his Spirit that dwelleth in us,"* Rom. 8. 11. This verse is parallel to the second clause of v. 13. Of the stomach and meats, it is said, God will destroy both it and them; of the Lord and the body it is said, As he raised up the one, he will also raise up the other. The cases, therefore, are widely different. The relation between our organs of digestion and food is temporary; the relation between Christ and the body is permanent. What concerns the former relation is a matter of indifference; what concerns the other touches the groundwork of our nature and the design for which we were created. On this destiny of the body compare 15, 15. 20. 35–56. Phil. 3, 21. Rom. 8, 11. 2 Cor. 4, 14. 1 Thess. 4, 14.

15. 16. Know ye not that your bodies are the members of Christ? shall I then take the members of Christ, and make (them) the members of an harlot? God forbid. What! know ye not that he which is joined to an harlot is one body? for two, saith he, shall be one flesh.

The design of these verses is to establish two points. First, that the relation between our bodies and Christ is of the intimate and vital character which had just been stated. And second, that the sin in question was inconsistent with that relation, and incompatible with it.

Know ye not that your bodies are the members of Christ? This is a conceded and familiar point of Christian doctrine, one with which they were supposed to be acquainted; and which proved all that the Apostle had said of the relation be

* Instead of the future ἐξεγερεῖ, *will raise up*, Lachmann and Tischendorf after A. D. read ἐξεγείρει, *he raises up*. Meyer after B. 67, prefers ἐξήγειρε, *he raised up*. According to this last reading the resurrection of believers is represented as involved in that of Christ. As they died when he died, so they rose when he rose. The common text however is the best supported, and gives a good sense.

tween the body and Christ. Our bodies are the members of Christ, because they belong to him, being included in the redemption effected by his blood; and also because they are so united to him as to be partakers of his life. It is one of the prominent doctrines of the Bible that the union between Christ and his people includes a community of life; and it is clearly taught that this life pertains to the body as well as to the soul, Rom. 8, 6–11. Eph. 2, 6. 7. 5, 30. This is the truth which the Apostle recalls to the minds of the Corinthians, and makes it the ground of his indignant condemnation of the sin of which he is speaking. That fornication is incompatible with the relation of the bodies of believers to Christ, arises out of the peculiar nature of that sin. The parties to it become partakers of a common life. Whether we can understand this or not, it is the doctrine of the Bible. Therefore as we cannot be partakers of the life of Christ, and of the life of Belial, so neither can our bodies be the members of Christ, and at the same time have a common life with "one who is a sinner," in the scriptural sense of that phrase.

17. But he that is joined unto the Lord is one spirit.

That is, has one Spirit with him. This does not mean has the same disposition or state of mind, but the same principle of life, v. 12, the Holy Spirit. The Holy Spirit is given without measure unto Christ, and from him is communicated to all his people who are thereby brought into a common life with him, Rom. 8, 9. 10. 1 Cor. 12, 13. John 17, 21. 23. Eph. 4, 4. 5, 30. This being the case, it imposes the highest conceivable obligation not to act inconsistently with this intimate and exalting relationship.

18. Flee fornication. Every sin that a man doeth, is without the body; but he that committeth fornication, sinneth against his own body.

This does not teach that fornication is greater than any other sin; but it does teach that it is altogether peculiar in its effects upon the body; not so much in its physical as in its moral and spiritual effects. The idea runs through the Bible that there is something mysterious in the commerce of the sexes, and in the effects which flow from it. Every other sin, however degrading and ruinous to the health, even drunkenness, is external to the body, that is, external to its life. But fornication, involving as it does a community of life, is a sin against the body itself, because incompatible, as the Apostle had just taught, with the design of its creation, and with its immortal destiny.

19. What! know ye not that your body is the temple of the Holy Ghost (which is) in you, which ye have of God, and ye are not your own?

There are two things characteristic of a temple. First, it is sacred as a dwelling-place of God, and therefore cannot be profaned with impunity. Second, the proprietorship of a temple is not in man, but in God. Both these things are true of the believer's body. It is a temple because the Holy Ghost dwells in it; and because it is not his own. It belongs to God. As it is a temple of the Holy Ghost, it cannot be profaned without incurring great and peculiar guilt. And as it belongs in a peculiar sense to God, it is not at our own disposal. It can only be used for the purposes for which he designed it.

20. For ye are bought with a price: therefore glorify God in your body, and in your spirit, which are God's.*

Ye are bought. The verb is in the past tense, ἠγοράσθητε, *ye were bought*, i. e. delivered by purchase. The deliverance of men from the power and condemnation of sin was not effected by power or by truth, but by a ransom. We were justly held in bondage. We were under the penalty of the law, and until that penalty was satisfied, we could not be delivered. The blood of Christ is our ransom, because it met all the demands of justice.

The proprietorship in believers asserted at the close of the preceding verse, does not arise from creation or preservation, but from redemption. 'Ye are not your own, for ye are bought with a price,' Rom. 6, 17. Gal. 3, 13. Eph. 3, 13. Acts

* The last clause of this verse is omitted by all the modern editors from Griesbach down. They are not found in the MSS. A. B. C. D. E. F. G., nor in several of the ancient versions.

20, 28. The price of redemption is the blood of Christ, Matt. 20, 28. Rom. 3, 24. Eph. 1, 7. 1 Pet. 1, 18. 19, and every where where the subject is spoken of in Scripture. *Therefore*, i. e. because redeemed, and because redeemed at such a price; *glorify God*, i. e. honour him, and so act as to cause him to be honoured by others. *In your body* as a temple consecrated to his worship, and employed only in his service.

The following words, *and in your spirit, which are God's*, may have been added, because the body alone is not the object of redemption, and therefore the obligation of the redeemed to be devoted to the service of God pertains also to the soul. As however these words are not found in the great majority of the oldest manuscripts, most modern editors omit them.

CHAPTER VII.

Instructions relative to marriage, vs. 1–17. The Gospel was not designed to interfere with the ordinary relations of men, vs. 18-24. Concerning virgins and widows, 25–40.

Instructions concerning marriage and other social relations. Vs. 1–24.

THE Corinthians had written to the Apostle, seeking his advice in reference to the state of things in their church. It appears from this chapter that one of the subjects about which they were in difficulty, and respecting which they sought direction, was marriage. On this subject the Apostle tells them, 1st. That, as they were situated, marriage was inexpedient to them. But as a general law every man should have his own wife, and every woman her own husband, vs. 1. 2. 2d. That the obligation of the parties to the marriage covenant is mutual; the one therefore has no right to desert the other. Temporary separation, for the purpose of devotion, is allowable; but nothing more, vs. 3–5. 3d. What he had said either in reference to marriage or temporary separation, was not to be considered as any thing more than advice. He could only tell them what, under the circumstances, was expedient; each one must act according to the grace given to him, vs. 6–9. 4th. With regard to the married the Lord had already taught that divorce was unlawful; the husband could not put away his wife, nor the wife her husband, vs. 10. 11. 5th. As to the case not specially contemplated in our Lord's instructions, where one of the parties was a Christian and the other a Jew or Pagan, the Apostle teaches, first, that if the unbelieving party is willing to remain in the marriage relation, it should not be dissolved. Secondly, that if the unbeliever departed, and refused to continue in the marriage connection, the marriage contract was thereby dissolved, and the believing party was at liberty, vs. 12–15. 6th. Such separations, however, are, if possible, to be avoided, because the gospel is a gospel of peace. It was not designed to break up any of the lawful relations of life. As a general rule, therefore, every man should continue in the same condition in which he was called. If a man was called being circumcised, his becoming a Christian did not impose upon him the obligation to become uncircumcised; and if called being uncircumcised, he was not required to be circumcised. In like manner, if a slave is called to be a Christian, he may remain a slave, because every slave is the Lord's free man, and every free man is the Lord's slave. These social distinctions do not affect our relation to Christ. Redemption, in raising all to the relation of slaves to Christ, that is, making them all his property, has raised them into a sphere where all earthly distinctions are insignificant. Therefore, let every man abide in the relation wherein he was called, vs. 16–24.

1. Now concerning the things whereof ye wrote unto me: (It is) good for a man not to touch a woman.

It is evident that there was a diversity of opinion on the subject of marriage among the Corinthian Christians. Probably some of them of Jewish origin thought it obligatory, while other members of the church thought it undesirable, if not wrong. Paul says, It is good for a man not to marry. The word *good* (καλόν) here means expedient, profitable, as it does frequently elsewhere, Matt. 17, 4. 18, 8. 9. 1 Cor. 9, 15. That the Apostle does not mean to teach either that marriage is morally an evil as compared with celibacy, or that as a general rule it is inexpedient, is evident. 1. Because in the following verse he declares directly the reverse. 2. Because in

v. 26 he expressly states that "the present distress," or the peculiar circumstances of trial and difficulty in which the Christians of that day were placed, was the ground of his advice on this subject. 3. Because in 1 Tim. 4, 3, he specifies "forbidding to marry" as one of the signs of the great apostasy which he predicted was to occur. 4. Because marriage is a divine institution, having its foundation in the nature of man, and therefore must be a good. God accordingly declared, "It is not good for man to be alone," i. e. to be unmarried, Gen. 2, 18. Paul cannot be understood in a sense which would make him directly contradict the word of God. 5. Because throughout the Scriptures marriage is spoken of as honourable, Heb. 13, 4, and is used to illustrate the relation between God and his people, and between Christ and his church. 6. Because all experience teaches that it is, as a general rule, necessary to the full development of the character of the individual, and absolutely essential to the virtue and the well-being of society. To depreciate marriage would be to go contrary both to nature and revelation, and such depreciation has never failed to be attended by the most injurious consequences to the church and to the world. If, therefore, Scripture is to be interpreted by Scripture, we must understand the Apostle as intending to say: 'Considering your peculiar circumstances, it is expedient for you not to marry.'

2. Nevertheless, (to avoid) fornication, let every man have his own wife, and let every woman have her own husband.

As a general rule, says the Apostle, let every man have his own wife, and every woman her own husband. Whatever exceptions there may be to this rule in particular cases, or in peculiar conditions of society or of the church, the rule itself stands. There is undoubtedly an increase of worldly care and anxiety connected with marriage, and therefore it may be expedient for those to remain single to whom freedom from such cares is specially important. This however does not alter the great law of God, that it is not good for man to be alone. Celibacy is to be the exception, not the rule.

3–5. Let the husband render unto the wife due

benevolence: * and likewise also the wife unto the husband. The wife hath not power of her own body, but the husband: and likewise also the husband hath not power of his own body, but the wife. Defraud ye not one the other, except (it be) with consent for a time, that ye may give yourselves to fasting and prayer; and come together again, that Satan tempt you not for your incontinency.

There is abundant evidence in the New Testament of the early manifestation of those principles of asceticism which soon produced such wide-spread effects, and which to so great a degree modified the reigning spirit of the church. The idea that marriage was a less holy state than celibacy, naturally led to the conclusion that married persons ought to separate; and it soon came to be regarded as an evidence of eminent spirituality when such separation was final. The Apostle teaches that neither party has the right to separate from the other; that no separation is to be allowed which is not with mutual consent, for a limited time, for the purpose of special devotion, and with the definite intention of reunion. Nothing can be more foreign to the mind of the Apostle than the spirit which filled the monasteries and convents of the mediæval church.

6. 7. But I speak this by permission, (and) not of commandment. For I would that all men were even as I myself. But every man hath his proper gift of God, one after this manner, and another after that.

The reference of the word *this* in v. 6, is a matter of doubt. Some refer it to the immediately preceding clause, 'Your coming together again I speak of as permitted, not as commanded.' But that clause is an entirely subordinate one; and the sense thus given to the passage is not consistent with the

* Instead of ὀφειλομένην εὔνοιαν of the received text, A. B. C. D. E. F. G. have the simpler reading, ὀφειλήν, which most editors adopt. The same authorities omit the words τῇ νηστείᾳ καί, in the latter part of the passage.

context. It was not a matter permitted, but commanded that husbands and wives should live together. Others refer it to the whole of v. 5. 'Your separating yourselves only by consent and for a limited time for the purpose of devotion, is a matter of permission, not of command; you may separate for other purposes and for an unlimited time.' But to this also it is an obvious objection, that it conflicts with the mandatory character of vs. 3. 4, and with the meaning of v. 5 itself; for that verse has not the form of a command. The reference to the 5th verse may be made under a different aspect. 'What I have said of your separating by consent for a season, is a matter of permission, not of command.' But this is not consistent with the reason assigned in the next verse. The most natural reference is to v. 2, and to what follows. His saying, 'Let every man have his own wife and every woman her own husband, and let them remember their mutual obligations,' was permissive and not a matter of command. Marriage, in other words, is permitted, not commanded. *For* I would that all were as I am. The sense is not materially different, if with many editors we read ϑέλω δέ instead of ϑέλω γάρ. 'Marriage is not commanded, but I would,' etc. The Apostle did not take sides with the extreme Jewish party, who regarded marriage as obligatory. He admitted the expediency of all remaining single in those times of persecution to whom God had given the requisite grace.

8. 9. I say therefore to the unmarried and widows, It is good for them if they abide even as I. But if they cannot contain, let them marry: for it is better to marry than to burn.

This is the application of the principle laid down in v. 1 to the Corinthians. 'I say to the unmarried and to the widows among you, it is well not to marry.' *The unmarried* is not to be limited to *widowers*, as is commonly done on account of the word *widows* following, because the word does not admit of that limitation; and because the word *married* in the following verse includes all classes. 'To the unmarried, and specially to widows, I say so; to the married I say so.'

If these verses and others of like import, are to be understood of men generally, and not of men in the peculiar circumstances of the early Christians, then it must be admitted that Paul depreciates marriage, and that he represents it as scarcely having any higher end than the sexual intercourse of brutes. This cannot be his meaning; not only because it is contrary to Scripture, but also because Paul elsewhere, Eph. 5, 22–33, represents marriage as a most ennobling spiritual union; which raises a man out of himself and makes him live for another; a union so elevated and refining as to render it the fit symbol of that bond between Christ and his people, by which they are exalted to the full perfection of their being. Marriage, according to Paul, does for man in the sphere of nature, what union with Christ does for him in the sphere of grace. The truth is that the apostle writes to the Corinthians as he would do to an army about to enter on a most unequal conflict in an enemy's country, and for a protracted period. He tells them, 'This is no time for you to think of marriage. You have a right to marry. And in general it is best that all men should marry. But in your circumstances marriage can only lead to embarrassment and increase of suffering.' This is the only view of the matter by which we can reconcile the apostle with himself, or with the truth of Scripture and of fact. This must therefore be borne in mind in the interpretation of this whole chapter.

10. 11. And unto the married I command, (yet) not I, but the Lord, Let not the wife depart from (her) husband: But and if she depart, let her remain unmarried, or be reconciled to (her) husband: and let not the husband put away (his) wife.

The first part of the 11th verse is a parenthesis, the construction goes on with the last clause. To the married I command, 'Let not the wife depart from her husband; and let not the husband put away his wife.' The distinction which he here and in v. 12 makes between his commands and those of the Lord, is not a distinction between what is inspired and what is not; nor is it a distinction between what Paul taught and what the Scriptures teach as Calvin understands it; but *Lord* here evidently refers to Christ; and the distinction intended is between what Christ had taught while on earth, and what Paul by his Spirit was inspired to teach. He tells the Corinthians that so far as the matter of divorce was concerned, they had no need to apply to him for instruction; Christ had already taught that the marriage bond could not be dissolved at the option of the parties. The wife had no right to leave her husband; nor had the husband the right to repudiate his wife. But although the marriage bond cannot be dissolved by any human authority, because it is, in virtue of the law of God, a covenant for life between one man and one woman; yet it can be annulled, not rightfully indeed, but still effectually. Adultery annuls it, because it is a breach of the specific contract involved in marriage. And so does, for the same reason, wilful desertion, as the apostle teaches in a following verse. This is the Protestant doctrine concerning divorce, founded on the nature of marriage and on the explicit instructions of our Lord, Matt. 5, 32. 19, 3–9. Mark 10, 2–12. Luke 16, 18. According to this doctrine nothing but adultery or wilful desertion is a legitimate ground of divorce, first, because the Scriptures allow of no other grounds; and secondly, because incompatibility of temper, cruelty, disease, crime, and other things of like kind, which human laws often make the occasion for divorce, are not in their nature a destruction of the marriage covenant. Romanists teach that divorce *a vinculo matrimonii*, where both parties were baptized, is never allowable. As this rule is contrary to Scripture, it is found injurious in practice; and therefore it is evaded by declaring marriages on frivolous grounds void *ab initio;* or by granting separation without dissolution of the marriage tie, for reasons not sanctioned by Scripture. The plain doctrine of the passage before us, as well as other portions of the word of God, is that marriage is an indissoluble covenant between one man and one woman for life, admitting neither of polygamy nor of divorce. If the covenant be annulled, it can only be by the sinful act of one of the parties.

But and if she depart. The law of Christ is that she should not depart; but if in violation of that law, or if from necessity she be obliged to depart, she has but two things to choose between,—she must remain unmarried, or she must be reconciled to her husband. This is not intended as an exception to the law, but it contemplates a case which may occur in despite of the law. 'In case a woman has actually departed, with or without just cause, then she must remain unmarried, or be reconciled to her husband.' There are cases undoubtedly which justify a woman in leaving her husband, which do not justify divorce. Just as there are cases which justify a child leaving, or being removed from, the custody of a parent. The apostle teaches, however, that in such cases of separation, the parties must remain unmarried.

12. 13. But to the rest speak I, not the Lord: If any brother hath a wife that believeth not, and she be pleased to dwell with him, let him not put her away. And the woman which hath an husband that believeth not, and if he be pleased to dwell with her, let her not leave him.

But to the rest; i. e. to those married persons not contemplated in the preceding class. The context makes it clear, that the distinction between the two classes was, that in the former, both parties were Christians; and in the latter, one was a Christian, and the other a Jew or heathen. With regard to these mixed marriages our Lord had given no specific command; therefore Paul says, I speak, not the Lord. The rule which the apostle lays down is, that such marriages are lawful, and therefore there is no obligation on the Christian party to dissolve the connection. And if he is not bound to do it, he has no right to do it. If, therefore, the unbelieving party consent (συνευδοκεῖ) to remain, the marriage may not be dissolved. The Christian husband is forbidden to repudiate (ἀφιέναι) his heathen wife; and the Christian wife is forbidden to repudiate her heathen husband. The same word is used in both cases, because, by the laws both of the Greeks and of the Romans, the woman as well as the man, had, on legal grounds, the right of divorce. Having said that these mixed marriages might be lawfully continued, he proceeds to remove the scruples which the Christian party might entertain on that point. He shows there is nothing unholy in such a connection.

14. For the unbelieving husband is sanctified by the wife, and the unbelieving wife is sanctified by the husband: else were your children unclean; but now are they holy.

The proof that such marriages may properly be continued, is, that the unbelieving party is sanctified by the believing; and the proof that such is the fact, is, that by common consent their children are holy; which could not be, unless the marriages whence they sprang were holy; or unless the principle that intimate communion with the holy renders holy, were a correct principle.

The assertion of the apostle is, that the unbelieving husband or wife is sanctified in virtue of the marriage relation with a believer. We have already seen that the word (ἁγιάζειν), *to sanctify*, means, 1. To cleanse. 2. To render morally pure. 3. To consecrate, to regard as sacred, and hence, to reverence or to hallow. Examples of the use of the word in the third general sense just mentioned, are to be found in all parts of Scripture. Any person or thing consecrated to God, or employed in his service, is said to be sanctified. Thus, particular days appropriated to his service, the temple, its utensils, the sacrifices, the priests, the whole theocratical people, are called holy. Persons or things not thus consecrated are called profane, common, or unclean. To transfer any person or thing from this latter class to the former, is to sanctify him or it. "What God hath cleansed (or sanctified), that call not thou common," Acts 10, 15. Every creature of God is good, and is to be received with thanksgiving, "For it is sanctified by the word of God and prayer," 1 Tim. 4, 5. This use of the word is specially frequent in application to persons and communities. The Hebrew people were sanctified (i. e. consecrated), by being selected from other nations and devoted to the service of the true God. They were, therefore, constantly called holy. All who joined them, or who were intimately connected with them, became in the same sense, holy. Their children were holy; so were their wives. "If the first-fruits be holy, the lump is also holy; and if the root be holy, so are also the branches," Rom. 11, 16. That is, if the parents be holy, so are also the children. Any child, the circumstances of whose birth secured it a place within the pale of the theocracy, or commonwealth of Israel, was, according to the constant usage of Scripture, said to be holy. In none of these cases does the word express any subjective or inward change. A lamb consecrated as a sacrifice, and therefore holy, did not differ in its nature from any other lamb. The priests or people, holy in the sense of set apart to the service of God, were in their inward state the same as other men. Children born within the theocracy, and therefore holy, were none the less conceived in sin, and brought forth in iniquity. They were by nature the children of wrath, even as others, Eph. 2, 3. When, therefore, it is said that the unbelieving husband is sanctified by the believing wife, and the unbelieving wife by the believing husband, the meaning is, not that they are rendered inwardly holy, nor that they are brought under a sanctifying influence, but that they were sanctified by their intimate union with a believer, just as the temple sanctified the gold connected with it; or the altar the gift laid upon it, Matt. 23, 17. 19. The sacrifice in itself was merely a part of the body of a lamb, laid upon the altar, though its internal nature remained the same, it became something sacred. Thus, the pagan husband, in virtue of his union with a Christian wife, although he remained a pagan, was sanctified; he assumed a new relation; he was set apart to the service of God, as the guardian of one of his chosen ones, and as the parent of children who, in virtue of their believing mother, were children of the covenant.

That this is so, the apostle proves from the fact, that if the parents are holy, the children are holy; if the parents are unclean, the children are unclean. This is saying literally what is expressed figuratively in Rom. 11, 16. "If the root be holy, so are the branches." It will be remembered that the words *holy* and *unclean*, do not in this connection express moral character, but are equivalent to *sacred* and *profane*. Those within the covenant are sacred, those without are profane, i. e. not consecrated to God. There are two views which may be taken of the apostle's argument in this verse. The most natural, and hence the most generally adopted view is this: 'The children of these mixed marriages are universally recognised as holy, that is, as belonging to the church. If this be correct, which no one disputes, the marriages themselves must be consistent with the laws of God. The unbelieving must be sanctified by the believing partner. Otherwise, your children would be unclean, i. e. born out of the pale of the church.' To this it is indeed objected by several modern commentators, that it takes for granted that the Corinthians had no scruples about the church-standing of the children of these mixed marriages. But this, it is said, is very improbable so soon after the establishment of the church, when cases of the kind must have been comparatively few. The principle in question, however, was not a new one, to be then first determined by Christian usage. It was, at least, as old as the Jewish economy; and familiar wherever Jewish laws and the facts of the Jewish history, were known. Paul circumcised Timothy, whose father was a Greek, while his mother was a Jewess, because he knew that his countrymen regarded circumcision in such cases as obligatory, Acts 16, 1–3. The apostle constantly assumes that his readers were familiar with the principles and facts of the Old Testament economy. Comp. 10, 1–13.

The other view of the argument is this: ‘If, as you admit, the children of believers be holy, why should not the husband or the wife of a believer be holy. The conjugal relation is as intimate as the parental. If the one relation secures this sacredness, so must the other. If the husband be not sanctified by his believing wife, children are not sanctified by believing parents.’ This, however, supposes a change in the persons addressed. Paul is speaking to persons involved in these mixed marriages. *Your* children naturally means the children of you who have unbelieving husbands or wives. Whereas this explanation supposes *your* to refer to Christians generally. In either way, however, this passage recognises as universally conceded the great scriptural principle, that the children of believers are holy. They are holy in the same sense in which the Jews were holy. They are included in the church, and have a right to be so regarded. The child of a Jewish parent had a right to circumcision, and to all the privileges of the theocracy. So the child of a Christian parent has a right to baptism and to all the privileges of the church, so long as he is represented by his parent; that is, until he arrives at the period of life when he is entitled and bound to act for himself. Then his relation to the church depends upon his own act. The church is the same in all ages. And it is most instructive to observe how the writers of the New Testament quietly take for granted that the great principles which underlie the old dispensation, are still in force under the new. The children of Jews were treated as Jews; and the children of Christians, Paul assumes as a thing no one would dispute, are to be treated as Christians. Some modern German writers find in this passage a proof that infant baptism was unknown in the apostolic church. They say that Paul could not attribute the holiness of children to their parentage, if they were baptized—because their consecration would then be due to that rite, and not to their descent. This is strange reasoning. The truth is, that they were baptized not to make them holy, but because they were holy. The Jewish child was circumcised because he was a Jew, and not to make him one. The Rabbins say: Peregrina si proselyta fuerit et cum ea filia ejus — si concepta fuerit et nata in sanctitate, est ut filia Israelita per omnia. See WETSTEIN *in loc.* To be born in holiness (i. e. within the church) was necessary in order to the child being regarded as an Israelite. So Christian children are not made holy by baptism, but they are baptized because they are holy.

15. But if the unbelieving depart, let him depart A brother or a sister is not under bondage in such (cases): but God hath called us to peace.

The command in the preceding verse was founded on the assumption, that the unbelieving party consented to remain in the marriage relation. If the unbeliever refused thus to remain, the believer was then free. The believer was not to repudiate the unbelieving husband or wife; but if the unbeliever broke up the marriage, the Christian partner was thereby liberated from the contract. This is the interpretation which Protestants have almost universally given to this verse. It is a passage of great importance, because it is the foundation of the Protestant doctrine that wilful desertion is a legitimate ground of divorce. And such is certainly the natural sense of the passage. The question before the apostle was, 'What is to be done in the case of these mixed marriages?' His answer is, 'Let not the believer put away the unbeliever, for Christ has forbidden a man to put away his wife for any cause except that of adultery, Matt. 5, 32. But if the unbeliever breaks up the marriage, the believer is no longer bound.' There is no conflict here between Christ's command and Paul's instructions. Both say, a man cannot put away his wife (nor of course a wife her husband) on account of difference of religion, or for any other reason but the one above specified. The apostle only adds that if the believing party be, without just cause, put away, he or she is free.

A brother or sister is not in bondage (οὐ δεδούλωται, equivalent to οὐ δέδεται, v. 39), i. e. *is not bound;* if the unbeliever consent to remain, the believer is bound; if the unbeliever will not consent, the believer is not bound. In the one case the marriage contract binds him; in the other case it does not bind him. This seems to be the simple meaning of the passage. Others understand the apostle as saying that the believer is not bound to continue the marriage—that is, is under no obligation to live with a partner who is unwilling to live with him. But the one part of the verse should be allowed to explain the other. An obligation which is said to exist in one case, Paul denies exists in another. If the unbeliever is willing to remain, the believer is bound by the marriage contract; but if she be unwilling, he is not bound.

But God hath called us in peace (ἐν εἰρήνῃ, i. e. ὥστε εἶναι ἐν εἰρήνῃ). Peace is the state in which the called should live. The gospel was not designed to break up families or to separate husbands and wives. Therefore, though the believer is free if deserted by his unbelieving partner, the separation should be avoided if possible. Let them live together if they can; and let all proper means be taken to bring the unbelieving party to a sense of duty, and to induce him to fulfil the marriage covenant. This is the common view of the meaning of this clause. Others understand it in a directly opposite sense, viz., as assigning a reason why the separation should take place, or at least why the attempt to detain an unwilling husband or wife should not be pressed too far. 'As God hath called us to live in peace, it is contrary to the nature of our vocation to keep up these ill-assorted connections.' This, however, is contrary to the whole animus of the apostle. He is evidently labouring throughout these verses to prevent all unnecessary disruptions of social ties.

16. For what knowest thou, O wife, whether thou shalt save (thy) husband? or how knowest thou, O man, whether thou shalt save (thy) wife?

The meaning of this verse depends on the interpretation given to the preceding. If Paul there said, 'Your call to live in peace forbids the continuance of the marriage relation with an unwilling husband or wife;' then this verse must give a further reason why (supposing one of the parties to be unwilling) such marriages should not be continued. That reason is, the utter uncertainty of any spiritual good flowing from them. 'Why persist in keeping up the connection, when, O wife, you know not whether you can save your husband?' If, however, the common interpretation of v. 15 be adopted, then the meaning is, 'Live in peace if possible, for how knowest thou whether thou shalt not save thy husband?' &c. We have here, therefore, an additional reason for avoiding separation in the case supposed. Compare 2 Sam. 12, 22. Joel 2, 14. Jonah 3, 9, in the Septuagint, where the phrase τίς οἶδεν εἰ, *who knows if*, is used to express hope. So here the idea is, 'Who knows, O wife, but that thou shalt save thy husband?'

17. But as God hath distributed to every man, as the Lord hath called every one,* so let him walk. And so ordain I in all churches.

Paul was not only averse to breaking up the conjugal relation, but it was a general ordinance of his that men should remain in the same social position after becoming Christians, which they had occupied before. We can very imperfectly appreciate the effect produced by the first promulgation of the gospel. The signs and wonders, and diverse miracles and gifts of the Holy Ghost by which it was attended; the perfect equality of men which it announced; the glorious promises which it contained; the insignificancy and ephemeral character which it ascribed to every thing earthly; and the certainty of the second coming of Christ which it predicted, produced a ferment in the minds of men such as was never experienced either before or since. It is not surprising, therefore, that men were in many instances disposed to break loose from their social ties; wives to forsake their unbelieving husbands, or husbands their wives; slaves to renounce the authority of their masters, or subjects the dominion of their sovereigns. This was an evil which called for repression. Paul endeavoured to convince his readers that their relation to Christ was compatible with any social relation or position. It mattered not whether they were circumcised or uncircumcised, bond or free, married to a Christian or married to a Gentile, their fellowship with Christ remained the same. Their conversion to Christianity involved, therefore, no necessity of breaking asunder their social ties. The gospel was not a revolutionary, disorganizing element; but one which was designed to eliminate what is evil, and to exalt and purify what is in itself indifferent.

As God (or *the Lord*) *hath distributed to every man*, i. e. whatever lot in life God has assigned any man. *As the Lord* (or *God*) *hath called every man*, i. e. whatever condition or station a man occupied when called by the word and Spirit of God, let him remain in it. His conversion, at least, does not

* The MSS., A. B. C. D. E. F. G., read *ὁ κύριος* with *ἐμέρισε*, and *ὁ θεός* with *κέκληκεν*.

render any change necessary. The principal difficulty with regard to this verse does not appear in our version. The words (εἰ μή), rendered *but* at the beginning of the verse, mean *except* or *unless*, and this meaning they have so uniformly that many commentators insist that they must be so rendered here. Some of them say the meaning is, 'What do you know *except* this, that every man should remain in the condition in which he was called?' But in this way the verse does not cohere with the preceding one. 'How knowest thou, O man, whether thou shalt save thy wife? *except* let every man remain as he was called.' This every one feels to be intolerably harsh. It would be better with others, to supply something at the beginning of the verse. 'What is to be done *except*.' 'Do not favour the separation of husbands and wives on account of difference in religion. God has called us to peace. The wife may save her husband, and the husband his wife. *What then is to be done*, except to remain in the condition in which you were called.' Others get over the difficulty by separating the εἰ and μή and connecting the latter with a verb understood. 'How knowest thou, O man, but that thou shalt save thy wife? If not, i. e. if thou shalt not save her, still the principle holds good that every man should remain in the state in which he was called.' This gives a good sense, but it would require εἰ δὲ μή. As it is undeniable that the Greek of the New Testament, especially in the use of the particles, is in a measure conformed to the usage of the Hebrew, a freer use of these particles is allowable, when the context requires it, than is common in classic writers. Most commentators therefore render the words in question as our translators have done. *And so I ordain in all the churches.* That is, this is the rule or order which I lay down in all churches. The apostles, in virtue of their plenary inspiration, were authorized not only to teach the doctrines of the gospel, but also to regulate all matters relating to practice.

18. Is any man called being circumcised? let him not become uncircumcised. Is any called in uncircumcision? let him not be circumcised.

This is the first application of the principle just laid down. Let every man remain as he is, circumcised or uncircumcised. The Jews were wont, when they abandoned their religion, to endeavour to obliterate the mark of circumcision. The Judaizers were disposed to insist on the circumcision of the Gentile converts. Both were wrong. Paul's command is that they should remain as they were. Instead of the interrogative form adopted in our version, the preferable translation is, "One was called (ἐκλήθη) being circumcised; let him not become uncircumcised. Another was called in uncircumcision; let him not be circumcised." *To call*, throughout the doctrinal portions of the New Testament, is to convert, to call effectually.

19. Circumcision is nothing, and uncircumcision is nothing, but the keeping of the commandments of God.

This is the reason why they should be treated with indifference. *They are nothing;* they have no influence either favourable or unfavourable on our relation to God. No man is either the better or worse for being either circumcised or uncircumcised. The gospel has raised men above all such things. The question to be asked is not whether a man is circumcised or uncircumcised; but whether he keeps the commandments of God. The things, therefore, about which the Christian ought to be solicitous, are not such external matters, which have no influence on his spiritual state, but conformity in heart and life to the revealed will of God. Rom. 2, 25. 29. Gal. 5, 6. "In Christ Jesus neither circumcision availeth any thing (is of any worth), nor uncircumcision; but faith which worketh by love." 'Faith that worketh by love,' and 'keeping the commandments of God,' are the same thing. They express the idea of holiness of heart and life under different aspects.

20. Let every man abide in the same calling wherein he was called.

This is a repetition of the sentiment contained in v. 17, which is again repeated in v. 24. The word calling (κλῆσις), always in the New Testament means the call of God, that efficacious operation of his Spirit by which men are brought into the kingdom of Christ. It is hard, however, to make it bear that sense here. The meaning is plain enough. 'As he was called, so let him remain.' But this is the idea detached from the form in which it is here expressed. The great majority of commentators agree in giving the word in this place the sense of *vocation*, as we use that word when we speak of the vocation of a mechanic or of a farmer. In whatever station or condition a man is called, therein let him remain. This of course is not intended to prohibit a man's endeavouring to better his condition. If he be a labourer when converted, he is not required always to remain a labourer. The meaning of the apostle evidently is, that no man should desire to change his status in life simply because he had become a Christian; as though he could not be a Christian and yet remain as he was. The gospel is just as well suited to men in one vocation as in another, and its blessings can be enjoyed in all their fulness equally in any condition of life. This is illustrated by an extreme case in the following verse.

21. Art thou called (being) a servant? care not for it: but if thou mayest be made free, use (it) rather.

Here again the general sense is plain. A man's being a slave, so far as his being a Christian is concerned, is a matter of no account. It need give him no concern. The interpretation of the latter part of the verse is somewhat doubtful. According to most of the Fathers the meaning is, 'Care not for being a slave; but even if you can be free, prefer to remain as you are.' This interpretation is adopted by several of the modern German commentators. It is urged in its favour that the original demands it. Paul does not say *but if* (ἀλλ' εἰ), but, *but if even* (ἀλλ' εἰ καί). 'Care not for your slavery; but if even you can be free, use it rather;' or, 'although (εἰ καί) thou canst be free, &c.' The English version overlooks the καί. Besides, it is said the common interpretation is in conflict with the context. The very thing the apostle has in view is to urge his readers to remain in the condition in which they were called. 'Art thou called being circumcised, remain circumcised; art thou called being free, remain free; art thou called being a slave, remain a slave.' There is not much force in this argument; because, as before remarked, Paul's object is not to exhort men not to improve their condition, but simply not to allow their social relations to disturb them; or imagine that their becoming Christians rendered it necessary to change those relations. He could, with perfect consistency with the context, say to the slave, 'Let not your being a slave give you any concern; but if you can become free, choose freedom rather than slavery.' A third argument urged in favour of the interpretation above mentioned, is that it is more consistent with the spirit of the apostle, with his exalted views of the equality of all men in Christ, and with his expectation that all earthly distinctions would soon be swept away. The advice to slaves to avail themselves of the opportunity to become free, it is said, would be trivial in the estimation of one who believed that those slaves might, at any moment, be exalted to be kings and priests to God. It must be admitted that this interpretation is plausible. It is not, however, demanded either by the language used, or by the context. The conjunction (καί), overlooked in our version, may be rendered *also.* 'Wast thou called being a slave? care not for it; but if also (i. e. in addition to your being called) thou canst become free, use it rather.' Luther, Calvin, Beza, and the great body of commentators from their day to this, understand the apostle to say that liberty was to be chosen if the opportunity to become free were offered. That the context does not conflict with this view of the passage, which our translators evidently adopted, has already been shown.

22. For he that is called in the Lord, (being) a servant, is the Lord's freeman: likewise also he that is called, (being) free, is Christ's servant.

The connection is with the first, not with the last clause of v. 21. 'Care not for your bondage, *for*,' &c. *He that is called in the Lord;* or, as the words stand, 'The slave called in the Lord.' That is, the converted slave. *Is the Lord's freeman*, i. e. is one whom the Lord has redeemed. The possession of that liberty with which Christ makes his people free, is so great a blessing, that all other things, even the condition of slavery, are comparatively of no account. Paul, in Rom. 8, 18–23, says that the afflictions of this life are not worthy to be compared with the glorious liberty of the sons of God, towards which the whole creation, now subject to vanity, looks with longing expectation. A man need care little about his external condition in this world, who is freed from the bondage of Satan, the curse of the law, the dominion of sin, and who is made a child and heir of God; that is, who is conformed to the image of his Son, and made a partaker of his exaltation and kingdom. *Likewise also he that is called, being free, is the Lord's servant* (i. e. slave, δοῦλος). The distinction between master and slave is obliterated. To be the Lord's freeman, and to be the Lord's slave, are the same thing.

The Lord's freeman is one whom the Lord has redeemed from Satan, and made his own; and the Lord's slave is also one whom Christ has purchased for himself. So that master and slave stand on the same level before Christ. Comp. Eph. 6, 9.

23. Ye are bought with a price; be not ye the ervants of men.

Ye (i. e. all Christians, bond and free,) *were bought with a price.* That is, purchased by Christ with his most precious blood, 1 Pet. 1, 18. 19. Ye belong to him; ye are his slaves, and should therefore act accordingly; and not be *the slaves of men.* The slave of one master cannot be the slave of another. One who is redeemed by Christ, who feels that he belongs to him, that his will is the supreme rule of action, and who performs all his duties, not as a man-pleaser, but as doing service as to the Lord, and not to men, Eph. 6, 6. 7, is inwardly free, whatever his external relations may be. This verse is a proper sequel to the preceding one. The apostle had exhorted all believers, even slaves, to be contented with their external condition. As a motive to such contentment, he had said they were all equally the subjects of redemption. They all belonged to Christ. To him their allegiance was due. They, therefore, whether bond or free, should act in obedience to him, and not in obedience to men. There is a very important sense in which even slaves are forbidden to be the servants of men—that is, they are not to be men-pleasers, but in all things should act from a sense of duty to God.

24. Brethren, let every man, wherein he is called, therein abide with God.

That is, as all these external relations are of no account, and especially, as a man may be a slave and yet a freeman, let every man be contented with the station which God has assigned him in this life. *With God* (παρὰ θεῷ); near him, perpetually mindful of his presence and favour. In other words, in communion with God. This would secure their contentment and happiness. They would find his favour to be life, and his loving-kindness to be better than life. To live near to God is, therefore, the apostle's prescription both for peace and holiness.

Of Virgins and Widows. Vs. 25–40.

In this portion of the chapter the apostle treats principally of the marriage of virgins—including, however, the young of both sexes. On this subject he says he was not authorized to speak with authority, but simply to advise, v. 25. His advice was, on account of the impending troubles, that they should not marry, vs. 26. 27. It was not wrong to marry, but it would expose them to greater suffering, v. 28. Besides, they should consider the transitory nature of all earthly ties. The fashion of the world was passing away, vs. 29–31. Still further, a single life was freer from worldly cares. The unmarried could consecrate themselves without distraction to the service of the Lord, vs. 32–35. To parents he says, that, if circumstances render it desirable, they might without hesitation give their daughters in marriage, v. 36. But if they were free to act on their own judgment, his advice was to keep them unmarried, vs. 37. 38. Marriage can only be dissolved by death. After the death of her husband, a woman is at liberty to marry again; but she should intermarry only with a Christian; and in Paul's judgment, her happiness would be promoted by remaining single, vs. 39. 40.

25. Now concerning virgins I have no commandment of the Lord: yet I give my judgment, as one that hath obtained mercy of the Lord to be faithful.

Now (δέ, *but*,) serves to resume the connection broken off by the preceding digression. 'But to resume my subject,' which in this chapter is marriage. *Concerning virgins*, (παρθένοι.) The word properly means *maidens*, though as an adjective it is used of both sexes, Rev. 14, 4. *I have no commandment of the Lord.* That is, neither Christ himself, nor the Spirit of Christ, by whom Paul was guided, had commissioned him to do any thing more than to counsel these persons. He was inspired, or led by the Spirit, in this matter, not to command, but to advise. His advice, however, was worthy of great deference. It was not merely the counsel of a wise and experienced man; but of one who had obtained mercy of the Lord to be *faithful*, i. e. worthy of confidence, one who could be trusted. This is a sense the word (πιστός) often has, as in the expressions, "faithful saying," "faithful witness." Paul felt himself indebted to the mercy of Christ for those inward graces and qualities which entitled him to the confidence of his readers. He recognised Christ as the giver of those gifts, and himself as undeserving of them. Had he been left to himself, instead of being the wise, disinterested, and faithful counsellor of Christians, he would have been a blaspheming persecutor. Philosophy would teach us that moral excellence must be self-acquired. The Bible teaches us that it is the gift of God; and being the gift of Christ, Christ must be God. As such, Paul blessed him for having been so merciful to him as to convert him, and bring him to the knowledge and obedience of the truth.

26. I suppose therefore that this is good for the present distress, (I say,) that (it is) good for a man so to be.

I suppose therefore, (νομίζω οὖν,) i. e. *I think then. The being so*, i. e. as you are, unmarried, is *good*, in the sense of expedient. There is a slight grammatical inaccuracy, or change of construction, in this verse. 'I think then this to be expedient on account of the coming necessity; that is, I think that it is expedient for a man so to be.' Paul here expressly states the ground of his opinion that it was inexpedient for his readers to marry. It was on account of *the present distress*, (ἐνεστῶσαν ἀνάγκην,) the distress standing near, whether actually present, or impending, depends on the context, Luke 21, 23. 2 Cor. 6, 4. 10, 12. 1 Thess. 3, 7. In the present case it was probably not so much the troubles in which Christians were then actually involved, as those which the apostle saw to be hanging over them, which he refers to. The Scriptures clearly predicted that the coming of Christ was to be preceded and attended by great commotions and calamities. These predictions had reference both to his first and second advent. The insight even of inspired men into the future was very imperfect. The ancient prophets searched diligently into the meaning of their own predictions, 1 Pet. 1, 10–12, and the apostles knew little of the times and seasons, Acts 1, 7. They knew that great calamities were to come on the earth, but how or when it was not given to them clearly to see. The awful desolation which was soon to fall upon Jerusalem and on the whole Jewish race, and which could not but involve more or less the Christians also, and the inevitable struggles and persecutions which, according to our Lord's predictions, his followers were to encounter, were surely enough to create a deep impression on the apostle's mind, and to make him solicitous to prepare his brethren for the coming storm. It is not necessary, therefore, to assume, as is so often done, that the apostle anticipated the second advent of Christ during that generation, and that he refers to the calamities which were to precede that event. Such expectation would not, indeed, be incompatible with his inspiration. It was revealed to him that Christ was to come the second time; and that he was to come as a thief in the night. He might, therefore, naturally look for it at any time. We know, however, that in the case of Paul at least, it was revealed, that the second advent was not to occur before the national conversion of the Jews, Rom. 11, 25; or before the great apostasy and rise of the man of sin, 2 Thess. 2, 2. 3. Still, he knew not when those events might occur, and therefore he knew not when Christ would come. It was not, however, to the calamities which are to precede the second advent, to which Paul here refers, but rather to those which it was predicted should attend the introduction of the gospel.

27. Art thou bound unto a wife? seek not to be loosed. Art thou loosed from a wife? seek not a wife.

Marriage, in the present circumstances of the church, will prove a burden. Although this fact will not justify the dissolution of any marriage, it should dissuade Christians from getting married.

28. But and if thou marry, thou hast not sinned; and if a virgin marry, she hath not sinned. Nevertheless such shall have trouble in the flesh: but I spare you.

If thou marry, or, 'If thou shalt have married, thou didst not sin; and *if a virgin shall have married*, she did not sin.' Marriage is inexpedient, not sinful. It is not because there is any thing wrong in getting married that Paul dissuades from it, but because *such shall have trouble* (θλῖψις, suffering) *in the flesh*; that is, external, as opposed to inward or spiritual afflictions. The reference is to the afflictions which must attend marriage in times of trouble. The word *flesh* is often used in this sense for what is external. John 6, 63. Eph. 6, 5.

2 Cor. 11, 18. *But I spare you.* The design of my dissuading you from marriage is to spare you these sufferings.

29-31. But this I say, brethren, the time (is) short; it remaineth, that both they that have wives be as though they had none; and they that weep, as though they wept not; and they that rejoice, as though they rejoiced not; and they that buy, as though they possessed not; and they that use this world, as not abusing (it): for the fashion of this world passeth away.

'This is another reason why you should not marry. You will soon have to leave your wives. It is nothing relating to your permanent and eternal interests which I urged you to forego, but only something which pertains to the fleeting relations of this changing world.'

But this I say, i. e. This I would have you bear in mind, as giving force to my advice. *The time*, i. e. the appointed time (καιρός, not χρόνος) *is short* (συνεσταλμένος). The verb properly means to *roll* or *wind up*, Acts 5, 6, then to *contract* or *shorten.* 'The time is shortened.' Comp. Matt. 24, 22. Mark 13, 20, where the idea is the same, though the word used is different. This interpretation is on the whole preferable to another almost equally common. 'The time is calamitous;' for this use of the word, however, no certain authority can be given. The words rendered, *it remaineth*, properly belong to the preceding clause. The meaning is not, 'It remaineth *that*,' but 'The time *henceforth* (τὸ λοιπόν) is short.' That is, the allotted time is brief. *That* does not depend on *This I say*, as though the sense were 'I say *that*;' but on what immediately precedes. 'The time is shortened *in order that*, &c.' It is the design of God in allowing us but a brief period in this world, or in this state, that we should set lightly by all earthly things; that those who have wives should be as though they had them not, and those that weep, as though they wept not; those who rejoice, as though they rejoiced not; those who buy, as though they possessed not; those using the world, as though they used it not.' We should set our affections on things above, and not on the things on the earth. Col. 3, 2. The clause rendered 'they that use this world as not abusing it,' is properly so translated, as καταχράομαι means *to use over-much.* The only reason for preferring the other translation is the analogy of the other passages. Either version is consistent with the usage of the word. *For the fashion of this world passeth away*, i. e. is in the act of passing away. *The fashion* (σχῆμα), the external form, the essence as it appears, the present state of things. The figure is derived from the scenes of a theatre, in the actual process of change. The fact that the present condition of the world is not to last long, and that our participation in its joys and sorrows is to be so short-lived, is the reason which the apostle urges why we should not be wedded to earthly things.

32. 33. But I would have you without carefulness. He that is unmarried careth for the things that belong to the Lord, how he may please the Lord: but he that is married careth for the things that are of the world, how he may please (his) wife.

This is the third reason why Paul wished the early Christians to remain unmarried. The first was, the increased suffering marriage would probably bring with it. The second was, the transitory nature of all earthly things. And the third is, the comparative freedom from care connected with a single life. The unmarried man may devote himself to the things of the Lord, i. e. to the service of Christ. Having no family to provide for and to protect in times of distress and persecution, he is less encumbered with worldly cares. Christ, and not his wife is, or may be, the great object of his solicitude.

34. There is difference (also) between a wife and a virgin. The unmarried woman careth for the things of the Lord, that she may be holy both in body and in spirit: but she that is married careth for the things of the world, how she may please (her) husband.

What is true of men is true also of women. *There is a difference between a wife and a virgin.* The difference is, that the virgin may devote her whole time to the Lord; the wife must be involved in worldly cares for the sake of her husband. The Greek literally rendered is, *Divided is a wife and a virgin.* Their interests are diverse. The one has a husband to divide her attention; the other is free from such distraction. The reading adopted by Lachmann and Rückert modifies the sense of this passage, and relieves some of its difficulties. They connect μεμέρισται with the preceding sentence, 'He that is married careth for the things of the world, how he may please his wife, and is divided, i. e. distracted between the service of the Lord and his social duties.' In the following clause they read 'ἡ γυνὴ ἡ ἄγαμος καὶ ἡ παρθένος ἡ ἄγαμος, the unmarried woman and the virgin care for the things of the Lord.' Jerome pronounces in favour of this reading, which he says he found in his Greek MSS., and it is also adopted by Calvin. The common text, however, is generally preferred. The virgin cares for the things of the Lord, *that she may be holy both in body and in spirit.* That is, that she be consecrated as to body and spirit. The word *holy* has the sense here that it has in v. 14, and so often elsewhere. It is not in purity and spirituality that the virgin is said to have the advantage of the wife; but in freedom from distracting cares. In v. 14, even the unbelieving husband or wife is said to be sanctified or made holy. And it is in the same general sense of consecration, that holiness is here predicated of virgins as distinguished from wives. It would be to impugn a divine ordinance, and to contradict all experience, to say that married women, because married, are less holy than the unmarried. Paul advances no such idea.

35. And this I speak for your own profit; not that I may cast a snare upon you, but for that which is comely, and that ye may attend upon the Lord without distraction.

The object of the apostle was their advantage. In urging them to remain single, he had no intention "to cast a snare upon them," i. e. to restrain their liberty. Or the meaning of the figure is, 'I do not wish to raise scruples, to make you afraid to move lest you fall into a snare.' The former explanation, however, is preferable. An animal ensnared was confined; it had no liberty of action. Paul did not wish to bring his readers into that state. They were perfectly free to do as they pleased. There was no moral obligation upon them to remain single; no superior holiness in celibacy. He was only saying what in his judgment would be most to their advantage under existing circumstances. That is, as he expresses it, his design was to promote what was *becoming and proper* in them; that is, to promote assiduous, undistracted devotion to the Lord. In other words, that they might be free from any thing to divert their minds from the service of the Lord. The literal translation is, 'For devotion to the Lord without distraction.' Every where the apostle is careful to show that celibacy was preferred merely on the grounds of expediency, and not on the ground of its being a higher state of virtue. All assumption or imposition of vows of celibacy, is a restriction of the liberty which the apostle was solicitous not to invade. Such vows are a snare; and those who take them are like an animal in a net.

36. But if any man think that he behaveth himself uncomely toward his virgin, if she pass the flower of (her) age, and need so require, let him do what he will, he sinneth not: let them marry.

This and the following verse are addressed to fathers, for with them, according to the usage both of Jews and Greeks, rested the disposal of the daughters of the family. Though the apostle regarded marriage at that time as inexpedient, he tells fathers that they were perfectly free to exercise their own judgment in giving their daughters in marriage, or keeping them single. *If any man* (i. e. any father) *thinketh he behaveth himself uncomely towards his virgin.* The word (ἀσχημονέω) may be taken either actively or passively. The meaning may therefore be, 'If any father think he exposes himself to disgrace by keeping his daughter unmarried;' as it was considered a reproach to be unmarried. Or, 'If he think that he exposes her to disgrace.' The latter interpretation is to be preferred because agreeable to the common use of the word, and because it is required by the preposition (ἐπί), which indicates the object of the action of the verb. *If she pass the flower of her age.* This is one of the conditions of the case on which Paul gives his advice. The daughter must be of full age; and secondly, there must be some reason why in her case marriage is necessary: *if need so require.* The daughter's happiness may be involved. Under these circumstances the father may *do what he will; he does not sin* in giving his daughter in marriage, and, therefore, *let them* (i. e. the parties) *marry.* In all cases of indifference, where no moral principle is concerned, our conduct must be regulated by a wise consideration of circumstances. But where a thing is in its own nature either right or wrong, there is no room for discretion.

37. Nevertheless he that standeth steadfast in his heart, having no necessity, but hath power over his own will, and hath so decreed in his heart that he will keep his virgin, doeth well.

He that standeth steadfast in his heart, i. e. whose judgment is settled and firm, being fully persuaded of the inexpediency of his daughter's marrying. *Having no necessity*, i. e. being controlled by no external necessity; nothing, in other words, rendering it necessary for him to act contrary to his own judgment. *But hath power over his own will*, i. e. is able to act as he pleases, or according to his judgment. *And hath so decreed in his heart*, i. e. has fully made up his mind, *to keep his virgin*, i. e. to keep his daughter unmarried; he doeth well.

38. So then he that giveth (her) in marriage doeth well; but he that giveth (her) not in marriage doeth better.

As there is no sin in marriage, and no superior virtue in celibacy, it is a mere question of expediency, to be determined by the circumstances of each particular case. All Paul says is that, other things being equal, it is *better* (i. e. wiser) not to marry than to marry; on account, as he before said, of impending calamities.

39. The wife is bound by the law as long as her husband liveth; but if her husband be dead, she is at liberty to be married to whom she will; only in the Lord.

The uniform doctrine of the New Testament is, that marriage is a contract for life, between one man and one woman, indissoluble by the will of the parties or by any human authority; but that the death of either party leaves the survivor free to contract another marriage. See Rom. 7, 1–3. Such being the doctrine of the Bible, no civil or ecclesiastical body can rightfully establish a different rule, or prescribe another or (as they pretend) a higher rule of morality. All attempts to be better than the Bible, on this or any other subject, only render men worse. Paul, therefore, teaches that a woman on the death of her husband, is free to marry whom she will—*only in the Lord.* There are two ways in which this restriction may be understood. First, that she should marry only one who is in the Lord, i. e. a Christian. Though mixed marriages between Christians and Jews or Gentiles should not, when formed, be broken up (as taught above, vs. 12–15); yet no such marriage ought to be contracted. Or, secondly, the phrase may be taken adverbially as expressing manner, *as becomes those who are in the Lord*, i. e. in a Christian manner. She is to marry as becomes a Christian. This interpretation includes the other. Compare Rom. 16, 2. 22. Eph. 6, 1, &c. The former explanation is the more simple and natural.

40. But she is happier if she so abide, after my judgment: and I think also that I have the Spirit of God.

Happier, freer from exposure to suffering, v. 28; and freer from worldly care, v. 32. *After my judgment;* it was an opinion founded, as he says, on the peculiar circumstances of the time, and not intended to bind the conscience or to interfere with the liberty of others, v. 35. Nevertheless, it was the opinion of a holy and inspired man, and therefore entitled to the greatest deference. *To have the Spirit*, means to be under the influence of the Spirit; whether as a Christian or as an apostle, depends on the context. The meaning here clearly is, that the apostle was led by the Spirit to give the advice in question; so that his advice is, so to speak, the advice of the Spirit. But is not the advice of the Spirit obligatory? Certainly, if he meant it to be so; but if he meant simply to lay down a general rule of expediency, and to leave every one to judge of its application to his or her peculiar case, then it leaves all concerned free. It would cease to be advice if men could not act contrary to it, without irreverence or disobedience. *I think* (δοκῶ) *I have*, is only, agreeably to Greek usage, an urbane way of saying *I have*, comp. Gal. 2, 6. 1 Cor. 12, 22. Paul was in no doubt of his being an organ of the Holy Ghost. *I also*, i. e. I as well as others. This is generally considered as referring (somewhat ironically) to the false pretenders in Corinth. 'I think I have the Spirit of God as well as those among you who make such high pretensions.'

CHAPTER VIII.

Eating of sacrifices offered to idols is not in itself wrong, vs. 1–7. But it should be avoided if it gave offence, vs. 8–13.

On eating of sacrifices. Vs. 1–13.

THE second subject on which the Corinthians had requested the advice of the apostle was the lawfulness of eating of the sacrifices offered to idols. To the discussion of that question in its different aspects the eighth, ninth and tenth chapters of this epistle are principally devoted. At the council of Jerusalem it was decided by the apostles, elders and brethren, that the Gentile converts should abstain "from meat offered to idols, from blood, and from things strangled, and from fornication," Acts 15, 29; and this decree was referred to the Holy Ghost as its author, v. 28. Yet Paul, though present in that council, not only does not refer to it, but goes directly against it. That decree forbade the eating of meat offered to idols; Paul, in ch. 10, tells the Corinthians that when exposed for sale in the market, or found on private tables, they might eat it without scruple. These facts do not prove any discrepancy between the apostles gathered in Jerusalem and Paul; nor that the decisions of that council were not obligatory on the church. They only serve to explain the true intent and meaning of those decisions. They show, 1. That there was no permanent moral ground for the prohibition of meat offered to idols. 2. That the ground of the prohibition being expediency, it was of necessity temporary and limited. It had reference to Christians in the midst of those to whom eating such meat was an abomination. It, therefore, ceased to be binding whenever and wherever the grounds of the prohibition did not exist. It is analogous to Paul's condemnation of women appearing in church without a veil. The decisions of that council, therefore, were no barrier to Paul's discussing the question on its merits. In this chapter the subject is viewed in two aspects; first, considered in itself; and secondly, in its bearing on the weaker or less enlightened class of Christians. Most of the questions which disturbed the early church had their origin in the conflicting prepossessions and prejudices of the Jewish and Gentile converts; or at least, of the more and less enlightened of the Christian converts. For it is probable that many of those who had been educated as heathen belonged to the class of weaker brethren. As a body, however, the Gentiles were disposed to latitudinarianism; and the Jews to superstitious scrupulousness. So far as general principles were concerned, Paul sided with the Gentile party. Their views about meats and drinks, and holy days, and ceremonies were derived from the apostle himself, and were therefore approved by him. But the spirit and practice of this party he severely condemns. Thus, in the present instance, he admits that an idol is nothing; that a sacrifice is nothing; that all enlightened Christians know this; that, consequently, eating of the heathen sacrifices was a matter of indifference, it made a man neither better nor worse; and yet eating of them might be, and in their case it was, sinful; because injurious to their weaker brethren. He begins the chapter with the admission, therefore, that all enlightened Christians have knowledge. He reminds them, however, that there is something higher than knowledge; that knowledge without love is, after all, only another form of ignorance. The main thing to be known is not apprehended, vs. 1–3. He admits, however, that Christians know that the gods of the heathen are vanities and lies, that there is but one only, the living and true God, v. 4. For although the heathen acknowledge a whole hierarchy of deities, celestial and terrestrial, Christians acknowledge but one God and one Mediator, v. 6. All this is admitted. It is, however, nevertheless true that many Christians, though they know that there is but one God, yet are not persuaded that the heathen deities are nothing, and therefore they stand in awe of them, and could not help believing that eating of sacrifices offered to idols was an act of worship, or in some way defiling, v. 7. The apostle also admits the second principle relied upon by the Gentile converts, viz., that meat does not commend us to God, that it can have no influence on our spiritual state, v. 8. It is not enough, however, that an act should be in its own nature indifferent to justify us in performing it. If our doing what is in itself innocent be the occasion of leading others into sin, it is for that reason sinful for us, v. 9. If, therefore, a weak brother should be led, against the convictions of his own mind, to join his stronger brethren in eating such sacrifices, he would bring himself into condemnation. It was, therefore, a breach of charity and a sin against Christ, to eat of the heathen sacrifices under circumstances which emboldened others to sin, vs. 10–12. The apostle avows his own determination never to eat meat at all, if by so doing he should cause his brethren to sin, v. 13.

1. Now as touching things offered unto idols, we know that we all have knowledge. Knowledge puffeth up, but charity edifieth.

The idolatry of the Greeks and Romans pervaded their whole life. Their social intercourse, their feasts, the administration of justice, the public amusements, the offices and honours of the government, were all more or less connected with religious services. Christians, therefore, were constantly exposed to the danger of being involved in some idolatrous homage without even knowing it. This gave rise to numerous and perplexing questions of conscience, which were often decided differently by different classes of Christians. One of the most perplexing of these questions related to the use of things offered to idols. Some had no scruples on this point; others thought it sinful to eat of such sacrifices under any circumstances. This was a question which it was necessary to have authoritatively settled, because it came up every day for decision. The victims offered in sacrifices were usually divided into three parts. One was consumed on the altar, another was given to the priest, and a third was retained by the offerer. The portion given to the priest, if not needed for himself, was sent to the market. The portion retained by the offerer was either eaten at his own table, or within the precincts of the temple. The Christians, therefore, if they bought meat in the market, or if invited to the houses of their heathen friends, or to the festivals in the temples, were liable to have these sacrifices placed before them. The two grounds on which the more liberal of them defended the use of such meat, were, first, that the idols were nothing, they were not really gods; and secondly, that meat cannot commend us to God. Both these principles are true, and therefore the apostle concedes them, but at the same time corrects the practical inferences which the Gentile converts drew from them. There were really two distinct questions relating to this subject. The first was, whether eating such sacrifices was lawful? the other, whether it was lawful to eat them within the precincts of the temple? The apostle does not distinguish these questions until the tenth chapter. Here he speaks of the subject only in its general aspects.

Now as touching things offered unto idols. Literally, *But, concerning idol-sacrifices.* The particle (δέ,) *but*, serves to introduce a new topic. As the fourth verse begins, *concerning therefore the eating things offered to idols*, the intervening words are a logical parenthesis. This parenthesis may begin immediately after the word *idols*, or after the word *knowledge*, so that the first two clauses of the verse are connected. "But concerning idol-sacrifices, we know we all have knowledge." This claim to knowledge, though a claim of the Corinthians, and the ground on which they defended the eating of those sacrifices, is not put forward as a point to be contested. The apostle adopts it, or makes it his own, and then proceeds to qualify and limit it, precisely as he did with the aphorism, "All things are lawful," in 6, 12; see also 10, 23. The subject of the two verbs *know* and *have* in this verse are not necessarily the same. The sense may be: 'I know we all have knowledge.' The knowledge intended is determined by the context. It is the knowledge concerning idols. In this verse Paul says, "We all have knowledge;" but in v. 7, he says, "This knowledge is not in all." This apparent contradiction may be explained by supposing, what is perfectly natural, that the apostle has reference to different classes of persons in the two passages. In v. 1 he may intend himself and his followers. *We all*, that is, all the stronger or more enlightened class of believers. Whereas, in v. 7, he may refer to Christians generally, including the strong and weak. 'This knowledge is not in all, for the weak have it not.' Or the distinction may be between theoretical and practical knowledge. All Christians admit, as a matter of theory, that an idol is nothing, but this knowledge is not in all believers practical and controlling. This also is natural and satisfactory. It is analogous to the statements of this same apostle in reference to the heathen. In Rom. 1, 23, he says, 'They know God,' but in 1 Cor. 1, 21, he says, they 'know not God.' These statements are perfectly consistent, because the word *know* has different senses. There is a sense in which all men know God; they all, from the constitution of their nature, and from the works of God, know that there is a being on whom they are dependent, and to whom they are responsible. But this is not the knowledge of God which is said to be "eternal life." It is therefore perfectly consistent to attribute the former knowledge to the heathen, though he denies to them the latter. So here it is consistent to say that all Christians have a theoretical knowledge of the truth that there is but one God, and that idols are nothing, and yet say that this knowledge is not practical and controlling in all. It is one of the great beauties of the Scriptures, that the sacred writers in the calm consciousness of truth, in the use of popular, as distinguished from philosophical language, affirm and deny the same verbal proposition, assured that the consistency and intent of their statements will make their way to the heart and conscience. That the apostle is here speaking of theoretical, as distinguished from true, practical knowledge, is plain from what he says of it. *It puffeth up.* The Greek word here used (φυσιόω,) is, in the New Testament, employed in the sense of the word (φυσάω,) which means *to blow, to fill with wind, to inflate;* and then, *to render vain and conceited.* Mere theoretical or speculative knowledge, that is, knowledge divorced from love, tends to inflate the mind, i. e. renders it vain and conceited. It is a great mistake, therefore, to suppose that mere knowledge, without religion, elevates and refines men, or can purify society. It is essential, but it is insufficient.

Charity edifieth. Charity is an inadequate and unhappy translation of the Greek word (ἀγάπη), because, agreeably to its Latin derivation, it properly means the feeling which arises from the perception of the wants and sufferings of others, and the consequent desire to relieve them. *Love* (ἀγάπη, a word peculiar to Hellenistic Greek,) is much more comprehensive than this, not only because it may have God for its object, but also because, when exercised towards men it includes complacency and delight as well as benevolence. It is of this comprehensive virtue the apostle treats at length in the thirteenth chapter of this epistle, and of which he here says, *it edifies.* It does not terminate on itself, as knowledge does, but goes out of itself, and seeks its happiness in another, and lives and acts for others. It is, therefore, something incomparably higher than knowledge, when the two are separated and distinguished.

2. And if any man think that he knoweth any thing, he knoweth nothing yet as he ought to know.

The knowledge which puffs up is not true knowledge. One is constantly astonished at the profound remarks which every where occur in the sacred writings; remarks which do not directly refer to the mysteries of the gospel, but philosophical remarks; that is, such as reveal the deepest insight into the nature of man and the workings of his constitution. Philosophy and theology are inseparably connected. The former is an element of the latter. A system of philosophy might be constructed by collecting and classifying the aphorisms of the Bible. And the reason why the philosophy which underlies Augustinianism has stood as a rock in the ocean, while other systems rise and fall like waves around it, is, that it is derived from the word of God, and not from the speculations of men. The relation between the cognitive and emotional faculties is one of the most difficult problems in philosophy. In many systems they are regarded as distinct. Paul here teaches, that with regard to a large class of objects, knowledge without feeling is nothing; it supposes the most essential characteristics of the object to be unperceived. And in the following verse he teaches that love is the highest form of knowledge. To know God is to love him; and to love him is to know him. Love is intelligent, and knowledge is emotional. Hence the apostle says, If a man thinketh that he knoweth any thing; that is, if he is proud or conceited, he is ignorant. He does not apprehend the true nature of the objects which he pretends to know. He does not see their vastness, their complexity, their majesty and excellence. These are the attributes of religious truths which are the most essential, and without the apprehension of which they cannot be known.

3. But if any man love God, the same is known of him.

To love is to know and to be known. Compare 1 John 4, 7. 8, "Every one that loveth is born of God, and knoweth God; he that loveth not, knoweth not God, for God is love."

This is the precise sentiment of the text. Love is essential to knowledge. He that loves God, knows God. The apostle in this connection interchanges love of the brethren and the love of God, because the love of the brethren is only one of the forms in which the love of God manifests itself. When he said, "Love edifieth," he meant love to the brethren, and without that love, he says, there can be no true knowledge; but if a man love God, (which includes love to the brethren,) *the same is known of him.* What is meant by this last expression, is not easy to determine. *To be known of God* may, according to scriptural usage, mean, 1. To be selected or approved by him, Exod. 33, 12. 17. Nahum 1, 7. Matt. 7, 23. 2. To be recognized as belonging to a particular class. So here, the sense may be, 'Is recognized by him as one of his disciples, or as one of his children. 3. To be the object of God's knowledge; but what this can mean in this connection, unless it include the idea of approbation, it is not easy to see. 4. According to others, the word (ἔγνωσται) is to be taken in a Hophal sense—'has been caused to know.' 'If any man loves God, the same has by him been brought to the true knowledge.' This view certainly suits the context. 'If a man is without love, he has not true knowledge; but if he love God, he has the right kind of knowledge.' The later grammarians deny that the passive form of Greek verbs ever has a causative sense analogous to the Hophal of Hebrew verbs. But as intransitive verbs in Greek often have a causative signification, (see Matt. 5, 45. 28, 19. 2 Cor. 2, 14,) it is not unreasonable that the passive form should be so used, if the context require it. In Gal. 4, 9, Paul says, "If after that ye have known God, or rather are known of God;" where the sense may be, 'or rather have been taught of God.' Whether the general principle be admitted or not, that the passive of Greek verbs can have this causative force, it is not improbable that Paul assumed that the particular verb γινώσκειν might mean *cognoscere facere*, (i. e. *to teach*,) a sense attributed to it by Stephanus in his Thesaurus; and if so, the passive as here used may mean, *was taught*. It is to be noticed, that it is only this verb that he appears to use in this way. If, however, this interpretation be rejected, as is done by the majority of modern commentators, as contrary to Greek usage, the first explanation given above gives a good sense. 'If any love God, the same is approved of him, i. e. is recognised as having the right kind of knowledge.'

4. As concerning therefore the eating of those things that are offered in sacrifice unto idols, we know that an idol (is) nothing in the world, and that (there is) none other God but one.

Concerning then. The particle (οὖν,) *then* serves to resume the subject of v. 1 after the interruption occasioned by the preceding parenthesis. For the general expression in v. 1, "Concerning idol-sacrifices," we have here the more definite one, "Concerning *the eating* of idol-sacrifices;" which was the point in dispute. To determine whether it was proper to eat of these sacrifices, it must be determined, first, what an idol is; and secondly, what effect the eating would have. As to the former, Paul says, there is no idol, (or an idol is nothing;) and as to the latter, that the eating could have no effect on our religious state; it could make us neither better nor worse, v. 8. From this it follows, that eating or not eating is a matter of indifference. Nevertheless, if our eating causes others to sin, we ought not to eat. It is worthy of remark that the apostle, in answering questions of conscience, does not give a categorical reply, but gives the reason for his decision. So here; and in ch. 11 he does not simply say it was wrong for Grecian women to appear in public unveiled, but he unfolds the principles valid for all time, on which the decision of that particular question rested.

As to the question, What is an idol? it is obvious that the word (εἴδωλον, *image*,) is used metonymically for the deity which the image was intended to represent. It is of such deity, or rather of the heathen gods generally, the apostle here speaks. His words are, "We know that οὐδὲν εἴδωλον ἐν κόσμῳ," which may mean, either, *an idol is nothing in the world;* or, *there is no idol in the world*, i. e. *the universe.* If the former version be adopted, the sense may be, either, 'these deities are nonentities,' they have no existence; or, they are powerless, they have no influence over the affairs of men. In favour of that translation is the analogy of Scripture. In the Old Testament the gods of the heathen are frequently said to be nothing, vanities, lies, &c., Is. 41, 24. 44, 8. 9. Jer. 10, 14. Ps. 115, 4. 8. So the Rabbis also said, Noverant utique Israelitae, idolum nihil esse, *Sanhdr.* 63. 2. But this explanation is not suitable here. As οὐδεὶς θεός in the next clause means *there is no God*, οὐδὲν εἴδωλον must mean, *there is no idol.* This does not mean that the heathen gods are either nonentities or powerless, for in 10, 19 Paul says they are demons. But it means, there are no such beings in the universe as the heathen conceived their gods to be. There was no Jupiter, Juno, or Mars. *There is no God*, no real divine being but one. The objects of heathen worship were neither what the heathen took them to be, nor were they gods in the true sense of that term.

5. For though there be that are called gods, whether in heaven or in earth, as there be gods many, and lords many,

This verse admits of two interpretations. It is commonly understood to mean, that although there are many imaginary gods in heaven and earth, i. e. beings whom the heathen regard as divinities, yet in fact there is but one God. When he says, there *are* many gods and many lords, he is to be understood to mean that such is the fact in the mythology of the heathen. A large number of commentators, however, understand the passage thus: 'There is but one true God; for although it be admitted that there are many beings called gods, as in fact there are gods many and lords many, yet to us there is but one.' The apostle concedes that, in the wide sense of the term, there are many gods and lords; and, therefore, if it should be admitted (what he does not admit) that the whole hierarchy of divinities, as conceived of by the heathen, actually existed, it is nevertheless true that there is but one God, the creator and end of all things. In favour of this interpretation is the usage of the O. T. Deut. 10, 17, "The Lord your God is God of gods and Lord of lords." Jos. 22, 22. Dan. 2, 47. Ps. 136, 2. 3. These passages show that the words *god* and *lord* are applied in a wide sense to other beings than to the true God. 2. The position and force of the words are in favour of this view. They mean, *Sunt qui dii dicuntur;* there *are* powers and beings who are called gods, as *there are* gods many, and lords many. To make this mean, there are *in the estimation of the heathen* many gods, is to insert something which is not in the text. 3. In 10, 19. 20, the apostle asserts that the objects of heathen worship are real and powerful beings. 4. The apparent contradiction between saying, *there is no idol in the world*, and saying, *there are many gods*, is easily removed. The meaning is, 'There is no such being in the universe as Jupiter or Mars; for although there is a multitude of supernatural beings, called gods and lords, not only by the heathen, but also in Scripture, yet there are no such beings as those which the heathen imagine.' The whole heathen mythology is a fable, the work of the imagination. There are no such gods in existence, though there are demons in abundance, of various ranks and powers, called gods. There are two things which the apostle means to deny. 1. The existence of such beings as the heathen conceived their gods to be. 2. That the supernatural beings who do really exist, and who are called gods, are really divine. They are mere creatures.

6. But to us (there is but) one God, the Father, of whom (are) all things, and we in him; and one Lord Jesus Christ, by whom (are) all things, and we by him.

Though there are many creatures called gods, there is but one true God, the creator of all things. *To us*, i. e. to Christians. *There is one God*, i. e. only one being who is eternal, self-existing and almighty. This one God is, first, *the Father;* not the first person of the Trinity, but our father. The word does not here express the relation of the first to the second person in the Godhead, but the relation of God as such to us as his children. When we say, "Our Father who art in heaven," the word Father designates the Supreme Being, the Triune Jehovah. Secondly, of this one God it is said, *of him are all things*. He, the one God, is the source of the whole universe, and all that it contains. He created all things by the word of his power. All other beings are his creatures. Thirdly, *we are to him*. He is our end; for his glory we were created and redeemed. Our version rendering the words εἰς αὐτόν, *in him*, is an unnecessary departure from their proper meaning.

As there is but one divine Being, so there is but one Lord, i. e. one administrator of the universe, into whose hands all power in heaven and earth has been committed, and who is the only mediator between God and man. This one Lord is *Jesus Christ*, Jesus the Messiah, the historical person, born in Bethlehem and crucified on Calvary. Of this one Lord it is said, first, *all things are by him*. The *all things* in this clause must be coextensive with the all things in the preceding one, i. e. the universe. Comp. Eph. 3, 9. Col. 1, 16. Heb. 1, 2. The universe was created *through* Jesus Christ, i. e. the energy of the one God was exercised *through* the Logos, who became flesh, assuming our nature into personal union with himself, and is therefore called Jesus Christ. This passage affords a striking illustration of the fact that the person of Christ may be denominated from his human nature, when what is affirmed of him is true only of his divine nature. He is here called Jesus Christ, though the work of creation attributed to him was the work of the Logos. Secondly, it is said of this one Lord, that *we are by him.* This does not mean we were created by him; for we Christians are included in the *all things.* It would be tautological to say, He created all things, and he created us. The meaning is, we as Christians (not, we as creatures, for that had been said before), we as the children of God are by him. We were redeemed by him; we are brought unto God by him.

7. Howbeit (there is) not in every man that knowledge: for some with conscience of the idol unto this hour eat (it) as a thing offered unto an idol; and their conscience being weak is defiled.

The context shows that (ἡ γνῶσις), *the* knowledge, means the particular kind of knowledge of which he had been speaking, viz. the knowledge that there is no idol in the world, or that the gods of the heathen are imaginary beings. Though the weaker believers knew that there is but one true God, they were still not fully persuaded that the gods of the heathen had no existence. *With conscience of an idol.* The word συνείδησις unites the meanings of our words *conscience* and *consciousness*, being sometimes the one and sometimes the other. Here the former meaning is better suited to the context. *Conscience of an idol* means a conscience under the influence of an idol; as in 1 Pet. 2, 19 *conscience of God* means a conscience under the influence of God.* The moral judgments and feelings of the persons referred to, were still influenced by the apprehension that the heathen gods might be real beings. *Unto this hour.* The words (ἕως ἄρτι) *until*

* Instead of συνειδήσει the MSS. A. B. 17. 46, and the Coptic, Ethiopic and Syrian versions read συνηθείᾳ, which reading is adopted by Lachmann and Tischendorf. The meaning would then be '*through custom of an idol,*' i. e. from being long accustomed to believe that there were such beings. The great weight of authority, however, is in favour of the common reading.

now, in the common Text stand after the word for *idol;* most modern editors of the Greek Testament, on the authority of the older MSS., place them before that word. In the one position, they naturally qualify the word *to eat;* '*until now they eat*,' i. e. they continue to eat. In the other, they qualify the word *conscience; with a conscience still under the influence of an idol*, which gives a better sense. Having this persuasion, or at least this apprehension of the reality of the idol, they eat the sacrifice as a sacrifice. That is, they do not regard it as ordinary meat, but as something which had a religious character and influence, from the fact of its having been offered in sacrifice. Hence *their conscience being weak was defiled.* A *weak* conscience is one which either regards as wrong what is not in fact so; or one which is not clear and decided in its judgments. According to the Scriptures, "whatever is not of faith is sin," Rom. 14, 23; therefore whatever a man does, thinking it is wrong, or doubtful whether it be wrong or not, to him it is sin. Thus the man who eats an idol-sacrifice, uncertain whether he is doing right or not, defiles his conscience. The conscience is said to be defiled, either when it approves or cherishes sin, or when it is burdened by a sense of guilt. The latter form of pollution is that here intended. The man who acts in the way supposed feels guilty, and is really guilty.

8. But meat commendeth us not to God: for neither, if we eat, are we the better; neither, if we eat not, are we the worse.

This verse is analogous to v. 1, in so far that it contains a principle adopted by the apostle as his own, which the Corinthians urged to justify their latitudinarian practice with regard to these sacrifices. It is not introduced as an objection, or as a point to be contested, but as an admitted truth, the application of which is to be regulated by other principles no less true. It is admitted that meat does not *commend us to God.* Literally, does not cause us to stand near to God; which involves the idea expressed in our version. *For* eating makes us neither better nor worse. It neither causes us to excel (περισσεύειν) nor to come behind (ὑστερεῖν).

There is another view of the bearing of this passage which has much to commend it, and which has many advocates. It is regarded as assigning a reason why the strong should have respect to the weak. 'If meat were a matter of importance, if it really commended us to God, there would be a valid reason why you should eat these sacrifices. But as it is a matter of indifference, you should not cause your brethren to offend.' This would be a natural interpretation if the caution which follows were introduced as an inference. That is, if the apostle had said, 'Eating is a matter of indifference, *therefore* you should use your liberty with due regard to your brethren.' His language, however, is, 'Meat does not commend us to God; it makes us neither better nor worse; *but* take heed how you use your liberty.' It is evidently a concession limited by what follows; comp. 6, 12, "All things are lawful, *but* all things are not expedient;" see also 10, 23.

9. But take heed lest by any means this liberty of yours become a stumblingblock to them that are weak.

Admitting you have the right to eat of these sacrifices, take care lest your eating become an occasion of sin to your weaker brethren. *Your liberty.* The word (ἐξουσία) means, 1. Ability or power. 2. Lawful power or right. 3. Authority; 'Who gave thee this authority?' 4. Power over others, dominion or rule. Here the second sense is the one in which the word is to be taken. *Stumblingblock*, (πρόσκομμα,) elsewhere rendered *offence*, in a moral sense is that which is an occasion to sin, or which causes men to fall. In the same sense the word (σκάνδαλον, literally, *a trap-stick*,) *scandal* is used, Luke 17, 1. Rom. 14, 13. 1 John 2, 10. *The weak* are the doubting, the undecided, those "not having knowledge," as is implied in the next verse.

10. For if any man see thee which hast knowledge sit at meat in the idol's temple, shall not the conscience of him which is weak be emboldened to eat those things which are offered to idols;

This verse is designed to show how eating these sacrifices might be an occasion of sin to others. *For* serves to introduce the illustration. *See thee having knowledge.* This is the description of the strong. They were those whose views were clear and their convictions decided. *Sit at meat*, (κατακείμενον,) literally, *lying down*, according to the ancient custom of reclining on a couch at table. The word ἀνάκειμαι, *to lie up*, is also used, as the couches were usually higher than the table. *In the idol's temple.* In the tenth chapter the apostle teaches, that as eating of things offered to idols was a matter of indifference, there was no harm in buying such meat in the market, or in partaking of it at a private table; but that to eat it within the precincts of the temple was an act of idolatry, and brought them into communion with demons, and therefore utterly broke off their connection with Christ. Here he views the matter simply under the aspect of *an offence*, or in reference to its effect on the weaker brethren, and therefore says nothing of the sinfulness of the act in itself. In like manner, in the eleventh chapter, speaking of it as a matter of decorum, he simply condemns women speaking in church *unveiled*, as though he had no objection to their speaking in public; but in the fourteenth chapter he condemns the thing itself, and not merely the manner of doing it. *Shall not the conscience of him being weak* (i. e. being uncertain whether he was doing right or wrong,) *be emboldened;* literally, *be edified.* This must either be understood ironically, which is out of keeping with the whole tone of the passage, or the word must be taken in the sense of *built up*, *carried forward* to the point (εἰς) of eating of the idol-sacrifices. That is, he might be led to do what his conscience secretly condemned.

11. And through thy knowledge shall the weak brother perish, for whom Christ died?

That is, shall your knowledge be the occasion of the perdition of a weak brother? There are three forms in which the apostle expresses the consequence of doing what the conscience is not satisfied is right. In v. 7 he says, the conscience is defiled; here, he says, the man perishes or is lost; in Rom. 14, 23, he says, "He that doubteth is damned (condemned) if he eat." All these forms of expression amount to the same thing. Guilt, condemnation and perdition are connected. The one implies the other. Whatever brings guilt on the conscience exposes to condemnation, and condemnation is perdition.

For whom Christ died. There is great power and pathos in these words. Shall we, for the sake of eating one kind of meat rather than another, endanger the salvation of those for whom the eternal Son of God laid down his life? The infinite distance between Christ and us, and the almost infinite distance between his sufferings and the trifling self-denial required at our hands, give to the apostle's appeal a force the Christian heart cannot resist. The language of Paul in this verse seems to assume that those may perish for whom Christ died. It belongs, therefore, to the same category as those numerous passages which make the same assumption with regard to the elect. If the latter are consistent with the certainty of the salvation of all the elect, then this passage is consistent with the certainty of the salvation of those for whom Christ specifically died. It was absolutely certain that none of Paul's companions in shipwreck was on that occasion to lose his life, because the salvation of the whole company had been predicted and promised; and yet the apostle said that if the sailors were allowed to take away the boats, those left on board could not be saved. This appeal secured the accomplishment of the promise. So God's telling the elect that if they apostatize they shall perish, prevents their apostasy. And in like manner, the Bible teaching that those for whom Christ died shall perish if they violate their conscience, prevents their transgressing, or brings them to repentance. God's purposes embrace the means as well as the end. If the means fail, the end will fail. He secures the end by securing the means. It is just as certain that those for whom Christ died shall be saved, as that the elect shall be saved. Yet in both cases the event is spoken of as conditional. There is not only a possibility, but an absolute certainty of their perishing if they fall away. But this is precisely what God has promised to prevent. This passage, therefore, is perfectly consistent with those numerous passages which teach that Christ's death secures the salvation of all those who were given to him in the covenant of redemption. There is, however, a sense in which it is scriptural to say that Christ died for all men. This is very different from saying that he died *equally* for all men, or that his death had no other reference to those who are saved than it had to those who are lost. To die *for one* is to die for his benefit. As Christ's death has benefited the whole world, prolonged the probation of men, secured for them innumerable blessings, provided a righteousness sufficient and suitable for all, it may be said that he died for all. And in reference to this obvious truth the language of the apostle, should any prefer this interpretation, may be understood, 'Why should we destroy one for whose benefit Christ laid down his life?'

All this is perfectly consistent with the great scriptural truth that Christ came into the world to save his people, that his death renders certain the salvation of all those whom the Father hath given him, and therefore that he died not only *for* them but *in their place*, and on the condition that they should never die.

12. But when ye sin so against the brethren, and wound their weak conscience, ye sin against Christ.

We sin against our brethren when we wound their weak conscience. The one phrase explains the other. To wound a man's conscience is to give it the pain of remorse. When we bring on him a sense of guilt we inflict on him the greatest evil in our power; not only because a wounded spirit is worse than a wounded body; but also because a sense of guilt alienates us from God and brings us under the power of Satan. He who thus sins against his brother, *sins against Christ.* This is true in two senses. An injury done to a child is an injury to the parent, both because proper regard for the parent would prevent one from injuring his child; and also because the parent suffers in the child. They are so united that the injury of the one is the injury of the other. So also it is a manifestation of want of love to Christ, an insult and injury to him, to injure his people; and moreover, he and they are so united that whatever of good or evil is done to them is done also to him. "Inasmuch as ye have done it unto one of the least of these my brethren, ye have done it unto me," Matt. 25, 40. If we believed this aright it would render us very careful not to wound our fellow Christians, and make us also feel it to be an honour to relieve their wants.

13. Wherefore, if meat make my brother to offend, I will eat no flesh while the world standeth, lest I make my brother to offend.

The word σκανδαλίζω means either to offend, or to cause to offend. That is, either to provoke, or to cause to sin. The English word is also used in both these senses. Matt. 17, 27, "That we may not offend them," i. e. provoke them. Matt. 5, 29, "If thy eye offend thee," i. e. cause thee to sin; and Matt. 18, 6, "Whoso shall offend (i. e. cause to sin) one of these little ones which believe in me, it were better for him that a mill-stone were hanged about his neck, and that he were drowned in the depth of the sea." This last quoted passage shows how serious a matter our Lord considers it to lead even the weakest Christian into sin. It is still worse to lead him into error, for error is the mother of many sins. It shows also how great an evil sin is, and justifies the strong language of the apostle that he would never eat flesh rather than cause his brother to offend. It is morally obligatory, therefore, to abstain from indulging in things indifferent, when the use of them is the occasion of sin to others. This is a principle the application of which must be left to every man's conscience in the fear of God. No rule of conduct, founded on expediency, can be enforced by church discipline. It was right in Paul to refuse to eat flesh for fear of causing others to offend; but he could not have been justly exposed to discipline, had he seen fit to eat it. He circumcised Timothy, and refused to circumcise Titus. Whenever a thing is right or wrong according to circumstances, every man must have the right to judge of those circumstances.

CHAPTER IX.

The apostle illustrates the duty of foregoing the exercise of our rights for the good of others, by a reference to his giving up his undoubted right to be supported by the church, vs. 1–18. He shows that in other ways he accommodated himself to the opinions and prejudices of others, 19–23. He reminds his readers that nothing good or great could be attained without self-denial, vs. 24–27.

The right of ministers to an adequate maintenance. The necessity of self-denial. Vs. 1–27.

Having in the preceding chapter urged on the strong the duty of foregoing the use of their rights for the sake of their weaker brethren, the apostle shows how he had acted on that principle. He was an apostle, and therefore had all the rights of an apostle. His apostleship was abundantly clear, because he had seen the Lord Jesus and was his immediate messenger; and his divine mission had been confirmed, at least among the Corinthians, beyond dispute. They were the seal of his apostleship, vs. 1–3. Being an apostle, he had the same right to be supported and to have his family supported, had he chosen to marry, as Peter or any other apostle, vs. 4–6. This right to adequate support he proves, First, from the principle which lies at the foundation of society, that the laborer is worthy of his reward, v. 7. Secondly, from the fact that this principle is recognized in the Old Testament, even in its application to brutes, vs. 8–10. Thirdly, from the principles of commutative justice, v. 11. Fourthly, from the fact that the Corinthians recognized this right in the case of other teachers, v. 12. Fifthly, from the universal recognition of the principle among all nations. Those who served the temple were supported from the temple, v. 13. Sixthly, from the express ordinance of Christ, who had ordained that those who preached the gospel should live by the gospel, v. 14. This undoubted right Paul had not availed himself of, and he was determined, especially at Corinth, not to avail himself of it in the future. By so doing he cut off occasion to question his motives, and gave himself a ground of confidence in resisting his opponents which he was determined not to relinquish, vs. 15–18. This was not, however, the only case in which he abstained from the exercise of his rights for the good of others. He accommodated himself to Jews and Gentiles in every thing indifferent, that he might gain the more, vs. 19–23. Such self-denial the heathen exercised to gain a corruptible crown—should not Christians do as much to gain a crown that is incorruptible? Without self-denial and effort the prize of their high calling could never be attained, vs. 24–27.

1. Am I not an apostle? am I not free? * have I not seen Jesus Christ our Lord? are not ye my work in the Lord?

The order of the first two of these questions is reversed by most editors on satisfactory external and internal evidence. *Am I not free?* That is, am I not a Christian, invested with all the liberties wherewith Christ has made his people free? Am I not as free as any other believer to regulate my conduct according to my own convictions of what is right; free from

* The MS. A. B., the great majority of the ancient versions, and many of the Fathers put ἐλεύθερος before ἀπόστολος, which is the natural order of the words, and which, after Griesbach, has been adopted by almost all editors.

any obligation to conform to the opinions or prejudices of other men? This, however, is a freedom which I have not availed myself of. Nay more, *Am I not an apostle?* Besides the rights which belong to all Christians, have I not all the prerogatives of an apostle? Am I not on a level with the chief of the apostles? Who of them can show a better title to the office? There were three kinds of evidence of the apostleship. 1. The immediate commission from Christ in the sight of witnesses, or otherwise confirmed. 2. Signs and wonders, and mighty deeds, 2 Cor. 12, 12. 3. The success of their ministry. No man could be an apostle who had not seen the Lord Jesus after his resurrection, because that was one of the essential facts of which they were to be the witnesses, Acts 1, 22. Neither could any man be an apostle who did not receive his knowledge of the gospel by immediate revelation from Christ, for the apostles were the witnesses also of his doctrines, Acts 1, 8. 10, 39. 22, 15. Gal. 1, 12. The necessity of this immediate mission and independent knowledge is insisted upon at length in the epistle to the Galatians. In proof of his apostleship Paul here appeals only to two sources of evidence; first, to his having seen the Lord Jesus; and second, to the success of his ministry. *Ye are my work in the Lord.* That is, either, you in the Lord, your being in the Lord (i. e. your conversion), is my work; or, the words (ἐν κυρίῳ) may mean *by the Lord*, i. e. by his co-operation. The former explanation is to be preferred, as the apostle's object is to state in what sense they were his work. It was as being in the Lord. The connection of this verse, and of the whole chapter, with what precedes is obvious. His design is to show that he had himself acted on the principle which he urged on others. Neither as a Christian nor as an apostle had he insisted upon his rights, without regard to the prejudices of others or the good of the church.

2. If I be not an apostle unto others, yet doubtless I am to you: for the seal of mine apostleship are ye in the Lord.

If to others, i. e. in the estimation of others, *I be not an apostle, surely I am to you.* Whatever pretence others may have to question my apostleship, you certainly can have none; *for the seal of my apostleship are ye in the Lord.* Your conversion is the seal of God to my commission. The conversion of men is a divine work, and those by whom it is accomplished are thereby authenticated as divine messengers. It is as much the work of God as a miracle, and therefore, when duly authenticated, has the same effect as an evidence of a divine commission. This, although valid evidence, and as such adduced by the apostle, is nevertheless very liable to be abused. First, because much which passes for conversion is spurious; and secondly, because the evidence of success is often urged in behalf of the errors of preachers, when that success is due to the truth which they preach. Still there are cases when the success is of such a character, so undeniable and so great, as to supersede the necessity of any other evidence of a divine call. Such was the case with the apostles, with the reformers, and with many of our modern missionaries.

3. Mine answer to them that do examine me is this:

That is, what precedes, and not what follows; for what follows is no answer to those who called his apostleship in question. Both the words here used, (ἀνακρίνω) *to examine*, and (ἀπολογία), *apology*, or *answer*, are forensic terms. Paul means that when any of his opponents undertook to question him, as it were, judicially, as to his apostleship, he answered, 'I have seen the Lord Jesus, and he has set his seal to my commission by the success with which he has crowned my labours.' This answer satisfied Peter, James and John, who gave to Paul the right hand of fellowship, seeing that to him had been committed the apostleship unto the Gentiles, Gal. 2, 8. 9.

4. Have we not power to eat and drink?

Power here as above, 8, 9, means *right*. Have we not the right to eat and drink? This, taken by itself, might mean, 'Have we not the same right that others have as to meats and drinks? All distinctions on this subject are abolished as much for us as for others. Are we not free?' The context shows, however, clearly that such is not the apostle's meaning. The right in question is that which he goes on to establish. It is the right to abstain from working, and of being supported by the church. Having proved his apostleship, he proves his right to be supported, and then shows that he had not availed himself of that right. He could, therefore, with the greater freedom urge the Corinthians to forego their right to eat of things offered to idols for the sake of their weaker brethren.

5. Have we not power to lead about a sister, a wife, as well as other apostles, and (as) the brethren of the Lord, and Cephas?

This is an amplification of the preceding verse. *Have we not the power*, i. e. the right. *To lead about*, a form of expression chosen because the apostles were not stationary ministers, each with his own parish or diocese, but were constantly travelling from place to place. *A sister*, i. e. a Christian woman. *A wife*, this determines the relation which this travelling companion sustained. It is as much as saying, 'A sister who is a wife.' Many of the Fathers explain this passage as referring to the custom of rich women attending the apostles on their journeys in order to minister to their support. In this interpretation they are followed by many Romanists in order to avoid the sanction which the ordinary and only legitimate interpretation gives to the marriage of the clergy. *As other apostles;* literally, "*the* other apostles." This does not necessarily imply that all the other apostles were married; but the implication is that as a body they were married men. Olshausen and others understand the apostle, in the vs. 4–6, as asserting his liberty as to three points; 1. As to meats, 'Have I not the same liberty that you claim as to eating and drinking?' 2. As to marriage, 'Have I not the right to marry?' 3. As to support. But this introduces more into the text than the connection warrants. There is no question about the right of marriage alluded to in the context; and what follows is a defence neither of his liberty to disregard the Jewish laws about meats and drinks, nor of his right to be married.

And the brethren of the Lord. Whether these were the children of Joseph and Mary, or the children of Mary, the sister of our Lord's mother, is a point very difficult to determine. Tradition, or the general voice of the church, is greatly in favour of the latter opinion. The former, however, is probably the opinion embraced by a majority of modern commentators. The discussion of this question belongs properly to the evangelical history.* The following passages may be compared on this subject: Matt. 1, 25. 12, 46. 13, 55. Luke

* The question is discussed by Neander, in his Planting of the Church, p. 554; by Winer, in Real Wörterbuch, under the head of Jacobus; by Prof. Schaf, who has devoted to it a volume; and by many other writers, ancient and modern.

2, 7. John 2, 12. Acts 1, 14. Gal. 1, 19. *And Cephas;* this is the name by which Peter is called whenever he is mentioned by Paul, except in the epistle to the Galatians; and Lachmann reads Cephas instead of Peter in Gal. 1, 18. 2, 9. 10. 14, leaving Gal. 2, 8. 9 the only exception. That Peter was married is clear from Matt. 8, 14. Mark 1, 30.

6. Or I only and Barnabas, have we not power to forbear working?

The power to forbear working; literally, *the right of not working.* 'Is there any reason why I and Barnabas should be the only exceptions to the rule that preachers of the word are to be supported by the churches?' From this it appears that Barnabas, while the apostle's missionary companion, followed his example in working with his own hands, that he might make the gospel of Christ without charge. Paul proceeds to demonstrate the right in question, not on grounds peculiar to the apostles or to that particular age of the church; but on grounds applicable to all ministers and to all ages. His first argument is from the universally recognized principle that labour is entitled to reward. This principle is illustrated in the following verse.

7. Who goeth a warfare any time at his own charges? who planteth a vineyard, and eateth not of the fruit thereof? or who feedeth a flock, and eateth not of the milk of the flock?

Here are three illustrations, taken from the common occupations of men, of the principle in question. The soldier, the agriculturist, the shepherd, all live by their labour; why should not the minister? His work is as engrossing, as laborious, and as useful as theirs; why should not it meet with a similar recompense? *Who goeth to war,* i. e. who serves in war, as a soldier, *at his own charges* (ἰδίοις ὀψωνίοις), on his own rations. What soldier in war is called upon to support himself? If you force him to do it, you make him a robber; and if ministers be required to support themselves, the danger is that they will be forced to become men of the world. It is not, however, the evil consequences, so much as the injustice of such a course, that the apostle has in view. What is true of the soldier is true of the farmer and of the shepherd, and of every other class of men.

8. Say I these things as a man? or saith not the law the same also?

Say I these things as a man? This phrase (κατὰ ἄνθρωπον λαλεῖν), *to speak as a man*, or after the manner of men, means in general, to speak as men are wont to speak, to utter their thoughts, or principles, or to use illustrations derived from their customs. Rom. 3, 5. Gal. 3, 15. comp. Rom. 6, 19. The apostle means here to ask whether it was necessary to appeal to the usages of men in support of the principle that labour should be rewarded. *Does not the law also say the same?* i. e. does not the word of God sanction the same principle? *The law* (ὁ νόμος) means in general that which binds. It is applied to the law of God, however revealed, whether in the heart, the decalogue, the Pentateuch, or in the whole Scriptures. The context must determine the specific reference in each particular case. Here the law of Moses is intended.

9. For it is written in the law of Moses, Thou shalt not muzzle the mouth of the ox that treadeth out the corn. Doth God take care for oxen?

For refers to the answer implied to the preceding question. 'Does not the law say the same? It does: *for* it is written,' &c. The passage quoted is found in Deut. 25, 4, where it is forbidden to put a muzzle on the oxen which draw the threshing machine over the corn, or which tread it out with their feet; as both methods of threshing were common in Palestine as well as the use of the flail or rods. Comp. Is. 28, 28. 41, 15. Hosea 10, 11. *Doth God take care of oxen?* It is perfectly certain that God does care for oxen; for he feeds the young ravens when they cry; Job 38, 41. Ps. 147, 9. Matt. 6, 26. Luke 12, 24. This, therefore, the apostle cannot intend to deny. He only means to say that the law had a higher reference. Although the proximate end of the command was that the labouring brute should be treated justly, yet its ultimate design was to teach men the moral truth involved in the precept. If God requires that even the ox, which spends his strength in our service, should not be defrauded of his reward, how much more strict will he be in enforcing the application of the same principle of justice to his rational creatures.

10. Or saith he (it) altogether for our sakes? For our sakes, no doubt, (this) is written: that he that plougheth should plough in hope; and that he that thresheth in hope should be partaker of his hope.

"He sayeth it *altogether*." This is not the meaning here; for this would make the apostle assert that the command in question had exclusive reference to men. The word (πάντως) should be rendered *assuredly*, as in Luke 4, 43. Acts 18, 21. 21, 22, and frequently elsewhere. 'This command was assuredly given, says the apostle, for *our sakes*,' i. e. for the sake of man—not, *for us ministers*, or *us apostles*. It was intended to enforce the principle that labour should have its reward, so that men may labour cheerfully. *That* (ὅτι); *because*. 'It is written on our account, *because* he that ploughs should (ὀφείλει, 2 Cor. 12, 11,) plough in hope,' i. e. of being rewarded. "And he that threshes should thresh in hope of partaking of his hope," i. e. of what he hoped for. The text is here doubtful. The reading preferred by most editors gives a simpler form to the passage*—'He that thresheth (should thresh) in hope of partaking,' (ἐπ' ἐλπίδι τοῦ μετέχειν). The sense is the same. Some of the ancient, and not a few of the most distinguished modern commentators assume that Paul gives an allegorical interpretation to the passage in Deuteronomy. They understand him to say that the passage is not to be understood of oxen, but of us, ministers. 'This command was given on account of us ministers, that we ploughers might plough in hope, and we threshers might thresh in hope.' But this is entirely foreign from the manner of the New Testament writers.† They never argue except from the true historical sense of Scripture. Gal. 4, 21–31, is no exception to this remark; for that passage is an illustration and not an argument.

* The common text is τῆς ἐλπίδος αὐτοῦ μετέχειν ἐπ' ἐλπίδι. Griesbach, Lachmann, Scholz and Tischendorf all read ἐπ' ἐλπίδι τοῦ μετέχειν, on the authority of the MSS. A. B. C.

† In reference to this mode of expounding the passage, Calvin says: Neque etiam quasi velit allegorice exponere praeceptum illud: quemadmodum nonnulli vertiginosi spiritus occasionem hinc arripiunt omnia ad allegorias transferendi: ita ex canibus faciunt homines, ex arboribus angelos, et totam Scripturam ludendo pervertunt.

11. If we have sown unto you spiritual things, (is it) a great thing if we shall reap your carnal things?

That is, if we have bestowed on you one class of benefits, is it unreasonable that we should receive from you another class? And if the benefits which we bestow are *spiritual*, such as knowledge, faith and hope, the fruits of the Spirit, and therefore of infinite value, is it much that we should derive from you *carnal* things, i. e. things necessary for the support of the body? On every principle of commutative justice, the minister's right to a support must be conceded.

12. If others be partakers of (this) power over you, (are) not we rather? Nevertheless we have not used this power; but suffer all things, lest we should hinder the gospel of Christ.

This is an argument directed specially to the Corinthians. They had recognized in other teachers the right to a support; they could not, therefore, with any show of reason, deny it to the apostle. *This power over you* (τῆς ὑμῶν ἐξουσίας), i. e. the right of which you are the objects. For this use of the genitive, (*power of you*, for *power over you*), compare Matt. 10, 1. John 17, 2. Undisputable as this right was in the case of Paul, he did not exercise it, *but suffered all things*, i. e. endured all kinds of privations. The word means *to bear in silence*. *Lest we should hinder* (place any hinderance in the way of,) *the gospel of Christ*. Under the circumstances in which Paul was placed, surrounded by implacable enemies, it would have hindered the gospel had he done any thing which gave the least ground to question the purity of his motives. He was willing to suffer any thing rather than to give his opponents the slightest pretext for their opposition to him.

13. Do ye not know that they which minister about holy things live (of the things) of the temple? and they which wait at the altar are partakers with the altar?

What Paul here says is true of all religions, though his reference is probably only to the Jewish. *Those which minister about holy things* (οἱ τὰ ἱερὰ ἐργαζόμενοι); *those who perform the sacred services*, i. e. those who offer sacrifices. *Eat of the temple*, i. e. they derive their support from the temple. *Those attending the altar share with the altar*, i. e. the priests receive a portion of the sacrifices offered on the altar. If this was an institution ordained by God himself, under the old dispensation, it has the sanction of divine authority. The apostle's concluding and conclusive argument on this subject is contained in the following verse.

14. Even so hath the Lord ordained that they which preach the gospel should live of the gospel.

Even so (οὔτω καί), *so also*, i. e. as God had ordained under the Old Testament, *so also* the Lord (i. e. Christ) had ordained under the New. Christ has made the same ordinance respecting the ministers of the gospel, that God made respecting the priests of the law. *The Lord hath ordained that*, &c., (διέταξε τοῖς), *he commanded those who preach*, &c. It was a command to ministers themselves not to seek their support from secular occupations; but *to live of the gospel*, as the priests lived of the temple. Matt. 10, 10. Luke 10, 8. This is the law of Christ, obligatory on ministers and people; on the latter to give, and on the former to seek a support from the church and not from worldly avocations. There are circumstances under which, as the case of Paul shows, this command ceases to be binding on preachers. These are exceptions, to be justified, each on its own merits; the rule, as a rule, remains in force. If this subject were viewed in this light, both by preachers and people, there would be little difficulty in sustaining the gospel, and few ministers would be distracted by worldly pursuits.

15. But I have used none of these things: neither have I written these things, that it should be so done unto me: for (it were) better for me to die, than that any man should make my glorying void.

None of these things, may refer to the various arguments above mentioned. 'I have availed myself of none of these arguments;' or, it may refer to the right itself, which was manifold, the right of a recompense for labour, v. 7; the right to an equivalent for benefits conferred, v. 11; the right to be treated as other ministers were, v. 12; the right to be dealt with according to the law of God in the Old Testament, and of Christ in the New. 'I have used none of these rights. *Neither have I written these things that it should* (in future) *be so done* (i. e. according to what I have written) *unto me* (ἐν ἐμοί), in my case. Paul had no intention of changing his course in this matter. The reason for this determination he immediately assigns. *For it were better for me to die than that any man should make my glorying void*, that is, deprive me of my ground of glorying. What enabled Paul to face his enemies with joyful confidence, was his disinterested self-denial in preaching the gospel without reward. And this he calls his (καύχημα), or ground of boasting. That this, and not merely preaching the gospel, was the proof of his integrity to which he could confidently refer, he shows in the following verses.

16. For though I preach the gospel, I have nothing to glory of: for necessity is laid upon me; yea, woe is unto me, if I preach not the gospel!

The reason why it was so important to him to refuse all remuneration as a minister was, that *although he preached the gospel* that was no (καύχημα), ground of boasting to him. That he was bound to do, yea, woe was denounced against him unless he did preach it. Nothing could be a ground of boasting, but something which he was free to do, or not to do. He was free to receive or to refuse a remuneration for preaching; and therefore his refusing to do so was a ground of glorying, that is, a proof of integrity to which he could with confidence appeal.

17. For if I do this thing willingly, I have a reward: but if against my will, a dispensation (of the gospel) is committed unto me.

This is the proof that preaching was no ground of boasting. If he preached *willingly*, i. e. if it were optional with him to preach or not to preach, then it would be a ground of boasting; but if he did it *unwillingly*, i. e. if it was not optional with him, (as was in fact the case), he was only discharging an official duty, and had nothing to boast of. That Paul preached the gospel willingly, that he esteemed it his highest joy and glory, is abundantly evident from his history and his writings. Rom. 1, 5. 11, 13. 15, 15. 16. 1 Cor. 15, 9. 10. Gal. 1, 15. 16. Eph. 3, 8. The difference, therefore, here expressed between (ἑκών and ἄκων), *willing* and *unwilling*, is not the difference between cheerfully and reluctantly, but between optional and obligatory. He says he had a dispensation or stewardship (οἰκονομία) committed to him. These stewards (οἰκονόμοι) were commonly slaves. There is a great difference between what a slave does in obedience to a command, and what a man volunteers to do of his own accord. And this is the precise difference to which the apostle here refers. The slave may feel honoured by the command of his master, and obey him gladly, still it is but a service. So Paul was commanded to preach the gospel, and he did it with his whole heart; but he was not commanded to refuse to receive a support from the churches. The former, therefore, was not a ground of boasting, not a thing for which he could claim the reward of special confidence; the latter was. He could appeal to it as a proof, not only of his obedience, but of the purity of the motive which prompted that obedience. A physician may attend the sick from the highest motives, though he receives a remuneration for his services. But when he attends the poor gratuitously, though the motives may be no higher, the evidence of their purity is placed beyond question. Paul's ground of glorying, therefore, was not preaching, for that was a matter of obligation; but his preaching gratuitously, which was altogether optional. If, says he, my preaching is optional, *I have a reward;* not in the sense of merit in the sight of God, but in the general sense of recompense. He gained something by it. He gained the confidence even of his enemies. But as preaching was not optional but obligatory, he did not gain confidence by it. Mere preaching, therefore, was not a (καύχημα) ground of boasting, but preaching gratuitously was. *A dispensation of the gospel is committed to me;* in the Greek it is simply, '*I am intrusted with a stewardship* (comp. Gal. 2, 7, i. e. an office), which I am bound to discharge. I am in this matter a mere servant.' The principle on which the apostle's argument is founded is recognized by our Lord, when he said, "When ye shall have done all those things which are commanded you, say, We are unprofitable servants: we have done that which was our duty to do," Luke 17, 10.

18. What is my reward then? (Verily) that, when I preach the gospel, I may make the gospel of Christ without charge, that I abuse not my power in the gospel.

To do what he was commanded was no ground of reward; but to preach the gospel without charge was something of which he could boast, i. e. make a ground of confidence. *What then is my reward?* i. e. what constitutes my reward? in the sense explained; what gives me a ground of boasting? The answer follows, (ἵνα being used instead of the exegetical infinitive; comp. John 15, 8. 1 John 4, 17.) *that preaching I should make the gospel free of charge.* In other words, *that I should not use my right in the gospel.* In other words, Paul's reward was to sacrifice himself for others. He speaks of his being permitted to serve others gratuitously as a reward. And so it was, not only because it was an honour and happiness to be allowed to serve Christ in thus serving his people; but also because it secured him the confidence of those among whom he laboured by proving his disinterestedness. The common version, *that I abuse not*, although agreeable to the common meaning of καταχράομαι, is not consistent with the context, and is not demanded by the usage of the word; see 7, 31. It was not the abuse, but the use of his right to be supported, that the apostle had renounced.

19. For though I be free from all (men), yet have I made myself servant unto all, that I might gain the more.

The apostle's self-denial and accommodation of himself to the weakness and prejudices of others, was not confined to the point of which he had been speaking. He constantly acted upon the principle of abstaining in things indifferent, from insisting on his rights. *Though free from all*, i. e. independent of all men, and under no obligation to conform my conduct to their opinions, *I subjected myself to all.* In what way he did this, and to what extent, is explained by what follows. His motive in thus accommodating himself to others, was, *that he might gain the more*, or the greater number, the majority; comp. 10, 5. No one was more yielding in matters of indifference, no one was more unyielding in matters of principle than this apostle. So long as things indifferent were regarded as such, he was ready to accommodate himself to the most unreasonable prejudices; but when they were insisted upon as matters of necessity, he would not give place, no not for an hour, Gal. 2, 5.

20. And unto the Jews I became as a Jew, that I might gain the Jews; to them that are under the law, as under the law, that I might gain them that are under the law;

To the Jews he became as a Jew, i. e. he acted as they acted, he conformed to their usages, observed the law, avowing at the same time that he did it as a matter of accommodation. Wherever the fair inference from his compliance would have been that he regarded these Jewish observances as necessary, he strenuously refused compliance. His conduct in relation to Timothy and Titus, before referred to, shows the principle on which he acted. The former he circumcised, because it was regarded as a concession. The latter he refused to circumcise, because it was demanded as a matter of necessity. There are two things, therefore, to be carefully observed in all cases of concession to the opinions and practices of others: first, that the point conceded be a matter of indifference; for Paul never yielded in the smallest measure to any thing which was in itself wrong. In this his conduct was directly the opposite to that of those who accommodate themselves to the sins of men, or to the superstitious observances of false religions. And secondly, that the concession does not involve any admission that what is in fact indifferent is a matter of moral obligation. The extent to which Paul went to conciliate the Jews may be learnt from what is recorded in Acts 21, 18–27.

To those under the law. These were not converted Jews, because they were already gained to the gospel, and did not need to be won, which is the sense in which the expression *to gain* is used in this verse, as he had just spoken of gaining the Jews. Perhaps *those under the law*, as distinguished from Jews, were proselytes, i. e. Gentiles who had embraced Judaism. But most of these proselytes were not strictly *under the law.* They acknowledged Jehovah to be the only true God, but did not subject themselves to the Mosaic institutions. The common opinion is, that this clause is only explanatory of the former, 'To the Jews, i. e. to those under the law, I became as a Jew, i. e. as one under the law.'

"Not being myself under the law," μὴ ὢν αὐτὸς ὑπὸ νόμον. This clause happened to be omitted from the Elziver edition of the Greek Testament from which our translation was made, and therefore fails in the common English version. It is found, however, in all the more ancient manuscripts, in many of the fathers and early versions, and is therefore adopted by most modern editors. The internal evidence is also in its favour. It was important for Paul to say that although acting *as* under the law, he was not under it; because it was a fundamental principle of the gospel which he preached, that believers are freed from the law. "We are not under law, but under grace," Rom. 6, 14. It was necessary, therefore, that his compliance with the Jewish law should be recognized as a matter of voluntary concession.

21. To them that are without law, as without law, (being not without law to God, but under the law to Christ,) that I might gain them that are without law.

Those without law were the heathen, who had no written revelation as the rule of their conduct; comp. Rom. 2, 12 As, however, the word (ἄνομος), *without law*, means also *reckless*, regardless of moral restraints, Paul is careful to explain in what sense he acted as without law. When among the Gentiles he did not conform to the Jewish law; in that sense, he was without law; but he did not act as *without law to God*, i. e. without regard to the obligation of the moral law; but as *under law to Christ*, i. e. as recognizing his obligation to obey Christ, whose will is the highest rule of duty. In other words, he was not under the Jewish law; but he was under the moral law. He disregarded the Jewish law that he *might gain those without law*, i. e. the Gentiles. When in Jerusalem, he conformed to the Jewish law; when in Antioch he refused to do so, and rebuked Peter for acting as a Jew among the Gentiles, Gal. 2, 11–21. It would have greatly impeded, if not entirely prevented, the progress of the gospel among the heathen, had it been burdened with the whole weight of the Jewish ceremonies and restrictions. Peter himself had told even the Jews that the Mosaic law was a yoke which neither they nor their fathers had been able to bear, Acts 15, 10. And Paul said to the Galatians, that he had resisted the Judaizers, in order that the truth of the gospel might remain with them, Gal. 2, 5.

22. To the weak became I as weak, that I might gain the weak: I am made all things to all (men), that I might by all means save some.

By *the weak* many understand the Jews and Gentiles considered under another aspect, i. e. as destitute of the power to comprehend and appreciate the gospel. The only reason for this interpretation is the assumption that *to gain* in this connection must mean to convert, or make Christians of, and therefore, those to be gained must be those who were not Christians. But the word means merely *to win over*, to bring to proper views, and therefore may be used in reference to weak and superstitious believers as well as of unconverted Jews and Gentiles. As in the preceding chapter *the weak* mean weak Christians, men who were not clear and decided in their views, and as the very design of the whole discussion was to induce the more enlightened Corinthian Christians to accommodate themselves to those weaker brethren, it is altogether more natural to understand it in the same way here. Paul holds himself up as an example. To the weak he became as weak; he accommodated himself to their prejudices that he might win them over to better views. And he wished the Corinthians to do the same. *I am made all things to all men.* This generalizes all that had been said. It was not to this or that class of men, that he was thus conciliatory, but to all classes, and as to all matters of indifference; that he might *at all events* (πάντως) *save some.*

23. And this I do for the gospel's sake, that I might be partaker thereof with (you).

This I do; or, according to the reading now generally adopted (πάντα instead of τοῦτο), *I do all things;* 'my whole course of action, not merely in thus accommodating myself to the prejudices of others, but in every thing else, is regulated for the promotion of the gospel.' This gives a better sense; for to say, *This I do*, would be only to repeat what is included in the preceding verse. Paul lived for the gospel. He did all things for it. *That I may be a joint-partaker thereof*, i. e. a partaker with others; not, *with you*, as there is nothing to confine the statement to the Corinthians. To be a partaker of the gospel, means, of course, to be a partaker of its benefits; the subject of the redemption which it announces. It is necessary to live for the gospel, in order to be a partaker of the gospel.

24. Know ye not that they which run in a race run all, but one receiveth the prize? So run, that ye may obtain.

An exhortation to self-denial and exertion, clothed in figurative language. As the exhortation is addressed principally to the Gentile converts, the imagery used is derived from the public games with which they were so familiar. These games, the Olympian and Isthmian, the latter celebrated every third summer in the neighbourhood of Corinth, were the occasions for the concourse of the people from all parts of Greece. The contests in them excited the greatest emulation in all classes of the inhabitants. Even the Roman emperors did not refuse to enter the lists. To be a victor was to be immortalized with such immortality as the breath of man can give. To Greeks, therefore, no allusions could be more intelligible, or more effective, than those to these institutions, which have nothing to answer to them in modern times.

Know ye not. He took for granted they were familiar with the rules of the games to which he referred. *That those running in a race;* literally in the *stadium* or *circus* in which the games were celebrated, so called because it was a *stadium* (a little more than two hundred yards) in length. *All run, but one obtains the prize.* It was not enough to start in this race; it was not enough to persevere almost to the end; it was necessary to outrun all competitors and be first at the goal. But one took the prize. *So run that ye may obtain.* That is, run as that one runs, *in order that* ye may obtain. The greatest self-denial in preparation, and the greatest effort in the contest, were necessary to success. In the Christian race there are many victors; but the point of the exhortation is, that all should run as the one victor ran in the Grecian games.

25. And every man that striveth for the mastery is temperate in all things. Now they (do it) to obtain a corruptible crown; but we an incorruptible.

Every one who striveth, &c. (πᾶς ὁ ἀγωνιζόμενος) *every one accustomed to contend*, i. e. every professional athlete. The word includes all kinds of contests, whether in running, wrestling or fighting. *Is temperate in all things*, i. e. controls himself as to all things. He exercises self-denial in diet, in bodily iudulgences, and by painful and protracted discipline. The ancient writers abound in rules of abstinence and exercise, to be observed by competitors in preparation for the games. *They indeed for a corruptible crown, we for an incorruptible.* If the heathen submitted to such severe discipline to gain a wreath of olive or garland of pine leaves, shall not Christians do as much for a crown of righteousness which fadeth not away?

26. I therefore so run, not as uncertainly; so fight I, not as one that beateth the air:

I therefore, i. e. because so much effort is necessary to success. *So run*, i. e. run not in such a manner as one who runs *uncertainly* (ἀδήλως). That may mean *unconspicuously*, not as one unseen, but as one on whom all eyes are fixed. Or more probably the idea is, not as one runs who is uncertain where or for what he is running. A man who runs uncertain as to his course or object, runs without spirit or effort. *So fight I.* The allusion is here to boxing, or fighting with the fist. *Not as one beating the air.* Here again the figure is doubtful. A man who is merely exercising, without an antagonist, may be said to smite the air. A man puts forth little strength in such a sham conflict. Or the man who aims at his antagonist, and fails to hit him, smites the air. This is the better explanation. VIRGIL has the same figure to express the same idea. He says of a boxer who missed his antagonist, "vires in ventum effudit." Æn. v. 446. In either way the meaning is the same. Nothing is accomplished. The effort is in vain. In 14, 9, the apostle says of those who speak in an unknown tongue, that they *speak into the air*. That is, they speak to no effect.

27. But I keep under my body, and bring (it) into subjection: lest that by any means, when I have preached to others, I myself should be a cast-away.

In opposition to the fruitless or objectless fighting just described, Paul says, *I keep under my body;* literally *I bruise my body.* (ὑπωπιάζω, *to smite under the eye*, *to bruise*, *to smite*, Luke 18, 5.) His antagonist was his body, which he so smote, i. e. so dealt with, as *to bring it into subjection ;* literally, *to lead about as a slave.* Perhaps in reference to the custom of the victor leading about his conquered antagonist as a servant; though this is doubtful. The body, as in part the seat and organ of sin, is used for our whole sinful nature. Rom. 8, 13. It was not merely his sensual nature that Paul endeavoured to bring into subjection, but all the evil propensities and passions of his heart. *Lest having preached to others* (κηρύξας). Perhaps the apostle means to adhere to the figure and say, 'Lest having acted the part of a herald, (whose office at the Grecian games was to proclaim the rules of the contest and to summon the competitors or combatants to the lists,) he himself should be judged unworthy of the prize.' As, however, the word is so often used for *preaching the gospel*, he may intend to drop the figure and say, 'He made these strenuous exertions, lest, having preached the gospel to others, he himself should become (ἀδόκιμος) a reprobate, one rejected.' What an argument and what a reproof is this! The reckless and listless Corinthians thought they could safely indulge themselves to the very verge of sin, while this devoted apostle considered himself as engaged in a life-struggle for his salvation. This same apostle, however, who evidently acted on the principle that the righteous scarcely are saved, and that the kingdom of heaven suffereth violence, at other times breaks out in the most joyful assurance of salvation, and says that he was persuaded that nothing in heaven, earth or hell could ever separate him from the love of God. Rom. 8, 38. 39. The one state of mind is the necessary condition of the other. It is only those who are conscious of this constant and deadly struggle with sin, to whom this assurance is given. In the very same breath Paul says, "O wretched man that I am;" and, "Thanks be to God who giveth us the victory," Rom. 7, 24. 25. It is the indolent and self-indulgent Christian who is always in doubt.

CHAPTER X.

A continuation of the exhortation to self-denial and caution, vs. 1–13. Express prohibition of joining in the sacrificial feasts of the heathen, vs. 14–22. Particular directions as to the use of meat sacrificed to idols, vs. 23–33.

The necessity of self-denial argued from the case of the Israelites. Vs. 1–13.

At the close of the preceding chapter the apostle had exhorted his readers to self-denial and effort, in order to secure the crown of life. He here enforces that exhortation, by showing how disastrous had been the want of such self-control in the case of the Israelites. They had been highly favoured as well as we. They had been miraculously guided by the pillar of cloud; they had been led through the Red Sea; they had been fed with manna from heaven, and with water from the rock; and yet the great majority of them perished, vs. 1–5. This is a solemn warning to Christians not to give way to temptation, as the Israelites did, v. 6. That is, not to be led into idolatry, v. 7, nor into fornication, v. 8, nor into tempting Christ, v. 9, nor into murmuring, v. 10. In all these points the experience of the Israelites was a warning to Christians; and therefore those who thought themselves secure should take heed lest they fall, vs. 11. 12. God is merciful, and would not suffer them to be too severely tempted, v. 13.

1. Moreover, brethren, I would not that ye should be ignorant, how that all our fathers were under the cloud, and all passed through the sea;

Moreover. The true reading is not (δέ) *moreover*, but (γάρ) *for*, which marks the connection with what precedes. 'We must use self-denial and effort; *for*, brethren, our fathers, notwithstanding all they experienced, perished.' *I would not have you ignorant*, Rom. 1, 10. 11, 25, a formula used when something specially important is to be presented. *That* (not *how that*). *All our fathers.* The emphasis is on *all*. 'All our fathers left Egypt; Caleb and Joshua alone entered the promised land.' All run, but one obtains the prize. The history of the church affords no incident better suited to enforce the necessity of guarding against false security, than that selected by the apostle. The Israelites doubtless felt, as they stood on the other side of the Red Sea, that all danger was over, and that their entrance into the land of promise was secured. They had however a journey beset with dangers before them, and perished because they thought there was no need of exertion. So the Corinthians, when brought to the knowledge of the gospel, thought heaven secure. Paul reminds them that they had only entered on the way, and would certainly perish unless they exercised constant self-denial. *Our fathers.* Abraham is our father, though we are not his natural descendants. And the Israelites were the fathers of the Corinthian Christians, although most of them were Gentiles. Although this is true, it is probable that the apostle, although writing to a church, many, if not most, of whose members were of heathen origin, speaks as a Jew to Jews; as he often addresses a congregation as a whole, when what he says has reference only to a part.

Were under the cloud, not underneath it, but under its guidance. Ex. 13, 21. "The Lord went before them by day in a pillar of cloud, to lead them; and by night in a pillar of fire to give them light, to go by day and night." See Num. 9, 15. 23. 14, 14. Deut. 1, 33. Ps. 78, 14. &c. No more decisive evidence could have been given of their election as a people, than this supernatural guidance. The symbol of the divine presence and favour was before their eyes day and night. If any people ever had reason to think their salvation secure, it was those whom God thus wonderfully guided. *They all passed through the sea.* Would God permit those to perish for whom he had wrought so signal a deliverance, and for whose sake he sacrificed the hosts of Egypt? Yet their carcasses were strewed in the wilderness. It is not enough, therefore, to be recipients of extraordinary favours; it is not enough to begin well. It is only by constant self-denial and vigilance, that the promised reward can be obtained. This is the lesson the apostle intends to inculcate.

2. And were all baptized * unto Moses in the cloud and in the sea;

Baptized unto Moses, i. e. in reference to Moses, so as by

* The MSS. A. C. D. E. F. G. all read ἐβαπτιϑήσαν, *were baptized*, instead of ἐβαπτίσαντο, *allowed themselves to be baptized*; and yet the majority of editors prefer the latter reading as the more difficult.

baptism to be made his disciples. See 1, 13. Rom. 6, 3. *In the cloud and in the sea.* The cloud and the sea did for them, in reference to Moses, what baptism does for us in reference to Christ. Their passage through the sea, and their guidance by the cloud, was their baptism. It made them the disciples of Moses; placed them under obligation to recognize his divine commission and to submit to his authority. This is the only point of analogy between the cases, and it is all the apostle's argument requires. One class of commentators says that they were immersed in the sea, and therefore it was a baptism; another says, the cloud rained upon them, and on that account they are said to have been baptized. Both suggestions are equally forced. For the people were baptized as much in the cloud as in the sea; but they were not immersed in the cloud nor sprinkled by the sea. There is no allusion to the mode of baptism. Neither is the point of analogy to be sought in the fact, that the cloud was vapour and the sea water. The cloud by night was fire. The point of similarity is to be found, not in any thing external, but in the effect produced. The display of God's power in the cloud and in the sea, brought the people into the relation of disciples to Moses. It inaugurated the congregation, and, as it were, baptized them to him, bound them to serve and follow him.

3. And did all eat the same spiritual meat;

As they had their baptism, so they had their eucharist; and they all had it. They all eat *the same* spiritual meat. They were all alike favoured, and had therefore equal grounds of hope. Yet how few of them reached the promised rest!

The reference is here obviously to the manna, which the apostle calls spiritual meat. Why it is so called is very doubtful. 1. The word *spiritual* may mean, partaking of the nature of spirit, a sense attributed to the word in 15, 44, where, "spiritual body" is assumed to mean a refined, aetherial body. The manna, according to this view, is called spiritual meat, because it was a refined kind of food; much in the way in which we use the word *celestial* as an epithet of excellence. This interpretation derives some support from Ps. 78, 25, where the manna is called "angels' food." By Josephus, *A.* III. 1, 6, it is called, "divine and wonderful food." 2. A second interpretation assumes that *spiritual* means having a spiritual import. "Spiritual meat" would then be equivalent to *typical.* They eat of that bread which was the type of the true bread from heaven.' Neither of these views, however, is consistent with the scriptural use of the word. *Spiritual* neither means refined nor typical. In 15, 44, "spiritual body" means a body adapted to the spirit as its organ. 3. Others give the word here its very common sense, *pertaining to the spirit;* as, in the preceding chapter, "carnal things" are things pertaining to the body, and "spiritual things" are things pertaining to the soul. The manna, according to this interpretation, was designed not only for the body, but for the soul. It was spiritual food; food intended for the spirit, because attended by the Holy Spirit and made the means of spiritual nourishment. This is a very commonly received interpretation. Calvin assumes it to be the only possible meaning of the passage, and founds on it an argument for his favourite doctrine, that the sacraments of the Old Testament had the same efficacy as those of the New. But this exalts the manna into a sacrament, which it was not. It was designed for ordinary food; as Nehemiah (9, 15) says, "Thou gavest them bread from heaven for their hunger, and broughtest forth for them water out of the rock for their thirst." And our Lord represents it in the same light, when he said, "Your fathers did eat manna in the wilderness and are dead." John 6, 49. He contrasts himself, as the true bread from heaven which gives life to the soul, with the manna which had no spiritual efficacy. 4. One of the most common meanings of the word *spiritual* in Scripture is, *derived from the Spirit.* Spiritual gifts and spiritual blessings are gifts and blessings of which the Spirit is the author. Every thing which God does in nature and in grace, he does by the Spirit. He garnished the heavens by the Spirit; and the Spirit renews the face of the earth. When therefore it is said, God gave them bread from heaven to eat, it means that the Spirit gave it; for God gave it through the Spirit. Thus God is said to renew and sanctify men, because the Spirit of God is the author of regeneration and sanctification. The manna therefore was spiritual food, in the same sense in which the special gifts of God are called spiritual gifts. That is, it was given by the Spirit. It was not natural food, but food miraculously provided. In the same sense, in the next verse, the water is called *spiritual drink*, because miraculously produced. In Gal. 4, 29, the natural birth of Isaac is said to have been *after the Spirit*, because due to the special intervention of God. As the miraculous deliverance and miraculous guidance of the Israelites was their baptism, so their being miraculously fed was their Lord's Supper. They were as signal marks of the divine presence and favour as sacraments are to us. If their privileges did not prevent their perishing in the wilderness, ours will not save us. If the want of self-denial and vigilance destroyed them, it will destroy us.

4. And did all drink the same spiritual drink; for they drank of that spiritual Rock that followed them: and that Rock was Christ.

The water which they drank was *spiritual*, because derived from the Spirit, i. e. by the special intervention of God. They all drank (ἔπιον) of it once when first provided, and they continued to drink (ἔπινον) of it, for it followed them. Whatever difficulties may be connected with the interpretation of this verse, two things are therein plainly taught. First, that the Israelites were constantly supplied in a miraculous manner with water; and secondly, that the source of that supply was Christ. The principal difficulties in the passage are, the declaration that the rock followed the Israelites; and that the rock was Christ. How are these statements to be understood? 1. Some take the passage literally, and assume that the rock smitten by Moses actually rolled after the Israelites during all their journey. Such was the tradition of the Jews, as is abundantly proved by the quotations from their writings, by Wetstein, Schoettgen and Lightfoot.* According to the local tradition, as old at least as the Koran, the rock smitten by Moses was not part of the mountain, but a detached rock, pierced with holes whence the water is said to have flowed. This view of the passage makes the apostle responsible for a Jewish fable, and is inconsistent with his divine authority. Those who adopt this interpretation do not suppose that the rock actually followed the Israelites, but that the apostle was misled by the tradition of his times. 2. Others say that by the rock following them is meant that the water out of the rock followed them. There is nothing unnatural in this. To say that the vines of France follow the people wherever they go, would be no violent figure to express the fact that the wine produced by those vines followed them. No man at least would be disposed to understand the expression literally.

* Fuit (ille puteus Num. 21, 16) sicut petra, sicut alveus apum et globosus, et volutavit, &c., et ivit cum ipsis in itineribus ipsorum. *Bammidhbar* R. S. 1.

In Ps. 105, 41, it is said, "He opened the rock, and the waters gushed out; they ran in dry places like a river," which at least proves that the supply of water was very copious, and flowed to a considerable distance. 3. It is not necessary, however, to assume that either the rock or the water out of the rock followed them. The rock that followed them was Christ. The Logos, the manifested Jehovah, who attended the Israelites in their journey, was the Son of God who assumed our nature, and was the Christ. It was he who supplied their wants. He was to them the fountain of living waters. He was the *spiritual* rock of which they drank. The word *spiritual* may have the same general force here as in the preceding clauses. The bread and water are called spiritual because supernatural. So the rock was a supernatural rock, though in a somewhat different sense. The manna was supernatural as to its origin; the rock, as to its nature. It is not uncommon for a word to be taken in the same connection in different, though nearly allied senses. Compare the use of this word *spiritual* in 2, 15 and 3, 1; and φθείρει and φθερεῖ in 3, 17. But in what sense was the rock Christ? Not that Christ appeared under the form of a rock; nor that the rock was a type of Christ, for that does not suit the connection. The idea is not that they drank of the typical rock; it was not the type but the antitype that supplied their wants. The expression is simply figurative. Christ was the rock in the same sense that he is the vine. He was the source of all the support which the Israelites enjoyed during their journey in the wilderness.

This passage distinctly asserts not only the preëxistence of our Lord, but also that he was the Jehovah of the Old Testament. He who appeared to Moses and announced himself as Jehovah, the God of Abraham, who commissioned him to go to Pharaoh, who delivered the people out of Egypt, who appeared on Horeb, who led the people through the wilderness, who dwelt in the temple, who manifested himself to Isaiah, who was to appear personally in the fulness of time, is the person who was born of a virgin, and manifested himself in the flesh. He is called, therefore, in the Old Testament, an angel, the angel of Jehovah, Jehovah, the Supreme Lord, the Mighty God, the Son of God—one whom God sent—one with him, therefore, as to substance, but a distinct person. Our Lord said, Abraham saw his day, for he was before Abraham, John 8, 58; John says, 12, 41, Isaiah beheld his glory in the temple; Paul says, the Israelites tempted him in the wilderness, 1 Cor. 10, 9, and that Moses suffered his reproach, Heb. 11, 26; Jude 5. says, the Lord, or (as Lachmann, after the ancient MSS. and versions, reads) Jesus, saved his people out of Egypt. This truth early impressed itself on the mind of the Christian church, as appears from the prayer in the ancient Liturgies, O Adonai (Supreme Lord), et Dux Domûs Israel, qui Mosi in igne flammeo rubi apparuisti, et ei in Sina aquam dedisti, veni ad redimendum nos in brachio extracto.

5. But with many of them God was not well pleased: for they were overthrown in the wilderness.

But, i. e. *notwithstanding* they had been thus highly favoured. *With many;* literally, with the greater number. *God was not well pleased*, that is, he was displeased. The proof of his displeasure was that they *were overthrown* in the wilderness. Literally, *they were strewed* as corpses *in the wilderness.* Their path through the desert could be traced by the bones of those who perished through the judgments of God.

6. Now these things were our examples, to the intent we should not lust after evil things, as they also lusted.

These things were our examples; literally, *our types. A type* is an impression; any thing produced by blows; then an impression which has a resemblance to something else; then a model to which some other person or thing should be, or in point of fact would be, conformed. The Israelites and the facts of their history were our types, because we shall be conformed to them if we do not exercise caution. Our doom will correspond to theirs. They therefore stand as warnings to us. The particular thing against which their fate was designed to warn us, is lusting after evil. According to Num. 11, 4, the people lusted after, i. e. they inordinately longed for, the flesh-pots of Egypt, and said, Who shall give us flesh to eat? God gave them their desire—"but while the flesh was yet between their teeth, he smote them with a great plague, and the place was called the 'graves of lust,' for there they buried the people that lusted," Num. 11, 34. Comp. Ps. 78, 27–31, and 105, 14. 15. This was a perpetual warning against the indulgence of inordinate desires for forbidden objects. It was specially appropriate as a warning to the Corinthians not to desire participation in the sacrificial feasts of the heathen in which they had been accustomed to indulge.

7. Neither be ye idolaters, as (were) some of them; as it is written, The people sat down to eat and drink, and rose up to play.

The Corinthians were as much exposed to temptation on this subject as the Israelites had been, and were quite as liable to fall into idolatrous practices. The Israelites did not consider themselves as idolaters when they made the golden calf; they did not believe that the second commandment forbade the worship of the true God by images, and it was Jehovah whom they designed to worship. The feast was proclaimed as a feast to Jehovah, Ex. 32, 6. They made the same excuse for the use of images as the Romanists now do; and the same in effect as that which the Corinthians made for their compliance with heathen usages. The latter did not consider the participation of the feasts in the idol's temple as an act of idolatry. As the Israelites perished for their sin, their excuse notwithstanding, so those who are in fact idolaters, whether they so regard themselves or not, must expect a like fate. It is not enough to make a thing right, that we think it to be so. Things do not change their nature according to our thoughts about them. Murder is murder, though man in his self-conceit and pride may call it justifiable homicide.

They sat down to eat and to drink, i. e. of the sacrifices offered to Jehovah in the presence of the golden calf, as a symbol of creative power—and rose up *to play*, i. e. to dance, as that amusement was, among the ancients, connected with their religious feasts. Homer, Od. 8, 251.

8. Neither let us commit fornication, as some of them committed, and fell in one day three and twenty thousand.

Idolatry and fornication have always been so intimately connected that the former seldom fails to lead to the latter. This was illustrated in the case of the Israelites. Num. 25, 1–9, "And the people began to commit whoredom with the daughters of Moab; and they called the people unto the sacrifices of their gods. . . . And Israel joined himself unto Baal-peor." This was a god of the Moabites, who was worshipped by the prostitution of virgins. Idolatry and fornication were in that case inseparable. In Corinth the principal temple was dedicated to Venus, and the homage paid to her was almost as corrupt as that rendered to Baal-peor. How could the Corinthians escape this evil if they allowed themselves to attend the sacrificial feasts within her temple—under the pretence that an idol is nothing?

And were slain in one day three and twenty thousand. In the Hebrew Scriptures, the Septuagint, by Philo, Josephus and the Rabbis, the number is given as twenty-four thousand. Both statements are equally correct. Nothing depended on the precise number. Any number between the two amounts may, according to common usage, be stated roundly as either the one or the other. The infallibility of the sacred writers consists in their saying precisely what the Spirit of God designed they should say; and the Spirit designed that they should speak after the manner of men—and call the heavens solid and the earth flat, and use round numbers, without intending to be mathematically exact in common speech. The Bible, although perfectly divine, because the product of the Spirit of God, is perfectly human. The sacred writers spoke and wrote precisely as other men in their circumstances would have spoken and written, and yet under such an influence as to make every thing they said correspond infallibly with the mind of the Spirit. When the hand of a master touches the organ we have one sound, and when he touches the harp we have another. So when the Spirit of God inspired Isaiah we had one strain, and when he inspired Amos, another. Moses and Paul were accustomed, like most other men, to use round numbers; and they used them when under the influence of inspiration just as they used other familiar forms of statement. Neither intended to speak with numerical exactness, which the occasion did not require. What a wonderful book is the Bible, written at intervals during a period of fifteen hundred years, when such apparitions of inaccuracy as this must be seized upon to impeach its infallibility!

9. Neither let us tempt Christ,* as some of them also tempted, and were destroyed of serpents.

* Instead of Χριστόν, the MSS. B. C., and the Coptic and Ethiopic versions read κύριον. The MS. A. has θεόν. The common text is sustained by the MSS. D. E. F. G. H. I. K., by the Syriac, Vulgate, the old Latin and Sahidic ver-

To tempt is to try, either in the sense of *attempting*, or of putting to the test, with a good or evil intent. God is said to tempt his people, when he puts their faith and patience to the test for the sake of exercising and strengthening those graces, Heb. 11, 17. Satan and evil men are said to tempt others, when they put their virtue to the test with the design of seducing them into sin, Gal. 6, 1. James 1, 3. Matt. 4, 1, &c. Men are said to tempt God when they put his patience, fidelity or power to the test. Acts 5, 9. Matt. 4, 7. Heb. 3, 9. It was thus the Israelites tempted him in the wilderness. They tried his forbearance, they provoked him. The exhortation is that we should not thus *tempt Christ.* This supposes that Christ has authority over us, that he is our moral governor to whom we are responsible, and who has the power to punish those who incur his displeasure. In other words, the passage assumes that we stand in the relation to Christ which rational creatures can sustain to God alone. Christ, therefore, is God. Whether the Corinthians are warned against tempting Christ by their impatience and discontent, as the Israelites did in the particular case here referred to; or whether they are cautioned against putting his fidelity to the test by running unnecessarily into danger (see Matt. 4, 7), is uncertain. Probably the former.

As some of them also tempted. As Christ is mentioned in the immediate context, it is most natural to supply the pronoun *him.* 'Let us not tempt Christ, as they tempted *him.*' This is not only the most natural explanation, but it is sustained by a reference to v. 4, and by the analogy of Scripture, as the Bible elsewhere teaches that the leader of the Israelites was the Son of God. It is only on theological grounds, that is, to get rid of the authority of the passage as a proof of our Lord's divinity, that others interpret the passage thus, 'Let us not tempt Christ, as they tempted God.' It is only one form of the argument, however, which is thus met. For according to this view the passage still teaches that we sustain the relation to Christ which the Israelites sustained to God. *And were destroyed of serpents.* Num. 21, 6. The people provoked God by their complaints and by their regretting their deliverance out of Egypt. "And the Lord sent fiery serpents

sions, and by Chrysostom and other Fathers. It is retained, therefore, by the majority of editors. As the more difficult reading it is the more likely to be the original one. The temptation was strong to change χριστόν into κύριον, but no one would be disposed to put the former word for the latter.

among the people, and they bit the people; and much people of Israel died." Similar judgments awaited the Corinthians if they exhausted the forbearance of the Lord.

10. Neither murmur ye, as some of them also murmured, and were destroyed of the destroyer.

To murmur is to complain in a rebellious spirit. The reference is to Num. 14, 2, "And all the children of Israel murmured against Moses and against Aaron: and the whole congregation said unto them, Would God we had died in the land of Egypt! or would God we had died in the wilderness." Vs. 11. 12, "And the Lord said unto Moses, How long will this people provoke me? and how long will it be ere they believe me for all the signs which I have shown among them? I will smite them with the pestilence, &c." V. 27, "How long shall I bear with this evil congregation which murmur against me? . . . Their carcasses shall fall in the wilderness." Or the reference is to Num. 16, in which the rebellion of Korah is related, and the subsequent murmuring of the people, v. 41, in consequence of which fourteen thousand and seven hundred were destroyed by a plague, v. 49. In both cases the offence and punishment were the same. *Were destroyed of the destroyer*, i. e. by an angel commissioned by God to use the pestilence as an instrument of destruction. Hence sometimes the destruction is referred to the pestilence, as in Num. 14, 14; sometimes to the angel, as here; and sometimes both the agent and the instrument are combined, as in 2 Sam. 24, 16. See Acts 12, 23.

11. Now all these things happened unto them for ensamples: and they are written for our admonition, upon whom the ends of the world are come.

All these happened (i. e. continued to happen) *to them for ensamples.* Literally, they were *types*, see v. 6. They were intended as historical pictures, to represent, as Calvin says, the effects of idolatry, fornication, murmuring, &c. *And they are written*, &c. They were recorded that we might have the benefit of these dispensations, so that we might be admonished to avoid the sins which brought such judgments upon them. *Upon whom the ends of the world* (literally, *of the ages*) *are come.* That is, upon us who live during the last ages. Duration is sometimes conceived of as one, and is therefore expressed by the singular αἰών; sometimes as made up of distinct periods, and is then expressed by the plural αἰῶνες. Hence we have the expressions συντέλεια τοῦ αἰῶνος, and τῶν αἰώνων, Matt. 24, 3. Heb. 9, 26, both signifying the completion of a given portion of duration, considered either as one or as made up of several periods. Sometimes these expressions refer to the close of the Jewish dispensation, and indicate the time of Christ's first coming; sometimes they refer to the close of the present dispensation, and indicate the time of his second advent. Matt. 13, 39, &c. See Eph. 1, 10, and Heb. 1, 1, for equivalent forms of expression. As in Heb. 9, 26, *the completion of the ages* means the end of the Jewish dispensation, so *the ends of the ages* may have the same meaning here. Or what, in this case, may be more natural, the meaning is that we are living during the last of those periods which are allotted to the duration of the world, or of the present order of things. One series of ages terminated with the coming of Christ; another, which is the last, is now passing.

12. Wherefore let him that thinketh he standeth, take heed lest he fall.

This indicates the design of the apostle in referring to the events above indicated in the history of the Israelites. There is perpetual danger of falling. No degree of progress we may have already made, no amount of privileges which we may have enjoyed, can justify the want of caution. *Let him that thinketh he standeth*, that is, let him who thinks himself secure. This may refer either to security of salvation, or against the power of temptation. The two are very different, and rest generally on different grounds. False security of salvation commonly rests on the ground of our belonging to a privileged body (the church), or to a privileged class (the elect). Both are equally fallacious. Neither the members of the church nor the elect can be saved unless they persevere in holiness; and they cannot persevere in holiness without continual watchfulness and effort. False security as to our power to resist temptation rests on an overweening self-confidence in our own strength. None are so liable to fall as they who, thinking themselves strong, heedlessly run into temptation. This probably is the kind of false security against which the apostle warns the Corinthians, as he exhorts them immediately after to avoid temptation.

13. There hath no tèmptation taken you but such as is common to man: but God (is) faithful, who will not suffer you to be tempted above that ye are able; but will with the temptation also make a way to escape, that ye may be able to bear (it).

No temptation, i. e. no trial, whether in the form of seductions or of afflictions, *has taken you but such as is common to man;* literally *human*, accommodated to human strength, such as men are able to bear. 'You have been subjected to no superhuman or extraordinary temptations. Your trials hitherto have been moderate; and God will not suffer you to be unduly tried.' This is the ordinary interpretation of this passage, and one which gives a simple and natural sense. It may, however, mean, 'Take heed lest ye fall. The temptations which you have hitherto experienced are moderate compared to those to which you are hereafter to be subjected.' In this view, it is not so much an encouragement, as a warning that all danger was not over. The apostle is supposed to refer to those peculiar trials which were to attend "the last times." As these times were at hand, the Corinthians were in circumstances which demanded peculiar care. They should not run into temptation, for the days were approaching when, if it were possible, even the elect would be deceived. As, however, there is no contrast between the present and the future intimated in the passage, the common interpretation is the more natural one.

But God is faithful. He has promised to preserve his people, and therefore his fidelity is concerned in not allowing them to be unduly tempted. Here, as in 1, 9, and every where else in Scripture, the security of believers is referred neither to the strength of the principle of grace infused into them by regeneration, nor to their own firmness, but to the fidelity of God. He has promised that those given to the Son as his inheritance, should never perish. They are kept, therefore, by the power of God, through faith, unto salvation, 1 Peter 1, 4. This promise of security, however, is a promise of security from sin, and therefore those who fall into wilful and habitual sin are not the subjects of the promise. Should they fall, it is after a severe struggle, and they are soon renewed again unto repentance. The absolute security of believers, and the necessity of constant watchfulness, are perfectly consistent.

Those whom God has promised to save, he has promised to render watchful. *Who will not suffer you to be tempted above that you are able*, i. e. able to bear. This is the proof of his fidelity. *But will with the temptation make a way of escape.* This means either, that when the temptation comes, God will make a way of escape; or, that when God brings the temptation he will also bring the way of escape. In the latter sense God is regarded as the author of the temptation, in the former he is not. The latter is to be preferred on account of the σύν, *with.* 'He will make *with* the temptation a way of escape,' i. e. he makes the one, he will make the other. The apostle James indeed says, "God cannot be tempted with evil, neither tempteth he any man," James 1, 3. *To tempt* there, however, means to solicit, or attempt to seduce into sin. In that sense God tempts no man. But he does often put their virtue to the test, as in the case of Abraham. And in that sense he tempts or tries them. What the apostle here says is, that when God thus tries his people it will not be beyond their strength, and that he will always make a way of escape *that they may be able to bear it.* This expresses the design of God in making a way of escape. (The genitive τοῦ δύνασθαι, &c., is the genitive of design).

Proof that attendance on sacrificial feasts in a heathen temple is idolatry. Vs. 14–22.

This whole discussion arose out of the question whether it was lawful to eat the sacrifices offered to idols. Paul, while admitting that there was nothing wrong in eating of such meat, exhorts the Corinthians to abstain for the sake of their weaker brethren. There was another reason for this abstinence; they might be led into idolatry. By going to the verge of the allowable, they might be drawn into the sinful. There was great danger that the Corinthians, convinced that an idol was nothing, might be induced to join the sacrificial feasts within the precincts of the temples. The danger was the greater, because such feasts, if held in a private house, lost their religious character, and might be attended without scruple. To convince his readers, that if the feast was held in a temple, attendance upon it was an act of idolatry, is the object of this section. The apostle's argument is from analogy. Attendance on the Lord's Supper is an act of communion with Christ, the object of Christian worship, and with all those who unite with us in the service. From its very nature, it brings all who partake of the bread and wine into fellowship with Christ and with one another, vs. 14–17. The same is true of Jewish sacrifices. Whoever eats of those sacrifices, is thereby brought into communion with the object of Jewish worship. The act is in its nature an act of worship, v. 18. The conclusion is too plain to need being stated—those who join in the sacrificial feasts of the heathen, join in the worship of idols. Such is the import of the act, and no denial on the part of those who perform it can alter its nature. It is not to be inferred from this mode of reasoning, that the objects of heathen worship are what the heathen suppose them to be. Because Paul argued that, as partaking of the Lord's Supper is an act of Christian worship, partaking of an idol-feast must be an act of heathen worship, it is not to be inferred that he regarded Jupiter or Juno as much real beings as Christ is. Far from it. What the heathen sacrifice, they sacrifice to demons; and therefore, to partake of their sacrifices under circumstances which gave religious significance to the act, brought them into communion with demons, vs. 19. 20. The two things are incompatible. A man cannot be a worshipper of Christ and a worshipper of demons, or in communion with the one while in communion with the other. Going to the Lord's table is a renunciation of demons; and going to the table of demons is a renunciation of Christ, v. 21. By this conduct the jealousy of the Lord would be excited against them, as of old it was excited against the Jews who turned aside after false gods, v. 22.

14. Wherefore, my dearly beloved, flee from idolatry.

Wherefore, i. e. because such severe judgments came upon the idolatrous Israelites; because you, as well as they, are in danger of being involved in that sin; and because your distinguished privileges can protect you neither from the sin nor from its punishment any more than their privileges protected them. *My dearly beloved.* Paul addresses them in terms of affection, although his epistle is so full of serious admonition and warning. *Flee from idolatry*, i. e. avoid it by fleeing from it. This is the only safe method of avoiding sin. Its presence is malarious. The only safety is keeping at a distance. This includes two things; first, avoiding what is questionable; that is, every thing which lies upon the border of what is allowable, or which approaches the confines of sin; and secondly, avoiding the occasion and temptations to sin; keeping at a distance from every thing which excites evil passion, or which tends to ensnare the soul.

15. I speak as to wise men; judge ye what I say.

Unto wise men; i. e. as to men of sense; men capable of seeing the force of an argument. Paul's appeal is not to authority, whether his own or that of the Scriptures. The whole question was, whether a given service came within the scriptural definition of idolatry. He was willing, as it were, to leave the decision to themselves; and therefore said, *judge ye what I say*, i. e. sit in judgment on the argument which I present. Should they differ from the apostle, that would not alter the case. The service was idolatrous, whatever they thought of it. But he takes this way of convincing them.

16. The cup of blessing which we bless, is it not the communion of the blood of Christ? The bread which we break, is it not the communion of the body of Christ?

It is here assumed that partaking of the Lord's Supper brings us into communion with Christ. If this be so, partaking of the table of demons must bring us into communion with demons. This is the apostle's argument. It is founded on the assumption, that a participation of the cup is a participation of the blood of Christ; and that a participation of the bread is a participation of the body of Christ. So far Romanists, Lutherans, and Reformed agree in their interpretation of this important passage. They all agree that a participation of the cup is a participation of the blood of Christ; and that a participation of the bread, is a participation of the body of Christ. But when it is asked, what is the nature of this participation, the answers given are radically different. The Reformed answer, negatively, that it is "not after a corporal or carnal manner." That is, it is not by the mouth, or as ordinary food is received. Affirmatively, they answer that it is by faith, and therefore by the soul. This, of course, determines the nature of the thing partaken of, or the sense in which the body and blood of Christ are received. If the reception is not by the mouth, but by faith, then the thing received is not the material body and blood, but the body and blood as a sacrifice, i. e. their sacrificial virtue. Hence all Reformed churches teach (and even the rubrics of the Church of England), that the body and blood of Christ are received elsewhere than at the Lord's table, and without the reception of the bread and wine, which in the Sacrament are their symbols and the organs of communication, as elsewhere the word is that organ. Another point no less clear as to the Reformed doctrine is, that since the body and blood of Christ are received by faith, they are not received by unbelievers.

Romanists answer the above question by saying, that the mouth is the organ of reception; that the thing received is the real body and blood of Christ, into the substance of which the bread and wine are changed by the act of consecration; and consequently, that believers and unbelievers are alike partakers. Lutherans teach, that although the bread and wine remain unchanged, yet, as the body and blood of Christ are locally present in the sacrament, in, with, and under the bread and wine, the organ of reception is the mouth; the thing received is the real body and blood of Christ; and that they are received alike or equally by believers and unbelievers; by the latter, however, to their detriment and condemnation; by the former, to their spiritual nourishment and growth in grace. Lutherans and Romanists further agree in teaching, that there is a reception of the body and blood of Christ in the Lord's Supper, which is elsewhere impossible.

These are the three great forms of doctrine which have prevailed in the Church on this subject; and this passage is interpreted by each party in accordance with their peculiar views. The passage decides no point of difference. If the Romish doctrine of transubstantiation can be elsewhere proved, then, of course, this passage must be understood in accordance with it. And if the Lutheran doctrine of consubstantiation can be established by other declarations of the Word of God, then this passage must be explained in accordance with that doctrine. But, if it can be clearly demonstrated from Scripture and from those laws of belief which God has impressed upon our nature, that those doctrines are false, then the passage must be understood as teaching a spiritual, and not a corporal participation of Christ's body and blood. All that the passage asserts is the fact of a participation, the nature of that participation must be determined from other sources.

The cup of blessing. The word (εὐλογέω), *to bless*, means, 1. To speak well of. 2. To praise and thank; as when we bless God. 3. To confer blessings, as when God blesses us. In virtue of the second of these meanings, the word is used interchangeably with (εὐχαριστέω), *to give thanks.* That is, the same act is sometimes expressed by the one word and sometimes by the other. In Matt. 26, 26 and Mark 14, 22, what is expressed by saying, *having blessed*, in Luke 22, 17. 19. and 1 Cor. 11, 25, is expressed by saying, *having given thanks.* And in the account of the Lord's Supper in Matthew and Mark, the one word is used in reference to the bread, and the other in reference to the cup. They therefore mean the same thing, or rather express the same act, for that act was both a benediction and thanksgiving; that is, it was an address to God, acknowledging his mercy and imploring his blessing, and therefore may be expressed either by the word benediction or thanksgiving. It is not necessary to infer that in these cases (εὐλογήσας) *having blessed* is used in the restricted sense of (εὐχαριστήσας) *having given thanks.* This cannot be the fact, because the object of (εὐλογήσας), at least in some of these passages, is not God, but the bread or the cup. The meaning is, 'having blessed the bread.' The phrase, therefore, the *cup of blessing*, so far as the signification of the words is concerned, may be rendered either—the cup of thanksgiving (the eucharistical cup), or the cup of benediction, the consecrated cup. The latter is no doubt the true meaning, because the explanation immediately follows, *which we bless.* The cup, and not God, is blessed. To take the phrase actively, *the cup which confers blessing* is not only inconsistent with usage, but incompatible with the explanation which immediately follows. The cup of blessing is the cup which we bless. In the Paschal service the cup was called "the cup of blessing," because a benediction was pronounced over it. The idea of consecration is necessarily included. Wine, as wine, is not the sacramental symbol of Christ's blood, but only when solemnly consecrated for that purpose. Even our ordinary food is said to "be sanctified by the word of God and prayer," 1 Tim. 4, 5, because it is set apart by a religious service to the end for which it was appointed. So the cup of blessing is the cup which, by the benediction pronounced over it, is "set apart from a common to a sacred use."

Which we bless. This is the explanation of the preceding clause. The cup of blessing is the cup which we bless; which can only mean the cup on which we implore a blessing; that is, which we pray may be blessed to the end for which it was appointed, viz. to be to us the communion of the blood of Christ. That is, the means of communicating to us the benefits of Christ's death. Just as we bless our food when we pray that God would make it the means of nourishing our bodies. The other interpretations of this clause are unnatural, because they require something to be supplied which is not in the text. Thus some say the meaning is, "taking which," or "holding which in our hands," or "over which," we give thanks. All this is unnecessary, as the words give a perfectly good sense as they stand (ὃ εὐλογοῦμεν), *which* (cup) *we bless.* This passage, therefore, seems to determine the meaning of such passages as Matt. 26, 26 and Mark 14, 22, "Having blessed (viz. the bread) he brake it." The bread or cup was the thing blessed. Comp. Luke 9, 16, where it is said our Lord, "having taken the five loaves and the two fishes, and having looked up to heaven, he blessed *them*." This also shows that "having given thanks" in such connections means "having with thanksgiving implored the blessing of God." The cup therefore is blessed by the prayer, in which we ask that God would make it answer the end of its appointment.

Is it not the communion of the blood of Christ? That is, is it not the means of participating of the blood of Christ? He who partakes of the cup, partakes of Christ's blood. This, of course, is true only of believers. Paul is writing to believers, and assumes the presence of faith in the receiver. Thus baptism is said to wash away sin, and the word of God is said to sanctify, not from any virtue in them; not as an external rite or as words addressed to the outward ear; not to all indiscriminately who are baptized or who hear the word; but as means of divine appointment, when received by faith and attended by the working of his Spirit. The believing reception of the cup is as certainly connected with a participation of Christ's blood, as the believing reception of the word is connected with an experience of its life-giving power. The whole argument of the apostle is founded on this idea. He wishes to prove that partaking of the sacrificial feasts of the heathen brought men into real communion with demons, because participation of the Lord's supper makes us really partakers of Christ. The word κοινωνία, *communion*, means *participation*, from the verb κοινωνέω, *to partake of;* in Heb. 2, 14, it is said, Christ took part of flesh and blood. Rom. 15, 17, the Gentiles took part in the spiritual blessings of the Jews. Hence we have such expressions as the following: participation of his Son, 1 Cor. 1, 9; participation of the Spirit, 2 Cor. 13, 13. Phil. 2, 1; participation of the ministry, 2 Cor. 8, 4; of the gospel, Phil. 1, 5; of sufferings, Phil. 3, 5. Of course the nature of this participation depends on the nature of its object. Participation of Christ is sharing in his Spirit, character, sufferings and glory; participation of the gospel is participation of its benefits; and thus participation of the blood of Christ is partaking of its benefits. This passage affords not the slightest ground for the Romish or Lutheran doctrine of a participation of the substance of Christ's body and blood. When in 1, 9 it is said, "We are called into the fellowship or participation of his Son," it is not of the substance of the Godhead that we partake. And when the Apostle John says, "We have fellowship one with another," i. e. we are (κοινωνοί) partners one of another, 1 John 1, 7, he does not mean that we partake of each other's corporeal substance. To share in a sacrifice offered in our behalf is to share in its efficacy; and as Christ's blood means his sacrificial blood, to partake of his blood no more means to partake of his literal blood, than when it is said his blood cleanses from all sin, it is meant that his literal corporeal blood has this cleansing efficacy. When we are said to receive the sprinkling of his blood, 1 Pet. 1, 1, it does not mean his literal blood.

The bread which we break, is it not the communion of the body of Christ? That is, by partaking of the bread we partake of the body of Christ. This is but a repetition of the thought contained in the preceding clause. The cup is the means of participation of his blood; the bread the means of participation of his body. *The body of Christ* cannot here mean the church, because his blood is mentioned in the same connection, and because in the institution of the Lord's supper the bread is the symbol of Christ's literal, and not of his mystical body. To partake of his body, is to partake of the benefits of his body as broken for us. *Which we break.* This is in evident allusion to the original institution of the sacrament. Our Lord "took bread, and having given thanks, he brake it and said, Take, eat; this is my body which is broken for you." 1 Cor. 11, 24. The whole service, therefore, is often called the "breaking of bread." Acts 2, 42. 20, 7. The custom, therefore, of using a wafer placed unbroken in the mouth of the communicant, leaves out an important significant element in this sacrament.

17. For we (being) many are one bread, (and) one body: for we are all partakers of that one bread.

Literally rendered this verse reads: *Since it is one bread, we the many are one body; for we are all partakers of one bread.* We are not said to be one bread; but we are one body because we partake of one bread. The design of the apostle is to show that every one who comes to the Lord's supper enters into communion with all other communicants. They form one body in virtue of their joint participation of Christ. This being the case, those who attend the sacrificial feasts of the heathen form one religious body. They are in religious communion with each other, because in communion with the demons on whom their worship terminates. Many distinguished commentators, however, prefer the following interpretation. "For we, though many, are one bread (and) one body." The participation of the same loaf makes us one bread, and the joint participation of Christ's body makes us one body. This is, to say the least, an unusual and harsh figure. Believers are never said to be one bread; and to make the ground of comparison the fact that the loaf is the joint product of many grains of wheat is very remote. And to say that we are literally one bread, because by assimilation the bread passes into the composition of the bodies of all the communicants, is to make the apostle teach modern physiology.

In the word κοινωνία, *communion*, as used in the preceding verse, lies the idea of joint participation. 'The bread which we break is a joint participation of the body of Christ; because (ὅτι) it is one bread, so are we one body.' The thing to be proved is the union of all partakers of that one bread. Instead of connecting this verse with the 16th, as containing a confirmation of what is therein stated, many commentators take it as an independent sentence introducing a passing remark. 'The Lord's supper brings us into communion with Christ. Because this is the case, we are one body *and should act accordingly.*' But this not only breaks the connection, but introduces what is not in the text. The idea is, 'Partaking of the sacrament is a communion, *because* we the many all partake of one bread.'

18. Behold Israel after the flesh: are not they which eat of the sacrifices partakers of the altar?

Israel after the flesh, i. e. the Jews, as a nation, as distinguished from Israel *after the Spirit*, or the spiritual Israel or true people of God. As Israel was a favourite term of honour, Paul rarely uses it for the Jews as a people without some such qualification. Comp. Rom. 2, 28. 9, 8. Gal. 4, 29. 6, 16.

Are not they which eat of the sacrifices. With the Jews, as with other nations, only a portion of most sacrifices was consumed upon the altar; the residue was divided between the priest and the offerer. Lev. 7, 15. 8, 31. Deut. 12, 18. To eat of the sacrifices in the way prescribed in the Law of Moses, was to take part in the whole sacrificial service. "Thou must eat them before the Lord thy God, in the place which the Lord thy God shall choose." Deut. 12, 18. Therefore the apostle says that those who eat of the sacrifices are *partakers of the altar*; that is, they are in communion with it. They become worshippers of the God to whom the altar is dedicated. This is the import and the effect of joining in these sacrificial feasts. The question is not as to the intention of the actors, but as to the import of the act, and as to the interpretation universally put upon it. To partake of a Jewish sacrifice as a sacrifice and in a holy place, was an act of Jewish worship. By parity of reasoning, to partake of a heathen sacrifice as a sacrifice, and in a holy place, was of necessity an act of heathen worship. As all who attended the Jewish sacrifices, to which none but Jews were admitted, professed to be Jews and to be the joint-worshippers of Jehovah, and as they could not be in communion with the altar without being in communion with each other, therefore all who attended the sacrificial feasts of the heathen brought themselves into religious communion with idolaters. It need hardly be remarked that this passage gives no ground for the opinion that the Lord's supper is a sacrifice. This is not the point of comparison. The apostle's argument does not imply that, because the Jewish and heathen feasts were sacrificial feasts, therefore the Christian festival had the same character. The whole stress lies on the word κοινωνία. 'Because participation of Christian ordinances involves communion with Christ, participation of heathen ordinances involves communion with devils.'

19. What say I then? that the idol is any thing, or that which is offered in sacrifice to idols is any thing?

This is evidently intended to guard against a false inference from this mode of reasoning. It was not to be inferred from what he had said, that he regarded the professed objects of heathen worship as having the same objective existence as the God whom Jews and Christians worshipped; or that he considered the heathen sacrifices as having any inherent power. The idol was nothing, and that which was offered to the idol was nothing. This however does not alter the case. For although there are no such beings as those whom the heathen conceive their gods to be, and although their sacrifices are not what they consider them, still their worship is real idolatry, and has a destructive influence on the soul. How this is, is explained in the following verse.

20. But (I say), that the things which the Gentiles sacrifice, they sacrifice to devils, and not to God: and I would not that ye should have fellowship with devils.

That is, 'I do not say the gods of the heathen have a real existence, that there are any such persons as Jupiter or Minerva; but I do say that the heathen worship is the worship of demons.' This verse presents two questions for consideration. First, in what sense does Paul here use the word δαιμόνια, translated *devils;* and secondly, in what sense can it be truly said that the heathen worship devils.

The words δαίμων and δαιμόνιον were used by the Greeks for any deity or god, or spirit, and generally for any object of reverence or dread. The only case in the New Testament where they have this sense is Acts 17, 18, ("He seems to be a setter forth of strange gods.") Elsewhere they always mean fallen angels. Our translators have not adhered to the distinction which in the New Testament is constantly made in the use of the words διάβολος and δαιμόνιον. They translate both terms by the word *devil*, and hence, when the latter occurs in the plural form, they render it *devils*. The former, however, is never applied in Scripture (except in its appellative sense of *accuser*) to any other being than Satan. He is the Devil, and the Scriptures never speak of more than one. By devils, therefore, in this case are to be understood *demons*, or the fallen angels or evil spirits. That this is the sense in which the Greek word is to be here taken is plain, 1. Because it is its only scriptural sense. The passage in Acts 17, 18, being the language of Athenians, proves nothing as to the usage of Jews speaking Greek. 2. In the Septuagint we have precisely the words used by the apostle, and in the same sense. Deut. 32, 17. See also Ps. 95, 5, where the Septuagint version is, ὅτι πάντες οἱ θεοὶ τῶν ἐθνῶν δαιμόνια, *all the gods of the heathen are devils*. It can hardly be doubted that the apostle meant to use the word in its established scriptural sense. Comp. also Rev. 9, 20. 3. The classical sense of the word does not suit the context. Paul had just said that the heathen gods were nothing; to admit now that there were *deities* in the Grecian sense of the word δαιμόνιον, would be to contradict himself. We must understand the apostle, therefore, as saying on the one hand, that the gods of the heathen were imaginary beings; and on the other, that their sacrifices were really offered to evil spirits. In what sense, however, is this true? The heathen certainly did not intend to worship evil spirits. Nevertheless they did it. Men of the world do not intend to serve Satan, when they break the laws of God in the pursuit of their objects of desire. Still in so doing they are really obeying the will of the great adversary, yielding to his impulses, and fulfilling his designs. He is therefore said to be the god of this world. To him all sin is an offering and an homage. We are shut up to the necessity of worshipping God or Satan; for all refusing or neglecting to worship the true God, or giving to any other the worship which is due to him alone, is the worshipping of Satan and his angels. It is true therefore, in the highest sense, that what the heathen offer they offer to devils. Although their gods have no existence, yet there are real beings, the rulers of the darkness of this world, wicked spirits in heavenly places (Eph. 6, 12), on whom their worship terminates.

And I would not that ye have fellowship with devils. By *fellowship* or communion, the apostle means here what he meant by the same term in the preceding verses. We are said to have fellowship with those between whom and us there are congeniality of mind, community of interest, and friendly intercourse. In this sense we have fellowship with our fellow Christians, with God and with his Son. And in this sense the worshippers of idols have fellowship with evil spirits. They are united to them so as to form one community, with a common character and a common destiny. Into this state of fellowship they are brought by sacrificing to them; that is, by idolatry, which is an act of apostasy from the true God, and of association with the kingdom of darkness. It was of great importance for the Corinthians to know that it did not depend on their intention whether they came into communion with devils. The heathen did not intend to worship devils, and yet they did it; what would it avail, therefore, to the reckless Corinthians, who attended the sacrificial feasts of the heathen, to say that they did not intend to worship idols? The question was not, what they meant to do, but what they did; not, what their intention was, but what was the import and effect of their conduct. A man need not intend to burn himself when he puts his hand into the fire; or to pollute his soul when he frequents the haunts of vice. The effect is altogether independent of his intention. This principle applies with all its force to compliance with the religious services of the heathen at the present day. Those who in pagan countries join in the religious rites of the heathen, are just as much guilty of idolatry, and are just as certainly brought into fellowship with devils, as the nominal Christians of Corinth, who, although they knew that an idol was nothing, and that there is but one God, yet frequented the heathen feasts. The same principle also applies to the compliance of Protestants in the religious observances of Papists. Whatever their intention may be, they worship the host if they bow down to it with the crowd who intend to adore it. By the force of the act we become one with those in whose worship we join. We constitute with them and with the objects of their worship one communion.

21. Ye cannot drink the cup of the Lord, and the cup of devils: ye cannot be partakers of the Lord's table, and of the table of devils.

The cup of the Lord is that cup which brings us into communion with the Lord, v. 16; *the cup of devils* is that cup which brings us into communion with devils. The reference is not exclusively or specially to the cup of libation, or to the wine poured out as an offering to the gods, but to the cup from which the guests drank at these sacrificial feasts. The whole service had a religious character; all the provisions, the wine as well as the meat, were blessed in the name of the idol, and thereby consecrated to him, in a manner analogous to that in which the bread and the wine on the Lord's table were consecrated to him; comp. 1 Sam. 9, 12. 13. *The table of the Lord* is the table at which the Lord presides, and at which his people are his guests. *The table of devils* is the table at which devils preside, and at which all present are their guests. What the apostle means to say is, that there is not merely an incongruity and inconsistency in a man's being the guest and friend of Christ and the guest and friend of evil spirits, but that the thing is impossible. It is as impossible as that the same man should be black and white, wicked and holy at the same time. In neither case is this attendance an empty, ineffective service. A man cannot eat of the table of demons without being brought under their power and influence; nor can we eat of the table of the Lord, without being brought into contact with him, either to our salvation or condemnation. If we come thoughtlessly, without any desire after communion with Christ, we eat and drink judgment to ourselves. But if we come with a humble desire to obey our divine master and to seek his presence, we cannot fail to be welcomed and blessed. Compare, in reference to this verse, 2 Cor. 6, 14–18.

22. Do we provoke the Lord to jealousy? are we stronger than he?

Jealousy is the feeling which arises from wounded love, and is the fiercest of all human passions. It is therefore employed as an illustration of the hatred of God towards idolatry. It is as when a bride transfers her affections from her lawful husband, in every way worthy of her love, to some degraded and offensive object. This illustration, feeble as it is, is the most effective that can be borrowed from human relations, and is often employed in Scripture to set forth the heinousness of the sin of idolatry. Deut. 32, 21. Ps. 78, 58 and elsewhere. *Or do we provoke*, i. e. is it our object to provoke the Lord to jealousy. The Corinthians ought not to attend these feasts unless they intended to excite against themselves in the highest measure the displeasure of the Lord. And they ought not thus to excite his anger, unless they were *stronger than he.* By *the Lord* is to be understood Christ, as the context requires. It was the Lord's table that was forsaken, and the same Lord that was provoked thereby to jealousy. Here, again, the relation in which Christians stand to Christ, is said to be analogous to that in which the Israelites stood to Jehovah. Christ is therefore our Jehovah. He is our husband, to whom our supreme affection is due, and who loves us as a husband loves his wife. "Thy maker is thy husband, Jehovah is his name," Is. 54, 5; see Eph. 5, 25–31.

Under what circumstances it was lawful to eat meat offered to idols. Vs. 23–33.

The apostle having, in the preceding paragraph, proved that eating of the sacrifices offered to idols under circumstances which gave a religious character to the act, was idolatry, comes to state the circumstances under which those sacrifices might be eaten without scruple. He begins by reverting to the general law of Christian liberty stated with the same limitations as in ch. 6, 12. The right to use things offered to idols, as well as other things in themselves indifferent, is limited by expediency. We should be governed in this matter by a regard to the good of others, and to our own edification, vs. 23. 24. If the meat of sacrifices be sold in the market, v. 25, or found at private tables, it may be eaten without any hesitation, v. 27. But if any one at a private table, from scruples on the subject, should apprise us that a certain dish contained part of a sacrifice, for his sake, and not for our own, we ought to abstain, v. 28. We should not make such a use of our liberty as to cause our good to be evil spoken of, v. 29. The general rule of action, not only as to meats and drinks, but as to all other things is, first, to act with a regard to the glory of God, v. 31; and secondly, so as to avoid giving offence (i. e. occasion for sin) to any class of men, v. 32. In this matter Paul presents himself as an example to his fellow-believers, v. 33.

23. All things are lawful for me, but all things are not expedient: all things are lawful for me, but all things edify not.

The apostle had already, in ch. 6, 12, and in ch. 8, conceded that eating of the sacrifices offered to idols, was, in itself, a matter of indifference. But the use of things indifferent is limited by two principles; first, a regard to the welfare of others; secondly, regard to our own welfare. The word (συμφέρει) *is expedient* expresses the one of these ideas, and (οἰκοδομεῖ) *edifieth* the other. All things are not expedient or useful to others; and all things are not edifying to ourselves. The latter phrase might indeed have reference to others as well as to ourselves—but as contrasted with the former clause, it appears to be used here with this restricted application. In this view it agrees with the clause, "I will not be brought under the power of any thing," in 6, 12.

24. Let no man seek his own, but every man another's (wealth).

That is, let every man, in the use of his liberty, have regard to the welfare of others. The maxim is indeed general. It is not only in the use of things indifferent, but in all other things we should act, not, in exclusive regard to our own interests, but also with a view to the good of others. Self, in other words, is not to be the object of our actions. The context, however, shows, that the apostle intended the maxim to be applied to the subject under discussion. Another's *wealth*, i. e. another's *weal* or welfare, according to the old meaning of the word wealth.

25. Whatsoever is sold in the shambles, (that) eat, asking no question for conscience' sake:

The general principle that sacrifices might be eaten under any circumstances which deprived the act of a religious character, is here, and in what follows, applied to particular cases. Meat, when exposed for public sale in the market, lost its character as a sacrifice, and might be eaten with impunity. The word μάκελλον is a Latin word which passed into the Greek, and means a *meat market*.

Eat, asking no questions for conscience' sake. This clause admits of three interpretations. 1. It may mean, 'When you go to the market, buy what you want, and make no matter of conscience about the matter. You need have no conscientious scruples, and therefore ask no questions as to whether the meat had been offered to idols or not.' This is the simplest and most natural interpretation. These verses contain the conclusion of the whole discussion. An idol is nothing; the sacrifices are nothing sacred in themselves; but as the heathen are really worshippers of evil spirits, to join in their worship by eating their sacrifices as sacrifices, is idolatry; but to eat them as meat is a matter of indifference; therefore do not make it a matter of conscience. This interpretation is confirmed by the following verse, which assigns the reason why we need have no scruples in the case. 2. Or, the meaning may be, Ask no questions, for fear of awakening scruples in your own mind. A man might eat with a good conscience of meat which he knew not was a sacrifice, when he would have serious scruples if informed that it had been offered to an idol. Therefore it was wise, for his own sake, to ask no questions. Paul, however, would not advise men to act blind fold. If a man thought it wrong to eat meat offered to idols, it would be wrong for him to run the risk of doing so by buying meat in the markets where sacrifices were exposed for sale. 3. Others say the apostle means to caution the strong against instituting such inquiries, for fear of giving rise to scruples in others. In favour of this view it is urged, that throughout the whole discussion the object of the apostle is to induce the strong to respect the conscientious scruples of the weak. And in v. 29 he says expressly, that he means the conscience of others. The former of these considerations has not much weight, for we have here general directions suited to all classes. Having shown in the preceding paragraph, that it was idolatrous to eat of these sacrifices under certain circumstances, it was perfectly natural that he should tell both the strong and the weak when they might be eaten without scruple. As to the second argument, it is rather against than in favour of this interpretation. For if, when he means the conscience of another, he expressly says so, the inference is, that when he makes no such explanation, he means the man's own conscience. Besides, the following verse gives the reason why we need not have any scruples in the case, and not why we should regard the scruples of others.

26. For the earth (is) the Lord's, and the fulness thereof.

This was the common form of acknowledgment among the Jews before meals. It was the recognition of God as the proprietor and giver of all things, and specially of the food provided for his children. The words are taken from Ps. 24, 1. *The fulness of the earth* is that by which it is filled; all the fruits and animals with which it is replenished; which were created by God, and therefore good. Nothing, therefore, can in itself be polluting, if used in obedience to the design of its creation. And as the animals offered in sacrifice were intended to be food for man, they cannot defile those who use them for that purpose. This is the reason which the apostle gives to show that, so far as God is concerned, the Corinthians need entertain no scruples in eating meat that had been offered to idols. It was a creature of God, and therefore not to be regarded as unclean. Comp. 1 Tim. 4, 4, where the same doctrine is taught, and for the same purpose.

27. If any of them that believe not bid you (to a feast), and ye be disposed to go; whatsoever is set before you, eat, asking no question for conscience' sake.

As the sacrifices lost their religious character when sold in the market, so also at any private table they were to be regarded not as sacrifices, but as ordinary food, and might be eaten without scruple. The apostle did not prohibit the Christians from social intercourse with the heathen. If invited to their tables, they were at liberty to go.

28. But if any man say unto you, This is offered in sacrifice unto idols, eat not for his sake that shewed it, and for conscience' sake: for the earth (is) the Lord's, and the fulness thereof:

This is an exception. They might without scruple eat any thing set before them. But if any of the guests apprised them that a particular dish contained meat which had been offered to an idol, out of regard to the conscientious scruples of him who made the intimation, they should abstain. *But, on the contrary, if any one.* That is, any of your fellow-guests. The only person likely to make the suggestion was a scrupulous Christian. *For his sake that showed it and for conscience' sake;* the latter clause is explanatory. 'On account of him making the intimation, i. e. on account of his conscience.' Though it is right to eat, and though you know it to be right, yet, to avoid wounding or disturbing the conscience of your weaker brother, it is your duty to abstain. The union of the most enlightened liberality with the humblest concession to the weakness of others, exhibited in this whole connection, may well excite the highest admiration. The most enlightened man of his whole generation, was the most yielding and conciliatory in all matters of indifference.

The clause, "For the earth is the Lord's and the fulness thereof," at the end of this verse, is not found in the best manuscripts, and therefore omitted in all the critical editions of the Greek Testament. They seem to be here entirely out of place. In verse 26 they assign the reason why the Corinthians might eat without scruple whatever was sold in the market. But here they have no connection with what precedes. The fact that the earth is the Lord's, is no reason why we should *not eat* of sacrificial meat out of regard to a brother's conscience. There is little doubt, therefore, that it should be omitted.

29, 30. Conscience, I say, not thine own, but of the other: for why is my liberty judged of another (man's) conscience? For if I by grace be a partaker, why am I evil spoken of for that for which I give thanks?

As in the preceding vs. 25. 27 the word conscience refers to one's own conscience, to prevent its being so understood in v. 28, Paul adds the explanation, 'Conscience, I say, not thine own, but of the other's.' That is, 'I do not mean your conscience, but the conscience of the man who warned you not to eat.' *For why is my liberty judged of another man's conscience?* These and the words following admit of three interpretations. 1. If connected with the preceding clause, they must give the reason why Paul meant "the conscience of the other." 'Conscience I say, not one's own, but of the other; *for* why is my liberty (or conscience) to be judged by another man's conscience? if I eat with thanksgiving (and with a good conscience, why am I blamed?') The obvious objection to this interpretation is, that it exalts a subordinate clause into the principal matter. It was plain enough that Paul did not mean the man's own conscience, and therefore it is unnecessary to take up two verses to prove that he did not. Besides, this interpretation makes the apostle change sides. He has from the beginning been speaking in behalf of the weak. This interpretation makes him here speak almost in terms of indignation in behalf of the strong, who certainly need no advocate. They did not require to be told that their liberty was not to be restricted by the scruples of the weak. 2. A much better sense is obtained by connecting this passage with the 28th verse. 'Do not eat out of regard to the conscience of your brother; for why should my (your) liberty be judged (i. e. condemned) by another conscience; why should I be blamed for what I receive with thanksgiving?' That is, why should I make such a use of my liberty as to give offence? This brings the passage into harmony with the whole context, and connects it with the main idea of the preceding verse, and not with an intermediate and subordinate clause. The very thing the apostle has in view is to induce the strong to respect the scruples of the weak. They might eat of sacrificial meat at private tables with freedom, so far as they themselves were concerned; but why, he asks, should they do it so as to give offence, and cause the weak to condemn and speak evil of them. 3. This passage is by some commentators regarded as the language of an objector, and not as that of the apostle. The strong, when told not to eat on account of the conscience of a weak brother, might ask, 'Why is my liberty judged by another's conscience—why should I be blamed for what I receive with thanksgiving?' (The γάρ, according to this view, is not *for*, but intensive, ἱνατί γάρ, *why then.*) This gives a very good sense, but it is not consistent with the following verse (which is connected with v. 30 by οὖν, and not by δέ). Paul does not go on to answer that objection, but considers the whole matter settled. The second interpretation is the only one consistent alike with what precedes and with what follows. 'Do not eat when cautioned not to do so; for why should you so use your liberty as to incur censure? Whether therefore you eat or drink, do all for the glory of God.' Why is my liberty *judged* (κρίνεται), i. e. judged unfavourably or condemned. *If I by grace am a partaker;* literally, *if I partake with thanksgiving.* The word χάρις, *grace*, is here used in the sense of *gratia*, *thanks*, as in the common phrase to *say grace.* See Luke 6, 32. 1 Tim. 1, 12, &c.

31. Whether therefore ye eat, or drink, or whatsoever ye do, do all to the glory of God.

This may mean either, 'Do all things with a view to the glory of God.' Let that be the object constantly aimed at;

or, 'Do all things in such a way that God may be glorified.' There is little difference between these modes of explanation. God cannot be glorified by our conduct unless it be our object to act for his glory. The latter interpretation is favoured by a comparison with 1 Peter 4, 11, "That God in all things may be glorified." See Col. 3, 17. All the special directions given in the preceding discussion are here summed up. 'Let self be forgotten. Let your eye be fixed on God. Let the promotion of his glory be your object in all you do. Strive in every thing to act in such a way that men may praise that God whom you profess to serve.' The sins of the people of God are always spoken of as bringing reproach on God himself. Rom. 2, 24. Ezek. 36, 20. 23. It is by thus having the desire to promote the glory of God as the governing motive of our lives, that order and harmony are introduced into all our actions. The sun is then the centre of the system. Men of the world have themselves for the end of their actions. Philosophers tell us to make the good of others the end; and thus destroy the sentiment of religion, by merging it into philanthropy or benevolence. The Bible tells us to make the glory of God the end. This secures the other ends by making them subordinate, while at the same time it exalts the soul by placing before it an infinite personal object. There is all the difference between making the glory of God (the personal Jehovah) the end of our actions, and the good of the universe, or of being in general, that there is between the love of Christ and the love of an abstract idea. The one is religion, the other is morality.

32. Give none offence, neither to the Jews, nor to the Gentiles, nor to the church of God:

Give none offence, i. e. give no occasion to sin. An offence is something over which men stumble. The exhortation is to avoid being the cause of sin to others, 8, 9. Rom. 14, 13. 21. They were to be thus careful with respect to all classes of men, Christians and non-Christians. The latter are divided into the two great classes, the Jews and Gentiles. *The church of God*, i. e. his people. Those whom God has called out of the world to be his peculiar possession. They are therefore distinguished as the κλητοί, *the called*, or, collectively considered, the ἐκκλησία, *the church*. The first great principle of Christian conduct is to promote the glory of God; the second is to avoid giving offence, or causing men to sin. In other words, love to God and love to men should govern all our conduct.

33. Even as I please all (men) in all (things), not seeking mine own profit, but the (profit) of many, that they may be saved.

What he urged them to do, he himself did. His object was not his own advantage, but the benefit of others. He therefore, in all things allowable, accommodated himself to all men, that they might be saved. "I am made all things to all men, that I might by all means save some." 9, 22.

The principle which the apostle here avows, and which he so strenuously recommends in the preceding chapters, is one which has often been lamentably perverted. On the plea of becoming all things to all men, Christians are tempted into sinful conformity with the habits and amusements of the world. On the same plea the church of Rome adopted heathen festivals, ceremonies and rites, until the distinction between Paganism and Christianity was little more than nominal. Heathen temples were called churches; pagan gods were baptized as saints, and honored as before. Modern Rome, in the apprehension of the people, is almost as polytheistic as ancient Rome. In like manner Romish missionaries accommodate themselves to such a degree to heathen ideas and forms, that the difference between what they call Christianity and the religion of the country is almost lost. Even Protestant missionaries are often perplexed how to decide between what is to be tolerated and what prohibited of the previous usages and ceremonies of their converts. That the principle on which Paul and the other apostles acted in reference to this matter, is radically different from that adopted by the church of Rome, is apparent from their different results. Rome has become paganized. The apostle so acted as to preserve the church from every taint of either Paganism or Judaism. The rules which guided the apostles may be easily deduced from the conduct and epistles of Paul. 1. They accommodated themselves to Jewish or Gentile usages only in matters of indifference. 2. They abstained from all accommodation even in things indifferent, under circumstances which gave to those things a religious import. They allowed sacrifices to be eaten; but eating within a temple was forbidden.

3. They conceded when the concession was not demanded as a matter of necessity; but refused when it was so regarded. Paul said circumcision was nothing and uncircumcision was nothing; yet he resisted the circumcision of Titus when it was demanded by the Judaizers. 4. The object of their concessions was not to gain mere nominal converts, nor to do away with the offence of the cross, Gal. 4, 11, but to save men. No concession therefore, whether to the manners of the world or to the prejudices of the ignorant, can plead the sanction of apostolic example, which has not that object honestly in view. 5. It is included in the above particulars that Paul, in becoming all things to all men, never compromised any truth or sanctioned any error.

XI., 1. Be ye followers of me, even as I also (am) of Christ.

This verse should belong to the tenth chapter, as it is the conclusion of the preceding discussion, and as a new subject is introduced with the following verse. Paul had referred to his own conciliatory conduct as an example to the Corinthians, and he exhorts them to imitate him, as he did Christ, who is the ultimate standard.

CHAPTER XI.

The impropriety of women appearing unveiled in the public assemblies, vs. 2–16. The improper manner of celebrating the Lord's Supper which prevailed in the Corinthian church, vs. 17–34.

On the impropriety of women appearing in public unveiled, vs. 2–16.

HAVING corrected the more private abuses which prevailed among the Corinthians, the apostle begins in this chapter to consider those which relate to the mode of conducting public worship. The first of these is the habit of women appearing in public without a veil. Dress is in a great degree conventional. A costume which is proper in one country, would be indecorous in another. The principle insisted upon in this paragraph is, that women should conform in matters of dress to all those usages which the public sentiment of the community in which they live demands. The veil in all eastern countries was, and to a great extent still is, the symbol of modesty and subjection. For a woman, therefore, in Corinth to discard the veil was to renounce her claim to modesty, and to refuse to recognize her subordination to her husband. It is on the assumption of this significancy in the use of the veil, that the apostle's whole argument in this paragraph is founded. He begins by praising the Corinthians for their obedience in general to his instructions, v. 2. He then reminds them of the divinely constituted subordination of the woman to the man, v. 3. Consequently it was disgraceful in the man to assume the symbol of subordination, and disgraceful in the woman to discard it, vs. 4. 5. If the veil were discarded as the symbol of subordination, it must also be discarded as the symbol of modesty. An unveiled woman, therefore, in Corinth proclaimed herself as not only insubordinate, but as immodest, v. 6. The man ought not to wear a veil because he represents the authority of God; but the woman is the glory of the man, v. 7. This subordination is proved by the very history of her creation. Eve was formed out of Adam, and made for him, vs. 8. 9. and, therefore, women should wear, especially in the religious assemblies where angels are present, the conventional symbol of their relation, v. 10. This subordination, however, of the woman is perfectly consistent with the essential equality and mutual dependence of the sexes. Neither is, or can be, without the other, vs. 11. 12. The apostle next appeals to their instinctive sense of propriety, which taught them that, as it is disgraceful in a man to appear in the costume of a woman, so it is disgraceful in a woman to appear in the costume of a man, vs. 13–15. Finally he appeals to authority; the custom which he censured was contrary to the universal practice of Christians, v. 16.

2. Now I praise you, brethren, that ye remember me in all things, and keep the ordinances, as I delivered (them) to you.

Now I praise you. The particle (δέ) rendered *now*, either simply indicates the transition to a new subject, or it is adversative. 'Though I exhort you to imitate me as though you were deficient, *yet* I praise you that you remember me.' The Corinthians, although backward in following the self-denial and conciliatory conduct of the apostle, were nevertheless in general mindful of the ordinances or rules which he had delivered to them. The word (παράδοσις) *tradition*, here rendered *ordinance*, is used not only for instructions orally transmitted from generation to generation, as in Matt. 15, 2. 3. 6, but for any instruction, whether relating to faith or practice, and whether delivered orally or in writing. 2 Thess. 2, 15. 3, 6. In reference to the rule of faith it is never used in the New Testament, except for the immediate instructions of inspired men. When used in the modern sense of the word *tradition*, it is always in reference to what is human and untrustworthy, Gal. 1, 14. Col. 2, 8, and frequently in the gospels of the traditions of the elders.

3. But I would have you know, that the head of every man is Christ; and the head of the woman (is) the man; and the head of Christ (is) God.

Though the apostle praised the Corinthians for their general obedience to his prescriptions, yet there were many things in which they were deserving of censure. Before mentioning the thing which he intended first to condemn, he states the principle on which that condemnation rested; so that, by assenting to the principle, they could not fail to assent to the conclusion to which it necessarily led. That principle is, that order and subordination pervade the whole universe, and is essential to its being. The head of the man is Christ; the head of the woman is the man; the head of Christ is God. If this concatenation be disturbed in any of its parts, ruin must be the result. The head is that on which the body is dependent, and to which it is subordinate. The obvious meaning of this passage is, that the woman is subordinate to the man, the man is subordinate to Christ, and Christ is subordinate to God. It is further evident, that this subordination is very different in its nature in the several cases mentioned. The subordination of the woman to the man is something entirely different from that of the man to Christ; and that again is at an infinite degree more complete than the subordination of Christ to God. And still further, as the subordination of the woman to the man is perfectly consistent with their identity as to nature, so is the subordination of Christ to God consistent with his being of the same nature with the Father. There is nothing, therefore, in this passage, at all inconsistent with the true and proper divinity of our blessed Lord. For a brief statement of the scriptural doctrine of the relation of Christ to God, see the comments on 3, 23. It need here be only further remarked, that the word Christ is the designation, not of the Logos or second person of the Trinity as such, nor of the human nature of Christ as such, but of the Theanthropos, the God-man. It is the incarnate Son of God, who, in the great work of redemption, is said to be subordinate to the Father, whose will he came into the world to do. *When Christ is said to be the head of every man*, the meaning is of every believer; because it is the relation of Christ to the church, and not to the human family, that is characteristically expressed by this term. He is the head of that body which is the church, Col. 1, 18. Eph. 1, 22. 23.

4. Every man praying or prophesying, having (his) head covered, dishonoureth his head.

Such being the order divinely established, (viz., that mentioned in v. 3,) both men and women should act in accordance with it; the man, by having the head uncovered, the woman by being veiled. As the apostle refers to their appearance in public assemblies, he says, *Every man praying or prophesying*, i. e. officiating in public worship. *Prophesying.* In the scriptural sense of the word, a prophet is one who speaks for another, as Aaron is called the prophet or *spokesman* of Moses. "Thou shalt speak unto him, and put words into his mouth, . . . and he shall be thy spokesman," Ex. 4, 15. 16; or, as he is called, 7, 1, *thy prophet.* The prophets of God, therefore, were his spokesmen, into whose mouth the Lord put the words which they were to utter to the people. To *prophesy*, in Scripture, is accordingly, to speak under divine inspiration; not merely to predict future events, but to deliver, as the organ of the Holy Ghost, the messages of God to men, whether in the form of doctrine, exhortation, consolation, or prediction. This public function, the apostle says, should not be exercised by a man with *his head covered;* literally, *having something on his head downward.* Among the Greeks, the priests officiated bareheaded; the Romans with the head veiled; the Jews (at least soon after the apostolic age) also wore the Tallis or covering for the head in their public services. It is not to be inferred from what is here said, that the Christian prophets (or inspired men) had introduced this custom into the church. The thing to be corrected was, women appearing in public assemblies unveiled. The apostle says, the veil is inconsistent with the position of the man, but is required by that of the women. Men are mentioned only for the sake of illustrating the principle.

Dishonoureth his head. It is doubtful whether we should read *his* or *his own* head, (αὐτοῦ or αὑτοῦ). This is a point the ancient manuscripts do not decide, as they are not furnished with the diacritical marks. It depends on the connection. It is also doubtful whether the apostle meant to say that he dishonoured Christ who is his head, or that he dishonoured himself. The latter, perhaps, is to be preferred, 1. Because, in the immediately preceding clause the word is used literally, 'If he cover his head, he dishonours his head.' 2. Because, in v. 5, the woman who goes unveiled is said to dishonour *her own* head, i. e. as what follows shows, *herself*, and not her husband. 3. It is more obviously true that a man who acts inconsistently with his station disgraces himself, than that he disgraces him who placed him in that station. A commanding military officer, who appears at the head of his troops in the dress of a common soldier, instead of his official dress, might more properly be said to dishonour himself than his sovereign. For a freeman to appear in the distinguishing dress of a slave, was a disgrace. So the apostle says, for a man to appear with the conventional sign of subjection on his head, disgraced himself. If the man be intended to represent the dominion of God, he must act accordingly, and not appear in the dress of a woman.

5. But every woman that prayeth or prophesieth with (her) head uncovered dishonoureth her head; for that is even all one as if she were shaven.

Praying and prophesying were the two principal exercises in the public worship of the early Christians. The latter term, as above stated, included all forms of address dictated by the Holy Spirit. It was Paul's manner to attend to one thing at a time. He is here speaking of the propriety of women speaking in public unveiled, and therefore he says nothing about the propriety of their speaking in public in itself. When that subject comes up, he expresses his judgment in the clearest terms, 14, 34. In here disapproving of the one, says Calvin, he does not approve of the other.

The veils worn by Grecian women were of different kinds. One, and perhaps the most common, was the *peplum*, or mantle, which in public was thrown over the head, and enveloped the whole person. The other was more in the fashion of the common eastern veil which covered the face, with the exception of the eyes. In one form or other, the custom was universal for all respectable women to appear veiled in public.—The apostle therefore says, that a woman who speaks in public with her *head uncovered, dishonoureth her head.* Here ἑαυτῆς is used, *her own* head; not her husband, but herself. This is plain, not only from the force of the words, but from the next clause, *for that is even all one as if she were shaven.* This is the reason why she disgraces herself. She puts herself in the same class with women whose hair has been cut off. Cutting off the hair, which is the principal natural ornament of women, was either a sign of grief, Deut. 21, 12, or a disgraceful punishment. The literal translation of this clause is: *she is one and the same thing with one who is shaven.* She assumes the characteristic mark of a disreputable woman.

6. For if the woman be not covered, let her also be shorn: but if it be a shame for a woman to be shorn or shaven, let her be covered.

That is, let her act consistently. If she wishes to be regarded as a reputable woman, let her conform to the established usage. But if she have no regard to her reputation, let her act as other women of her class. She must conform either to the reputable or disreputable class of her sex, for a departure from the one is conforming to the other. These imperatives are not to be taken as commands, but rather as expressing what consistency would require. *Shorn* or *shaven*, the latter is the stronger term; it properly means to cut with a razor.

7. For a man indeed ought not to cover (his) head, forasmuch as he is the image and glory of God: but the woman is the glory of the man.

The woman, and the woman only, ought to be veiled; *for* the man ought not to cover his head. This does not mean, he is not bound to do it, but should not do it. The negative belongs not to ὀφείλει, but to κατακαλύπτεσθαι. The reason is that *he is the image and glory of God.* The only sense in which the man, in distinction from the woman, is the image of God, is that he represents the authority of God. He is invested with dominion. When, in Genesis 1, 26. 27, it is said God created man in his own image, the reference is as much to woman as to man; for it is immediately added, "male and female created he them." So far, therefore, as the image of God consists in knowledge, righteousness and holiness, Eve as truly, and as much as Adam, bore the likeness of her Maker. But in the dominion with which man was invested over the earth, Adam was the representative of God. He is the glory of God, because in him the divine majesty is specially manifested. *But the woman is the glory of the man.* That is, the woman is in this respect subordinate to the man. She is not designed to reflect the glory of God as a ruler. She is the glory of the man. She receives and reveals what there is of majesty in him. She always assumes his station; becomes a queen if he is a king, and manifests to others the wealth and honour which may belong to her husband.

8. 9. For the man is not of the woman; but the woman of the man. Neither was the man created for the woman; but the woman for the man.

The subordination of the woman to the man is here proved from two facts recorded in the history of their creation. First, the woman was formed out of the man, and derived her origin from him. He, and not she, was created first. Secondly, she was created on his account, and not he on hers. In this way does the New Testament constantly authenticate, not merely the moral and religious truths of the Old Testament, but its historical facts; and makes those facts the grounds or proofs of great moral principles. It is impossible, therefore, for any Christian who believes in the inspiration of the apostles to doubt the divine authority of the Old Testament Scriptures, or to confine the inspiration of the ancient writers to their doctrinal and preceptive statements. The whole Bible is the word of God.

10. For this cause ought the woman to have power on (her) head because of the angels.

There is scarcely a passage in the New Testament which has so much taxed the learning and ingenuity of commentators as this. After all that has been written, it remains just as obscure as ever. The meaning which it naturally suggests to the most superficial reader, is regarded by the most laborious critics as the only true one. By ἐξουσία, *power*, the apostle means the sign or symbol of authority; just as *Diodorus Sic.*, 1. 47, speaks of an image as "having three kingdoms on its head." The apostle had asserted and proved that the woman is subordinate to the man, and he had assumed as granted that the veil was the conventional symbol of the man's authority. The inference is that the woman ought to wear the ordinary symbol of the power of her husband. As it was proper in itself, and demanded by the common sense of propriety, that the woman should be veiled, it was specially proper in the worshipping assemblies, for there they were in the presence not merely of men but of angels. It was, therefore, not only out of deference to public sentiment, but from reverence to those higher intelligences that the woman should conform to all the rules of decorum. This is the common and only satisfactory interpretation of the passage. Of those who dissent from this view, some propose various conjectural emendations of the text; others vainly endeavour to prove that the word ἐξουσία may be made to mean a veil; others take the word literally. And as to the last clause, instead of taking the word *angels* in its ordinary sense, some say it here means the angels, or presiding officers, of the church; others, that it means messengers or spies from the heathen who came to observe the mode in which the Christians worshipped, and would report any thing they observed to their disadvantage. The great majority of commentators acquiesce in the interpretation stated above, which satisfies all the demands of the context.

11. Nevertheless, neither is the man without the woman, neither the woman without the man, in the Lord.

That is, although there is this subordination of the woman to the man, they are mutually dependent. The one cannot exist without the other. *In the Lord.* This does not mean that the one is not in the Lord to the exclusion of the other. The apostle is not here speaking of the spiritual equality of the sexes. In Galatians 3, 28 and elsewhere he abundantly teaches that in Christ Jesus there is neither male nor female; that the one is as fully a partaker of all the benefits of redemption as the other. And it is also true that he teaches that this equality of Jews and Greeks, bond and free, before God is perfectly consistent with the social inequalities existing in this world. But these truths, however important, and however they distinguish the Christian doctrine of the equality and dignity of woman from all other forms of religious doctrine on the subject, are foreign to this connection. The apostle's single object is to show the true nature and limitations of the subordination of the woman to the man. It is a real subordination, but it is consistent with their mutual dependence; the one is not without the other. And this mutual dependence is ἐν κυρίῳ, i. e. by divine appointment—according to the will of the Lord. These words are used here, as so frequently elsewhere, as an adverbial qualification, meaning *religiously*, *after a Christian manner*, or *divinely*, i. e. *by divine appointment.* The same idea is substantially expressed by those who explain the words in *the Lord* as tantamount to "in Christianity;" in the sense that it is a Christian doctrine that the man and the woman are thus mutually dependent.

12. For as the woman (is) of the man, even so (is) the man also by the woman; but all things of God.

The one is not without the other, *for* as the woman was originally formed out of the man, so the man is born of the woman. This is a proof, not of the admitted equality of the sexes in the kingdom of God, but of their mutual dependence in the kingdom of nature. It therefore confirms the interpretation given of the preceding verse. *But all things are of God;* these subordinate relations of one creature to another are merged, as it were, in the supreme causality of God. It matters little whether the man was of the woman or the woman of the man, as both alike are of God; just as he before said, it matters little whether a man were a Jew or Gentile, bond or free, since all are alike before God.

13. Judge in yourselves: is it comely that a woman pray unto God uncovered?

This is an appeal to their own sense of propriety. The apostle often recognizes the intuitive judgments of the mind as authoritative. Rom. 1, 32. 3, 8. The constitution of our nature being derived from God, the laws which he has impressed upon it, are as much a revelation from him as any other possible communication of his will. And to deny this, is to deny the possibility of all knowledge. *Is it comely* (πρέπον ἐστί), *is it becoming* or *decorous?*

14. 15. Doth not even nature itself teach you, that, if a man have long hair, it is a shame unto him? But if a woman have long hair, it is a glory to her: for (her) hair is given her for a covering.

Doth not nature itself. The word (φύσις), *nature*, sometimes means *essence* or *substance*, sometimes *the laws of nature* or *of our natural constitution;* sometimes, the instinctive feelings or judgments which are the effects of those laws. The form which these feelings assume is necessarily determined in a great measure by education and habit. The instinctive sense of propriety in an eastern maiden prompts her, when surprised by strangers, to cover her face. In an European it would not produce that effect. In writing, therefore, to eastern females, it would be correct to ask whether their native sense of propriety did not prompt them to cover their heads in public. The response would infallibly be in the affirmative. It is in this sense the word *nature* is commonly taken here. It may, however, mean the laws or course of nature. Nature gives the man short hair and the woman long hair; and therefore nature itself teaches that long hair is a disgrace to the one and an ornament to the other; for it is disgraceful in a man to be like a woman, and in a woman to be like a man. Wearing long hair was contrary to the custom both of the Hebrews and Greeks. The Nazarites, as a distinction, allowed their hair to grow. Num. 6, 8; see also Ezek. 44, 20. It was considered so much a mark of effeminacy for men to wear long hair, that it was not only ridiculed by Juvenal, but in after times seriously censured by church councils. To a woman, however, in all ages and countries, long hair has been considered an ornament. It is given to her, Paul says, as a *covering*, or as a natural veil; and it is a glory to her *because* it is a veil. The veil itself, therefore, must be becoming and decorous in a woman.

16. But if any man seem to be contentious, we have no such custom, neither the churches of God.

The arguments against the custom of women appearing in public unveiled having been presented, the apostle says, if any man, notwithstanding these arguments, is disposed to dispute the matter, or appears to be contentious, we have only further to say, *that we* (the apostles) *have no such custom, neither have the churches of God. To be contentious*, i. e. disposed to dispute for the sake of disputation. With such persons all argument is useless. Authority is the only end of controversy with such disturbers of the peace. The authority here adduced is that of the apostles and of the churches. The former was decisive, because the apostles were invested with authority not only to teach the gospel, but also to organize the church, and to decide every thing relating to Christian ordinances and worship. The authority of the churches, although not coercive, was yet great. No man is justified, except on clearly scriptural grounds, and from the necessity of obeying God rather than man, to depart from the established usages of the church in matters of public concern.

Calvin, and many of the best modern commentators, give a different view of this passage. They understand the apostle to say, that if any one seems to be disputatious, neither we nor the churches are accustomed to dispute. It is not our wont to waste words with those who wish merely to make contention. The only reason assigned for this interpretation, is Paul's saying *we have* no such custom; which they say cannot mean the custom of women going unveiled. But why not? The apostles and the churches constituted a whole—neither the one nor the other, neither the churches nor their infallible guides, sanctioned the usage in question. Besides, no other custom is mentioned in the context than the one which he has been discussing. "If any one appear contentious," is not a custom and suggests nothing to which the words *such a custom* can naturally refer.

Celebration of the Lord's Supper, vs. 17–34.

This section relates to the disorders connected with the celebration of the Lord's supper. These disorders were of a kind which, according to our method of celebrating that sacrament, seems almost unaccountable. It was, however, the early custom to connect the Lord's supper in the strict sense of the words with an ordinary meal. As this sacrament was instituted by our Lord at the close of the Paschal supper, so it appears to have been customary at the beginning for the Christians to assemble for a common meal and to connect with it the commemoration of the Redeemer's death. Intimations of this usage may be found in such passages as Acts 2, 42. "They continued steadfastly in the apostle's doctrine and fellowship, and in breaking of bread, and in prayer." In v. 46 it is said, this breaking of bread was from house to house. In Acts 20, 7, it is said, "The disciples came together on the first day of the week to break bread," which, from the narrative which follows, appears to have been an ordinary meal. Whatever may be thought of these passages, it is clear from the paragraph before us that at Corinth at least, the sacrament of the Lord's supper was connected with a regular meal. This may have arisen, not so much from the original institution of the Eucharist in connection with the Paschal supper, as from the sacred festivals both of the Jews and Greeks. Both classes had been accustomed to unite with their sacrifices a feast of a more or less public character. It is also evident that, agreeably to a familiar Grecian custom, the persons assembled brought their own provisions, which being placed on the table formed a common stock. The rich brought plentifully, the poor brought little or nothing. It was, however, essential to the very idea of a Christian feast, that it should be a communion; that all the guests at the table of their common Lord should be on the terms of equality. Instead of this fraternal union, there were divisions among the Corinthians even at the Lord's table. The rich eating by themselves the provisions which they had brought, and leaving their poorer brethren mortified and hungry. It is to the correction of these disorders that the concluding portion of this chapter is devoted.

It was no matter of praise that the assemblies of the Corinthians made them worse rather than better, v. 17. The prominent evil was, that there were schisms even in their most sacred meetings; an evil necessary in the state in which they were, and which God permitted in order that the good might be made manifest, vs. 18. 19. The evil to which he referred was not merely that they had degraded the Lord's supper into an ordinary meal, but that in that meal they were divided into parties, some eating and drinking to excess, and others left without any thing, vs. 20. 21. This was not only making the Lord's supper a meal for satisfying hunger—contrary to its original design, but a cruel perversion of a feast of love into a means of humiliating and wounding their poorer brethren, v. 22. In order to show how inconsistent their conduct was with the nature of the service in which they professed to engage, the apostle recounts the original institution of the Lord's supper, vs. 23–25. From this account it follows, first, that the Lord's supper was designed not as an ordinary meal, but as a commemoration of the death of Christ; secondly, that to participate in this ordinance in an unworthy manner, was an offence against his body and blood, the symbols of which were so irreverently treated; thirdly, that no one ought to approach the Lord's table without self-examination, in order that with due preparation and with a proper understanding of the ordinance, he may receive the bread and wine as the symbols of Christ's body and blood, vs. 26–29. In this way they would escape the judgments which the Lord had brought upon them on account of their profanation of his table, vs. 30–32. In conclusion, he exhorts them to use their houses for their ordinary meals, and to make the Lord's supper a real communion, vs. 33. 34.

17. Now in this that I declare (unto you) I praise (you) not, that ye come together not for the better, but for the worse.

In v. 2 he said, *I praise you.* His praise was consistent with grave disapprobation of many things in their condition as a church. He did not praise them for the manner in which they conducted their public worship. Their assemblies were disgraced not only by women appearing unveiled, contrary to the established rules of decorum, but also by the unfraternal and irreverent manner of celebrating the Lord's supper—and also by the disorderly manner in which they used their spiritual gifts. These evils he takes up in their order. Having dispatched the first, he comes now to the second.

*Now in this that I declare unto you.** The Greek is not *in this*, but *this.* The passage may be rendered, *Declaring this I do not applaud.* To this, however, it is objected that

* The common Text here reads παραγγέλλων οὐκ ἐπαινῶ. Lachmann and Tischendorf read παραγγέλλω οὐκ ἐπαινῶν on the authority of the Mss. A. C. F. G. and others of later date, and the Syriac, Vulgate, and Ethiopic versions. The common reading is preferred by the majority of editors.

παραγγέλλειν in the New Testament never means *to declare*, but always *to command.* Hence, the better translation is, *Commanding* or *enjoining this I do not applaud.* It is doubtful whether *this* refers to what precedes or to what follows. If the former, then the sense is, 'While I command what precedes respecting women appearing veiled, I do not praise you, that,' &c. If the latter, the meaning is, 'Commanding what follows, I do not praise,' &c. *That ye come together not for the better, but for the worse.* That is, your public assemblies are so conducted that evil rather than good results. The censure is general, embracing all the grounds of complaint which are specified in this and the following chapters.

18. For first of all, when ye come together in the church, I hear that there be divisions among you; and I partly believe it.

For first of all, or, *For in the first place.* Paul often begins an enumeration which he does not follow out. There is nothing to answer to these words in what follows. According to one view the first censure is directed against the divisions, and the second against their mode of celebrating the Lord's supper. But the only divisions which he here refers to are those connected with their public worship, and especially with the celebration of the sacrament. Besides, the subject of divisions was treated in the beginning of the epistle. He is here speaking of their assemblies. The second ground of censure is to be found in the following chapter. *When ye come together in the church.* The word (ἐκκλησία) *church* never means in the New Testament, a building. The meaning is, when ye come together in convocation, or assemble as a church. *I hear that there be divisions among you.* Literally, *schisms.* For the meaning of that word, see 1, 10. The nature of these schisms is described in what follows. They were *cliques*, not sects, but parties, separated from each other by alienation of feeling. It is evident that the rich formed one of these parties, as distinguished from the poor. And probably there were many other grounds of division. The Jewish converts separated from the Gentiles; those having one gift exalted themselves over those having another. It is not outward separation, but inward alienation, which is here complained of. *And I partly believe it.* Paul intimates that he was loath to believe all he had heard to their disadvantage in this matter; but he was forced to believe enough to excite his serious disapprobation.

19. For there must be also heresies among you, that they which are approved may be made manifest among you.

This is the reason why he believed what he had heard. He knew that such things must happen, and that God had a wise purpose in permitting them; comp. Matt. 18, 7, "It must needs be that offences come." Evil as well as good is included in the divine purpose. It is purposed not as evil, but for the sake of the good which infinite wisdom evolves from it. *Also heresies.* This does not mean heresies in addition to schisms, as something different from them. But heresies as well as other evils. 'I hear there are divisions (σχίσματα) among you, and I believe it, for such divisions (αἱρέσεις) must occur.' What in the one verse are called *schisms*, in the next are called *heresies;* both words having the general sense of divisions. The nature of these divisions is to be determined by the context. The word (αἵρεσις) *heresy* means literally *an act of choice*, then a chosen way of life, a sect or party; not always in a bad sense, but in the sense of schools; as, "the heresies of philosophers" means "the schools or different classes of philosophers." So in the New Testament it is repeatedly used of "the *sect* of the Pharisees," or "of the Sadducees," Acts 15, 5. 5, 17. Here and in Gal. 5, 20 it means *dissension.* The ecclesiastical sense of the word *heresy*, is, the choice of an opinion different from that of the church, or a doctrine contrary to Scripture. There is nothing to favour the assumption that such is its meaning here.

That they which are approved may be made manifest. This is the end which God has in view in permitting the occurrence of such divisions. It is, *that they which are approved* (οἱ δόκιμοι), *the tried*, those who have stood the test, and are worthy of approbation. The opposite class are called (ἀδόκιμοι) *reprobate.* By the prevalence of disorders and other evils in the church, God puts his people to the test. They are tried as gold in the furnace, and their genuineness is made to appear. It is a great consolation to know that dissensions, whether in the church or in the state, are not fortuitous, but are ordered by the providence of God, and are designed, as storms, for the purpose of purification.

20. When ye come together therefore into one place, (this) is not to eat the Lord's supper.

Ye coming together then into one place. Verse 19 is an interruption. The connection with v. 18 is resumed by the particle (οὖν) *then.* When you assemble *it is not to eat the Lord's supper.* This is not the real, though it is your professed purpose. 'You come together for a common, and that too, a disorderly, unbrotherly meal.' The words, however, admit of two other interpretations. We may supply, as our translators have done, the word *this.* 'This is not to eat the Lord's supper; your meal does not deserve that sacred character.' Or, 'Ye cannot eat the Lord's supper.' The substantive verb (ἔστι) followed by an infinitive often means *can;* οὐκ ἔστιν εἰπεῖν, *one cannot say;* οὐκ ἔστι φαγεῖν, *one cannot eat.* 'Coming together as you do it is impossible to celebrate the Lord's supper.' This gives a very pertinent sense. *The Lord's supper* is the supper instituted by the Lord, one to which he invites the guests, and which is celebrated in commemoration of his death. That was a very different service from the Agapae, or love feasts, as they were afterwards called, and which, on account of the disorders attending them, were subsequently prohibited by the Council of Carthage. These Agapae were feasts to which each one brought his contributions, during and after which (the bread *during,* and the cup *after*) the consecrated elements were distributed. See *Augusti's* Antiquities of the Christian Church, I. p. 299; and *Pool's* Synopsis on Matt. 26, 26. *Coleman's* Ancient Christianity, p. 443.

21. For in eating every one taketh before (other) his own supper: and one is hungry, and another is drunken.

For, i. e. the reason why the Corinthian suppers were not the Lord's supper, is (so far as here stated) that there was no communion, or eating together. They were not all partakers of one bread, 10, 17. They did not wait for each other. Comp. v. 33. On the contrary, each one took beforehand, i. e. before others could join with him, *his own supper,* i. e. that which he had brought. The consequence was, that *one was hungry;* the poor had nothing; while another *was drunk.* Such is the meaning of the word. Whether the apostle intended to say that any of the Corinthians actually became intoxicated at the table which they called the table of the Lord, or whether he meant simply to say, that while one had more, another had less, than enough, it is not easy to decide. As they seem to have accommodated their service to the sacrificial feasts to which they had, while yet heathens, been accustomed, it is the less improbable that in some cases they were guilty of actual excess. "It is wonderful, and well nigh portentous," says Calvin, "that Satan could have accomplished so much in so short a time. We may learn from this example, what is the worth of mere antiquity; that is, what authority is due to custom unsustained by the word of God. . . . Yet this is the firmest foundation of Popery: it is ancient; it was done of old, therefore it has divine authority!" If, within twenty years of its institution, the Corinthians turned the Lord's supper into a disorderly feast, although the apostles were then alive, we need not wonder at the speedy corruption of the church after their death.

22. What! have ye not houses to eat and to drink in? or despise ye the church of God, and shame them which have not? What shall I say to you? shall I praise you in this? I praise (you) not.

The two grounds on which the apostle condemned this conduct of the Corinthians were, first, that it was a perversion of the Lord's supper; and secondly, that it was disrespectful and mortifying to their poorer brethren. It was a perversion of the Lord's supper, because it made it an ordinary meal designed to satisfy hunger. For that purpose they had their own houses. The church comes together to worship God and to celebrate his ordinances, not for the purpose of eating and drinking. It is important that the church, as the church, should confine itself to its own appropriate work, and not as such undertake to do what its members, as citizens or members of families, may appropriately do. The church does not come together to do what can better be done at home. *Or despise ye the church of God?* This was the second ground of condemnation. Their conduct evinced contempt of their brethren. They treated them as unfit to eat with them. Yet the poor were constituent members of the church of God. They were his people; those whom he had chosen, whom he had made kings and priests unto himself. These persons, thus highly honoured of God, the richer Corinthians treated with contempt; and that too at the Lord's table, where all external distinctions are done away, and the master is not a hair's breadth above his slave. *And shame those who have not. To shame*, i. e. to mortify and humble, by rendering conscious of inferiority. *Those who have not* may mean, either those who have not houses to eat or drink in, or simply *the poor*. Those who have, are the rich; those who have not, are the poor. The latter interpretation is not only consistent with the Greek idiom, but gives a better sense. Even the poorer members of the church did not, and ought not, come to the Lord's table for the sake of food. Much as Paul was disposed to praise the Corinthians, in this matter he could not praise them.

23. For I have received of the Lord that which also I delivered unto you, That the Lord Jesus, the (same) night in which he was betrayed, took bread:

'I cannot praise you, *for* your manner of celebrating the Lord's supper is utterly inconsistent with its original institution.' They were the more inexcusable in departing from the original mode of celebrating this ordinance, first, because the account of its original institution had been received by Paul from the Lord himself; and secondly, because he had delivered it to them. Their sin was therefore one of irreverent disobedience, without the excuse of ignorance. *For I have received of the Lord.* Paul asserts that he received from the Lord the account here given. The whole context shows that he intends to claim for this narrative the direct authority of the Lord himself. As with regard to his doctrines generally, so with regard to the institution and design of this ordinance, he disclaims all indebtedness to tradition or to the instructions of men, and asserts the fact of a direct revelation to himself. Of the gospel he says, "I neither received it of man, neither was I taught it, but by the revelation of Jesus Christ," Gal. 1, 12. To this interpretation, however, it is objected, 1. That he uses the preposition ἀπό, which properly expresses a mediate derivation (i. e. through the instrumentality of others), and not παρά, which would imply a direct communication. This objection supposes a refinement in the use of the Greek particles, which is not consistent with the character of the Greek of the New Testament. The Apostle John says: "This is the message which we have heard of him (ἀπ' αὐτοῦ)," 1 John 1, 5, which certainly does not refer to an indirect communication received through others. In this place ἀπὸ τοῦ κυρίου, *from the Lord*, is evidently opposed to ἀπ' ἀνθρώπων, *from men*. He received his knowledge from the Lord, and not from men. Comp. Gal. 1, 12. So in Gal. 1, 1, he says he was an apostle *not by men* (οὐκ ἀπ' ἀνθρώπων), but *by Jesus Christ* (διὰ Ἰησοῦ Χριστοῦ). Must it be inferred from this latter expression that Christ was only the medium of Paul's call to the apostleship, because διά expresses the instrumental cause? This would be as reasonable as to infer from the use of ἀπό in the text, that the knowledge of Paul was derived indirectly from the Lord. The apostle however says in Gal. 1, 1, that he received his apostleship, not only *through Jesus Christ*, but also *through God the Father*; must this also mean *through the instrumentality* of God? is God the Father a mere instrument? No writer uses language with such strict grammatical accuracy as this objection supposes; much less did Jews writing Greek. It is of course important to adhere as far as possible to the exact meaning of the words; but to sacrifice the sense and obvious intent of the writer to such niceties is unreasonable. The use of ἀπό, in this case, probably arose from the desire to avoid the triple repetition of παρά; παρέλαβον, παρά, παρέδωκα. 2. It is objected that, as the Lord's supper had been celebrated without interruption from the time of its institution, the facts concerning it must have been universally known, and therefore needed no direct revelation. The same objection might be made to a special revelation of the gospel to Paul. Why might he not have been allowed to learn it from the other apostles? Besides, Paul, as he shows in the first and second chapters of his epistle to the Galatians, had no communication with the other apostles for three years after his conversion. 3. It is objected that ideas and truths may be communicated by visions and inward influences, but not historical facts. Then a large part of the prophecies of the Old Testament must be fabulous. The evidence is so strong from the context, that Paul claims independent authority for what he here says, that many who bow to the force of the Greek preposition, say that the account received by Paul from Christ through others, was authenticated to him by an inward revelation. But this is not what he says. He says he received it from Christ, which, in the connection, can only mean that he received it directly from Christ; for his object is to give authority to his account of the ordinance. It was not only of importance for the Corinthians, but for the whole church, to be assured that this account of the Lord's supper, was communicated immediately by Christ to the apostle. It shows the importance which our Lord attributes to this ordinance.

The account which Paul received was, *That the same night in which he was betrayed*, i. e. while he was being betrayed—while the traitorous scheme was in progress. Under these affecting circumstances the ordinance was instituted. This fact, which Christ saw fit to reveal to Paul, must be of permanent interest to his people. It is not a matter of indifference, that this sacred rite was instituted on the last night of our Redeemer's life, and when he knew what the morrow was to bring forth. This fact gives a peculiar solemnity and interest to the institution. Romanists, in answer to the objections made by Protestants to the mass, that it is a departure from the original mode of celebrating the Lord's supper, say that if the example of Christ be obligatory, we should celebrate the ordinance at night, after a meal, and at a table covered with provisions, &c. Protestants, however, do not hold that the church in all ages is bound to do whatever Christ and the apostles did, but only what they designed should be afterwards done. It is not apostolic example which is obligatory, but apostolic precept, whether expressed in words or in examples declared or evinced to be preceptive. The example of Christ in celebrating the Lord's supper is binding as to every thing which enters into the nature and significancy of the institution; for those are the very things which we are commanded to do. They constitute the ordinance.

Took bread. Matt. 26, 26, it is said, "as they were eating," i. e. during the repast, "Jesus took bread," that is, he took of the bread lying on the table; and as it was at the time of the Passover, there is no doubt that the bread used was unleavened. It was the thin Passover bread of the Jews, But as no part of the significancy of the rite depends on the kind of bread used, as there is no precept on the subject, and as the apostles subsequently in the celebration of the ordinance used ordinary bread, it is evidently a matter of indifference what kind of bread is used. It was however for a long time a subject of bitter controversy. At first the Latins and Greeks used leavened bread; when the Latins introduced the unleavened wafer from superstitious fear of any of the fragments being dropped, the Greeks retained the use of fermented bread, and accused the Latins of Judaizing. Romanists and Lutherans use unleavened wafers; Protestants generally ordinary bread.

24. And when he had given thanks, he brake (it), and said, Take, eat; this is my body, which is broken for you: this do in remembrance of me.

Having given thanks. In Matt. 26, 26, and Mark 14, 22, it is, "Having blessed *it*." In Luke 22, 19, it is as here. The two expressions mean the same thing. Both express the act of consecration, by a grateful acknowledgment of God's mercy and invocation of his blessing. See the remarks on 10, 16. *He brake* it. This circumstance is included in all the accounts; in those of Matthew, Mark, and Luke, as well as in Paul's. This is one of the significant parts of the service, and ought not to be omitted as is done by Romanists, by the Greek church and by Lutherans. *And said.* The words uttered by our blessed Lord at this moment are differently reported by the different evangelists. In Matt. 26, 26, it is, "Take, eat." In Mark 14, 22, the latter word (according to the best authorities) is omitted. In Luke 22, 19, both are omitted. Here, although both are found in the common text, yet, as they are wanting in the oldest MSS., they should probably be omitted; so that Paul's account agrees as to this point with that of Luke. The proper inference from this diversity is, that the words were uttered by our Lord; but as the ideas which they express were sufficiently indicated by the gesture of reaching the bread to his disciples, they were omitted by some of the narrators as unnecessary. The idea, whether expressed by words or gesture, is however of importance. The bread was to be taken and eaten.—There must be a distribution of the elements to those participating in the service. Otherwise it is not a communion. This distribution is omitted by Romanists in the ordinary celebration of the Mass. The priest alone eats the consecrated wafer. The next words, *this is my body*, are found in all the accounts. Probably the history of the world does not furnish a parallel to the controversies occasioned by these simple words. The ordinary and natural interpretation of them is, that the pronoun *this* refers to the bread. 'This bread which I hold in my hand, and which I give to you, is my body.' That is, is the symbol of my body; precisely as we say of a statue, it is the person which it represents; or as the Scriptures say that the sign is the thing of which it is the symbol, Ez. 5, 4. 5. Gal. 4, 24; or as our Saviour says, I am the vine, ye are the branches. I am the door; or as in the preceding chapter it was said, "that rock was Christ;" or as in John 1, 32, the dove is said to be the Holy Ghost; or as baptism is said to be regeneration. This is a usage so familiar to all languages that no one disputes that the words in question will bear this interpretation. That they must have this meaning, would seem to be plain, 1. From the impossibility of the bread in Christ's hand being his literal body then seated at the table; and the wine the blood then flowing in his veins. 2. From the still more obvious impossibility of taking the words "this cup is the New Testament" in a literal sense. In Matt. 26, 28 it is said, "this (cup) is my blood." But Romanists do not hold to a transubstantiation of the *cup*, but only of the wine. But if the words are to be taken literally, they necessitated the belief of the one as well as of the other. 3. From the utter subversion of all the rules of evidence and laws of belief necessarily involved in the assumption that the bread in the Lord's supper is literally the crucified body of Christ. 4. From the infidelity on the one hand, and the superstitious idolatry on the other, which are the unavoidable consequences of calling upon men to believe so glaring a contradiction. It is only by denying all distinction between matter and spirit, and confounding all our ideas of substance and qualities, that we can believe that wine is blood, or bread flesh.

The Romish interpretation of these words is, that the bread is the body of Christ, because its whole substance is changed into the substance of his body. The Lutherans say, It is his body, because his body is locally present in and with the bread. Calvin says, It is his body in the same sense that the dove (John 1, 32) was the Holy Ghost. The Holy Ghost appeared under the form of a dove, which was the pledge of his presence. So the bread is the symbol of Christ's body, because with the one we receive the other. What is received, however, and what Calvin calls Christ's body, and sometimes the substance of his body, is not the body itself, which, he admits, is in heaven only, but a life-giving power (vim vivificam) which flows to us from the glorified body of our Lord. The only presence of Christ's body in the sacrament admitted by

Calvin was this presence of power.* The Reformed churches teach that the bread is called the body of Christ in the same sense that the cup is called the new covenant. He who in faith receives the cup, receives the covenant of which it was the pledge; and he who receives in faith the bread receives the benefits of Christ's body as broken for sin. The one is the symbol and pledge of the other.

Broken for you. In Luke it is, *given for you.* In Matthew and Mark these words are omitted. In some manuscripts † the word (κλώμενον), *broken*, is wanting in this passage; so that it would read simply *for you*, leaving the participle to be supplied from the context. *Broken* or *given* for you means slain, or given unto death for you. The sacrificial character of the death of Christ enters essentially into the nature of this ordinance. It is the commemoration of his death, not as a teacher, or a benefactor, but as a sacrifice; so that if this idea be kept out of view the sacrament loses all its significance and power.

This do in remembrance of me. These words are not found in Matthew or Mark. They occur in Luke 22, 19, as they do here. *This* do, i. e. 'Do what I have just done; take bread, consecrate it, break it, distribute and eat it. *In remembrance of me*, i. e. that I may be remembered as he who died for your sins. This is the specific, definite object of the Lord's Supper, to which all other ends must be subordinate, because this alone is stated in the words of institution. It is of course involved in this, that we profess faith in him as the sacrifice for our sins; that we receive him as such; that we acknowledge the obligations which rest upon us as those who have been redeemed by his blood; and that we recognize ourselves as constituent members of his church and all believers as our brethren. We are thus, as taught in the preceding chapter, brought into a real communion with Christ and with all his people by the believing participation of this ordinance.

25. After the same manner also (he took) the cup, when he had supped, saying, This cup is the new testa-

* Hæc communicatio corporis Christi, quam nobis in coena exhiberi dico, nec localem praesentiam, nec Christi descensum, nec infinitam extensionem, nec aliud quicquam tale flagitat. . . . Locum non mutat, ut nobis adsit, sed e coelo praesentem in nos carnis suae virtutem transmittat.

† The MSS. A. B. C. omit κλώμενον, Griesbach questioned its genuineness, Lachmann and Tischendorf reject it.

ment in my blood: this do ye, as oft as ye drink (it), in remembrance of me.

This second part of the service is introduced by Luke with the same words which are here used, though our translators there render them *Likewise also the cup, after supper.* This latter version is the literal and simple rendering of the original. In Matthew and Mark it is said, "Having taken the cup, and having given thanks." This explains what Paul and Luke mean by *likewise*, or *after the same manner.* They intend to say that Christ did with the cup what he had done with the bread, i. e. he took it, and pronounced over it the eucharistical benediction, i. e. a blessing connected with thanksgiving. In this particular there is a slight departure in our mode of administering this ordinance, from the example of Christ. With us there is generally but one eucharistical blessing at the introduction of the service, having reference both to the bread and to the cup. Whereas it seems that our Lord blessed the bread, and having broken, distributed it to his disciples; and then took the cup, and having blessed it, gave it to them to drink. *After supper*, i. e. after the conclusion of the paschal supper.

Saying, This cup is the New Testament in my blood. The same words occur in Luke 22, 20. In Matthew and Mark the corresponding expression is, "This is my blood of the New Testament." The sense must be the same. "The blood of the covenant" means here, as in Ex. 24, 8, the blood by which the covenant was ratified and its blessings secured. The passage referred to in Exodus shows the manner in which covenants were anciently ratified in the East. A victim was slain and the blood sprinkled upon the contracting parties, by which they were solemnly bound to their mutual engagements. The word διαθήκη so constantly, after the Vulgate, rendered Testament by our translators, always in the New Testament means a covenant, unless Heb. 9, 16 be an exception. Here that sense is required by the context, as a covenant and not a testament was ratified by blood. This covenant is called *new* in reference to the Mosaic covenant. The latter was ratified by the blood of animals; the new, by the blood of the eternal Son of God; the one in itself could secure only temporal benefits and the remission of ceremonial offences; the other secures eternal redemption, and the remission of sin in the sight of God. As the Hebrews entered into covenant with God when the blood of the heifer was sprinkled upon them, and thereby bound themselves to be obedient to the Mosaic institutions, and as God thereby graciously bound himself to confer upon them all its promised blessings on condition of that obedience; so, in the Lord's supper, those who receive the cup profess to embrace the covenant of grace, and bind themselves to obedience to the gospel; and God binds himself to confer on them all the benefits of redemption. In receiving the cup, therefore, they receive the pledge of their salvation. The death of Christ, which is so often compared to a sin-offering, is here, as well as in the Epistle to the Hebrews, compared to a federal sacrifice. The two, however, do not differ. The death of Christ is the latter only in virtue of its being the former. It ratifies the covenant of grace and secures its benefits, only because it was a propitiation, i. e. because it was a satisfaction to divine justice, as is so clearly taught in Rom. 3, 25. 26. Every time, therefore, the consecrated wine touches the believer's lips, he receives anew the application of the blood of Christ for the remission of his sins and his reconciliation with God. If the Bible says we are sprinkled with the blood of Jesus, 1 Peter 1, 2, why may we not be said to receive his blood? If the former expression means the application of the benefits of his sacrificial death, why may not the latter mean the reception of those benefits? Here, as elsewhere, the difficulty is the want of faith. He who by faith appropriates a divine promise recorded in the word, receives the blessing promised; and he who in the exercise of faith receives the sacramental cup receives the benefits of the covenant of which that cup is the symbol and the pledge. But what is faith? or rather, what is it that we are required to believe, in order to experience all this? 1. We must believe that Jesus is the Son of God, and that he loved us and gave himself for us. 2. That his blood cleanses from all sin. 3. That in the sacrament he offers us, with the symbols of his broken body and his shed blood, the benefits of his death; and that he will certainly convey those benefits to all those who hold out even a trembling hand to receive them.

In Luke, after the words *in my blood*, it is added, *which is shed for you*. In Mark the explanation is, *which is shed for many;* and in Matthew, still more fully, *which is shed for many for the remission of sins.* These are different forms of expressing the sacrificial character of the death of Christ. Though it was the blood of the covenant, yet it was at the same time *shed for many*, not merely for their benefit in the general, but for the specific object of securing *the remission of sins.* It was, therefore, truly a sin-offering. Thus does Scripture explain Scripture. What is said concisely in one place is more fully and clearly stated in another.

This do, as oft as ye drink it, in remembrance of me. These words do not occur in Luke. In Matthew the words are, *Drink ye all of it.* Mark says, *They all drank of it.* In each account the fact is made plain that the cup was distributed to all at the table and that all drank of it. The words *This do* are to be understood here as in v. 25, 'Do what I have done, i. e. bless the cup and distribute it among yourselves.' *As oft as ye drink of it.* This does not mean that every time Christians drank wine together they should do it in commemoration of Christ's death; but, 'as often as this ordinance is celebrated, do what I have done, to commemorate my death.' The Lord's Supper is a commemoration of Christ's death, not only because it was designed for that purpose, but also because the bread and wine are the significant symbols of his broken body and shed blood. In this ordinance therefore Christ is set forth as a sacrifice which at once makes expiation for sin and ratifies the covenant of grace.

26. For as often as ye eat this bread, and drink this cup, ye do shew the Lord's death till he come.

What Paul had received of the Lord is recorded in the preceding verses. Here and in what follows we have his own inferences from the account which the Lord had given him. The first of those inferences is, that the Lord's supper is, and was designed to be, a proclamation of the death of Christ to continue until his second advent. Those who come to it, therefore, should come, not to satisfy hunger, nor for the gratification of social feelings, but for the definite purpose of bearing their testimony to the great fact of redemption, and to contribute their portion of influence to the preservation and propagation of the knowledge of that fact. *For* indicates the connection with what precedes. 'It is a commemoration of his death, *for* it is in its very nature a proclamation of that great fact.' And it was not a temporary institution, but one designed to continue until the consummation. As the Passover was a perpetual commemoration of the deliverance out of Egypt, and a prediction of the coming and death of the

Lamb of God, who was to bear the sins of the world; so the Lord's supper is at once the commemoration of the death of Christ and a pledge of his coming the second time without sin unto salvation.

27. Wherefore whosoever shall eat this bread, and drink (this) cup of the Lord, unworthily, shall be guilty of the body and blood of the Lord.

This is the second inference. *Wherefore*, i. e. so that, hence it follows. If the Lord's Supper be in its very nature a proclamation of the death of Christ. it follows that those who attend upon it as an ordinary meal, or in an irreverent manner, or for any other purpose than that for which it was appointed, are guilty of the body and blood of the Lord. That is, they contract guilt in reference to the body and blood of Christ. See James 2, 10. The man who tramples on the flag of his country, insults his country; and he who treats with indignity the representative of a sovereign, thereby offends the sovereign himself. In like manner, he who treats the symbols of Christ's body and blood irreverently is guilty of irreverence towards Christ. The idea that he is so evil that he would have joined in the crucifixion of the Lord; or that he makes himself a partaker of the guilt of his death, does not lie in the words. It is also obvious that this passage affords no ground for either the Romish or Lutheran view of the local presence of Christ's body in the sacrament, since an insult to the appointed symbol of his body, is an insult to his body itself. Neither does the passage countenance the doctrine held by both Romanists and Lutherans, that unbelievers receive the body and blood of Christ. If they do not receive them, it is asked, how can they be guilty in respect to them? By treating them, in their appointed symbols, irreverently. It is not necessary, therefore, in order to the guilt here spoken of, either that the body of Christ should be locally present, or that the unworthy receiver be a partaker of that body, which is received by faith alone. In our version it is, "whosoever shall eat this bread *and* drink this cup;" in the Greek it is (ἢ) *or*, not *and*. And this the sense requires. The irreverent use of either the bread or the cup in this ordinance involves the guilt of which the apostle here speaks; because the indignity extends to the whole service.

But what is it to eat and drink *unworthily?* It is not to

eat and drink with a consciousness of unworthiness, for such a sense of ill-desert is one of the conditions of acceptable communion. It is not the whole, but the consciously sick whom Christ came to heal. Nor is it to eat with doubt and misgiving of our being duly prepared to come to the Lord's table; for such doubts, although an evidence of a weak faith, indicate a better state of mind than indifference or false security. In the Larger Catechism of our Church, in answer to the question, whether one who doubts of his being in Christ, may come to the Lord's supper, it is said, "One who doubteth of his being in Christ, or of his due preparation to the sacrament of the Lord's supper, may have true interest in Christ, though he be not yet assured thereof; and in God's account hath it, if he be duly affected with the apprehension of the want of it, and unfeignedly desires to be found in Christ, and to depart from iniquity; in which case (because promises are made, and this sacrament is appointed, for the relief even of weak and doubting Christians) he is to bewail his unbelief, and labour to have his doubts resolved; and so doing, he may and ought to come to the Lord's supper, that he may be further strengthened." To eat or drink *unworthily* is in general to come to the Lord's table in a careless, irreverent spirit, without the intention or desire to commemorate the death of Christ as the sacrifice for our sins, and without the purpose of complying with the engagements which we thereby assume. The way in which the Corinthians ate unworthily was, that they treated the Lord's table as though it were their own; making no distinction between the Lord's supper and an ordinary meal; coming together to satisfy their hunger, and not to feed on the body and blood of Christ; and refusing to commune with their poorer brethren. This, though one, is not the only way in which men may eat and drink unworthily. All that is necessary to observe is, that the warning is directly against the careless and profane, and not against the timid and the doubting.

28. But let a man examine himself, and so let him eat of (that) bread, and drink of (that) cup.

This is the third inference from the account of the Lord's supper which Paul had received. It requires self-examination and preparation in order to being worthily received. If it be a commemoration of Christ's death; if we are therein "made partakers of his body and blood;" if we contract such guilt by eating and drinking unworthily; in other words, if such blessings attend the worthy receiving, and such guilt the unworthy receiving of this ordinance, it is evident that we should not approach it without due self-inspection and preparation. *Let a man examine himself.* In other words, let him ascertain whether he has correct views of the nature and design of the ordinance, and whether he has the proper state of mind. That is, whether he desires thankfully to commemorate the Lord's death, renewedly to partake of the benefits of that death as a sacrifice for his sins, publicly to accept the covenant of grace with all its promises and obligations, and to signify his fellowship with his brethren as joint members with himself of the body of Christ. *And so let him eat.* That is, after this self-examination, and, as is evidently implied, after having ascertained that he possesses the due preparation. It is not essential, however, to this preparation, as before remarked, that we should be assured of our good estate, but simply that we have the intelligent desire to do what Christ requires of us when we come to his table. If we come humbly seeking him, he will bid us welcome, and feed us with that bread whereof if a man eat, he shall never die.

29. For he that eateth and drinketh unworthily,* eateth and drinketh damnation to himself, not discerning the Lord's body.

This verse assigns the reason why self-examination in preparation for the Lord's supper is necessary. It is because he that eateth and drinketh unworthily (in the sense before explained), *eateth and drinketh judgment to himself.* That is, he incurs the manifestation of God's displeasure by the act of eating. The word *damnation*, used in our version, originally and properly means simply condemnation, and not hopeless and final perdition, which is its modern and popular sense. In the original the word is κρίμα without the article, and there-

* The word ἀναξίως, *unworthily*, is omitted by the MSS. A. C., and is rejected by Lachmann and Tischendorf. If discarded, the sense of the passage is either, 'The eater and drinker, i. e. he who eats and drinks at the Lord's table as at an ordinary meal, eats judgment to himself;' or, 'He that eats, not discerning the Lord's body, eats judgment to himself.' The common text has in its support the majority of ancient MSS., and is followed by most editors.

fore simply *judgment*, not *the* judgment. The meaning obviously is, that the unworthy eater contracts guilt; he exposes himself to the judgments of God. What kind of judgments the apostle had in his mind is plain from the next verse, where he refers to sickness and death.* This verse is only a repetition of the sentiment expressed in v. 27, where he who eats unworthily is said to contract guilt in reference to the body of the Lord. *Not discerning*, i. e. because he does not discern *the Lord's* body. The word διακρίνω, translated *to discern*, means *to separate*, then to cause to differ, as 4, 7; and also, judge of, either in the sense of discriminating one thing from another, or in the sense of estimating aright. This passage may therefore mean, not discriminating the Lord's body, i. e. making no difference between the bread in the sacrament and ordinary food; or, it may mean, not estimating it aright, not reverencing it as the appointed symbol of the body of the Lord. In either case the offence is the same. The ground of the condemnation incurred is, regarding and treating the elements in the Lord's supper as though there was nothing to distinguish them from ordinary bread and wine. Here, as before, it is the careless and profane who are warned. There is, therefore, nothing in these passages which should surround the Lord's table with gloom. We are not called unto the mount covered with clouds and darkness, from which issue the signs of wrath, but unto Mount Zion, to the abode of mercy and grace, where all is love—the dying love of him who never breaks the bruised reed.

30. For this cause many (are) weak and sickly among you, and many sleep.

For this cause, that is, because those who partake of the Lord's supper unworthily incur the judgment of God; *many are weak and sickly*. The distinction between these words made by commentators, is, that the former designates those whose strength decays as it were of itself, and the latter, those rendered *infirm* by sickness. The latter term is the stronger of the two. *And many sleep*, i. e. have already died. As there is nothing in the context to intimate that these terms

* BENGEL's remark on this clause is: κρίμα sine articulo judicium aliquod, morbum, mortemve corporis, ut qui Domini corpus non discernunt, corpore suo luant. Non dicit τὸ κατάκριμα, condemnationem.

are used figuratively of moral infirmities and spiritual declension, they should be taken in their literal sense. Paul knew that the prevailing sickness and frequent deaths among the Christians of Corinth were a judgment from God on account of the irreverent manner in which they had celebrated the Lord's supper.

31. For if we would judge ourselves, we should not be judged.

For, i. e. these afflictions are judgments from God, because of your sin in this matter; for, if *we judge ourselves*, that is, if we examine ourselves (see v. 28) and prepare ourselves for the Lord's table, *we should not be judged*, i. e. thus afflicted. It is because we do not sit in judgment on ourselves, that God judges us.

32. But when we are judged, we are chastened of the Lord, that we should not be condemned with the world.

These judgments were chastisements designed for the benefit of those who suffered, to bring them to repentance, that they might not be finally condemned with the world; that is, with unbelievers. The world often means mankind as distinguished from the church, or those chosen out of the world. "They are not of the world, even as I am not of the world," John 17, 16. What Paul says of the design of these judgments, proves that even the extreme irreverence with which he charges the Corinthians in reference to the Lord's supper, was not an unpardonable sin.

33. 34. Wherefore, my brethren, when ye come together to eat, tarry one for another. And if any man hunger, let him eat at home; that ye come not together unto condemnation. And the rest will I set in order when I come.

The two great evils connected with the observance of the Lord's supper at Corinth were, first, that it was not a communion, one took his supper before another, v. 21; and secondly, that they came to the Lord's table to satisfy their hunger. That is, they made it an ordinary meal. They thus sinned against their brethren, v. 22, and they sinned against Christ, v. 27. In the conclusion, therefore, of the whole discussion, he exhorts them to correct these evils; to wait for each other, and make it a joint service; and to satisfy their hunger at home, and come together only to commemorate the Lord's death. Mildly as this exhortation is expressed, it is enforced by the solemn warning already given, *that ye come not together to condemnation*, that is, so as to incur the displeasure of God. *The rest will I set in order when* (*whenever* ὡς ἄν) *I may come.* There were, it seems, other irregularities of less importance than those above mentioned, which the apostle leaves to be corrected until he should again visit Corinth. The epistles of Paul abound in evidence of the plenary authority exercised by the apostles over the churches. The word διατάσσω, *to set in order*, implies authoritative direction; see 7, 17. 16, 1. Matt. 11, 1. The apostles were rendered infallible, as the representatives of Christ, to teach his doctrines, to organize the church and determine its form of government, and to regulate its worship. And what they ordained has binding force on the church to this day. What Paul teaches in this chapter concerning the nature and mode of celebrating the Lord's supper, has determined the views and practice of evangelical Christians in every part of the world. It is not at all wonderful, considering that the festivals of the Jews, and especially the Passover, as well as the sacrificial feasts of the Gentiles, were social repasts, and especially considering that our Lord instituted this ordinance in connection with the Paschal supper, that the early Christians should have so generally combined it with a social meal; or that this custom should have continued so long in the church. Nor is it a matter of surprise, that the social element in this combined service should so often have prevailed over the religious one. That this was to a lamentable degree the case in Corinth, is evident from this chapter; and it is probable from Jude 12, that the evil was by no means confined to Corinth. That apostle, speaking of certain sensual persons, says, "These are spots in your feasts of charity, when they feast with you without fear." Hence the unspeakable importance of the instructions and directions given by St. Paul, which are specially designed to separate the Lord's supper as a religious rite from the social element with which it was combined. The apostle urges that neither the sacrament itself, nor any feast with which it might be connected, should be regarded as the occasion of satisfying hunger. The communion of saints and the commemoration of the death of Christ as a sacrifice for our sins, are the only legitimate objects which could be contemplated in the service. And by exhibiting the intimate fellowship with the Lord involved in the right use of this ordinance, and the dreadful consequences of unworthily participating, he has raised it to a purely religious service, and made it the highest act of worship. From one extreme the church gradually passed over to the opposite. From regarding it as it had been in Corinth, little more than an ordinary meal, it came to be regarded as an awful mystery, a sacrifice which the people were to witness, and in which they were to adore the Redeemer as locally present in his corporeal nature under the form of a wafer! So strong a hold had this unscriptural view taken of the mind of the church, that Luther found it impossible to emancipate himself from the belief of the local presence of Christ's real body in this sacrament. And even Calvin could not divest himself of the conviction, not only of its supernatural character, which all admit who regard it as a means of grace, but also of its being truly miraculous. It was only after a severe struggle that the Reformed church got back to the simple, yet sublime view of the ordinance presented by the apostle Paul. The danger has often since been that the church should go back to the Corinthian extreme, and look upon the Lord's supper as a simple commemoration, involving nothing supernatural either in its nature or effects. Our only safety is in adhering strictly to the teachings of the Scriptures. The apostle tells us, on the authority of a direct revelation from the Lord himself, that while the ordinance is designed as a memorial of Christ's death, it involves a participation of his body and blood, not of their material substance, but of their sacrificial efficacy, so that, "although the body and blood of Christ are not corporally or carnally present in, with, or under the bread and wine in the Lord's supper; and yet are spiritually present to the faith of the receiver, no less truly and really than the elements themselves are to their outward senses; so they that worthily communicate in the sacrament of the Lord's supper, do therein feed upon the body and blood of Christ, not after a corporal or carnal, but in a spiritual manner; yet truly and really, while by faith they receive and apply unto themselves Christ crucified and all the benefits of his death." *Larger Catechism.*

CHAPTER XII.

Of Spiritual Gifts, vs. 1–31.

THE ancient prophets had clearly predicted that the Messianic period should be attended by a remarkable effusion of the Holy Spirit. "And it shall come to pass in those days," it is said in the prophecies of Joel, "saith God, I will pour out of my Spirit upon all flesh; and your sons and your daughters shall prophesy, and your young men shall see visions, and your old men shall dream dreams." Our Lord, before his crucifixion, promised to send the Comforter, who is the Holy Ghost, to instruct and guide his church, John 14, &c. And after his resurrection he said to his disciples, "These signs shall follow them that believe. In my name shall they cast out devils; they shall speak with new tongues; they shall take up serpents; and if they drink any deadly thing it shall not hurt them; they shall lay hands on the sick and they shall recover," Mark 16, 17. 18. And immediately before his ascension he said to the disciples, "Ye shall be baptized with the Holy Ghost not many days hence," Acts 1, 5. Accordingly, on the day of Pentecost, these promises and prophecies were literally fulfilled. The peculiarity of the new dispensation consisted, in the first place, in the general diffusion of these gifts. They were not confined to any one class of the people, but extended to all classes; male and female, young and old; and secondly, in the wonderful diversity of these supernatural endowments. Under circumstances so extraordinary it was unavoidable that many disorders should arise. Some men would claim to be the organs of the Spirit, who were deluded or impostors; some would be dissatisfied with the gifts which they had received, and envy those whom they regarded as more highly favoured; others would be inflated, and make an ostentatious display of their extraordinary powers; and in the public assemblies it might be expected that the greatest confusion would arise from so many persons being desirous to exercise their gifts at the same time. To the correction of these evils, all of which had manifested themselves in the church of Corinth, the apostle devotes this and the two following chapters. It is impossible to read these chapters without being deeply impressed by the divine wisdom with which they are pervaded. After contrasting the condition of the Corinthians, as members of that body which was instinct with the life-giving Spirit of God, with their former condition as the senseless worshippers of dumb idols, he, First, lays down the criterion by which they might decide whether those who pretended to be the organs of the Spirit were really under his influence. How do they speak of Christ? Do they blaspheme, or do they worship him? If they openly and sincerely recognize Jesus as the Supreme Lord, then they are under the influence of the Holy Ghost, vs. 1–3. Secondly, these gifts, whether viewed as graces of the Spirit, or as forms of ministering to Christ, or the effects of God's power, that is, whether viewed in relation to the Spirit, to the Son, or to the Father, are but different manifestations of the Holy Ghost dwelling in his people, and are all intended for the edification of the church, vs. 4–7. Thirdly, he arranges them under three heads, 1. The word of wisdom and the word of knowledge. 2. Faith, the gift of healing, the power of working miracles, prophesying, and the discerning of spirits. 3. The gift of tongues and the interpretation of tongues, vs. 8–10. Fourthly, these gifts are not only all the fruits of the Spirit, but they are distributed according to his sovereign will, v. 11. Fifthly, there is therefore in this matter a striking analogy between the church and the human body. For, 1. As the body is one organic whole, because animated by one spirit, so the church is one because of the indwelling of the Holy Ghost as the principle of its life. 2. As the unity of life in the body is manifested in a diversity of organs and members; so the indwelling of the Spirit in the church is manifested by a diversity of gifts and offices. 3. As the very idea of the body as an organization supposes this diversity in unity, the same is true in regard to the church. 4. As in the human body the members are mutually dependent, and no one exists for itself alone but for the body as a whole, so also in the church there is the same dependence of its members on each other, and their various gifts are not designed for the exclusive benefit of those who exercise them, but for the edification of the whole church. 5. As in the body the position and function of each member are determined not by itself, but by God, so also these spiritual gifts are distributed according to the good pleasure of their author. 6. In the body the least attractive parts are those which are indispensable to its existence, and so in the church it is not the most attractive gifts which are the most useful. Sixthly, the apostle draws from this analogy the following inferences. 1. Every one should be contented with the gift which he has received of the Lord, just as the hand and foot are contented with their position and office in the body. 2. There should be no exaltation of one member of the church over others, on the ground of the supposed superiority of his gifts. 3. There should, and must be mutual sympathy between the members of the church, as there is between the members of the body. One cannot suffer without all the others suffering with it. No one lives, or acts, or feels for itself alone, but each in all the rest, vs. 12–27. In conclusion the apostle shows that what he had said with regard to these spiritual gifts, applies in all its force to the various offices of the church, which are the organs through which the gifts of the Spirit are exercised, vs. 28–31.

1. Now concerning spiritual (gifts),. brethren, I would not have you ignorant.

Instead of beginning with, *in the second place*, in continuance of the enumeration begun in 11, 17, he passes to the second ground of censure, by the simple *now* (δέ) as the particle of transition. The misuse of the spiritual gifts, especially of the gift of tongues, was the next topic of rebuke. *Concerning spiritual*, whether *men* or *gifts*, depends on the context, as the word may be either masculine or neuter. The latter is the more natural and common explanation, because the gifts rather than the persons are the subject of discussion; and because in v. 31, and 14, 1, the neuter form is used. *I would not have you ignorant*, i. e. I wish you to understand the origin and intent of these extraordinary manifestations of divine power, and to be able to discriminate between the true and false claimants to the possession of them.

2. Ye know that ye were Gentiles, carried away unto these dumb idols, even as ye were led.

Here, as in Ephesians 2, 11, the apostle contrasts the former with the present condition of his readers. Formerly, they were Gentiles, now they were Christians. Formerly, they were the worshippers and consulters of dumb idols, now they worshipped the living and true God. Formerly, they were swayed by a blind, unintelligent impulse, which carried them away, they knew not why nor whither; now they were under the influence of the Spirit of God. Their former condition is here adverted to as affording a reason why they needed instruction on this subject. It was one on which their previous experience gave them no information.

Ye know that ye were Gentiles.* This is the comprehensive statement of their former condition. Under it are included the two particulars which follow. First, they were addicted to the worship of *dumb* idols, i. e. voiceless, comp. Hab. 2, 18. 19, "Woe unto him that saith unto the wood, Awake; unto the dumb stone, Arise, it shall teach," and Ps. 115, 5. 135, 16. To worship dumb idols, gods who could neither hear nor save, expresses in the strongest terms at once their folly and their misery. Secondly, they were *carried away* to this worship *just as they were led*, i. e. they were controlled by an influence which they could not understand or resist. Compare, as to the force of the word here used, Gal. 2, 13. 2 Pet. 3, 17. It is often spoken of those who are led away to judgment, to prison, or to execution. Mark 14, 53. John 18, 13. Matt. 27, 21. Paul means to contrast this (ἀπάγεσθαι) *being carried away*, as it were, by force, with the (ἄγεσθαι πνεύματι), *being led by the Spirit.* The one was an irrational influence controlling the understanding and will; the other is an influence from God, congruous to our nature, and leading to good.

3. Wherefore I give you to understand, that no man speaking by the Spirit of God calleth Jesus accursed: and (that) no man can say that Jesus is the Lord, but by the Holy Ghost.

Wherefore, i. e. because I would not have you ignorant on this subject. The first thing which he teaches is the criterion or test of true divine influence. This criterion he states first negatively and then positively. The negative statement is, that *no man speaking by the Spirit of God calleth Jesus accursed.* To speak by (or *in*) the Spirit, is to speak under the influence of the Spirit, as the ancient prophets did. Matt. 22, 43. Mark 12, 36. *No one speaking* (λαλῶν, *using his voice*), *calleth* (λέγει *pronounces*) *Jesus to be accursed.* Or, according to another reading, utters the words, "Jesus is accursed."

* The common text is ὅτι, the MSS. A. C. D. E. F. I., and many of the versions and Fathers have ὅτι ὅτε (*that when*), which reading is adopted by Lachmann, Scholz, and Tischendorf. The construction is then irregular.

By *Jesus*, the historical person known among men by that name is indicated. And, therefore, Paul uses that word and not *Christ*, which is a term of office. *Accursed*, i. e. anathema. This word properly means something consecrated to God; and as among the Jews what was thus consecrated could not be redeemed, but, if a living thing, must be put to death, Lev. 27, 28. 29, hence the word was used to designate any person or thing devoted to destruction; and then with the accessory idea of the divine displeasure, something devoted to destruction as accursed. This last is its uniform meaning in the New Testament. Rom. 9, 3. Gal. 1, 8. 9. 1 Cor. 16, 22. Hence to say that Jesus is anathema, is to say he was a malefactor, one justly condemned to death. This the Jews said who invoked his blood upon their heads. The affirmative statement is, *no man can say Jesus is the Lord, but by the Holy Ghost.* The word κύριος, LORD, is that by which the word Jehovah is commonly rendered in the Greek version of the Old Testament. To say Jesus is the Lord, therefore, in the sense of the apostle, is to acknowledge him to be truly God. And as the word *Jesus* here as before designates the historical person known by that name, who was born of the Virgin Mary, to say that Jesus is Lord, is to acknowledge that that person is God manifest in the flesh. In other words, the confession includes the acknowledgment that he is truly God and truly man. What the apostle says, is that no man can make this acknowledgment but by the Holy Ghost. This of course does not mean that no one can utter these words unless under special divine influence; but it means that no one can truly believe and openly confess that Jesus is God manifest in the flesh. unless he is enlightened by the Spirit of God. This is precisely what our Lord himself said, when Peter confessed him to be the Son of God. "Blessed art thou, Simon Bar-jona; for flesh and blood hath not revealed it unto thee, but my Father who is in heaven." Matt. 16, 17. The same thing is also said by the apostle John. "Hereby know ye the Spirit of God; every spirit that confesseth that Jesus Christ is come in the flesh is of God: and every spirit that confesseth not that Jesus Christ is come in the flesh is not of God," 1 John 4, 2. 3; and in v. 15, "Whosoever shall confess that Jesus is the Son of God, God dwelleth in him, and he in God." To blaspheme Christ, *maledicere Christo*, Plin. Epist. X. 97, was the form for renouncing Christianity before the Roman tribunals; and saying, "I believe that Jesus is the Son of God," Acts 8, 37, was the form of professing allegiance to Christ. Men acknowledged themselves to be Christians, by acknowledging the divinity of Christ. These passages, therefore, teach us first, whom we are to regard as Christians, viz., those who acknowledge and worship Jesus of Nazareth as the true God; secondly, that the test of the divine commission of those who assume to be teachers of the gospel, is not external descent, or apostolic succession, but soundness in the faith. If even an apostle or angel teach any other gospel, we are to regard him as accursed, Gal. 1, 8. And Paul tells the Corinthians that they were to discriminate between those who were really the organs of the Holy Ghost, and those who falsely pretended to that office, by the same criterion. As it is unscriptural to recognize as Christians those who deny the divinity of our Lord; so it is unscriptural for any man to doubt his own regeneration, if he is conscious that he sincerely worships the Lord Jesus.

4–6. Now there are diversities of gifts, but the same Spirit. And there are differences of administrations, but the same Lord. And there are diversities of operations, but it is the same God which worketh all in all.

The second thing which the apostle teaches concerning these gifts is, their diversity of character in connection with the unity of their source and design. He is not, however, to be understood as here dividing these gifts into three classes, under the heads of *gifts*, *ministrations*, and *operations;* but as presenting them each and all under three different aspects. Viewed in relation to the Spirit, they are gifts; in relation to the Lord, they are ministrations; and in relation to God, they are operations, i. e. effects wrought by his power. And it is the same Spirit, the same Lord, and the same God who are concerned in them all. That is, the same Spirit is the giver; it is he who is the immediate and proximate author of all these various endowments. It is the same Lord in whose service and by whose authority these various gifts are exercised. They are all different forms in which he is served, or ministered to. And it is the same God the Father, who having exalted the Lord Jesus to the supreme headship of the church, and having sent the Holy Ghost, works all these effects in the minds of men. There is no inconsistency between this statement and v. 11, where the Spirit is said to work all these gifts; because God works by his Spirit. So in one place we are said to be born of God, and in another to be born of the Spirit. Thus, the doctrine of the Trinity underlies the whole scheme of redemption in its execution and application as well as in its conception.

Those who understand this passage as describing three distinct classes of gifts, one as derived from the Spirit, the other from the Son, and the other from the Father, suppose that to the first class belong wisdom, knowledge, and faith; to the second, church-offices; and to the third, gift of miracles. But this view of the passage is inconsistent with the constant and equal reference of these gifts to the Holy Spirit; they all come under the head of "spiritual gifts;" and with what follows in vs. 8–10, where a different classification is given. That is, the nine gifts there mentioned are not classified in reference to their relation to the Father, Son, and Spirit; and therefore it is unnatural to assume such a classification here. They are all and equally gifts of the Spirit, modes of serving the Son, and effects due to the efficiency of the Father.

7. But the manifestation of the Spirit is given to every man to profit withal.

But, i. e. notwithstanding these gifts have the same source, they are diverse in their manifestations. *To each one*, i. e. to every believer, or every recipient of the Holy Ghost, *is given a manifestation of the Spirit.* That is, the Spirit who dwells in all believers as the body of Christ, manifests himself in one way in one person, and in another way in another person. The illustration which the apostle subsequently introduces is derived from the human body. As the principle of life manifests itself in one organ as the faculty of vision, and in another as the faculty of hearing, so the Holy Ghost manifests himself variously in the different members of the church; in one as the gift of teaching, in another as the gift of healing. This is one of those pregnant truths, compressed in a single sentence, which are developed in manifold forms in different parts of the word of God. It is the truth of which this whole chapter is the exposition and the application. *To profit withal* (πρὸς τὸ συμφέρον), i. e. for edification. This is the common object of all these gifts. They are not designed exclusively or mainly for the benefit, much less for the gratification of their recipients; but for the good of the church. Just as the power of vision is not for the benefit of the eye, but for the man. When, therefore, the gifts of God, natural or supernatural, are perverted as means of self-exaltation or aggrandizement, it is a sin against their giver, as well as against those for whose benefit they were intended.

With regard to the gifts mentioned in the following verses, it is to be remarked, first, that the enumeration is not intended to include all the forms in which the Spirit manifested his presence in the people of God. Gifts are elsewhere mentioned which are not found in this catalogue; comp. Rom. 12, 4–8, and v. 28 of this chapter. Secondly, that although the apostle appears to divide these gifts into three classes, the principle of classification is not discernible. That is, we can discover no reason why one gift is in one class rather than in another; why, for example, prophecy, instead of being associated with other gifts of teaching, is connected with those of healing and working miracles. The different modes of classification which have been proposed, even when founded on a real difference, cannot be applied to the arrangement given by the apostle. Some would divide them into natural and supernatural. But they are all supernatural, although not to the same degree or in the same form. There are gifts of the Spirit which are ordinary and permanent, such as those of teaching and ruling, but they are not included in this enumeration, which embraces nothing which was not miraculous, or at least supernatural. Others, as Neander, divide them into those exercised by word, and those exercised by deeds. To the former class belong those of wisdom, knowledge, prophecy, and speaking with tongues; and to the latter the gifts of healing and miracles. Others, again, propose a psychological division, i. e. one founded on the different faculties involved in their exercise. Hence they are distinguished as those which concern the feelings, those which pertain to the intelligence, and those which relate to the will. But this is altogether arbitrary, as all these faculties are concerned in the exercise of every gift. It is better to take the classification as we find it, without attempting to determine the principle of arrangement, which may have been in a measure, so to speak, fortuitous, or determined by the mere association of ideas, rather than by any characteristic difference in the gifts themselves. The Scriptures are much more like a work of nature than a work of art; much more like a landscape than a building. Things spring up where we cannot see the reason why they are there, rather than elsewhere, while every thing is in its right place.

8. For to one is given by the Spirit the word of wisdom; to another the word of knowledge by the same Spirit;

In v. 7, he had said, "To each one is given a manifestation of the Spirit," *for* to one is given one gift, and to another, another. What follows, therefore, is the illustration and confirmation of what precedes. The point to be illustrated is the diversity of forms in which the same Spirit manifests himself in different individuals. "To one is given the word of wisdom, to another the word of knowledge." The *word* of wisdom, is the gift of speaking or communicating wisdom; and the *word* of knowledge is the gift of communicating knowledge. As to the difference, however, between wisdom and knowledge, as here used, it is not easy to decide. Some say the former is practical, and the latter speculative. Others, just the reverse; and passages may be cited in favour of either view. Others say that wisdom refers to what is perceived by intuition, i. e. what is apprehended (as they say) by the reason; and knowledge what is perceived by the understanding. The effect of the one is spiritual discernment; of the other, scientific knowledge; i. e. the logical nature and relations of the truths discerned. Others say that wisdom is the gospel, the whole system of revealed truth, and the *word* of wisdom is the gift of revealing that system as the object of faith. In favour of this view are these obvious considerations, 1. That Paul frequently uses the word in this sense. In ch. 2 he says, we speak wisdom, the wisdom of God, the hidden wisdom which the great of this world never could discover, but which God has revealed by his Spirit. 2. That gift stands first as the most important, and as the characteristic gift of the apostles, as may be inferred from v. 28, where the arrangement of offices to a certain extent corresponds with the arrangement of the gifts here presented. Among the gifts, the first is the word of wisdom; and among the offices, the first is that of the apostles. It is perfectly natural that this correspondence should be observed at the beginning, even if it be not carried out. This gift in its full measure belonged to the apostles alone; partially, however, also, to the prophets of the New Testament. Hence apostles and prophets are often associated as possessing the same gift, although in different degrees. "Built on the foundation of the apostles and prophets," Eph. 2, 20. "As now revealed unto the holy apostles and prophets by the Spirit," Eph. 3, 5; see also 4, 11. The characteristic difference between these classes of officers was, that the former were endowed with permanent and plenary, the latter with occasional and partial, inspiration. By the *word of knowledge*, as distinguished from *the word of wisdom*, is probably to be understood the gift which belonged to teachers. Accordingly, they follow the apostles and prophets in the enumeration given in v. 28. *The word of knowledge* was the gift correctly to nnderstand and properly to exhibit the truths revealed by the apostles and prophets. This agrees with 13, 8, where the gift of knowledge is represented as pertaining to the present state of existence. *By the same Spirit*, literally, *according to* the same Spirit, i. e. according to his will, or as he sees fit; see v. 11. The Spirit is not only the author, but the distributor of these gifts. And therefore sometimes they are said to be given (διά) *by*, and sometimes (κατά) *according to*, the Spirit.

9. To another faith by the same Spirit; to another the gifts of healing by the same Spirit;

There is a distinction indicated in the Greek which is not expressed in our version. The main divisions in this enumeration seem to be indicated by ἕτερος, and the subordinate ones by ἄλλος, though both words are translated by *another;* the former, however, is a stronger expression of difference. Here, therefore, where ἑτέρῳ is used, a new class seems to be introduced. To the first class belong the word of wisdom and the word of knowledge; to the second, all that follow except the last two. *To another faith.* As faith is here mentioned as a gift peculiar to some Christians, it cannot mean saving faith, which is common to all. It is generally supposed to mean the faith of miracles to which our Lord refers, Matt. 17, 19. 20, and also the apostle in the following chapter, "Though I have all faith, so that I could remove mountains," 13, 2. But to this it is objected, that the gift of miracles is mentioned immediately afterwards as something different from the gift of faith. Others say it is that faith which manifests itself in all the forms enumerated under this class, that is, in miracles, in healing, in prophecy, and in discerning of spirits. But then it is nothing peculiar; it is a gift common to all under this head, whereas it is as much distinguished from them, as they are from each other. Besides, no degree of faith involves inspiration which is supposed in prophecy. In the absence of distinct data for determining the nature of the faith here intended, it is safest, perhaps, to adhere to the simple meaning of the word, and assume that the gift meant is a higher measure of the ordinary grace of faith. Such a faith as enabled men to become confessors and martyrs, and which is so fully illustrated in Heb. 11, 33–40. This is something as truly wonderful as the gift of miracles. *To another the gifts of healing*, i. e. gifts by which healing of the sick was effected, Acts 4, 30. This evidently refers to the miraculous healing of diseases.

10. To another the working of miracles; to another prophecy; to another discerning of spirits; to another (divers) kinds of tongues; to another the interpretation of tongues:

Working of miracles, literally, *effects which are miraculous*, or which consist in miracles. This is more comprehensive than the preceding gift. Some had merely the gift of healing the sick, while others had the general power of working miracles. This was exemplified in the death of Ananias, in raising Dorcas, in smiting Elymas with blindness, and in many other cases.

To another prophecy. The nature of this gift is clearly exhibited in the 14th ch. It consisted in occasional inspiration and revelations, not merely or generally relating to the future, as in the case of Agabus, Acts 11, 28, but either in some new communications relating to faith or duty, or simply an immediate impulse and aid from the Holy Spirit, in presenting truth already known, so that conviction and repentance were the effects aimed at and produced; comp. 14, 25. The difference, as before stated, between the apostles and prophets, was, that the former were permanently inspired, so that their teaching was at all times infallible, whereas the prophets were infallible only occasionally. The ordinary teachers were uninspired, speaking from the resources of their own knowledge and experience.

To another discerning of spirits. It appears, especially from the epistles of the apostle John, that pretenders to inspiration were numerous in the apostolic age. He therefore exhorts his readers, "to try the spirits, whether they be of God; for many false prophets are gone out into the world," 1 John 4, 1. It was therefore of importance to have a class of men with the gift of discernment, who could determine whether a man was really inspired, or spoke only from the impulse of his own mind, or from the dictation of some evil spirit. In 14, 29, reference is made to the exercise of this gift. Compare also 1 Thess. 5, 20. 21.

To another divers *kinds of tongues.* That is, the ability to speak in languages previously unknown to the speakers. The nature of this gift is determined by the account given in Acts 2, 4–11, where it is said, the apostles spoke "with *other* tongues as the Spirit gave them utterance;" and people of all the neighbouring nations asked with astonishment, "Are not all these that speak Galileans? And how hear we every man in our own tongue wherein we were born?" It is impossible to deny that the miracle recorded in Acts consisted in enabling the apostles to speak in languages which they had never learnt. Unless, therefore, it be assumed that the gift of which Paul here speaks was something of an entirely different nature, its character is put beyond dispute. The identity of the two, however, is proved from the sameness of the terms by which they are described. In Mark 16, 17, it was promised that the disciples should speak "with *new* tongues." In Acts 2, 4, it is said they spoke "with *other* tongues." In Acts 10, 46, and 19, 6, it is said of those on whom the Holy Ghost came, that "they spake with tongues." It can hardly be doubted that all these forms of expression are to be understood in the same sense; that to speak "with tongues" in Acts 10, 46, means the same thing as speaking "with other tongues," in Acts 2, 4, and that this again means the same as speaking "with new tongues," as promised in Mark 16, 17. If the meaning of the phrase is thus historically and philologically determined for Acts and Mark, it must also be determined for the Epistle to the Corinthians. If *tongues* means languages in the former, it must have the same meaning in the latter. We have thus two arguments in favour of the old interpretation of this passage. First, that the facts narrated in Acts necessitate the interpretation of the phrase "to speak with other tongues" to mean to speak with foreign languages.

Second, that the interchange of the expressions, *new* tongues, *other* tongues, and *tongues*, in reference to the same event, shows that the last mentioned (to speak with tongues) must have the same sense with the two former expressions, which can only mean to speak in new languages. A third argument is, that the common interpretation satisfies all the facts of the case. Those facts are, 1. That what was spoken with tongues was intelligible to those who understood foreign languages, as appears from Acts 2, 11. Therefore the speaking was not an incoherent, unintelligible rhapsody. 2. What was uttered were articulate sounds, the vehicle of prayer, praise, and thanksgiving, 1 Cor. 14, 14–17. 3. They were edifying, and therefore intelligible to him who uttered them, 1 Cor. 14, 4. 16. 4. They admitted of being interpreted, which supposes them to be intelligible. 5. Though intelligible in themselves, and to the speaker, they were unintelligible to others, that is, to those not acquainted with the language used; and consequently unsuited for an ordinary Christian assembly. The folly which Paul rebuked was, speaking in Arabic to men who understood only Greek. The speaker might understand what he said, but others were not profited, 1 Cor. 14, 2. 19. 6. The illustration employed in 1 Cor. 14, 7. 11, from musical instruments, and from the case of foreigners, requires the common interpretation. Paul admits that the sounds uttered were "not without signification," v. 10. His complaint is, that a man who speaks in an unknown tongue is to him a foreigner, v. 11. This illustration supposes the sounds uttered to be intelligible in themselves, but not understood by those to whom they were addressed. 7. The common interpretation is suited even to those passages which present the only real difficulty in the case; viz., those in which the apostle speaks of the understanding as being unfruitful in the exercise of the gift of tongues, and those in which he contrasts praying with the spirit and praying with the understanding, 14, 14. 15. Although these passages, taken by themselves, might seem to indicate that the speaker himself did not understand what he said, and even that his intellect was in abeyance, yet they may naturally mean only that the understanding of the speaker was unprofitable to others; and speaking with the understanding may mean speaking intelligibly. It is not necessary, therefore, to infer from these passages, that to speak with tongues was to speak in a state of ecstasy, in a manner unintelligible to any human being. 8. The common interpretation is also consistent with the fact that the gift of interpretation was distinct from that of speaking with tongues. If a man could speak a foreign language, why could he not interpret it? Simply, because it was not his gift. What he said in that foreign language, he said under the guidance of the Spirit; had he attempted to interpret it without the gift of interpretation, he would be speaking of himself, and not "as the Spirit gave him utterance." In the one case he was the organ of the Holy Ghost, in the other he was not.

Fourth argument. Those who depart from the common interpretation of the gift of tongues, differ indefinitely among themselves as to its true nature. Some assume that the word *tongues* (γλῶσσαι) does not here mean languages, but *idioms* or peculiar and unusual forms of expression. To speak with tongues, according to this view, is to speak in an exalted poetic strain, beyond the comprehension of common people. But it has been proved from the expressions *new* and *other* tongues, and from the facts recorded in Acts, that the word γλῶσσαι (*tongues*) must here mean languages. Besides, to speak in exalted language is not to speak unintelligibly. The Grecian people understood the loftiest strains of their orators and poets. This interpretation also gives to the word γλῶσσαι a technical sense foreign to all scriptural usage, and one which is entirely inadmissible, at least in those cases where the singular is used. A man might be said to speak in "phrases," but not in "a phrase." Others say that the word means the tongue as the physical organ of utterance; and to speak *with the tongue* is to speak in a state of excitement in which the understanding and will do not control the tongue, which is moved by the Spirit to utter sounds which are as unintelligible to the speaker as to others. But this interpretation does not suit the expressions *other tongues* and *new tongues*, and is irreconcilable with the account in Acts. Besides it degrades the gift into a mere frenzy. It is out of analogy with all Scriptural facts. The spirits of the prophets are subject to the prophets. The Old Testament seers were not beside themselves, and the apostles in the use of the gift of tongues were calm and rational, speaking the wonderful works of God in a way which the foreigners gathered in Jerusalem easily understood. Others, again, admit that the word *tongues* means languages, but deny that they were languages foreign to the speaker. To speak with tongues, they say, was to speak in an incoherent, unintelligible manner, in a state of ecstasy, when the mind is entirely abstracted from the external world, and unconscious of things about it, as in a dream or trance. This, however, is liable to the objections already adduced against the other theories. Besides, it is evident from the whole discussion, that those who spake with tongues were self-controlled. They could speak or not as they pleased. Paul censures them for speaking when there was no occasion for it, and in such a manner as to produce confusion and disorder. They were, therefore, not in a state of uncontrollable excitement, unconscious of what they said or did. It is unnecessary to continue this enumeration of conjectures; what has already been said would be out of place if the opinions referred to had not found favour in England and in our own country.

The arguments against the common view of the nature of the gift of tongues, (apart from the exegetical difficulties with which it is thought to be encumbered,) are not such as to make much impression upon minds accustomed to reverence the Scriptures. 1. It is said the miracle was unnecessary, as Greek was understood wherever the apostles preached. This, no doubt, is in a great degree true. Greek was the language of educated persons throughout the Roman empire, but it had not superseded the national languages in common life; neither was the preaching of the apostles confined to the limits of the Roman empire. Besides, this supposes that the only design of the gift was to facilitate the propagation of the gospel. This was doubtless one of the purposes which it was intended to answer; but it had other important uses. It served to prove the presence of the Spirit of God; and it symbolized the calling of the Gentiles and the common interest of all nations in the gospel. See the remarks on Acts 2, 4. 2. It is said God is not wont by miracles to remove difficulties out of the way of his people, which they can surmount by labour. 3. Others pronounce it impossible that a man should speak in a language which he had never learnt. But does it thence follow that God cannot give him the ability? 4. It appears that Paul and Barnabas did not understand the speech of Lycaonia, Acts 14, 11–14. The gift of tongues, however, was not the ability to speak all languages. Probably most of those who received the gift, could speak only in one or two. Paul thanked God that he had the gift in richer measure than any of the Corinthians. 5. The gift does not appear to have been made subservient to the missionary work. It certainly was in the first instance, as recorded in Acts, and may have been afterwards. 6. Paul, in 1 Cor. 14, 14–19, does not place speaking with tongues and speaking in one's own language in opposition; but speaking with the understanding and speaking with the spirit; and therefore to speak with tongues, is to speak without understanding, or in a state of ecstasy. This is a possible interpretation of this one passage considered in itself, but it is in direct contradiction to all those passages which prove that speaking with tongues was not an involuntary, incoherent, ecstatic mode of speaking. The passage referred to, therefore, must be understood in consistency with the other passages referring to the same subject. Though there are difficulties attending any view of the gift in question, arising from our ignorance, those connected with the common interpretation are incomparably less than those which beset any of the modern conjectures.

To another, the interpretation of tongues. The nature of this gift depends on the view taken of the preceding. Commonly, at least, the man using a foreign language was able to understand it, see 14, 2. 4. 16, and may have had the gift of interpretation in connection with the gift of tongues. It is possible, however, that in some cases he did not himself understand the language which he spoke, and then of course he would need an interpreter. But even when he did understand the language which he used, he needed a distinct gift to make him the organ of the Spirit in its interpretation. If speaking with tongues was speaking incoherently in ecstasy, it is hard to see how what was said could admit of interpretation. Unless coherent it was irrational, and if irrational, it could not be translated.

11. But all these worketh that one and the selfsame Spirit, dividing to every man severally as he will.

But all these, &c., i. e. notwithstanding the diversity of these gifts they have a common origin. They are wrought by the same Spirit. What therefore in v. 6 is referred to the efficiency of God, is here referred to the efficiency of the Spirit. This is in accordance with constant scriptural usage. The same effect is sometimes attributed to one, and sometimes to another of the persons of the Holy Trinity. This supposes that, being the same in substance (or essence) in which divine power inheres, they coöperate in the production of these effects. Whatever the Father does, he does through the Spirit. The Holy Ghost not only produces these gifts in the minds of men, but he distributes them *severally* (ἰδίᾳ) *to every man as he will*, i. e. not according to the merits or wishes of men, but according to his own will. This passage clearly proves that the Holy Spirit is a person. *Will* is here attributed to him, which is one of the distinctive attributes of a person. Both the divinity and personality of the Holy Ghost are therefore involved in the nature of the work here ascribed to him.

12. For as the body is one, and hath many members, and all the members of that one body, being many, are one body: so also (is) Christ.

For introduces an illustration of the truth taught in the preceding verses. Every organism, or organic whole, supposes diversity and unity. That is, different parts united so as to constitute one whole. The apostle had taught that in the unity of the church there is a diversity of gifts. This is illustrated by a reference to the human body. It is one, yet it consists of many members. And this diversity is essential to unity; for unless the body consisted of many members, it would not be a (σῶμα) *body*, i. e. an organic whole. *So also is Christ*, i. e. the body of Christ, or the Church. As the body consists of many members and is yet one; so it is with the church, it is one and yet consists of many members, each having its own gift and office. See Rom. 12, 4. 5. Eph. 1, 23, and 4, 4. 16.

13. For by one Spirit are we all baptized into one body, whether (we be) Jews or Gentiles, whether (we be) bond or free; and have been all made to drink into one Spirit.

This is the proof of what immediately precedes. The church is one, *for* by one Spirit we were all baptized into one body. The word is not in the present tense, but in the aorist. 'We *were*, by the baptism of the Spirit, constituted one body.' This is commonly, and even by the modern commentators, understood of the sacrament of baptism; and the apostle is made to say that by the Holy Ghost received in baptism we were made one body. But the Bible clearly distinguishes between baptism with water and baptism with the Holy Ghost. "I indeed baptize you with water . . . but he shall baptize you with the Holy Ghost," Matt. 3, 11. "He that sent me to baptize with water, the same said unto me, Upon whom thou shalt see the Spirit descending, and remaining on him, the same is he which baptizeth with the Holy Ghost," John 1, 33. "John truly baptized with water, but ye shall be baptized with the Holy Ghost, not many days hence," Acts 1, 5. These passages not only distinguish between the baptism of water and the baptism of the Spirit, but they disconnect them. The baptism to which Acts 1, 5 refers took place on the day of Pentecost, and had nothing to do with the baptism of water. It is not denied that the one is sacramentally connected with the other; or that the baptism of the Spirit often attends the baptism of water; but they are not inseparably connected. The one may be without the other. And in the present passage there does not seem to be even an allusion to water baptism, any more than in Acts 1, 5. Paul does not say that we are made one body by baptism, but by the baptism of the Holy Ghost; that is, by spiritual regeneration. Any communication of the Holy Spirit is called a baptism, because the Spirit is said to be poured out, and those upon whom he is poured out, whether in his regenerating, sanctifying, or inspiring influences, are said to be baptized. In all the passages above quoted the expression is ἐν πνεύματι, *by the Spirit*, as it is here.* It is not therefore by baptism as an external rite, but by the communication of the Holy Spirit that we are made members of the body of Christ. *Unto one body* means *so as to constitute one body* (εἰς, *unto*, expressing the result). No matter how great may have been the previous difference, whether they were Jews or Gentiles, bond or free, by this baptism of the Spirit, all who experience it are merged into one body; they are all intimately and organically united as partaking of the same life. Comp. Gal. 3, 28. And this is the essential point of the analogy between the human body and the church. As the body is one because pervaded and animated by one soul or principle of life, so the church is one because pervaded by one Spirit. And as all parts of the body which partake of the common life belong to the body, so all

* It may be remarked in passing that βαπτίζεσθαι ἐν πνεύματι cannot mean *to be immersed in the* Spirit, any more than βαπτίζεσθαι ὕδατι, Luke 3, 16, Acts 1, 5, can by possibility mean *to be immersed in water*.

those in whom the Spirit of God dwells are members of the church which is the body of Christ. And by parity of reasoning, those in whom the Spirit does not dwell are not members of Christ's body. They may be members of the visible or nominal church, but they are not members of the church in that sense in which it is the body of Christ. This passage, therefore, not only teaches us the nature of the church, but also the principle of its unity. It is one, not as united under one external visible head, or under one governing tribunal, nor in virtue of any external visible bond, but in virtue of the indwelling of the Holy Spirit in all its members. And this internal spiritual union manifests itself in the profession of the same faith, and in all acts of Christian fellowship.

And have all been made to drink into one Spirit. This is a difficult clause. *To drink into* is an unexampled phrase, whether in English or Greek. The text varies. In some MSS. it is εἰς ἓν πνεῦμα, *into one Spirit*, in others, ἓν πνεῦμα, *one Spirit.* The latter is adopted by Lachmann and Tischendorf. If this be preferred, the sense is, 'We have all drank one Spirit.' That is, we have all been made partakers of one Spirit. Compare John 7, 37, and other passages, in which the Spirit is compared to water of which men are said to drink. The meaning of the passage according to this reading is simple and pertinent. 'By the baptism of the Holy Ghost we have all been united in one body and made partakers of one Spirit.' If the common text be preferred, the most natural interpretation would seem to be, 'We have all been made to drink so as to become one Spirit.' The words (εἰς ἓν πνεῦμα) *unto one Spirit*, would then correspond to (εἰς ἓν σῶμα) *unto one body.* The allusion is supposed by Luther, Calvin and Beza to be to the Lord's Supper. 'By baptism we become one body, and by drinking (of the cup, i. e. by the Lord's Supper) we become one body.' But this allusion is not only foreign to the context, but is not indicated by the words. How can the simple word ἐποτίσθημεν, *made to drink*, in such a connection, mean to partake of the Lord's Supper? Besides, as the modern commentators all remark, the tense of the verb forbids this interpretation. It must express the same time with the preceding verb. 'We were all baptized (ἐβαπτίσθημεν), and we were all made to drink (ἐποτίσθημεν).' It is something done in the past, not something continued in the present that the word expresses. If any thing is to be supplied it is not the word *cup*, but *the Spirit*, i. e. the water of life. 'We have been made to drink (i. e. of the Spirit) so as to become one spirit.' Another interpretation of the common text supposes that the preposition (εἰς) *into* belongs to the construction of the verb—*to drink into* being equivalent to *drink of*. The sense is then the same as in the reading without the εἰς, 'We have all drank of one Spirit.' The doctrine taught is clear, viz., that by receiving the Spirit we are all made members of the body of Christ, and that it is in virtue of the indwelling of the Spirit that the church is one.

14. For the body is not one member, but many.

This is a proof that diversity of gifts and members is necessary to the unity of the church. The church no more consists of persons all having the same gifts, than the body is all eye or all ear. As the body is not one member, but many, so the church is not one member, but many. The word *member* means a constituent part having a function of its own. It is not merely a multiplicity of parts that is necessary to the body; nor a multiplicity of persons that is necessary to the church; but in both cases what is required is a multiplicity of members in the sense just stated. To a certain extent what Paul says of the diversity of gifts in individual members of the church, may, in the existing state of things, be applied to different denominations of Christians. No one is perfect or complete in itself; and no one can say to the others, I have no need of you. Each represents something that is not so well represented in the others. Each has its own function to exercise and work to perform, which could not so well be accomplished without it. As, therefore, harmony and coöperation, sympathy and mutual affection, are required between individual Christians as constituent members of Christ's body, so also should they prevail between different denominations. It is only when the hand undertakes to turn the foot out of the body, that the foot is bound in self-defence and for the good of the whole, to defend its rights.

15. 16. If the foot shall say, Because I am not the hand, I am not of the body; is it therefore not of the body? And if the ear shall say, Because I am not the eye, I am not of the body; is it therefore not of the body?

The first and most obvious conclusion from the view which Paul had given of the nature of the church is the duty of contentment. It is just as unreasonable and absurd for the foot to complain that it is not the hand, as for one member of the church to complain that he is not another; that is, for a teacher to complain that he is not an apostle; or for a deaconess to complain that she is not a presbyter; or for one who had the gift of healing to complain that he had not the gift of tongues. This, as the apostle shows, would destroy the very idea of the church.

17. If the whole body (were) an eye, where (were) the hearing? If the whole (were) hearing, where (were) the smelling?

The obvious meaning of this verse is, that the very existence of the body as an organization depends on the union of members endowed with different functions. And the application of this idea to the church is equally plain. It also requires to its existence a diversity of gifts and offices. If all were apostles where would be the church?

18. But now hath God set the members every one of them in the body, as it hath pleased him.

But now, i. e. as the matter actually is. Instead of the body being all one member, God has arranged and disposed the parts each in its place so as to constitute one living organic whole. The eye did not give itself the power of vision, nor the ear its ability to discriminate sounds. Each member occupies in the body the position which God has seen fit to assign it, and which is most conducive to the good of the whole. It is so also in the church; the position and the gifts of every member are determined by the Lord. One has one gift and another another; one is a pastor and another is a missionary; one labours in a city, another in the wilderness, not according to their relative merits, nor in virtue of their own selection, but as God wills and orders. It is therefore as inconsistent with the idea of the church that each member should decide on his own position and functions, as that the members of the body should arrange themselves according to their own notions. The nature of the church supposes, that as in the body the principle of life manifests itself under one form in the eye, and in another form in the ear, so the Spirit of God dwelling in the church manifests himself under one form in one member and under a different form in another; and that the selection of his organs and distribution of his gifts are according to his sovereign pleasure. We are contending against him, therefore, when we contend against the position and the office which he has assigned us in the church. It is easy to give this principle a wider application. One is born in Europe, another in Asia; one in America, another in Africa; one is rich, another poor; one has ten talents, another one; not because one is better than the other, but simply because God has so ordained. His will, as thus manifested, is not only sovereign but infinitely wise and benevolent. It is on this diversity, whether in the world, in the church, or in the human body, that the life and the good of the whole depend. This verse thus contains the second practical inference from the nature of the church as the body of Christ. The place and gifts of each member are determined by the Lord.

19. 20. And if they were all one member, where (were) the body? But now (are they) many members, yet but one body.

These verses are a repetition of the idea that diversity of organs in the body is essential to its nature as a body, i. e. as an organization; and that this diversity is perfectly consistent with unity.

21. And the eye cannot say unto the hand, I have no need of thee: nor again the head to the feet, I have no need of you.

The third inference from the doctrine taught above, is the mutual dependence of the members of the church. As in the body the eye cannot dispense with the hand, nor the head with the feet, so in the church the most highly gifted are as much dependent on those less favoured as the latter are on the former. Every thing like pride, therefore, is as much out of place in the church as discontent.

22. 23. Nay, much more those members of the body, which seem to be more feeble, are necessary: and those (members) of the body, which we think to be less honourable, upon these we bestow more abundant honour; and our uncomely (parts) have more abundant comeliness.

The fourth inference from the apostle's doctrine is, that the least attractive gifts are the most important. As in the human frame the heart is more important than the tongue, so in the church the gift of prayer is more important than eloquence. Those who in the closet, however obscure, wrestle with God, often do more for his glory and for the advancement of his kingdom than those who fill the largest space in the public eye. What would the tongue do without the lungs, which are neither seen nor heard? God's thoughts are not as our thoughts. The childish Corinthians prized the gift of tongues, which, as they used it, could edify no one, to the gift of prophecy by which the whole body of Christ could be instructed and comforted. And those persons and offices in the church which are most admired or coveted, are often of little account in the sight of God. There is another idea presented in these verses. It is an instinct of nature to adorn most the least comely portions of the body; and it is an instinct of grace to honour most those members of the church who least attract admiration. *Those members of the body which we think to be less honourable*, i. e. less likely to be honoured; *on those we bestow the more abundant honour*, i. e. we on that account honour them the more. It is thus with a mother. The child which is the least admired, she cherishes with special affection. And it is thus with the church. The true people of God are only the more disposed to honour those of their number who are undervalued or despised. In the body, as the apostle says, *our uncomely parts* have (i. e. they receive) *more abundant comeliness*, i. e. are specially adorned.

24. For our comely (parts) have no need: but God hath tempered the body together, having given more abundant honour to that (part) which lacked:

Our comely parts have no need, i. e. of being thus adorned. The face is uncovered; the feet are clothed and decked. The former needs no adorning, the latter does. *God hath tempered the body together*, i. e. he has so adjusted it and combined its several members, as to secure the result that more abundant honour should be given to those which lacked. By making the uncomely parts essential to the well-being of the rest, and by diffusing a common life through all the members, he has made the body a harmonious whole.

25. 26. That there should be no schism in the body; but (that) the members should have the same care one for another. And whether one member suffer, all the members suffer with it; or one member be honoured, all the members rejoice with it.

God has so constituted the body *that there should be no schism in it*, i. e. no diversity of feeling or interest. *Schism* means simply *division*, but when spoken of an organized body, or of a society, it commonly includes the idea of alienation of feeling. Such was the schism which existed among the Corinthians, see 1, 10. 11, 18. *But that the members should have the same care one for another.* That is, that one member should have the same care for another member that it has for itself. The body is so constituted that the eye is as solicitous for the welfare of the foot as it is for its own well-being. The consequence is that if one member suffers all the members suffer with it; and if one member be honoured, all the members rejoice with it. This is the law of our physical nature. The body is really one. It has a common life and consciousness. The pain or pleasure of one part is common to the whole.

27. Now ye are the body of Christ, and members in particular.

That is, collectively ye are the body of Christ; individually or severally, ye are members. This is the application of the preceding analogy to the case of the Corinthians. What had been said of the body, of its unity; of the diversity of its members; of their mutual dependence; of the greater importance of the weaker than of the stronger members; of the community of feeling and interest that pervades the whole; is all true in its application to the church. The body of Christ is really one, pervaded by one and the same spirit; it consists of many members of different gifts and functions, each according to the will of the Spirit; these members are mutually dependent; the humble and obscure are more necessary to the being and welfare of the church than those distinguished by attractive gifts; and the law of sympathy pervades the whole, so that if one Christian suffers all his fellow Christians suffer with him, and if one believer is honoured, all believers rejoice with him. It is to be observed that Paul is not speaking of what ought to be, but of what is. He does not say that it is the duty of one member of the human body to care for another member, but that it does thus care. Such is the law of our nature. The want of this sympathy in any part with all the rest, would prove that it was a mere excrescence which did not partake of the common life. The same is true with regard to the body of Christ. It is not merely the duty of one Christian to have sympathy with another, to suffer when he suffers, and to rejoice when he is honoured; but such is the nature of their relation that it must be so. The want of this sympathy with our fellow Christians, no matter by what name they may be called, is proof that we do not belong to the body of Christ. In this, as in all other respects, Christians are imperfect. The time has not yet come when every believer shall have the same care for another that he has for himself, and rejoice in his joy and grieve in his sorrow as though they were his own. The ideal is here set before us, and blessed are those who approach nearest to the standard.

28. And God hath set some in the church, first apostles, secondarily prophets, thirdly teachers, after that miracles, then gifts of healings, helps, governments, diversities of tongues.

In Eph. 4, 11, Paul says, "God gave *some* apostles, *some* prophets," &c. He began here to use the same form, 'God hath set *some* in the church,' but varies the construction, and says, First, apostles. This verse is an amplification of the preceding one. In v. 27 he said the church is analogous to the human body. He here shows that the analogy consists in the common life of the church, or the indwelling Spirit of God, manifesting itself in a diversity of gifts and offices, just as the common life of the body manifests itself in different organs and members. In the church some were apostles, i. e. immediate messengers of Christ, rendered infallible as teachers and rulers by the gift of plenary inspiration. Secondly, prophets, i. e. men who spoke for God as the occasional organs of the Spirit. Thirdly, *teachers*, i. e. uninspired men who had received the gift of teaching. Fourthly, *miracles;* here and in what follows abstract terms are used for concrete—*miracles* mean men endowed with the power of working miracles. Fifthly, *gifts of healing*, i. e. persons endowed with the power of healing diseases. Sixthly, *helps*, i. e. persons qualified and appointed to help the other officers of the church, probably in the care of the poor and the sick. These, according to the common understanding from Chrysostom to the present day, were deacons and deaconesses. Seventhly, *governments*, i. e. men who had the gift and authority to rule. As this gift and office are distinguished from those of teachers, it cannot be understood of the presbyters or bishops who were required "to be apt to teach." It seems to refer clearly to a class of officers distinct from teachers, i. e. rulers, or as they are called in the Reformed churches, "ruling elders," and in the ancient church, *seniores plebis*. Finally, *diversities of tongues*, i. e. persons having the gift of speaking in foreign lauguages. This is put last probably because it was so unduly valued and so ostentatiously displayed by the Corinthians.

On this enumeration it may be remarked, first, that it was not intended to be exhaustive. Gifts are mentioned in vs. 8–10, and elsewhere, which have nothing to correspond to them here. Secondly, every office necessarily supposes the corresponding gift. No man could be an apostle without the gift of infallibility; nor a prophet without the gift of inspiration; nor a healer of diseases without the gift of healing. Man may appoint men to offices for which they have not the necessary gifts, but God never does, any more than he ordains the foot to see or the hand to hear. If any man, therefore, claims to be an apostle, or prophet, or worker of miracles, without the corresponding gift, he is a false pretender. In the early church, as now, there were many false apostles, i. e. those who claimed the honour and authority of the office without its gifts. Thirdly, the fact that any office existed in the apostolic church is no evidence that it was intended to be permanent. In that age there was a plenitude of spiritual manifestations and endowments demanded for the organization and propagation of the church, which is no longer required. We have no longer prophets, nor workers of miracles, nor gifts of tongues. The only evidence that an office was intended to be permanent is the continuance of the gift of which it was the organ, and the command to appoint to the office those who are found to possess the gift. The only evidence that God intended the eye to be a permanent organ of the body, is, that he has perpetuated the faculty of vision. Had the gift of sight been discontinued, it would avail little that men should call the mouth and nose eyes, and demand that they should be recognized as such. This is precisely what Romanists and others do, when they call their bishops apostles, and require men to honour and obey them as though they were. Fourthly, the only evidence of a call to an office, is the possession of the requisite gifts. If a man received the gift of prophecy, he was thereby called to be a prophet; or if he received the gift of healing, he was thereby called to exercise that gift. So if any man has received ministerial gifts, he has received a call to the ministry. What those gifts are the Bible has taught us. They are such as these: soundness in the faith, competent knowledge, ability to teach, the love of Christ and zeal for his glory, an intelligent conviction of an obligation to preach the gospel, and in short the qualifications which are necessary in one who is to be an example and guide of the flock of Jesus Christ. The office of the church in the matter is, first to examine whether the candidate for the ministry really possesses ministerial gifts; and then, if satisfied on that point, authoritatively to declare its judgment in the appointed way. The same remarks may be made in reference to a call to the missionary work or to any other department of labour in the church of Christ. The fundamental idea is that the church is the body of Christ, filled by his Spirit, and that the Spirit distributes to every one severally as he wills, the gifts which he designs him to exercise for the edification of the whole.

29. 30. (Are) all apostles? (are) all prophets? (are) all teachers? (are) all workers of miracles? Have all the gifts of healing? do all speak with tongues? do all interpret?

As in the body all is not eye, or all ear, so in the church all have not the same gifts and offices. And as it would be preposterous in all the members of the body to aspire to the same office, so it is no less preposterous in the members of the church that all should covet the same gifts. It is the design of the apostle to suppress, on the one hand, all discontent and envy, and on the other, all pride and arrogance. God distributes his gifts as he pleases; all are necessary, and the recipients of them are mutually dependent.

31. But covet earnestly the best gifts: and yet shew I unto you a more excellent way.

All cannot have every gift, *but* covet earnestly the better ones. *To covet* (ζηλόω) is *earnestly to desire*, with the implication of corresponding effort to obtain. The extraordinary gifts of the Spirit were bestowed according to his own good pleasure. But so also are his saving benefits. Yet both may be, and should be sought in the use of the appointed means. *The best gifts;* literally, *the better gifts*, by which is meant, as appears from 14, 5, those which were the more useful. The Corinthians had a very different standard of excellence; and coveted most the gifts which were the most attractive, although the least useful. *And yet* (or, *moreover*) *I shew you an excellent way.* The expression is not in itself comparative, *more* excellent; but simply *a way according to excellence*, i. e. an excellent way. Whether it is excellent compared to something else, or most excellent, depends on the context. Here no comparison is implied. The idea is not that he intends to show them a way that is better than seeking gifts, but a way *par excellence* to obtain those gifts. The other view is indeed adopted by Calvin and others, but it supposes the preceding imperative (*covet ye*) to be merely concessive, and is contrary to 14, 1, where the command to seek the more useful gifts is repeated. The sense is, 'Seek the better gifts, and *moreover* I show you an excellent way to do it.'

CHAPTER XIII.

Christian Love. Vs. 1–13.

Love is superior to all extraordinary gifts. It is better than the gift of tongues, v. 1; than the gifts of prophecy and knowledge, v. 2; and than the gift of miracles, v. 2. All outward works of charity without it are worthless, v. 3. Love has this superiority, first, because of its inherent excellence; and secondly, because of its perpetuity. As to its superior excellence, it implies or secures all other excellence. 1. It includes all the forms of kindness. 2. It is humble and modest. 3. It is unselfish. 4. It sympathizes with all good, vs. 4–7. It is perpetual—all the extraordinary gifts mentioned in the preceding chapter were designed for the present state of existence, or were temporary. Love is never to cease, v. 8. Knowledge, as a special gift, and perhaps also in the form in which it exists in this world, is to pass away. It is now the apprehension of truth as through a mirror—hereafter it will be lost in immediate vision, vs. 9–12. The permanent graces are faith, hope, and love, and the greatest of these is Love, v. 13.

This chapter, although devoted to a single Christian grace, and therefore not to be compared with the eighth chapter of Romans, or with some chapters in the epistle to the Ephesians, as an unfolding of the mysteries of redemption, still has ever been considered as one of the jewels of Scripture. For moral elevation, for richness and comprehensiveness, for beauty and felicity of expression, it has been the admiration of the church in all ages.—With regard to the word *charity*, as the translation of the Greek ἀγάπη, it has already been remarked in the comment on 8, 1, that it is peculiarly unhappy. Neither in its primary signification, nor in the sense which usage has attached to it, does it properly answer to the Greek term. The latter occurs about one hundred and sixteen times in the New Testament, and is translated *love* in all places except twenty-three; and in those the departure from the common usage is altogether arbitrary. The word charity is just as inappropriate in this chapter as it would be in such phrases as, "the Son of his charity," or, "the charity of God is shed abroad in our hearts," or, "the charity of Christ." The Greek word ἀγάπη is not of heathen origin. The heathen had no conception of the grace which in the Scriptures is expressed by that term; neither ἔρως nor φιλία answers to the Scriptural sense of ἀγάπη; nor do the Latin words *amor* or *caritas*. It was the unsuitableness of the former that induced Jerome to adopt the latter as the more elevated of the two. The one properly expresses love founded on sympathy; the latter came to mean love founded on respect. Its English derivative (*charity*) retains more of the original force of the Latin word. Caritas (from carus, *a carendo*, *dear*, i. e. costly) is properly dearness or costliness; and then it came to express the feeling arising from the sight of want and suffering. And this is the common meaning still attached to the English word, which renders it unsuitable as the substitute of the comprehensive word love. Many have been led to think that almsgiving covers a multitude of sins, because charity is said to have that effect; and that kindness to the poor and the sick is the sum of all religion, because Paul exalts charity above faith and hope. It is not of charity, but of love, of which the Bible thus speaks.

Superiority of Love to all other gifts.

1. Though I speak with the tongues of men and of angels, and have not charity, I am become (as) sounding brass, or a tinkling cymbal.

The gift of tongues, on which the Corinthians so much valued themselves, is mentioned first, because it was the prominent subject in this whole discussion. *The tongues of men* are the languages which men speak. As this is the obvious meaning of the expression, it serves to prove that the gift of tongues was the gift of speaking foreign languages. *The tongues of angels* are the languages which angels use. A mode of expression equivalent to 'all languages human or divine.' Paul means to say, that the gift of tongues in its highest conceivable extent without love is nothing. *Without love I am become*, i. e. the mere want of love has reduced me, notwithstanding the gift in question, to a level with *sounding brass;* not a musical instrument made of brass, which has some dignity about it, but to a piece of clattering brass which makes a senseless noise; or, at least, to a *tinkling cymbal*, the lowest and least expressive of all musical instruments. *Tinkling* (ἀλαλάζον), properly *clanging*, expressive of the loud shrill noise made by the cymbal. These instruments were of two kinds, one small, worn on the thumb and middle finger, answering, it is thought, to the modern *castanets;* the other large, broad plates, like our common cymbals. Joseph. Ant. 7. 12. 3. Both kinds are perhaps referred to in Ps. 150, 5, where the Septuagint distinguishes them as the *sweet-toned* and the *loud.* The latter is the kind here specified. The illustration was probably adopted from the shrill, discordant noise made by the speakers with their tongues, each endeavouring to drown the voice of all the others, as seems from what follows to have been the case with the Corinthians. Paul says, 14, 23, the meetings for worship in Corinth, if all spoke with tongues, would be so confused as to make strangers think they were mad.

2. And though I have (the gift of) prophecy, and understand all mysteries, and all knowledge; and though I have all faith, so that I could remove mountains, and have not charity, I am nothing.

There are three gifts here referred to, prophecy, "the word of knowledge," and miracles. 'Though I have the gift of prophecy, so as to understand all mysteries, and (though I have) all knowledge, and all faith,' &c. As the particle ἐάν, *though*, by which the distinction of gifts is indicated in the context, is here omitted, the first two clauses are commonly combined. 'Though I have the gift of prophecy, so as to understand all mysteries, and *so as to possess* all knowledge.' There are two objections to this. The passage literally reads, 'that I may know all mysteries and all knowledge;' so that the words *mysteries* and *knowledge* grammatically depend on (εἰδῶ), *I may know*. But this would make Paul use an unexampled phrase, 'to know knowledge.' Something, therefore, must be supplied, and it is as natural to borrow from the context the words, *though I have*, as simply, *that I may have*. And secondly, Paul distinguishes between prophecy and knowledge as distinct gifts, v. 8 and 12, 8–10. The understanding or apprehension of mysteries, and not the possession of knowledge, in its distinctive sense, was the result of the gift of prophecy. *Mysteries* are secrets, things undiscoverable by human reason, which divine revelation alone can make known. And the gift of prophecy was the gift of revelation by which such mysteries were communicated; see 14, 30. *All mysteries*, therefore, here means, *all the secret purposes of God* relating to redemption. This limitation is required by the context. Paul intends to say, that though he was the recipient of all the revelations which God ever designed to make concerning the plan of salvation and the kingdom of Christ, without love he would be nothing.

And all knowledge, i. e. and though I have all knowledge. By knowledge is meant the intellectual apprehension or cognition of revealed truth. It was the prerogative of the prophet to reveal, of the teacher to know and to instruct. Compare 14, 6, where Paul connects revelation with prophecy, and knowledge with doctrine or teaching. *And all faith*, i. e. all degrees of the faith of miracles, so that the greatest wonders, such as removing mountains, could be thereby accomplished. Compare our Lord's language in Matt. 21, 21. *I am nothing*, i. e. worthless. Neither intellectual gifts nor attainments, nor power, without love, are of any real value. They do not elevate the character or render it worthy of respect or confidence. Satan may have, and doubtless has, more of intelligence and power than any man ever possessed, and yet he is Satan still. Those, therefore, who seek to exalt men by the mere cultivation of the intellect, are striving to make satans of them.

3. And though I bestow all my goods to feed (the poor), and though I give my body to be burned, and have not charity, it profiteth me nothing.

Paul here advances one step further. All outward acts of beneficence are of no avail without love. A man may give away his whole estate, or sacrifice himself, and be in no sense the gainer. He may do all this from vanity, or from the fear of perdition, or to purchase heaven, and only increase his condemnation. Religion is no such easy thing. Men would gladly compound by external acts of beneficence, or by penances, for a change of heart; but the thing is impossible. Thousands indeed are deluded on this point, and think that they can substitute what is outward for what is inward, but God requires the heart, and without holiness the most liberal giver or the most suffering ascetic can never see God. The original word (ψωμίζω) here used, literally means, *to feed by morsels*. It is generally followed by two accusatives, *to feed a person with something*. Here the accusative of the person is omitted, so that the passage stands, 'Though I feed out my property,' i. e. distribute it in food. *And though I give my body to be burned*, i. e. though I make the most painful sacrifice of myself. A man may not only give his property but his life, and be nothing the better. It is not probable that the apostle refers to martyrdom, or that the idea is, that a man may, from wrong motives, submit to be a martyr. The context requires that the reference should be to a sacrifice made for the good of others. Some suppose that the reference is to the branding of slaves to indicate their ownership. The meaning would then be, 'Though I not only give away all my goods, but should sell myself as a slave for the sake of the poor, it would profit me nothing.' Had Paul intended to say this, he would probably have used the appropriate term for branding. We do not express the idea that an animal was branded, by saying it was burnt. There is no necessity for departing from the simple sense of the words. 'Though I give my body to be burnt for others, i. e. though I should die for them, without love it profiteth me nothing.'

4. Charity suffereth long, (and) is kind; charity envieth not; charity vaunteth not itself, is not puffed up,

Almost all the instructions of the New Testament are suggested by some occasion, and are adapted to it. We have not in this chapter a methodical dissertation on Christian love, but an exhibition of that grace as contrasted with extraordinary gifts which the Corinthians inordinately valued. Those traits of love are therefore adduced which stood opposed to the temper which they exhibited in the use of their gifts. They were impatient, discontented, envious, inflated, selfish, indecorous, unmindful of the feelings or interests of others, suspicious, resentful, censorious. The apostle personifies love, and places her before them and enumerates her graces, not in logical order, but as they occurred to him in contrast to the deformities of character which they exhibited.

Love suffereth long; i. e. is long-minded, or slow to be roused to resentment. It patiently bears with provocation, and is not quick to assert its rights or resent an injury. *It is kind*, i. e. is inclined to perform good offices; is good-natured. The root of the verb (χρηστός, from χράομαι) means *useful*, and hence its primary sense is, *disposed to be useful*. The excellence here indicated is the positive side of that already mentioned. Love is not quick to resent evil, but is disposed to do good. *It envieth not*. The word (ζηλόω) here used may express any wrong feeling excited in view of the good of others; not only envy, but hatred, emulation, and the like. *It vaunteth not itself* (περπερεύεται), this includes all forms of the desire to gain the applause of others. Love does not seek to win admiration and applause. *Is not puffed up*, i. e. conceited. This is the root of the preceding. The man who has a high conceit of himself is apt to be boastful and desirous of praise. Love, on the other hand, is modest and humble; modest because humble.

5. Doth not behave itself unseemly, seeketh not her own, is not easily provoked, thinketh no evil;

Doth not behave itself unseemly, i. e. does nothing of which one ought to be ashamed. Its whole deportment is decorous and becoming. *Seeketh not her own*; is disinterested, 10, 33. *Is not easily provoked*, i. e. is not quick tempered; or, does not suffer itself to be roused to resentment. And, therefore, *it thinketh no evil*, or rather, *it does not think evil.* This may mean, 1. It does not plan or devise evil. But the expression is (τὸ κακόν) *the* evil, and not (κακά) *evil.* Comp. Matt. 9, 4. 2. It does not impute evil, i. e. attribute evil motives to others, or is not suspicious. The sense is good in itself, but not so suitable to the connection as, 3. It does not lay the evil which it suffers to the charge of the wrong-doer. Instead of being resentful, it is forgiving.

6. Rejoiceth not in iniquity, but rejoiceth in the truth;

The general sentiment of this verse is, that love does not sympathize with evil, but with good. *It rejoiceth not in iniquity*, i. e. in any thing which is not conformed to the standard of right. The word is usually translated unrighteousness; but this is not to be limited to injustice, but includes all forms of moral evil. *Truth* is often used antithetically in Scripture to *unrighteousness*, as it is here. Rom. 1, 8. comp. John 3, 21. 1 John 1, 6, and other passages, in which men are said to do the truth. Hence it is commonly interpreted in such cases as meaning *righteousness.* 'Love does not rejoice in unrighteousness, but it rejoices together with (συγχαίρει) righteousness,' i. e. sympathizes with it, and has a common joy with it. As, however, the word so commonly in Paul's epistles stands for religious truth as revealed in the gospel, perhaps the majority of commentators so understand it here. 'Love rejoices together with the truth.' This, how ever, not only destroys the antithesis, but introduces a disturb ing element into the description; for it is of love as a virtue of which Paul is speaking. Its sympathy with the gospel, therefore, does not seem to be appropriate in this connection.

7. Beareth all things, believeth all things, hopeth all things, endureth all things.

Beareth all things. This may either mean, bears in silence all annoyances and troubles, or *covers up all things* (as στέγω may have either meaning), in the sense of concealing or excusing the faults of others, instead of gladly disclosing them. The latter interpretation harmonizes better with what follows, but it is contrary to Paul's usage as to this word. See 9, 12. 1 Thess. 3, 1. 5. With him the word always means *to bear patiently.* Further, love *believes all things,* is not suspicious, but readily credits what men say in their own defence. *Hopeth all things,* i. e. hopes for the best with regard to all men. It would be contrary to the context to understand the faith and hope here spoken of as referring to the truths and promises of the gospel. *Endureth all things.* The word (ὑπομένω) is properly a military word, and means to sustain the assault of an enemy. Hence it is used in the New Testament to express the idea of sustaining the assaults of suffering or persecution, in the sense of bearing up under them, and enduring them patiently. 2 Tim. 2, 10. Heb. 10, 32. 12, 2. This clause, therefore, differs from that at the beginning of the verse; as that had reference to annoyances and troubles, this to suffering and persecutions.

8. Charity never faileth: but whether (there be) prophecies, they shall fail; whether (there be) tongues, they shall cease; whether (there be) knowledge, it shall vanish away.

Love never fails, i. e. it endures for ever. It is not designed and adapted, as are the gifts under consideration, merely to the present state of existence, but to our future and immortal state of being. *Whether* there be *prophecies,* or *be it prophecies, they shall fail,* i. e. be done away with. The gift shall cease to be necessary, and therefore shall not be continued. *Be it tongues,* &c., i. e. the gift of tongues shall cease. *Be it knowledge, it shall vanish away,* i. e. cease to exist. It is the same word as that used above in reference to prophecies. It is not knowledge in the comprehensive sense of the term that is to cease, but knowledge as a gift; as one of the list of extraordinary endowments mentioned above, 12, 8–11. Knowledge, considered as the intellectual apprehension of truth, is, as the apostle immediately states, hereafter to be rendered perfect. But the λόγος γνώσεως, *the word of knowledge,* 12, 8,

i. e. knowledge in that form in which it was the foundation of the office of teacher, is to be done away with. Whether this means that hereafter there will be no need of the office of teacher, and therefore that the gift which qualified for that office shall cease; or whether Paul means to say that the immediate vision of truth is to be hereafter so different from our present discursive, obscure, and imperfect mode of cognition, that it deserves to be called by a different name, may be matter of doubt. Both are probably true. There will be no ignorance in heaven to be removed through the intervention of human instructors; and there will probably be as great a difference between knowledge hereafter and what we call knowledge here, as there is between hearing of an object and seeing it. We may hear a description of a person or place and have thereby a certain form of knowledge of him or it; but that form passes away, or is merged in a higher, as soon as we see what we had before only heard about.

9. 10. For we know in part, and we prophesy in part. But when that which is perfect is come, then that which is in part shall be done away.

This is the reason why knowledge and prophecy are to cease. They are partial or imperfect, and therefore suited only to an imperfect state of existence. The revelations granted to the prophets imparted mere glimpses of the mysteries of God; when those mysteries stand disclosed in the full light of heaven, what need then of those glimpses? A skilful teacher may by diagrams and models give us some knowledge of the mechanism of the universe; but if the eye be strengthened to take in the whole at a glance, what need then of a planetarium or of a teacher? The apostle employs two illustrations to teach us the difference between the present and the future. The one is derived from the difference between childhood and maturity; the other from the difference between seeing a thing by imperfect reflection, or through an obscure medium, and seeing it directly.

11. When I was a child, I spake as a child, I understood as a child, I thought as a child: but when I became a man, I put away childish things.

When I was a child; not an infant, but as opposed to one

of mature age, *a child. I spake as a child.* This does not refer to the gift of tongues as something childish, but simply to the mode of speaking characteristic of children. *I understood as a child*, rather, *I felt and acted* as a child; otherwise too little distinction is made between this and the next clause. *I thought as a child.* My language, feelings and thoughts were all childish. The words (φρονέω and λογίζομαι), however, are so comprehensive that the two clauses may be rendered, 'I had the opinions of a child and I reasoned as a child.' The former word, however, is so often used to express feeling, Matt. 16, 23. Rom. 8, 5. Phil. 3, 19. Col. 3, 2, that the first mentioned interpretation is to be preferred. *When I became a man*, or having become a man, I have put away *childish things*, i. e. my former childish mode of speaking, feeling and thinking. The feelings and thoughts of a child are true and just, in so far as they are the natural impression of the objects to which they relate. They are neither irrational nor false, but inadequate. The impression which the sight of the heavens makes on the mind of the child, is for the child a just and true impression. The conception which it forms of what it sees is correct in one aspect of the great object contemplated. Yet that impression is very different from that which is made on the mind of the astronomer. In like manner our views of divine things will hereafter be very different from those which we now have. But it does not thence follow that our present views are false. They are just as far as they go, they are only inadequate. It is no part of the apostle's object to unsettle our confidence in what God now communicates by his word and Spirit to his children, but simply to prevent our being satisfied with the partial and imperfect.

12. For now we see through a glass, darkly; but then face to face: now I know in part; but then shall I know even as also I am known.

This is a confirmation of what precedes. Our present knowledge is imperfect, *for* we now see *through a glass.* These words admit of three interpretations. 1. The preposition (διά) may have its ordinary instrumental sense, we see *by means* of a glass; or, 2. It may have its local sense, *through.* Then, assuming *glass* (ἐσόπτρον) to mean a window, the meaning is, we see as through a window; and as the windows were commonly made of mica, and therefore imperfectly transparent, to see through a window was to see dimly. As the word, however, properly means a mirror, James 1, 23, the best interpretation probably is, 3. We see as through a mirror; the optical impression is that the object is behind the mirror, and the spectator seems to look through it. The ancient mirrors were of imperfectly polished metal, and the reflection which they gave was very obscure. *Darkly*, literally, *in an enigma*. This may be taken adverbially, as by our translators, *we see enigmatically*, i. e. obscurely; or the idea may be that we see divine things as it were wrapped up in enigmas. We do not see the things themselves, but those things as set forth in symbols and words which imperfectly express them. The reference seems to be to Num. 12, 8. Of an ordinary prophet God said, "I will make myself known unto him in a vision, and speak to him in a dream;" but of Moses he says, "With him will I speak mouth to mouth, even apparently, and not in dark sayings," i. e. in enigmas. (The Septuagint version is δι' αἰνιγμάτων). The clearest revelation of the things of God in words is as an enigma, when compared to sight. Every thing is comparative. The revelations made to Moses were clear in comparison to the communications made to others by visions and dreams. Paul says the writings of Moses were enigmas compared to the revelations contained in the gospel, 2 Cor. 3, 12. 13. And the gospel itself is obscure compared to the lucid medium through which we shall see hereafter. *But then face to face*, i. e. no longer through a mirror, but immediately. Comp. Gen. 32, 31. Num. 12, 8. The word of God is a mirror wherein even now we behold the glory of the Lord (2 Cor. 3, 18), but what is that to seeing him face to face!

Now I know in part (imperfectly), *but then shall I know even as I am known*, i. e. perfectly. As we are required to be perfect as our Father in heaven is perfect, Matt. 5, 48, so we may be said to know even as we are known. We may be perfect in our narrow sphere, as God is perfect in his; and yet the distance between him and us remain infinite. What Paul wishes to impress upon the Corinthians is, that the gifts in which they so much prided themselves, were small matters compared to what is in reserve for the people of God.

13. And now abideth faith, hope, charity, these three; but the greatest of these (is) charity.

The words *and now* may either indicate time, *now*, during the present state; or they may be inferential, *now*, i. e. *since things are so, rebus sic stantibus.* In the latter case, the sense is, 'Since these extraordinary gifts are to pass away, faith, hope, and love abide.' The former are temporary, the latter are permanent. The only objection to this interpretation arises from the apostle's speaking of faith and hope abiding in a future state, whereas elsewhere, Rom. 8, 24. 2 Cor. 5, 7, and Heb. 11, 1, faith and hope seem to be represented as pertaining only to our present state of existence, and as being hereafter merged, the one in sight, and the other in fruition. This apparent inconsistency arises from the comprehensiveness of the terms. The state of mind indicated by faith and hope as now exercised, will not continue in the future life; but the state of mind, so to speak, of the saints in heaven, may be designated by these same terms, because confidence and expectation will continue for ever. Faith in one form, ceases when merged in sight; but in another form it continues; and the same is true of hope. Or perhaps the same idea may be more correctly expressed by saying that some exercises of faith and hope are peculiar to the present state, while others will never cease. Certain it is that there will always be room even in heaven for confidence in God, and for hope of the ever advancing and enlarging blessedness of the redeemed.

If, however, (νυνὶ δέ), *but now*, be taken, as is commonly done, as relating to time, the meaning is, 'Now, i. e. so long as we continue in this world, there remain faith, hope and love.' These are the three great permanent Christian graces, as opposed to the mere temporary gifts of prophecy, miracles, and tongues. But this does not seem to be consistent with what precedes. The contrast is not between the more or less permanent gifts pertaining to our present state; but between what belongs exclusively to the present, and what is to continue for ever. In v. 8 it is said of love, as a ground or reason of its pre-eminence, that *it never fails;* and here the same idea is expressed by saying, *it abides.* 'To abide,' therefore, must mean, that it continues for ever. The same permanence is attributed to faith, hope, and love. They are all contrasted with the temporary gifts, and they are all said to abide. The one is to continue as long as the others. The former interpretation is, therefore, to be preferred.

The greatest of these is love. In what sense is love greater than faith? Some say, because it includes, or is the root of faith and hope. It is said that we believe those whom we love, and hope for what we delight in. According to Scripture, however, the reverse is true. Faith is the root of love. It is the believing apprehension of the glory of God in the face of Jesus Christ, that calls forth love to him. Others say, the ground of superiority is in their effects. But we are said to be sanctified, to be made the children of God, to overcome the world, to be saved, by faith. Christ dwells in our hearts by faith; he that believes hath eternal life, i. e. faith as including knowledge, is eternal life. There are no higher effects than these so far as we are concerned. Others say that love is superior to faith and hope, because the latter belong to the present state only, and love is to continue for ever. But, according to the true interpretation of the verse, all these graces are declared to abide. The true explanation is to be found in the use which Paul makes of this word *greater*, or the equivalent term *better*. In 12, 31, he exhorts his readers to seek *the better* gifts, i. e. the more useful ones. And in 14, 5, he says, 'Greater is he that prophesies, than he that speaks with tongues;' i. e. he is more useful. Throughout that chapter the ground of preference of one gift to others is made to consist in its superior usefulness. This is Paul's standard; and judged by this rule, love is greater than either faith or hope. Faith saves ourselves, but love benefits others.

CHAPTER XIV.

Superiority of the gift of prophecy to that of tongues, vs. 1–25. Special directions for the conduct of public worship, vs. 26–40.

Superiority of the gift of prophecy to that of tongues. Vs. 1–25.

THE superiority of the gift of prophecy to that of tongues is founded, 1. On the consideration that he who speaks with tongues speaks to God, whereas, he who prophesies, speaks to men, vs. 2. 3. 2. That he who speaks with tongues edifies only himself, whereas, he who prophesies edifies the church, vs. 4. 5. That this must be so, is proved, 1. By an appeal to their own judgment and experience. If Paul came to them speaking in a way which they could not understand, what good could it do them? But if, as a prophet, he brought them a revelation from God, or as a teacher, set before them a doctrine, they would be edified, v. 6. 2. From the analogy of musical instruments. It is only when the sounds are understood, that they produce the desired effect. If a man does not know that a given note of the trumpet is a signal for battle, he will not prepare himself for the conflict, vs. 7–9. 3. From their experience in intercourse with strangers. If a man comes to me speaking a language which I cannot understand, no matter how polished or significant that language may be, he is a barbarian to me, and I to him, vs. 10. 11. In their zeal, therefore, for spiritual gifts, they should have regard to the edification of the church, v. 12. Hence, he who had the gift of tongues should pray for the gift of interpretation; as without the latter gift, however devotional he might be, his prayers could not profit others, vs. 13. 14. It was not enough that the prayers and praises should be spiritual, they must be intelligible; otherwise those who were unlearned could not join in them, vs. 15–17. For himself, the apostle says, although more richly endowed with the gift of tongues than any of his readers, he would rather speak five words so as to be understood, than ten thousand words in an unknown tongue, vs. 18. 19. It was mere childishness in the Corinthians to be so delighted with a gift which they could not turn to any practical account, v. 20. They should learn wisdom from the experience of the Hebrews. It was as a judgment that God sent among them teachers whom they could not understand. So long as they were obedient, or there was hope of bringing them to repentance, he sent them prophets speaking their own language, vs. 21. 22. Their experience would not be dissimilar. If they came together, each speaking in an unknown tongue, the effect would be only evil. But if, when they assembled, all the speakers spoke so as to be understood, and under the influence of the Spirit, then men would be convinced and converted, and God glorified, vs. 23–25.

In the comment on 12, 10, reasons have already been presented for adhering to the common view, that the gift of tongues, of which the apostle here speaks, was the gift miraculously conferred, of speaking in foreign languages. Every one must feel, however, the truth of the remark of Chrysostom in his commentary on this chapter: "This whole passage is very obscure; but the obscurity arises from our ignorance of the facts described, which, though familiar to those to whom the apostle wrote, have ceased to occur." That this gift should be specially connected with prophesying, as in Acts 19, 6, "they spake with tongues and prophesied," and elsewhere, is to be explained from the fact that all speaking under divine, supernatural influence, was included under the head of prophesying; and as all who spake with tongues "spake as the Spirit gave them utterance," in the wide sense of the word they all prophesied. But it is not so easy to understand why this gift should have been so common, nor why it should so often attend on conversion; see Acts 10, 46. 19, 6. There are many things also in this chapter which it is not easy to understand on any theory of the nature of the gift. Under these circumstances it is necessary to hold fast what is clear, and to make the certain our guide in explaining what is obscure. It is clear, 1. That the word *tongues* in this connection, as already proved, means languages. 2. That the speaker with tongues was in a state of calm self-control. He could speak, or be silent, 14, 28. 3. That what he said was intelligible to himself, and could be interpreted to others. 4. That the unintelligibleness of what was said, arose not from the sounds uttered being inarticulate, but from the ignorance of the hearer. The interpretation of particular passages must, therefore, be controlled by these facts.

1. Follow after charity, and desire spiritual (gifts), but rather that ye may prophesy.

In the preceding chapters Paul had taught, 1. That all the extraordinary gifts of the Spirit were proper objects of desire. 2. That they were of different relative importance. 3. That love was of greater value than any gift. In accordance with these principles, the apostle exhorts his readers to *follow after love*; i. e. to press forward towards it, as men do towards the goal in a race, Phil. 3, 12. 14. Pursue it earnestly as the greatest good. But at the same time, *desire spiritual* gifts. Because love is more important than miraculous gifts, it does not follow that the latter were not to be sought. The same word is used here as in 12, 31. *But rather that ye may prophesy.* The two gifts specially in the apostle's mind were the gift of speaking with tongues, and that of prophecy, i. e. the gift of speaking as the organ of the Spirit in a manner adapted to instruct and edify the hearer. Of these two gifts, he says, the latter is to be preferred. The reason for this preference is given in what follows.

2. For he that speaketh in an (unknown) tongue speaketh not unto men, but unto God: for no man understandeth (him); howbeit in the spirit he speaketh mysteries.

What is here taught is, First, that he who speaks with tongues speaks not to men, but to God. Second, that this means that men do not understand *him*. Thirdly, that the reason of his not being understood is in the medium of communication, not in the things communicated. *Speaketh not unto men, but unto God;* or, speaks not *for* men, but *for* God. Sibi canit et musis, according to the Latin proverb. CALVIN. His communion is with God, and not with man. *For no man understandeth* him. Literally, *no man hears*, i. e. hears any articulate sounds. He hears the sound, but does not distinguish the words. This, however, does not imply that the sounds uttered were in themselves unintelligible, so that no man living (unless inspired) could understand them. When the apostles spake with tongues on the day of Pentecost, what they said was understood. The meaning is, not that no man *living*, but that no man *present*, could understand. It is not the use of the gift of tongues that he censures, but the use of that gift when no one was present who understood the language employed. *Howbeit in the spirit he speaketh mysteries. Spirit* does not mean the man's own spirit as distinguished from his understanding. The Scriptures do not distinguish between the νοῦς and πνεῦμα as distinct faculties of the human intelligence. The latter is not the higher spiritual powers of our nature, but the Holy Spirit; comp. 2, 14. In favour of this interpretation is, 1. The prevailing use of the word *spirit* in reference to the Holy Ghost in all Paul's epistles, and especially in this whole connection. 2. That the expression to speak *in* or *by* the Spirit, is an established Scriptural phrase, meaning to speak under the guidance of the Holy Spirit. 3. When *spirit* is to be distinguished from the *understanding*, it designates the affections; a sense which would not at all suit this passage. 4. The meaning arrived at by this interpretation is natural, and suitable to the connection. 'Although he who speaks with tongues is not understood, yet, guided by the Spirit, he speaks mysteries. *Mysteries* mean divine truths; things which God has revealed. In Acts 2, 11, they are called "the wonderful things (τὰ μεγαλεῖα) of God." To make the word mean, things not understood by the hearer, is contrary to the usage of the word. A secret disclosed, is no longer a secret; and a mystery revealed ceases to be a mystery, for a mystery is something hidden. Besides, Paul would then say, 'No man understands him, yet he speaks what is not understood.'* The meaning obviously is, that although not understood, yet what he utters contains divine truth. The difficulty was in the language used, not in the absence of meaning, or in the fact that inarticulate sounds were employed. This verse, therefore, contains nothing inconsistent with the commonly received view of the nature of the gift in question. 'He who speaks with tongues, speaks to God and not to men, for no one (in the case supposed) understands him, although what he says is replete with the highest meaning.' The implication is that these *tongues* were foreign to the hearers; and therefore it is said, 'no man understands him.'

3. But he that prophesieth speaketh unto men (to) edification, and exhortation, and comfort.

The prophet spoke in the native language of his hearers; the speaker with tongues in a foreign language. This made the difference between the cases. The one was understood and the other was not. The prophet spoke with a view to *edification*. This is a general term including the sense of the two following. He edified the church either by exhortation or comfort; either by arousing believers to do or suffer, or by pouring into their hearts the consolations of the Spirit.

4. He that speaketh in an (unknown) tongue edifieth himself; but he that prophesieth edifieth the church.

* Calvin says, *Mysteria* et res occultas, ideoque nullius utilitatis. Mysteria hic Chrysostomus accepit honorifice, pro eximiis Dei revelationibus: ego vero in malam partem pro aenigmatibus obscuris et involutis, quasi diceret, loquitur quod nemo percipiat. Calvin's view of the gift of tongues seems to have been very little higher than that of some of the moderns.

This follows from what had been said. The speaker with tongues did not edify the church, because he was not understood; he did edify himself, because he understood himself. This verse, therefore, proves that the understanding was not in abeyance, and that the speaker was not in an ecstatic state.

5. I would that ye all spake with tongues, but rather that ye prophesied: for greater (is) he that prophesieth than he that speaketh with tongues, except he interpret, that the church may receive edifying.

I would that ye all spake with tongues. It was not to be inferred from what he had said, that the apostle undervalued this gift. He admitted its importance as one of the manifestations of the Spirit, and he subsequently, v. 18, gives thanks that he himself possessed it in rich measure. From this it is evident that it was something of a higher nature than modern theories wonld represent it. *But rather that ye prophesied,* (θέλω ἵνα). *I would that.* The same particle often follows verbs of wishing, praying, exhorting, &c. *For greater is he that prophesieth,* &c., i. e. he is more useful than the speaker with tongues, unless the latter interpret. "Nam si accedat interpretatio, jam erit prophetia." CALVIN. Speaking under the supernatural influence of the Spirit was common to both gifts; the only difference was in the language used. If the speaker interpreted, then he prophesied. *That the church may receive edification.* This proves that the contents of these discourses, delivered in an unknown tongue, were edifying; and therefore did not consist in mysteries in the bad sense of that term; i. e. in enigmas and dark sayings. This passage also proves that the gift of interpretation, although distinct from that of tongues, might be, and doubtless often was, possessed by the same person, and consequently, that he understood what he said. The absence of the gift of interpretation does not prove that the speaker himself in such cases was ignorant of what he uttered. It only proves that he was not inspired to communicate in another language what he had delivered. Had he done so, it would have been on his own authority, and not as an organ of the Spirit. It is conceivable that a man might speak connectedly in a foreign language under the inspiration of the Spirit, so as to be perfectly understood by those acquainted with the language, though he himself did not understand a word of what he uttered. But this hypothesis, though it would suit some passages in this chapter, is inconsistent with others, and therefore cannot be adopted.

6. Now, brethren, if I come unto you speaking with tongues, what shall I profit you, except I shall speak to you either by revelation, or by knowledge, or by prophesying, or by doctrine?

Now (νυνὶ δέ), *since things are so*, i. e. since speaking with tongues without interpreting is unedifying, what shall I profit you, asks the apostle, if I should come to you speaking in a language which you do not understand? He then varies the question, 'What shall I profit you unless I speak to you as a prophet, by (or rather *with*, ἐν) a revelation, or as a teacher, with a doctrine.' There are not four, but only two modes of address contemplated in this verse. Revelation and prophecy belong to one; and knowledge and doctrine to the other. He who received revelations was a prophet, he who had "the word of knowledge" was a teacher.

7. And even things without life giving sound, whether pipe or harp, except they give a distinction in the sounds, how shall it be known what is piped or harped?

This verse in Greek begins with the word ὅμως, *yet*, which is variously explained. The most natural interpretation is to assume that the word here, as in Gal. 3, 15, is out of its logical place, and that the sentence should read thus: 'Things without life giving sound, *yet*, unless they give a distinction of sound, how shall it be known," &c. The obvious design of the illustration is to show the uselessness of making sounds which are not understood. But what is the point of the analogy? According to some it is this, as musical instruments emit a mere jargon of sounds, unless the regular intervals be observed, so the speakers with tongues utter a mere jargon. The sounds which they utter are not articulate words, but a confused noise.* From this it is inferred that the speaking with tongues was not the gift of speaking foreign languages. This would make Paul wish (v. 5) that all the Corinthians would utter unmeaning sounds, and give thanks that he produced more such jargon than any of them! It is plain from what follows, as well as from the drift of the whole discourse, that the simple point of the analogy is, that as we cannot know what is piped or harped, or be benefited by it, unless we can discriminate the sounds emitted; so we cannot be benefited by listening to one who speaks a language which we do not understand. It is not the nature of the gift, but the folly of the use made of it, which is the point which the apostle has in view.

8. For if the trumpet give an uncertain sound, who shall prepare himself to the battle?

This is a confirmation of the last clause of the preceding verse. The sound emitted does not produce its proper effect if it be unintelligible or uncertain. This teaches us the point of the whole illustration. The trumpet may sound the battle call, but if that call is not understood, who will heed it? So the speaker with tongues may announce the most important truths, he may unfold mysteries, or pour forth praises as from a harp of gold, what can it profit those who do not understand him?

9. So likewise ye, except ye utter by the tongue words easy to be understood, how shall it be known what is spoken? for ye shall speak into the air.

This is the application of the preceding illustration, and affords another proof of what the apostle intended to illustrate. It was not the nature of the sounds uttered, but their unintelligibleness to the hearer, which was to be considered. *By the tongue*, i. e. by means of the tongue as the organ of speech. *Words easy to be understood*, or rather, *an intelligible dis-*

* Acsi diceret: Non potest homo dare citharae aut tibiae animam: vocem tamen affingit ita temperatam, ut discerni queat; quam igitur absurdum est, homines ipsos intelligentiae praeditos confusum nescio quid sonare?—Calvin. This would seem to mean that the speaker with tongues uttered a confused noise, with no more meaning in it than thrumming on a harp.

course. This does not imply, as is contended by the advocates of the modern theories, that those who spoke with tongues uttered inarticulate sounds. The opposite of εὔσημος, is not inarticulate, but unintelligible, i. e. what is not in fact understood. *Ye shall speak into the air*, i. e. in vain. Your words are lost in the air, no ear receives them. In 9, 26, the man who struck in vain is said to smite the air.

10. There are, it may be, so many kinds of voices in the world, and none of them (is) without signification.

There are, it may be, so many kinds of voices. The words (εἰ τύχοι), properly rendered, *it may be*, are often used to render a statement indefinite, where precision is impossible or unimportant. It was no matter, so far as the apostle's object was concerned, whether the "kinds of sound" in the world were more or less. *There are so many*, or, as we should say, 'There are *ever so many*, it may be, languages in the world.' *Kinds of voices.* Calvin understands this of the voices or natural cries of animals. All animated nature is vocal; no living creature is mute or utters unintelligible sounds: tota igitur naturæ series quæ est a Deo ordinata, nos ad distinctionem invitat. The context, however, shows that the reference is to human speech, therefore the words (γένη φωνῶν) should be translated *kinds of languages*, Gen. 1, 11. And no one of them *is without signification*, i. e. inarticulate. The phrase is (φωνὴ ἄφωνος), *a language which is no language*, that is, without significancy, which is the essence of a language. The illustration contained in this verse goes to prove that speaking with tongues was to speak in foreign languages. The very point is that as all languages are significant, so the languages used by those who spoke with tongues were significant. The difficulty was not in the language used, but in the ignorance of the hearer. This is still plainer from what follows.

11. Therefore if I know not the meaning of the voice, I shall be unto him that speaketh a barbarian, and he that speaketh (shall be) a barbarian unto me.

Therefore, i. e. because the sounds uttered are significant; because the man does not make a mere senseless noise, but speaks a real language, therefore, if I know not the meaning of the voice (i. e. the language), I shall stand in the relation of a foreigner to him and he to me. Otherwise it would not be so. If a man utters incoherent, inarticulate sounds, which no man living could understand, that would not make him a foreigner. It might prove him to be deranged, but not a stranger. The word *barbarian* means simply one of another country. All other people, whether civilized or not, were barbarians to the Greeks, or to the Romans. As ancient civilization came to be confined to those nations, not to be a Greek or Roman, was to be uncivilized, and hence barbarian or foreigner came to mean without civilization. Just as the true religion being confined to the Jews, *Gentile* (one not a Jew) came to be synonomous with *heathen.* In this passage, however, barbarian means simply foreigner. Comp. Rom. 1, 14. Acts 28, 24. Col. 3, 11.

12. Even so ye, forasmuch as ye are zealous of spiritual (gifts), seek that ye may excel to the edifying of the church.

Even so ye. That is, as the man who speaks a language which I do not understand, is a foreigner to me and I to him, so are ye. You too are foreigners to those who do not understand the language which you use. As all such unintelligible speaking is worthless, the apostle exhorts them to seek to edify the church. *As ye are zealous of spiritual* gifts; literally, *of spirits.* The most probable explanation of this expression is to be sought from 12, 7, where it is said that "to every one is given a manifestation of the Spirit." One and the same Spirit manifests himself in different ways in different persons; and these different manifestations are called spirits. Somewhat analogous are the expressions, "spirits of the prophets," v. 32; "discernment of spirits," 12, 11; "try the spirits," 1 John 4, 1; and "the seven Spirits of God," spoken of in the Apocalypse. In all these cases *spirits* mean manifestations of the Spirit, or forms under which the Spirit manifests himself. It is not an unusual metonomy when the effect receives the name of its cause. Comp. Gal. 5, 17, "The spirit lusteth against the flesh," where *spirit* may mean the renewed principle produced by the Spirit.

Seek that ye may excel (or *abound*) *to the edifying of the church.* This is the common explanation of this clause. But taking the words in their order the passage reads, 'Seek (these gifts) with a view to the edification of the church, in order that ye may excel.' The former explanation is the more natural. The end or object to be sought is not *that they might excel;* that is not the ultimate object, but the edification of the church. The words ζητεῖτε ἵνα, κτλ., therefore, naturally go together. 'Seek that ye may abound unto the edification of the church,' i. e. that ye may possess in rich abundance those gifts which are useful.

13. Wherefore let him that speaketh in an (unknown) tongue pray that he may interpret.

This is an inference not only from the preceding verse but from the whole preceding argument, which was designed to show how useless it is to speak in a language which no one present understands. The verse admits of two interpretations. It may mean that the speaker with tongues should pray for the gift of interpretation; or, that he should pray with the purpose (ἵνα) of interpreting what he said. The principal reason for this latter interpretation is the assumption that the gift of tongues was exercised only in prayer and praise; in other words, that it consisted in an ecstatic but unintelligible and unintelligent pouring out of the heart to God. It is therefore inferred that "to speak with a tongue," v. 13, and "to pray with a tongue," v. 14, mean exactly the same thing; the former being no more comprehensive than the latter. But this whole assumption is not only gratuitous but contrary to Scripture. The gift of tongues was, according to Acts 2, 5–11, exercised in declaring the "wonderful works of God." It is also apparent from what is said in this chapter, vs. 22–25, and v. 27, that the gift in question was not confined to acts of devotion. The former interpretation is therefore to be preferred. 'Let him pray that (ἵνα) he may interpret.' For this use of ἵνα after verbs of *entreating*, &c., see Robinson's Greek Lex. p. 352.

14. For if I pray in an (unknown) tongue, my spirit prayeth, but my understanding is unfruitful.

This is the reason why the speaker with tongues should pray for the gift of interpretation. Unless he interprets his prayer can do no good; or, as the same idea is expressed in vs. 16, 17, those who are unlearned cannot join in it. Praying with a tongue is specified, by way of example, as one mode of speaking with tongues. Though the general meaning of this verse is thus plain, it is the most difficult verse in the whole chapter. What does Paul mean by saying, His spirit prays? There are three answers given to this question. 1. That *spirit* (my spirit) here means the higher intellectual powers of the soul, as distinguished from the understanding. This verse and those which immediately follow, are the principal foundation of the theory that the speaker with tongues was in a state of ecstatic excitement in which his understanding was not exercised, so that he knew not what he said or did. How inconsistent this theory is with the facts of the case has already been shown. This view of the passage, therefore, cannot be admitted. Besides, it has already been remarked, that the Scriptures know nothing of this distinction between the *reason* and the *understanding*. 2. Others say that *spirit* here means the affections. 'My feelings find utterance in prayer, but my understanding is unfruitful.' This would give a good sense; but this meaning of the word spirit is of rare occurrence. In most of the passages quoted by lexicographers as examples of this use of the term, it really means the Holy Spirit. And in this whole discussion, *spirit* is not once used for the feelings. 3. *My spirit* may mean the Holy Spirit in me; that is, my spiritual gift; or, my spirit as the organ of the Spirit of God. Each man has his own spirit, (comp. v. 12) i. e. his own spiritual gift. And Paul means to say, that when a man prays in an unknown tongue, his spiritual gift is indeed exercised; in other words, the Holy Spirit is active in him, but others are not profited. The speaker with tongues is not to be set down as an enthusiast, or as a man in a frenzy, or, as the mockers said, as a man full of new wine. He is really the organ of the Holy Ghost. But as the influence of the Spirit under which he acts, is not irresistible, he should not exercise his gift where it can do no good to others. He may pray in silence, v. 28. This interpretation seems much more in accordance with the use of the word and with the whole drift of the chapter.

What is meant by saying, *my understanding is unfruitful?* It may mean, My understanding is not profited, gains no fruit; that is, I do not understand what I say. Though the words in themselves may have this meaning, this interpretation contradicts all those passages which teach that the speaker with tongues did understand himself. The words, therefore, must be understood to mean, 'my understanding produces no fruit,' i. e. it does not benefit others. This is in accordance with all that precedes, and with the uniforn use of the word, Eph. 5, 11. Tit. 3, 14. 2 Pet. 1, 8. Matt. 13, 22. Paul had, from the beginning, been urging his readers to have regard to the edification of the church, and he here says, that if he prayed in an unknown tongue, though he acted under the guidance of the Spirit, his prayer could not profit others.* This interpretation is confirmed by vs. 16. 17, as remarked above, where the same idea is expressed by saying, the unlearned could not say Amen to such a prayer. By his understanding being unfruitful is therefore meant, that others did not understand what he said.

The great objection to the preceding interpretation is, that *my* spirit and *my* understanding must be explained in the same way. If the latter means *my own* understanding, the former must mean *my own* spirit. The Holy Ghost, it is said, never is, and cannot be called *my* spirit, for the very reason that it is distinct from the spirit of man. The interpretation given above, however, does not suppose that *my spirit* means the Holy Spirit as a person, but the Holy Spirit as a manifestation; it is the way in which the Spirit manifests himself in me. In other words, it is my spiritual gift. The objection, if it have any force, bears as much against the conceded meaning of the phrase, "the spirits of the prophets," as it does against the explanation just given of the expression, "my

* CALVIN says, Sensus planus est. Si ergo idiomate mihi ignoto preces concipiam, ac spiritus mihi verba suppeditet: ipse quidem spiritus qui linguam meam gubernat, orabit; sed mens mea vel alibi vagabitur, vel saltem non erit orationis particeps. This implies, that the gift of tongues, at least when disjoined from the gift of interpretation, was the power to speak in a language which the speaker himself did not at the time understand. Accordingly just before he had asked, Si donum linguae ab intelligentia separetur, ita ut qui pronuntiat, sit ipse sibi barbarus, quid proficiet sic balbutiendo? Yet Calvin himself regarded this as ridiculous. Quam ridiculum fuisset, linguam hominis Romani formari Dei Spiritu ad pronuntiandas voces Graecas, quae loquenti essent prorsus ignotae: qualiter psittaci, et picae, et corvi humanas voces fingere docentur? It is very certain, however, that the gift of tongues was possessed by those who had not the gift of interpretation, and yet, even in those cases, it was edifying to the speaker. It therefore follows, that this view of the nature of the gift must be erroneous. Those speaking with tongues were not parrots or ravens. The expression in the text, *my understanding is unfruitful*, consequently cannot mean, "I do not myself understand what I say."

spirit." The spirits of the prophets means the Holy Ghost as manifested in the prophets, or the spiritual influence of which they were the subjects. And that is just the meaning of *my spirit* in this passage.

15. What is it then? I will pray with the spirit, and I will pray with the understanding also: I will sing with the spirit, and I will sing with the understanding also.

What is it then? i. e. what is the practical conclusion from what has been said? That conclusion is expressed by Paul's avowal of his own purpose. The interpretation of this verse of course depends on that of the preceding. Accordingly, some say, the meaning is, I will pray not only with the reason, but with the understanding also, i. e. not only with the higher powers of my nature in exercise, but also with such a command of the understanding as to be able to comprehend and to interpret what I say.* 2. Others say the passage means, 'I will pray with the heart and with the understanding; my mind and feelings shall unite in the exercise.' A very good sense, but entirely foreign to the context. The sentiment is correct in itself, but it is not what Paul here says. 3. According to the third interpretation the sense is, 'I will not only pray in the exercise of my spiritual gift, but so as to be understood by others;' i. e. not only spiritually but intelligibly. If τῷ νοΐ, *with the understanding*, may mean, as the moderns say it does, 'with a view to interpret' (MEYER); it certainly may mean, 'with a view to be understood.' That is, this is what is implied and intended in what the apostle says. When a man spoke τῷ πνεύματι, *with the Spirit*, the Spirit was the *principium movens*, the moving principle, determining him to speak, and what to say. When he spake with τῷ νοΐ, *with the understanding*, the understanding was that controlling principle. These two could be combined. The man could so speak under the guidance of the Spirit as to be intelligible to others.

* This view of the subject supposes the speakers with tongues to have been in a state somewhat analogous to that of somnambulists; whose spiritual nature is in activity, but their ordinary intellectual consciousness is suspended, so that when they are recovered, they do not remember any thing they said or did when in their somnambulistic condition.

I will sing. The word (ψάλλειν) means *to touch ;* then *to touch the cords* of a stringed instrument, i. e. to play upon it ; then to sing or chant in harmony with such instrument ; and then to sing or chant. This last is its New Testament meaning. It appears from this as well as from other passages, that singing was from the beginning a part of Christian worship. Pliny, about forty years later, says, Christianos solitos fuisse canere antelucanos hymnos Christo.

16. 17. Else, when thou shalt bless with the spirit, how shall he that occupieth the room of the unlearned say Amen at thy giving of thanks, seeing he understandeth not what thou sayest? For thou verily givest thanks well, but the other is not edified.

Else, i. e. since in that case. That is, in case you do not speak intelligibly (τῷ νοΐ as well as τῷ πνεύματι). *If thou shalt bless with the spirit.* That is, bless God, including praise and thanksgiving. The word translated *to give thanks*, in the last clause of the verse expresses the same idea. *By the Spirit*, i. e. under the influence of the Spirit, or in the exercise of your spiritual gift, as in the preceding verse. *How shall he that occupieth the place of the unlearned*, i. e. (ἰδιώτου) *of a private person.* The word is used to designate one out of office in opposition to officers; and in general, one who does not possess the distinguishing characteristic of the class to which it is opposed. It here designates the ungifted in opposition to those who had the gift of tongues; or rather, it is applicable to any one who was ignorant of the language used by the speaker. Comp. vs. 23. 24. Acts 4, 13. 2 Cor. 11, 6. The context shows that Paul does not refer to laymen in opposition to church officers; for the officers were just as likely to be (ἰδιῶται) *unlearned* as to the language used as others. *To fill the place* means to occupy the position; not a particular part of the place of assembly assigned to laymen, but to sustain the relation to the speaker of one unacquainted with the tongue which he uses. *Say Amen at thy giving of thanks*, i. e. assent or respond to it. *Amen* is a Hebrew adjective signifying *true* or *faithful*, often used adverbially at the end of a sentence to express assent to what is said, in the sense of *so let it be.* In the Jewish synagogue it was the custom for the people to respond to the prayers by audibly saying Amen, by which they signified their assent and participation in the petitions which had been offered. *Buxtorf's* Talm. Lexicon, *Vitringa* de Synag. Great importance was attached by the Jews to saying Amen. Schoettgen quotes numerous passages to show to what a superstitious extreme this was carried. "He who says Amen is greater than he that blesses." "Whoever says Amen, to him the gates of Paradise are opened." "Whoever says Amen shortly, his days shall be shortened; whoever answers Amen distinctly and at length, his days shall be lengthened." According to Justin Martyr, Apolog. ii. 97, the custom passed over to the Christian church. This seems also intimated in this passage; the expression is, "Say *the* Amen," i. e. utter the familiar formula of assent. The unlearned cannot thus assent, *since he knows not what thou sayest.* Men cannot assent to what they do not understand, because assent implies the affirmation of the truth of that to which we assent. It is impossible, therefore, to join in prayers uttered in an unknown tongue. The Romish church persists in the use of the Latin language in her public services not only in opposition to the very idea and intent of worship, but also to the express prohibition of the Scriptures. For the very thing here prohibited is praying in public in a language which the people do not understand. It is indeed said that words may touch the feelings which do not convey any distinct notions to the mind. But we cannot say Amen to such words, any more than we can to a flute. Such blind, emotional worship, if such it can be called, stands at a great remove from the intelligent service demanded by the apostle. *Thou verily givest thanks well*, i. e. in a way acceptable to God and profitable to yourself. This proves that the speaker must have understood what he said. For if the unintelligible is useless, it must be so to the speaker as well as to the hearer. If it was necessary that they should understand in order to be edified, it was no less necessary that he should understand what he said in order to be benefited. This verse is therefore decisive against all theories of the gift of tongues which assume that those who used them did not understand their own words. The Scriptures recognize no unintelligent worship of God, or any spiritual edification (in the case of adults) disconnected from the truth; whether that edification be sought by sounds or signs, whether by prayers or sacraments.

18. 19. I thank my God, I speak with tongues

more than ye all: yet in the church I had rather speak five words with my understanding, that (by my voice) I might teach others also, than ten thousand words in an (unknown) tongue.

That Paul should give thanks to God that he was more abundantly endowed with the gift of tongues, if that gift consisted in the ability to speak in languages which he himself did not understand, and the use of which, on that assumption, could according to his principle benefit neither himself nor others, is not to be believed. Equally clear is it from this verse that to speak with tongues was not to speak in a state of mental unconsciousness. The common doctrine as to the nature of the gift, is the only one consistent with this passage. Paul says that although he could speak in foreign languages more than the Corinthians, he would rather speak five words *with his understanding*, i. e. so as to be intelligible, than ten thousand words in an unknown tongue. *In the church*, i. e. in the assembly. *That I might teach others also*, (κατηχέω) to instruct orally, Gal. 6, 6. This shows what is meant by speaking *with the understanding*. It is speaking in such a way as to convey instruction.

20. Brethren, be not children in understanding: howbeit in malice be ye children, but in understanding be men.

There are two characteristics of children; the one a disposition to be pleased with trifles, or to put a false estimate on things; the other, comparative innocence. There is a great difference as to every thing evil between a little child and a full-grown man. The former of these characteristics the apostle wished the Corinthians to lay aside. The latter he wished them to cultivate. They had displayed a childish disposition in estimating the gift of tongues above more useful gifts, and in using it when it could answer no good purpose. A little child, however, is some thing so lovely, and is so often held up in Scripture for imitation, that he could not say, without qualification, *Be not children.* He therefore says, Be not children *as to understanding;* but as *to malice*, a comprehensive word for evil dispositions, *be ye children.* So our Lord said, Except ye be converted, and become as little children, ye shall not enter into the kingdom of heaven, Matt. 18, 3.

21. In the law it is written, With (men of) other tongues and other lips will I speak unto this people; and yet for all that will they not hear me, saith the Lord.

In the law. The word *law* signifies that which binds; especially that which binds the conscience as a rule of faith and practice. That rule may be revealed in our hearts, in the whole Scriptures, in the Pentateuch, or in the moral law; and hence the word as used in Scripture may refer to any one of these forms in which the will of God is made known; or it may include them all. The context must decide its meaning in each particular case. Here, as in John 10, 34. Rom. 3, 20, and elsewhere, the reference is not to the Pentateuch, but to the Old Testament. The passage quoted is Is. 28, 11. 12, which in our version stands thus, "For with stammering lips, and another tongue, will he speak to this people. To whom he said, This is the rest wherewith ye may cause the weary to rest; and this is the refreshing: yet they would not hear." The apostle gives the 11th verse in a free translation, and the concluding words of the 12th. He does not quote the passage as having any prophetic reference to the events in Corinth; much less does he give an allegorical interpretation of it in order to make it a condemnation of speaking with tongues. It is a simple reference to a signal event in the Jewish history from which the Corinthians might derive a useful lesson. The Jews had refused to hear the prophets speaking their own language, and God threatened to bring upon them a people whose language they could not understand. This was a judgment; a mark of displeasure designed as a punishment and not for their conversion. From this the Corinthians might learn that it was no mark of the divine favour to have teachers whose language they could not understand. They were turning a blessing into a curse. The gift of tongues was designed, among other things, to facilitate the propagation of the gospel, by enabling Christians to address people of various nations each in his own language. Used for this purpose it was a blessing; but to employ it for the sake of display, in addressing those who could not understand the language employed, was to make it a curse. The Spirit of God often confers gifts on men, and then holds them responsible for the way in which they exercise them.

22. Wherefore tongues are for a sign, not to them that believe, but to them that believe not: but prophesying (serveth) not for them that believe not, but for them which believe.

There are two inaccuracies in this version which obscure the sense. The first is the introduction of the word *serveth* after prophesying. The clauses are parallel. Tongues are for a sign to one class, and prophesying to another. Nothing need be supplied; what is implied is, that prophesying *is for a sign.* The introduction of the word *serveth* is not only unnecessary, but contrary to the context. The second inaccuracy is expressing the force of the datives (πιστεύουσι and ἀπίστοις) by *to* in the first member of the verse, and by *for* in the second member. There is no reason for this change. The relation expressed is the same in both cases. 'Tongues are *for* the one, prophesying are *for* the other;' or, 'Tongues are for a sign *to* the one, and prophesying *to* the other.' The connection between this verse and what precedes is indicated by the word *wherefore*, or *so that.* The inference may be drawn either from the immediately preceding clause, viz., "For all that they will not hear me, saith the Lord;" or from the historical fact referred to in the whole verse. If the former, then the design of the apostle is to show that as teaching the Hebrews by men of other tongues did not render them obedient; so speaking in other tongues would not profit the Corinthians. If the latter, then the design is to show, that as sending foreigners among the Hebrews was a mark of God's displeasure, so speaking in the Christian assemblies in foreign languages would be a curse and not a blessing. The latter view is demanded by the whole context.

The inference from the preceding verse is that tongues are a sign not to the believing but to the unbelieving, and prophesying just the reverse. This difficult verse is variously explained. 1. The word *sign* is taken in the sense of *mark* or *proof*, as when it is said, "the signs of an apostle," 2 Cor. 12, 12, that is, the tokens by which an apostle may be known. Comp. Luke 2, 12. 2 Thess. 3, 17. The meaning of the passage would then be, 'Tongues are a proof that those among whom they are used are not believers, but unbelievers; and prophesying is a proof that they are believers, and not unbelievers.' But when the word is used in this sense, the thing of which it is a sign is put in the genitive. It is a sign *of*, not *to* or *for*. 2. It may mean a *prodigy* or *wonder*. This is a very common sense of the word, as in the familiar phrase, "signs and wonders." The meaning is then commonly made to be, 'Tongues are a wonder designed not for the benefit of believers, but for unbelievers; and on the other hand, prophesy is a wonder designed not for the benefit of unbelievers, but for the benefit of believers.' But this is neither true nor in accordance with v. 24. It is not true that the gift of tongues was designed exclusively for the conversion of unbelievers. Why should not that gift be exercised for the edification, as well as for the conversion of men? Their conversion would not enable them to understand the native language of the apostles. Much less is it true that prophecy was designed exclusively for the edification of believers. The prophets and apostles were sent forth for the conversion of the world. And in v. 24 the conversion of unbelievers is specified as the very effect to be anticipated from the use of this gift. A still more decisive objection to this interpretation is, that it does not give the true conclusion from the preceding verse. The nature of the premises must decide the nature of the inference. It is not a fair inference from the fact that although God sent foreigners to teach the Hebrews they still continued disobedient, that foreign tongues were designed for the conversion of unbelievers. The very opposite conclusion would naturally follow from that fact. 3. *Sign* may here mean *a warning* or sign of punishment. 'Tongues are a warning, designed not for believers, but for unbelievers,' who are understood to be, not those merely without faith, but positive infidels, or obstinate rejectors of the truth. To this, however, it may be objected, that the word unbeliever (ἄπιστος) is used in v. 24 for those without faith, and that to assume a change of meaning in the same context is most unnatural. A still more serious objection is, that this interpretation cannot be carried out. It cannot be said that prophecy is a warning designed for believers. The two members of the sentence are so related that whatever is said of the gift of tongues, must be true, *mutandis mutatis*, of prophecy. If the one be a punishment designed for unbelievers, the other must be a punishment designed for believers. 4. The most satisfactory explanation is to take *sign* in the general sense of any indication of the divine presence. 'Tongues are a manifestation of God, having reference, not to believers, but to unbelievers; and prophecy is a similar manifestation, having reference, not to unbelievers, but to believers.' By *tongues*, however, is not to be understood the gift of tongues, but, as v. 21 requires, foreign languages, i. e. languages unknown to the hearers. The meaning is, that when a people are disobedient, God sends them teachers whom they cannot understand; when they are obedient, he sends them prophets speaking their own language. This is the natural conclusion from the premises contained in v. 21. When the Hebrews were disobedient God sent foreigners among them; when obedient, he sent them prophets. *Wherefore*, i. e. hence it follows, that unintelligible teachers are for the unbelieving; those who can be understood are for the believing. This view is also consistent with what follows, which is designed to show that speaking in a language which those who hear cannot understand is the cause of evil; whereas speaking intelligibly is the source of good. It must be remembered that it is not the gift of tongues of which the apostle speaks, but speaking to people in a language which they do not understand. And therefore this interpretation does not imply any disparagement of the gift in question. When used aright, that is, when employed in addressing those to whom the language used was intelligible, it was prophecy. The obscurity of the passage arises in a great measure from the ambiguity of the expression *to speak with tongues*. It means to speak in foreign or unknown languages. But a language may be said to be unknown either in reference to the speaker or to the hearer. It is said to be unknown to the speaker, if not previously acquired; and it is said to be unknown to the hearers if they do not understand it. The apostle uses the expression sometimes in one sense and sometimes in the other. When it is said that the apostles, on the day of Pentecost, spake with tongues, it means that they used languages which they had never learned; but when Paul says he would rather speak five words intelligibly than ten thousand words with a tongue, he means in a language unknown to the hearers. Speaking with tongues in the one sense, was a grace and a blessing; in the other sense, it was a folly and a curse. It was of speaking with tongues in the latter sense the apostle treats in these verses.

23. If therefore the whole church be come together into one place, and all speak with tongues, and there come in (those that are) unlearned, or unbelievers, will they not say that ye are mad?

If *therefore.* The inference from the preceding representation is, that speaking in languages not understood by the people is undesirable and useless. To show the justness of this conclusion the apostle supposes the case which follows. *If the whole church be come together in one place.* That is, if all the Christians of the place, or the whole congregation, be assembled. This is one of the conditions of the hypothesis. Another is, that *all should speak with tongues.* This does not necessarily imply either that all present had the gift of tongues, or that all who possessed the gift spoke at one and the same time, although from vs. 27 and 30 it may be inferred that this was sometimes done. All that the words here require is that all who spoke used foreign languages. *To speak with tongues* must mean to speak in languages unknown to the hearers. The third condition of the case supposed is, that unlearned and unbelievers should come into the meeting. Who are the (ἰδιῶται), *the unlearned* here intended? 1. Some say they were Christians ignorant of the gift of tongues, because they are distinguished from *unbelievers*, or those not Christians. 2. Others say that the *unlearned* are those who were ignorant of Christianity, and the (ἄπιστοι) *unbelieving*, are those who knew and rejected it, i. e. infidels. This is giving to the word a force which it has not in itself, and which the context does not give it. 3. The simplest explanation is that the *unlearned* were those ignorant of the language spoken, and the *unbelieving* those not Christians, whether Jews or Gentiles. Such persons were doubtless often led, from curiosity or other motives, to attend the Christian assemblies. The two classes (the unlearned and the unbelieving) are not so distinguished that the same person might not belong to both classes. The same persons were either ἰδιῶται or ἄπιστοι, according to the aspect under which they were viewed. Viewed in relation to the languages spoken, they were *unlearned;* viewed in relation to Christianity, they were *unbelievers.* The apostle asks what impression such persons, in the case supposed, would receive? Would they not say *ye are mad?* John 12, 20. Acts 12, 15. 26, 24.

24. 25. But if all prophesy, and there come in one that believeth not, or (one) unlearned, he is convinced of all, he is judged of all: and thus are the secrets of his heart made manifest; and so falling down on (his)

face he will worship God, and report that God is in you of a truth.

This is another part of the inference from what was said in vs. 21. 22. Speaking in languages unknown to the hearers is not adapted to do good; speaking intelligibly is suited to produce the happiest effects. *If all prophesy*, i. e. if all the speakers speak under the guidance of the Spirit in a language which the hearers can understand. *If one that believeth not, or one unlearned.* From these words it is manifest that the unlearned were not Christians as distinguished from Jews or Gentiles here called unbelievers, for the same effect is said to be produced on both. The unlearned were therefore as much the subjects of conversion as the unbelieving. The meaning is, if any person, either ignorant or destitute of faith, should come in, he would be *convinced by all.* That is, what he heard from all would carry conviction to his mind. He would be convinced of the truth of what he heard; convinced of sin, of righteousness and of judgment, John 16, 8; convinced that Jesus is the Christ, the Son of the living God, Acts 9, 20. 22; and that it is a faithful saying, and worthy of all acceptation, that Jesus Christ is come into the world to save sinners, 1 Tim. 1, 15. *He is judged of all*, i. e. examined, searched into (ἀνακρίνεται); for the word of God is a discerner (κριτικός) of the thoughts and intents of the heart, Heb. 4, 12. The result of this searching examination is, *that the secrets of his heart are made manifest;* that is, they are revealed to himself. His real character and moral state, with regard to which he was before ignorant, are made known to him. The effect of this is humility, contrition, self-condemnation, and turning unto God. This is expressed by saying, *so* i. e. in this condition of a convinced sinner who has been brought to the knowledge of himself, *falling down on his face, he will worship God.* The first step in religion is entire self-abasement; such a conviction of sin, i. e. of guilt and pollution, as shall lead to self-condemnation and self-abhorrence, and to a complete renunciation of all dependence on our own righteousness and strength. When the soul is thus humbled God reveals himself sooner or later, in mercy, manifesting himself as reconciled in Jesus Christ; and then we *worship him.* This expresses reverence, love and confidence. It is the return of the soul to the favour and fellowship of God. One who has had such an experience cannot keep it to himself. The apostle therefore describes the convert as *declaring*, i. e. *proclaiming aloud that God is in you of a truth.* "With the heart man believeth unto righteousness, and with the mouth confession is made unto salvation," Rom. 10, 10. It is not enough to believe the truth, it must be publicly professed; because confession is the natural fruit of faith. When there is a proper apprehension of the value of the truth, and a sincere appropriation of the promises of God to ourselves, there will be the desire to acknowledge his goodness and to proclaim the truth to others. The thing acknowledged is, *that God is in you*, i. e. that Christianity is divine; that Christians are not deluded fanatics, but the true children of God, in whom he dwells by his Spirit. The convert therefore joins himself to them to share their fate, to take part in whatever of reproach or persecution falls to their lot. This confession is made with confidence. *Declaring that God is in you of a truth.* It is not a mere conjecture, but a firm conviction, founded on experience, i. e. on the demonstration of the Spirit, 2, 4.

Special directions as to the mode of conducting their public assemblies, vs. 26–40.

The apostle concludes this chapter with certain practical directions derived from the principles which he had laid down. He neither denied the reality of the extraordinary gifts with which the Corinthians were so richly endowed, nor forbade their exercise. He only enjoined that mutual edification should be the end aimed at, v. 26. With regard to those having the gift of tongues, he directed that not more than two, or at most three, should speak, and that in succession, while one interpreted. But in case no interpreter was present, there was to be no speaking with tongues, vs. 27. 28. Of the prophets also only two or three were to speak, and the rest were to sit in judgment on what was said. In case a new revelation was made to one of the prophets, he was not to interrupt the speaker, but wait until he had concluded; or the one was to give way to the other. Both were not to speak at the same time, for God did not approve of confusion. As the influence of which the prophets were the subjects did not destroy their self-control, there could be no difficulty in obeying this injunction, vs. 29–33. Women were not to speak in public; but to seek instruction at home. This prohibition rests on the divinely established subordination of the women, and on the instinct of propriety, vs. 34. 35. The Corinthians were not to act in this matter as though they were the oldest or the only church, v. 36. The apostle requires all classes, no matter how highly gifted, to regard his directions as the commands of Christ, vs. 37. 38. He sums up the chapter in two sentences. 1. Earnestly to seek the gift of prophecy, and not to prohibit the exercise of the gift of tongues. 2. To do all things with decency and order.

26. How is it then, brethren? when ye come together, every one of you hath a Psalm, hath a doctrine, hath a tongue, hath a revelation, hath an interpretation. Let all things be done unto edifying.

How is it then? i. e. as in v. 15, What is the conclusion from what has been said? What is the condition of things among you? How, in point of fact, do you conduct your public worship? *When ye come together.* That is, as often as ye come together. *Every one of you hath*, &c. *Every one* is used distributively; one has this and another that. *A psalm*, a song of praise to God. This can hardly mean one of the Psalms of the Old Testament; but something prepared or suggested for the occasion. One was impelled by the Spirit to pour forth his heart in a song of praise. Comp. v. 15. *Hath a doctrine*, i. e. comes prepared to expound some doctrine. *Hath a tongue*, i. e. is able and impelled to deliver an address or to pray in an unknown tongue. *Hath a revelation*, i. e. as a prophet he has received a revelation from God which he desires to communicate. *Hath an interpretation*, i. e. is prepared to give the interpretation of some discourse previously delivered in an unknown tongue. This passage, and indeed the whole chapter, presents a lively image of an early Christian assembly. Although there were officers in every church, appointed to conduct the services and especially to teach, yet as the extraordinary gifts of the Spirit were not confined to them or to any particular class, any member present who experienced the working of the Spirit in any of its extraordinary manifestations, was authorized to use and exercise his gift. Under such circumstances confusion could hardly fail to ensue. That such disorder did prevail in the public assemblies in Corinth is clear enough from this chapter. To correct this evil is the apostle's design in this whole passage. It was only so long as the gifts of tongues, of prophecy, of miracles, and others of a like kind continued in the church that the state of things here described prevailed. Since those gifts have ceased, no one has the right to rise in the church under the impulse of his own mind to take part in its services. The general rule which the apostle lays down, applicable to all gifts alike, is that every thing *should be done unto edifying.* That is, that the edification of the church should be the object aimed at in the exercise of these gifts. It was not enough that a man felt himself the subject of a divine influence; or that acting under it would be agreeable or even profitable to himself, he must sit in silence unless the exercise of his gift would benefit the brethren as a worshipping assembly.

27. If any man speak in an (unknown) tongue, (let it be) by two, or at the most (by) three, and (that) by course; and let one interpret.

As to the use of the gift of tongues, the directions were that only two or three having that gift should speak; that they were not to speak together, but in succession; and that one should interpret what the others said.

28. But if there be no interpreter, let him keep silence in the church; and let him speak to himself, and to God.

If neither the speaker himself, nor any other person present, have the gift of interpretation, the former was to keep *silence in the church*, i. e. in the public assembly. *And let him speak to himself, and to God*, or, *for* himself, and *for* God. That is, let him commune silently with God in the exercise of his gift. As, according to Paul, all true worship is intelligent, it is evident that if in the exercise of the gift of tongues, there was communion with God, the understanding could not have been in abeyance. In that gift, not only the words, but also the thoughts and the accompanying emotion were communicated or excited by the Spirit. Those having that gift spake as the Spirit gave them utterance, Acts 2, 4.

29. 30. Let the prophets speak two or three, and let the others judge. If (any thing) be revealed to another that sitteth by, let the first hold his peace.

The number of prophets who were to speak at any one

meeting was also limited to two or three. The others were *to judge*, i. e. exercise the gift of "the discerning of spirits," 12, 10. From this passage it may be inferred that this latter gift was a concomitant of the gift of prophecy; for the other prophets, i. e. those who did not speak were to sit in judgment on what was said, in order to decide whether those claiming to be prophets were really inspired. The case, however, might occur that a communication from the Spirit might be made to one prophet while another was speaking. What was to be done then? As it was contrary to order for two to speak at the same time, the one speaking must either at once stop, or the receiver of the new revelation must wait until his predecessor had concluded his discourse. The imperative form of the expression (ὁ πρῶτος σιγάτω), *let the first be silent*, is in favour of the former view. This would suppose that the fact of a new communication being made, indicated that it was entitled to be heard at once. There are two reasons, however, which may be urged for the second view. The interruption of a speaker was itself disorderly, and therefore contrary to the whole drift of the apostle's directions; and secondly, what follows is most naturally understood as assigning the reason why the receiver of the new revelation should wait. The meaning may be, 'Let the first be silent *before the other begins*.'

31. For ye may all prophesy one by one, that all may learn, and all may be comforted.

This verse assigns the reason why two prophets should not speak at the same time. They could all have the opportunity of speaking one by one. Not indeed at the same meeting, for he had before limited the number of speakers to two or three for any one occasion. *That all may learn, and all may be comforted.* This is the end to be attained by their all speaking. The discourse of one might suit the wants of some hearers; and that of another might be adapted to the case of others. Thus all hearers would receive instruction and consolation. The latter word (*consolation*), however, is not so comprehensive as the original, which means not only to comfort, but also to exhort and to admonish.

32. And the spirits of the prophets are subject to the prophets.

This verse is connected by *and* to the preceding as containing an additional reason for the injunction in v. 31. 'You need not speak together, because you can all have the opportunity of speaking successively, *and* you are not compelled to speak by any irresistible impulse.' *The spirits of the prophets.* The word *spirit* is used here (comp. vs. 12. 14. 15) for the divine influence under which the prophets spoke. That influence was not of such a nature as to destroy the self-control of those who were its subjects. It did not throw them into a state of frenzy analogous to that of a heathen pythoness. The prophets of God were calm and self-possessed. This being the case, there was no necessity why one should interrupt another, or why more than one should speak at the same time. The one speaking could stop when he pleased; and the one who received a revelation could wait as long as he pleased. The spirits of the prophets are subject to the prophets, i. e. under their control. According to another interpretation the *spirits of the prophets* means their own *spirits* (or minds), considered as the organs of the Holy Spirit. But this is contrary to the use of the word in the context; and moreover it is inconsistent with the sense assigned to the word by the advocates of this interpretation. They say that *spirit* means the higher powers of the mind in distinction from the understanding. In this sense every man, whether the subject of divine influence or not, has a spirit. In other words, according to their theory it is not because the higher powers of the mind are the organs of the Spirit of God that they are called *spirits.* It is therefore inconsistent to assign that reason for the use of the word here. The interpretation above given of this verse is the one commonly adopted. Many commentators, however, understand the apostle to say, that the spirits of the prophets are subject to one another, i. e. to other prophets; and therefore if one is speaking he should yield to another who wishes to speak. This idea is not suited to the context. It would suggest merely a reason why one *ought* to yield to the other. What the apostle says and wishes to prove is, that one *can* yield to the other. A prophet was not forced to speak by the spirit which he had received.

33. For God is not (the author) of confusion, but of peace, as in all churches of the saints.

This is the reason why the spirits of the prophets must be

assumed to be subject to the prophets. They are from God; but God is not a God of disorder or of commotion, but of peace. Therefore every spirit which is from him, must be capable of control. He never impels men to act contrary to the principles which he has ordained. If he wills order to prevail in the church, he never impels men to be disorderly. This is a truth of wide application. When men pretend to be influenced by the Spirit of God in doing what God forbids, whether in disturbing the peace and order of the church, by insubordination, violence or abuse, or in any other way, we may be sure that they are either deluded or impostors.

34. Let your women keep silence in the churches: for it is not permitted unto them to speak; but (they are commanded) to be under obedience, as also saith the law.

The words *as in all the churches of the saints*, if connected with verse 33, contain a proof of what had just been said. 'I may appeal to all the churches of the saints in proof that God is the God not of commotion, but of peace.' Most commentators, however, connect them with v. 34. 'As in all the churches of the saints, let your women keep silence in the churches; for it is not permitted to them to speak; but *they are commanded* to be under obedience, as also saith the law.' The reasons for preferring this connection are, 1. That verse 33 has an appropriate conclusion in the words "God is not a God of confusion but of peace." 2. The words *as in all the churches of the saints*, if connected with v. 33, do not give a pertinent sense. The apostle would be made to prove a conceded and undeniable truth by an appeal to the authority or experience of the church. 3. If connected with v. 34, this passage is parallel to 11, 16, where the custom of the churches in reference to the deportment of women in public is appealed to as authoritative. The sense is thus pertinent and good. 'As is the case in all other Christian churches, let your women keep silence in the public assemblies.' The fact that in no Christian church was public speaking permitted to women was itself a strong proof that it was unchristian, i. e. contrary to the spirit of Christianity. Paul, however, adds to the prohibition the weight of apostolic authority, and not of that only but also the authority of reason and of Scripture. *It is not permitted to them to speak.* The speaking intended is public speaking, and especially in the church. In the Old Testament it had been predicted that "Your sons and your daughters shall prophesy;" a prediction which the apostle Peter quotes as verified on the day of Pentecost, Acts 2, 17; and in Acts 21, 9 mention is made of four daughters of Philip who prophesied. The apostle himself seems to take for granted, in 11, 5, that women might receive and exercise the gift of prophecy. It is therefore only the public exercise of the gift that is prohibited. The *rational* ground for this prohibition is that it is contrary to the relation of subordination in which the woman stands to the man that she appear as a public teacher. Both the Jews and Greeks adopted the same rule; and therefore the custom, which the Corinthians seemed disposed to introduce, was contrary to established usage. The *scriptural* ground is expressed in the words *as also saith the law*, i. e. the will of God as made known in the Old Testament. There, as well as in the New Testament, the doctrine that women should be in subjection is clearly revealed.

35. And if they will learn any thing, let them ask their husbands at home: for it is a shame for women to speak in the church.

The desire for knowledge in women is not to be repressed, and the facilities for its acquisition are not to be denied them. The refinement and delicacy of their sex, however, should be carefully preserved. They may learn all they wish to know without appearing before the public. *For it is a shame for women to speak in the church.* The word used is αἰσχρός, which properly means *ugly*, *deformed*. It is spoken of any thing which excites disgust. As the peculiar power and usefulness of women depend on their being the objects of admiration and affection, any thing which tends to excite the opposite sentiments should for that reason be avoided.

36. What! came the word of God out from you? or came it unto you only?

That is, Are you the mother church? or are you the only church? *The word of God* here means the gospel. Paul means to ask, whether the gospel took its rise in Corinth?

The disregard which the people of that church manifested for the customs of their sister churches seemed to evince an assuming and arrogant temper. They acted as though they were entitled to be independent, if not to prescribe the law to others. Paul takes the authority of the church for granted. He assumes that any thing contrary to the general sentiment and practice of the people of God is wrong. This he does because he understands by the church the body of Christ, those in whom the Holy Spirit dwells, and whose character and conduct are controlled and governed by his influence.

37. If any man think himself to be a prophet, or spiritual, let him acknowledge that the things that I write unto you are the commandments of the Lord.

If any man think, &c. That is, If any man, with or without just reason, assumes to be *a prophet*, i. e. inspired; or *spiritual*, i. e. the possessor of any gift of the Spirit, let him prove himself what he claims to be by submitting to my authority. Here, as in 1 John 4, 6, ("He that knoweth God, heareth us; he that is not of God, heareth not us,") submission to the infallible authority of the apostles is made the test of a divine mission and even of conversion. This must be so. If the apostles were the infallible organs of the Holy Ghost, to disobey them in any matter of faith or practice is to refuse to obey God. The inference which Romanists draw from this fact is, that as the apostleship is a permanent office in the church, and as the prelates are the bearers of that office, therefore to refuse submission in matters of faith or practice to the bishops is a clear proof that we are not of God. This is the chain with which Rome binds the nations to her car which she drives whithersoever she wills. The inference which Protestants draw from the fact in question is, that as we have the infallible teaching of the prophets and apostles in the Bible, therefore any man who does not conform in faith and practice to the Scriptures cannot be of God. This is the rule by which Protestants try all who claim to have a divine commission. It is nothing to them what their ecclesiastical descent may be. He that heareth not the Scriptures, is not of God. *The things which I write.* There is not only no reason for confining these words, as some do, to the preceding verse, but every reason against it. It is not merely for the prohibition against women speaking in the church for which the apostle claims divine authority. The specification of prophets and spiritual persons shows that the reference is primarily to the whole contents of this chapter. All the directions which he had given with respect to the exercise of spiritual gifts were of divine authority. What is true, however, of this chapter, is no less true of all apostolical instructions; because they all rest on the same foundation. *Are the commandments of the Lord*, i. e. of Christ, because he is the person known in the Christian church as Lord. The continued influence of Christ by the Spirit over the minds of his apostles, which is a divine prerogative, is here assumed or asserted.

38. But if any man be ignorant, let him be ignorant.

That is, if any man be ignorant or refuses to acknowledge the divine authority of my instructions, let him be ignorant. Paul would neither attempt to convince him, nor waste time in disputing the point. Where the evidence of any truth is abundant and has been clearly presented, those who reject it should be left to act on their own responsibility. Further disputation can do no good.

39. Wherefore, brethren, covet to prophesy, and forbid not to speak with tongues.

Prophecy and the gift of tongues are the two gifts of which this chapter treats. The former is to be preferred to the latter. The one is to be coveted, i. e. earnestly desired and sought after; the exercise of the other, even in Christian assemblies, was not to be prohibited; provided, as stated above, any one be present who possessed the gift of interpretation.

40. Let all things be done decently and in order.

Decently, i. e. in such a way as not to offend against propriety. The adjective, the adverbial form of which is here used, means *well-formed*, *comely;* that which excites the pleasing emotion of beauty. The exhortation therefore is, so to conduct their worship that it may be beautiful; in other words, so as to make a pleasing impression on all who are right-minded. *And in order* (κατὰ τάξιν), not tumultuously as in a mob, but as in a well-ordered army, where every one keeps his place, and acts at the proper time and in the proper way. So far as external matters are concerned, these are the two principles which should regulate the conduct of public worship. The apostle not only condemns any church acting independently of other churches, but also any member of a particular church acting from his own impulses, without regard to others. The church as a whole, and in every separate congregation, should be a harmonious, well-organized body.

CHAPTER XV.

The Resurrection of the Dead.

In treating this subject the apostle first proves the fact of Christ's resurrection, vs. 1–11. He thence deduces, first, the possibility, and then the certainty of the resurrection of his people, vs. 12–34. He afterwards teaches the nature of the resurrection, so far as to show that the doctrine is not liable to the objections which had been brought against it, vs. 35–58.

The Resurrection of Christ as securing the Resurrection of his People, vs. 1–34.

THAT certain false teachers in Corinth denied the resurrection of the dead is plain, not only from the course of argument here adopted but from the explicit statement in v. 12. Who these persons were, and what were the grounds of their objections, can only be conjectured from the nature of the apostolic argument. The most common opinion is that the objectors were converted Sadducees. The only reason for this opinion is that the Sadducees denied the doctrine of the resurrection, and that Paul, as appears from Acts 24, 6–9 and 26, 6–8, had been before brought into collision with them on this subject. The objections to this view are of no great weight. It is said that such was the hostility of the Sadducees to the gospel that it is not probable any of their number were among the converts to Christianity. The case of Paul himself proves that the bitterest enemies could, by the grace of God, be converted into friends. It is further objected that Paul could not, in argument with Sadducees, make the resurrection of Christ the basis of his proof. But he does not assume that fact as conceded, but proves it by an array of the testimony by which it was supported. Others suppose that the opponents of the doctrine were Epicureans. There is, however, no indication of their peculiar opinions in the chapter. In v. 32 Epicurean carelessness and indulgence are represented as the consequence, not the cause, of the denial of the resurrection. Nothing more definite can be arrived at on this point than the conjecture that the false teachers in question were men of Grecian culture. In Acts 17, 32 it is said of the Athenians that "some mocked" when they heard Paul preach the doctrine of the resurrection. From the character of the objections answered in the latter part of the chapter, vs. 35–58, it is probable that the objections urged against the doctrine were founded on the assumption that a material organization was unsuited to the future state. It is not unlikely that oriental philosophy, which assumed that matter was the source and seat of evil, had produced an effect on the minds of these Corinthian sceptics as well as on the Christians of Colosse. The decision of the question as to what particular class of persons the opponents of the doctrine of the resurrection belonged, happily is of no importance in the interpretation of the apostle's argument. As in 2 Tim. 2, 17. 18 he speaks of Hymeneus and Philetus as teaching that the resurrection was passed already, it is probable that these errorists in Corinth also refused to acknowledge any other than a spiritual resurrection.

After reminding the Corinthians that the doctrine of the resurrection was a primary principle of the gospel, which he had preached to them, and on which their salvation depended, vs. 1–3, he proceeds to assert and prove the fact that Christ rose from the dead on the third day. This event had been predicted in the Old Testament. Its actual occurrence is proved, 1. By Christ appearing after his resurrection, first to Peter and then to the twelve. 2. By his appearing to upward of five hundred brethren at one time, most of whom were still alive. 3. By a separate appearance to James. 4. And then again to all the apostles. 5. Finally by his appearance to Paul himself. There never was a historical event established on surer evidence than that of the resurrection of Christ, vs. 4–8. This fact, therefore, was included in the preaching of all the apostles, and in the faith of all Christians, v. 11. But if this be so, how can the doctrine of the resurrection be denied by any who pretend to be Christians? To deny the resurrection of the dead is to deny the resurrection of Christ; and to deny the resurrection of Christ, is to subvert the gospel, vs. 12–14; and also to make the apostles false witnesses, v. 15. If Christ be not risen, our faith is vain, we are yet in our sins, those dead in Christ are perished, and all the hopes of Christians are destroyed, vs. 16–19. But if Christ be risen, then his people will also rise, because he rose as a pledge of their resurrection. As Adam was the cause of death, so Christ is the cause of life; Adam secured the death of all who are *in* him, and Christ secures the life of all who are *in* him, vs. 20–22. Although the resurrection of Christ secures the resurrection of his people, the two events are not contemporaneous. Christ rose first, his people are to rise when he comes the second time. Then is to be the final consummation, when Christ shall deliver up his providential kingdom as mediator to the Father, after all his enemies are subdued, vs. 23. 24. It is necessary that Christ's dominion over the universe, to which he was exalted after his resurrection, should continue until his great work of subduing or restraining evil was accomplished. When that is done, then the Son (the Theanthropos, the Incarnate Logos), will be subject to the Father, and God as God, and not as Mediator, reign supreme, 25–28.

Besides the arguments already urged, there are two other considerations which prove the truth or importance of the doctrine of the resurrection. The first is, "the baptism for the dead" (whatever that means) prevailing in Corinth, assumes the truth of the doctrine, v. 29. The other is, the intimate connection between this doctrine and that of a future state is such, that if the one be denied, the other cannot, in a Christian sense, be maintained. If there be no resurrection, there is for Christians no hereafter, and they may act on the principle, "Let us eat and drink for to-morrow we die," vs. 30–32. The apostle concludes this part of the subject by warning his readers against the corrupting influence of evil associations. Whence it is probable that the denial of the doctrine had already produced the evil effects referred to among those who rejected it, vs. 33. 34.

1. 2. Moreover, brethren, I declare unto you the gospel which I preached unto you, which also ye have received, and wherein ye stand; by which also ye are

saved, if ye keep in memory what I have preached unto you, unless ye have believed in vain.

There is no connection between this and the preceding chapter. The particle δέ, rendered *moreover*, indicates the introduction of a new subject. *I declare unto* (γνωρίζω), literally, *I make known* to you, as though they had never heard it before. 'Moreover, brethren, I proclaim to you the gospel.' This interpretation is more consistent with the signification of the word, and more impressive than the rendering adopted by many, 'I remind you.' Comp. however, 12, 3. 2 Cor. 8, 1. Of this gospel Paul says, 1. That he had preached it. 2. They had received it, i. e. embraced it as true. 3. That they then professed it. They still stood firm in their adherence to the truth. It was not the Corinthians as a body, but only "some among them," v. 12, who denied the doctrine of the resurrection. 4. That by it they *are saved*. The present tense is used to express either the certainty of the event, or the idea that believers are in this life partakers of salvation. They are already saved. There is to them no condemnation. They are renewed and made partakers of spiritual life. Their salvation, however, is conditioned on their perseverance. If they do not persevere, they will not only fail of the consummation of the work of salvation, but it becomes manifest that they never were justified or renewed. 'Ye are saved (εἰ κατέχετε) *if ye hold fast*.' The word does not mean, *if ye keep in memory*. It simply means, *if ye hold fast;* whether that be by a physical holding fast with the hand, or a retaining in the memory, or a retaining in faith, depends on the connection. Here it is evident that the condition of salvation is not retaining in the memory, but persevering in the faith. 'The gospel saves you,' says the apostle, 'if you hold fast the gospel which I preached unto you.'

The only difficulty in the passage relates to the words τίνι λόγῳ, literally, *with what discourse;* which in our version is expressed by the word *what*. This may express the true sense. The idea is, 'If you hold fast to the gospel *as* I preached it to you.' The principal objection to this interpretation is the position of the words. The order in which they stand is, 'With what discourse I preached unto you if ye hold fast.' The interpretation just mentioned reverses this order. This clause is therefore by many connected with the first words of the chapter. 'I bring to your knowledge, brethren, the gospel which I preached unto you, which ye received, wherein ye stand, by which ye are saved, (I bring to your knowledge, I say,) how, *qua ratione*, I preached, if ye hold fast.' This, however, breaks the connection. It is, therefore, better to consider the words τίνι λόγῳ as placed first for the sake of emphasis. 'You are saved if you hold fast (the gospel) as I preached it to you.' *Unless ye have believed in vain.* The word εἰκῇ, *in vain*, may mean either *without cause*, Gal. 2, 18, or *without effect*, i. e. to no purpose, Gal. 3, 4. 4, 11. If the former, then Paul means to say, 'Unless ye believed without evidence, i. e. had no ground for your faith.' If the latter, the meaning is, 'Unless your faith is worthless.' The clause may be connected with the preceding words, 'If ye hold fast, which ye do, or will do, unless ye believed without cause.' The better connection is with the words *ye are saved*, &c. 'Ye are saved, if ye persevere, unless indeed faith is worthless.' If, as the errorists in Corinth taught, there is no resurrection, Paul says, v. 14, our faith is vain; it is an empty, worthless thing. So here he says, the gospel secures salvation, unless faith be of no account.

3. For I delivered unto you first of all that which I also received, how that Christ died for our sins according to the Scriptures:

For introduces the explanation of '*what* he had preached.' *I delivered unto you first of all; first*, not in reference to time; nor *first* to the Corinthians, which would not be historically true, as Paul did not preach first at Corinth; but ἐν πρώτοις means, among the first, or principal things. The death of Christ for our sins and his resurrection were therefore the great facts on which Paul insisted as the foundation of the gospel. *Which also I received*, i. e. by direct revelation from Christ himself. Comp. 11, 23. Gal. 1, 12. "I did not receive it (the gospel) from man, neither was I taught it; but by revelation of Jesus Christ." The apostle, therefore, could speak with infallible confidence, both as to what the gospel is and as to its truth. *That Christ died for our sins*, i. e. as a sacrifice or propitiation for our sins. Comp. Rom. 3, 23–26. Some commentators remark that as ὑπὲρ ἁμαρτιῶν, *for sin*, cannot mean in *the place of* sin, therefore ὑπὲρ ἡμῶν, *for us*, cannot mean *in our place.* This remark, however, has no more force in reference to the Greek preposition, ὑπέρ, than it has in relation to the English preposition, *for*. Whether the phrase, *to die for any one*, means to die for his benefit, or in his place, is determined by the connection. It may mean either or both; and the same is true of the corresponding scriptural phrase.

According to the Scriptures, i. e. the fact that the Messiah was to die as a propitiation for sin had been revealed in the Old Testament. That the death of Christ as an atoning sacrifice was predicted by the law and the prophets is the constant doctrine of the New Testament. Our Lord reproved his disciples for not believing what the prophets had spoken on this subject, Luke 24, 25. 26. Paul protested before Festus, that in preaching the gospel he had said "none other things than those which Moses and the prophets say should come; that Christ should suffer, and that he should be the first that should rise from the dead, and should show light unto the people, and to the Gentiles," Acts 26, 22. 23. He assured the Romans that his gospel was "witnessed (to) by the law and the prophets," Rom. 3. 21. The epistle to the Hebrews is an exposition of the whole Mosaic service as a prefiguration of the office and work of Christ. And the fifty-third chapter of Isaiah is the foundation of all the New Testament exhibitions of a suffering and atoning Messiah. Paul and all other faithful ministers of the gospel, therefore, teach that atonement for sin, by the death of Christ, is the great doctrine of the whole word of God.

4. And that he was buried, and that he rose again the third day according to the Scriptures:

There are two things taught in this, as in the preceding verse. First, the truth of the facts referred to; and secondly, that those facts had been predicted. It is true that Christ was buried, and that he rose again on the third day. These facts were included in the revelation made to Paul, and the truth of which he proceeds to confirm by abundant additional testimony. That these facts were predicted in the Old Testament, is taught in John 20, 9. Acts 26, 23. The passage especially urged by the apostles as foretelling the resurrection of Christ, is Ps. 16, 10. Peter proves that that Psalm cannot be understood of David, because his body was allowed to see corruption. It must, he says, be understood of Christ, who was raised from the dead, and "saw no corruption," Acts 13, 34-37. The prophetic Scriptures, however, are full of this doctrine; for on the one hand they predict the sufferings and death of the Messiah, and on the other his universal and perpetual dominion. It is only on the assumption that he was to rise from the dead that these two classes of prediction can be reconciled.

5. And that he was seen of Cephas, then of the twelve:

As the resurrection of Christ is an historical fact, it is to be proved by historical evidence. The apostle therefore appeals to the testimony of competent witnesses. All human laws assume that the testimony of two witnesses, when uncontradicted, and especially when confirmed by collateral evidence, produces such conviction of the truth of the fact asserted as to justify even taking the life of a fellow-creature. Confidence in such testimony is not founded on experience, but on the constitution of our nature. We are so constituted that we cannot refuse assent to the testimony of good men to a fact fairly within their knowledge. To render such testimony irresistible it is necessary, 1. That the fact to be proved should be of a nature to admit of being certainly known. 2. That adequate opportunity be afforded to the witnesses to ascertain its nature, and to be satisfied of its verity. 3. That the witnesses be of sound mind and discretion. 4. That they be men of integrity. If these conditions be fulfilled, human testimony establishes the truth of a fact beyond reasonable doubt. If, however, in addition to these grounds of confidence, the witnesses give their testimony at the expense of great personal sacrifice, or confirm it with their blood; if, moreover, the occurrence of the fact in question had been predicted centuries before it came to pass; if it had produced effects not otherwise to be accounted for, effects extending to all ages and nations; if the system of doctrine with which that fact is connected so as to be implied in it, commends itself as true to the reason and conscience of men; and if God confirms not only the testimony of the original witnesses to the fact, but also the truth of the doctrines of which that fact is the necessary basis, by the demonstration of his Spirit, then it is insanity and wickedness to doubt it. All these considerations concur in proof of the resurrection of Christ, and render it the best authenticated event in the history of the world.

The apostle does not refer to all the manifestations of our

Lord after his resurrection, but selects a few which he details in the order of their occurrence. The first appearance mentioned is that to Cephas; see Luke 24, 34. The second occurred on the same day "to the eleven and those who were with them," Luke 24, 33–36. To this Paul refers by saying, "then to the twelve;" comp. also John 20, 19. On this occasion, when the disciples were terrified by his sudden appearance in the midst of them, he said, "Why are ye troubled? and why do thoughts arise in your hearts? Behold my hands and my feet, that it is I myself: handle me, and see; for a spirit hath not flesh and bones, as ye see me have. And when he had thus spoken, he showed them his hands and his feet." Luke 24, 38–40. The apostles collectively, after the apostasy of Judas, are spoken of as the twelve according to a common usage, although at the time there were only eleven.

6. After that, he was seen of above five hundred brethren at once; of whom the greater part remain unto this present, but some are fallen asleep.

There is no distinct record of this event in the evangelical history. It may have taken place on the occasion when Christ met his disciples in Galilee. Before his death he told them, "After I am risen again, I will go before you into Galilee," Matt. 26, 32. Early in the morning of his resurrection he met the women who had been at his tomb, and said to them, "Be not afraid; go tell my brethren, that they go into Galilee, and there shall they see me," Matt. 28, 10; and accordingly in v. 16, it is said, "Then the eleven went away into Galilee, into a mountain where Jesus had appointed them." This, therefore, was a formally appointed meeting, and doubtless made known as extensively as possible to his followers, and it is probable, therefore, that there was a concourse of all who could come, not only from Jerusalem, but from the surrounding country, and from Galilee. Though intended specially for the eleven, it is probable that all attended who knew of the meeting, and could possibly reach the appointed place. Who would willingly be absent on such an occasion? Others think that this appearance took place at Jerusalem, where, in addition to the one hundred and twenty who constituted the nucleus of the church in the holy city, there were probably many disciples gathered from all parts of Judea in attendance on the passover. The special value of this testimony to the fact of

Christ's resurrection, arises not only from the number of the witnesses, but from Paul's appeal to their testimony while the majority of them were still alive. *Some have fallen asleep.* This is the Christian expression for dying, v. 18, and 11, 30. Death to the believer is a sleep for his body; a period of rest to be followed by a glorious day.

7. After that, he was seen of James; then of all the apostles.

Which James is here intended cannot be determined, as the event is not elsewhere recorded. The chronological order indicated in this citation of witnesses, renders it improbable that the reference is to our Lord's interview with the two disciples on their way to Emmaus, and is inconsistent with the tradition preserved by Jerome, that Christ appeared to James immediately after his resurrection. It has been inferred that the James intended was James the brother of our Lord, who presided over the church in Jerusalem, because he was so conspicuous and universally known. *Then to all the apostles.* This, for the reason given above, probably does not refer to the appearance of Christ to the eleven on the day in which he rose from the dead. It may refer to what is recorded in John 20, 26; or to the interview mentioned in Acts 1, 4. Whether James was one of the apostles is not determined by any thing in the verse. The word πᾶσιν may be used to indicate that the appearance was to the apostles collectively; and this, from its position, is the most natural explanation. Or the meaning may be, he appeared to James separately, and then to all the apostles including James. If the James intended was James of Jerusalem; and if that James were a different person from James the son of Alpheus (a disputed point), then the former interpretation should be preferred. For "the apostle" answers to "the twelve," and if James of Jerusalem was not the son of Alpheus, he was not one of the twelve.

8. And last of all he was seen of me also, as of one born out of due time.

Last of all may mean last of all the apostles; or, as is more probable, *last of all* means *the very last. As to an abortion, he appeared to me.* Such is Paul's language concerning himself. Thus true is it, that unmerited favours produce self-abasement. Paul could never think of the distinction conferred on him by Christ, without adverting to his own unworthiness.

9. For I am the least of the apostles, that am not meet to be called an apostle, because I persecuted the Church of God.

The least, not because the last in the order of appointment, but in rank and dignity. *Who am not worthy to be called an apostle.* See Matt. 3, 11. Luke 3, 16. This deep humility of the apostle, which led him to regard himself as the least of the apostles, was perfectly consistent with the strenuous assertion of his official authority, and of his claim to respect and obedience. In 2 Cor. 11, 5 and 12, 11, he says, he was "not behind the very chiefest apostles;" and in Gal. 2, 6–9, he claims full equality with James, Cephas and John. Those of his children whom God intends to exalt to posts of honour and power, he commonly prepares for their elevation by leading them to such a knowledge of their sinfulness as to keep them constantly abased. *Because I persecuted the church of God.* This is the sin which Paul never forgave himself. He often refers to it with the deepest contrition, 1 Tim. 1, 13–15. The forgiveness of sin does not obliterate the remembrance of it; neither does it remove the sense of unworthiness and ill-desert.

10. But by the grace of God I am what I am: and his grace which (was bestowed) upon me was not in vain; but I laboured more abundantly than they all: yet not I, but the grace of God which was with me.

Christian humility does not consist in denying what there is of good in us; but in an abiding sense of ill-desert, and in the consciousness that what we have of good is due to the grace of God. *The grace of God*, in this connection, is not the love of God, but the influence of the Holy Spirit considered as an unmerited favour. This is not only the theological and popular, but also the scriptural sense of the word *grace* in many passages. *By the grace of God I am what I am.* That is, divine grace has made me what I am. 'Had I been left to myself, I should have continued a blasphemer, a persecutor, and injurious. It is owing to his grace that I am now an apostle, preaching the faith which I once destroyed.' The grace of which he was made the subject, he says, *was not in vain*, i. e. without effect. *But*, on the contrary, *I laboured more abundantly than they all.* This may mean either, more than any one of the apostles, or more than all of them together. The latter is more in keeping with the tone of the passage. It serves more to exalt the grace of God, to which Paul attributes every thing good; and it is historically true, if the New Testament record is to be our guide. *Yet not I*, i. e. the fact that I laboured so abundantly is not to be referred to me; I was not the labourer—*but the grace which was with me.* By some editors the article is omitted in the last clause, ἡ σὺν ἐμοί. The sense would then be *with me*, instead of, *which was* with me. In the one case grace is represented as co-operating with the apostle; in the other, the apostle loses sight of himself entirely, and ascribes every thing to grace. 'It was not I, but the grace of God.' Theologically, there is no difference in these different modes of statement. The common text is preferred by most editors on critical grounds; and the sense, according to the common reading, is more in accordance with the spirit of the passage, and with Paul's manner; comp. Rom. 7, 17. True, he did co-operate with the grace of God, but this co-operation was due to grace —so that with the strictest propriety he could say, 'Not I, but the grace of God.'

11. Therefore whether (it were) I or they, so we preach, and so ye believed.

This verse resumes the subject from which vs. 9. 10 are a digression. 'Christ appeared to the apostles and to me; whether therefore I or they preached, we all proclaimed that fact, and ye all believed it.' The resurrection of Christ was included in the preaching of all ministers, and in the faith of all Christians.

12. 13. Now if Christ be preached that he rose from the dead, how say some among you that there is no resurrection of the dead? But if there be no resurrection of the dead, then is Christ not risen:

The admission of the resurrection of Christ is inconsistent with the denial of the resurrection of the dead. What has happened, may happen. The actual is surely possible. This mode of arguing shows that the objections urged in Corinth bore equally against the resurrection of Christ, and against the general doctrine of the resurrection. They, therefore, could not have been founded on the peculiar difficulties attending the latter doctrine. They must have been derived from the assumption that the restoration to life of a body once dead, is either an impossibility, or an absurdity. Most probably, these objectors thought, that to reunite the soul with the body was to shut it up again in prison; and that it was as much a degradation and retrocession, as if a man should again become an unborn infant. 'No,' these philosophers said, 'the hope of the resurrection "is the hope of swine." The soul having once been emancipated from the defiling encumbrance of the body, it is never to be re-imprisoned.'

The argument of the apostle does not imply that the objectors admitted the resurrection of Christ. He is not arguing with them, but against them. His design is to show that their objections to the resurrection proved too much. If they proved any thing, they proved what no Christian could admit, viz., that Christ did not rise from the dead. The denial of the resurrection of the dead involves the denial of the resurrection of Christ. The question discussed throughout this chapter is not the continued existence of the soul after death, but the restoration of the body to life. This is the constant meaning of the expression "resurrection of the dead," for which the more definite expression "resurrection of the body" is often substituted. Whether the false teachers in Corinth, who denied the doctrine of the resurrection, also denied the immortality of the soul, is uncertain. The probability is that they did not. For how could any one pretend to be a Christian, and yet not believe in an hereafter? All that is certain is, that they objected to the doctrine of the resurrection on grounds which logically involved the denial of the resurrection of Christ.

14. And if Christ be not risen, then (is) our preaching vain, and your faith (is) also vain.

This is the first consequence of denying the resurrection of Christ. The whole gospel is subverted. The reason why this fact is so essential, is, that Christ rested the validity of all his claims upon his resurrection. If he did rise, then he is truly the Son of God and Saviour of the world. His sacrifice has been accepted, and God is propitious. If he did not rise, then none of these things is true. He was not what he claimed to be, and his blood is not a ransom for sinners. In Rom. 1, 3, the apostle expresses this truth in another form, by saying that Christ was by his resurrection demonstrated to be the Son of God. It was on account of the fundamental importance of this fact that the apostles were appointed to be the witnesses of Christ's resurrection, Acts 1, 22. *Then*, i. e. in case Christ be not risen, *our preaching is vain*, i. e. empty, void of all truth, reality, and power. *And your faith is also vain*, i. e. empty, groundless. These consequences are inevitable. For, if the apostles preached a risen and living Saviour, and made his power to save depend on the fact of his resurrection, of course, their whole preaching was false and worthless, if Christ were still in the grave. The dead cannot save the living. And if the object of the Christian's faith be the Son of God as risen from the dead and seated at the right hand of God in heaven, they believed a falsehood if Christ be not risen.

15. Yea, and we are found false witnesses of God; because we have testified of God that he raised up Christ: whom he raised not up, if so be that the dead rise not.

This is the second consequence. The apostles were false witnesses. They were guilty of deliberate falsehood. They testified that they had seen Christ after his resurrection; that they had handled him, felt that he had flesh and bones; that they had put their hands into his wounds, and knew assuredly that it was their Lord. *We are found*, i. e. we are detected or manifested as being *false witnesses;* not such as falsely claim to be witnesses; but those who bear witness to what is false, Matt. 26, 60. *Because we testified of God;* literally, *against* God. We said he did, what in fact he did not do, *if so be the dead rise not.* Here again it is assumed that to deny that the dead rise is to deny that Christ has risen. But why is this? Why may not a man admit that Christ, the incarnate Son of God, arose from the dead, and yet consistently deny that there is to be a general resurrection of the dead?

Because the thing denied was that the dead could rise. The denial was placed on grounds which embraced the case of Christ. The argument is, If the dead cannot rise, then Christ did not rise; for Christ was dead.

16. For if the dead rise not, then is not Christ raised:

This is a reassertion of the inseparable connection between these two events. If there be no resurrection, Christ is not risen. If the thing be impossible, it has never happened. The sense in which Christ rose, determines the sense in which the dead are said to rise. As it is the resurrection of Christ's body that is affirmed, so it is the resurrection of the bodies of the dead, and not merely the continued existence of their souls which is affirmed. The repetition in this verse of what had been said in v. 13, seems to be with the design of preparing the way for v. 17.

17. And if Christ be not raised, your faith (is) vain; ye are yet in your sins.

This is the third consequence of the denial of Christ's resurrection. In v. 14 it was said, your faith is κενή, *empty;* here it is said to be ματαία, *fruitless.* In what sense the following clause explains; *ye are yet in your sins*, i. e. under the condemnation of sin. Comp. John 8, 21, "Ye shall die in your sins." As Christ's resurrection is necessary to our justification, Rom. 4, 25, if he did not rise, we are not justified. To teach, therefore, that there is no resurrection, is to teach that there is no atonement and no pardon. Errorists seldom see the consequences of the false doctrines which they embrace. Many allow themselves to entertain doubts as to this very doctrine of the resurrection of the body, who would be shocked at the thought of rejecting the doctrine of atonement. Yet Paul teaches that the denial of the one involves the denial of the other.

18. Then they also which are fallen asleep in Christ are perished.

This is the fourth disastrous consequence of the denial of the doctrine in question. All the dead in Christ are lost. *To*

14*

fall asleep in Christ is to die in faith, or in communion with Christ for salvation. See 1 Thess. 4, 14. Rev. 14, 13. *Are perished;* rather, *they perished.* 'They perished when they died.' Perdition, according to Scripture, is not annihilation, but everlasting misery and sin. It is the loss of holiness and happiness for ever. If Christ did not rise for the justification of those who died in him, they found no advocate at the bar of God; and have incurred the fate of those who perish in their sins. Rather than admit such conclusions as these, the Corinthians might well allow philosophers to say what they pleased about the impossibility of a resurrection. It was enough for them that Christ had risen, whether they could understand how it can be that the dead should rise, or not.

19. If in this life only we have hope in Christ, we are of all men most miserable.

Not only the future, but even the present is lost, if Christ be not risen. Not only did the departed sink into perdition when they died, but we, who are alive, are more miserable than other men. This is the last conclusion which the apostle draws from the denial of the resurrection. *If in this life only*, the word μόνον, *only*, admits of a threefold connection. Although it stands at the end of the clause it may be connected, as in our translation, with the words "in this life." 'If in this life only.' That is, if all the good we expect from Christ is to be enjoyed in this life, we are more miserable than other men. We are constantly exposed to all manner of persecutions and sufferings, while they are at their ease. 2. It may be connected with the word *Christ.* This is a very natural construction, according to the position of the words in the common text, for (ἐν Χριστῷ μόνον), *in Christ only*, stand together. The sense would then be, 'If we have set all our hopes on Christ, *and he fails us*, we are of all men most miserable.' This, however, supposes the important clause, on which every thing depends (*if he fails us*), to be omitted. It also leaves the words *in this life* without importance. 3. Recent editors, following the older manuscripts, place ἐν Χριστῷ before the verb, and make μόνον qualify the whole clause. 'If we have only hoped in Christ, and there is to be no fulfilling of our hopes, we are more miserable than others.' Or, 'If we are only such (nothing more than such) who in life, and not in death, have hope in Christ,' &c. The apposition between the dead in v. 18, and the living in this verse, is in favour of the first-mentioned explanation. 'Those who died in Christ, perished when they died. And we, if all our hopes in Christ are confined to this life, are the most miserable of men.' *We have hoped.* The Greek is ἠλπικότες ἐσμέν, which, as the commentators remark, expresses not what we do, but what we are. *We are hopers.* This passage does not teach that Christians are in this life more miserable than other men. This is contrary to experience. Christians are unspeakably happier than other men. All that Paul means to say is, that if you take Christ from Christians, you take their all. He is the source not only of their future, but of their present happiness. Without him they are yet in their sins, under the curse of the law, unreconciled to God, having no hope, and without God in the world; and yet subject to all the peculiar trials incident to a Christian profession, which in the apostolic age often included the loss of all things.

20. But now is Christ risen from the dead, (and) become the first-fruits of them that slept.

But now, νυνὶ δέ, i. e. as the matter actually stands. All the gloomy consequences presented in the preceding verses follow from the assumption that Christ did not rise from the dead. But as in point of fact he did rise, these things have no place. Our preaching is not vain, your faith is not vain, ye are not in your sins, the dead in Christ have not perished, we are not more miserable than other men. The reverse of all this is true. Christ has not only risen, but he has risen in a representative character. His resurrection is the pledge of the resurrection of his people. He rose as *the first-fruits of them that slept*, and not of them only, but as the first-fruits of all who are ever to sleep in Jesus. The apostle does not mean merely that the resurrection of Christ was to precede that of his people; but as the first sheaf of the harvest presented to God as a thank-offering, was the pledge and assurance of the ingathering of the whole harvest, so the resurrection of Christ is a pledge and proof of the resurrection of his people. In Rom. 8, 23 and 11, 16, the word ἀπαρχή, *first-fruits*, has the same force. Comp. also Col. 1, 18, where Christ is called "the first begotten from the dead," and Rev. 1, 5. Of the great harvest of glorified bodies which our earth is to yield Christ is the first-fruits. *As* he rose, *so* all his people must; as certainly and as gloriously, Phil. 3, 21. The nature of this causal connection between the resurrection of Christ and that of his people, is explained in the following verses.

21. For since by man (came) death, by man (came) also the resurrection of the dead.

The connection between this verse and the preceding is obvious. The resurrection of Christ secures the resurrection of his people, *for* as there was a causal relation between the death of Adam and the death of his descendants, so there is a causal relation between the resurrection of Christ and that of his people. What that causal relation is, is not here expressed. It is simply asserted that as death is δι' ἀνθρώπου, *by means of a man;* so the resurrection is δι' ἀνθρώπου, *by means of a man.* Why Adam was the cause of death, and why Christ is the cause of life, is explained in the following verse, and abundantly elsewhere in Scripture, but not here. By *death*, in this verse, is meant the death of the body; and by *the resurrection* is meant the restoration of the body to life. This, however, only proves that the death of which Adam was the cause includes physical death, and that the life of which Christ is the cause includes the future life of the body. But as the life which we derive from Christ includes far more than the life of the body, so the death which flows from Adam includes far more than physical death.

22. For as in Adam all die, even so in Christ shall all be made alive.

This is the reason why Adam was the cause of death, and why Christ is the cause of life. We die *by means of* Adam, because we were *in* Adam; and we live *by means of* Christ, because we are *in* Christ. Union with Adam is the cause of death; union with Christ is the cause of life. The nature of this union and its consequences are more fully explained in Rom. 5, 12–21. In both cases it is a representative and vital union. We are in Adam because he was our head and representative, and because we partake of his nature. And we are in Christ because he is our head and representative, and because we partake of his nature through the indwelling of his Spirit. Adam, therefore, is the cause of death, because his sin is the judicial ground of our condemnation; and because we derive from him a corrupt and enfeebled nature. Christ is the cause of life, because his righteousness is the judicial ground of our justification; and because we derive from him the Holy Ghost, which is the source of life both to the soul and body. Comp. Rom. 8, 9–11.

That the word *all* in the latter part of this verse is to be restricted to all believers (or rather, to all the people of Christ, as infants are included) is plain, 1. Because the word in both clauses is limited. It is the all who are in Adam that die; and the all who are in Christ who are made alive. As union with Christ is made the ground of the communication of life here spoken of, it can be extended only to those who are in him. But according to the constant representation of the Scriptures, none are in him but his own people. "If any man be in Christ, he is a new creature," 2 Cor. 5, 17. 2. Because the verb (ζωοποιέω) here found is never used of the wicked. Whenever employed in reference to the work of Christ it always means to communicate to them that life of which he is the source, John 5, 21. 6, 63. Rom. 8. 11. 1 Cor. 15, 45. Gal. 3, 21. The real meaning of the verse therefore, is, 'As in Adam all die, so in Christ shall all be made partakers of a glorious and everlasting life.' Unless, therefore, the Bible teaches that all men are in Christ, and that all through him partake of eternal life, the passage must be restricted to his own people. 3. Because, although Paul elsewhere speaks of a general resurrection both of the just and of the unjust, Acts 24, 15, yet, throughout this chapter he speaks only of the resurrection of the righteous. 4. Because, in the parallel passage in Rom. 5, 12–21, the same limitation must be made. In v. 18 of that chapter it is said, "As by the offence of one judgment came upon all men to condemnation; even so by the righteousness of one the free gift came upon all men to justification of life." That is, as for the offence of Adam all men were condemned, so for the righteousness of Christ all men are justified. The context and the analogy of Scripture require us to understand this to mean, as all who are in Adam are condemned, so all who are in Christ are justified. No historical Christian church has ever held that all men indiscriminately are justified. For whom God justifies them he also glorifies, Rom. 8, 30.

There are two other interpretations of this verse. According to one, the verb, *shall be made alive,* is taken to mean no more than *shall be* raised from the dead. But this, as already remarked, is not only inconsistent with the prevailing use of the word, but with the whole context. Others, admitting that the passage necessarily treats of a resurrection to glory and blessedness, insist that the word *all* must be taken to include all men. But this contradicts the constant doctrine of the Bible, and has no support in the context. It is not absolutely all who die through Adam, but those only who were in him; so it is not absolutely all who live through Christ, but those only who are in him.

23. But every man in his own order: Christ the first-fruits; afterward they that are Christ's at his coming.

In his own *order*. The word τάγμα is properly a concrete term, meaning *a band*, as of soldiers. If this be insisted upon here, then Paul considers the hosts of those that rise as divided into different cohorts or companies; first Christ, then his people, then the rest of mankind. But the word is used by later writers, as Clemens in his Epistle to the Corinthians I. 37, and 41, in the sense of τάξις, *order of succession*. And this best suits the context, for Christ is not a band. All that Paul teaches is, that, although the resurrection of Christ secures that of his people, the two events are not contemporaneous. First Christ, then those who are Christ's. There is no intimation of any further division or separation in time in the process of the resurrection. The resurrection of the people of Christ is to take place *at his coming*, 1 Thess. 3, 13. 4, 14–19.

24. Then (cometh) the end, when he shall have delivered up the kingdom to God, even the Father; when he shall have put down all rule, and all authority and power.

This is a very difficult passage, and the interpretations given of it are too numerous to be recited. The first question is, What is the end here spoken of? The common answer is, That it is the end of the world. That is, the close of the present order of things; the consummation of the work of redemption. In favour of this view, it may be urged, 1. That where there is nothing in the context to determine otherwise, *The end* naturally means the end of all things. There is nothing here to limit the application, but the nature of the subject spoken of. 2. The analogy of Scripture is in favour of this explanation. In 1 Pet. 4, 7 we find the expression "the end of all things is at hand." Matt. 24, 6, "The end is not yet;" v. 14, "Then shall the end come." So in Mark 13, 7. Luke 21, 9. In all these passages *the end* means the end of the world. 3. The equivalent expressions serve to explain the meaning of this phrase. The disciples asked our Lord, "What shall be the sign of thy coming, and of the end of the world?" (i. e. the consummation of the present dispensation.) In answer to this question, our Lord said certain things were to happen, but "the end is not yet;" and afterwards, "then shall the end come." See Matt. 24, 3. 6. 14. The same expression occurs in the same sense, Matt. 13, 39. 28, 20, and elsewhere. "The end," therefore, means the end of the world. In the same sense the phrase "until the restoration of all things" is probably used in Acts 3, 21. 4. What immediately follows seems decisive in favour of this interpretation. The end is, when Christ shall deliver up his kingdom, after having subdued all his enemies; i. e. after having accomplished the work of redemption.

Many commentators understand by *the end*, the end of the resurrection. That work, they say, is to be accomplished by distinct stages. First the resurrection of Christ, then that of his people, then that of the wicked. This last, they say, is expressed by *then cometh the end*, viz., the end of the resurrection. Against this view, however, are all the arguments above stated in favour of the opinion that *the end* means the end of the world. Besides, the doctrine that there are to be two resurrections, one of the righteous and another of the wicked, the latter separated from the former by an unknown period of time, is entirely foreign to the New Testament, unless what is said in the 20th chapter of Revelation teaches that doctrine. Admitting that a twofold resurrection is there spoken of, it would not be proper to transfer from that passage an idea foreign to all Paul's representations of the subject. If that fact was revealed to John, it does not prove that it was revealed to Paul. All that the most stringent doctrine of inspiration requires is, that the passages should not contradict each other. The passage in Revelation, however, is altogether too uncertain to be made the rule of interpretation for the plainer declarations of the epistolary portions of the New Testament. On the contrary, what is doubtful in the former should be explained by what is clearly taught in the latter, Secondly, it is clearly taught in the gospels and epistles that the resurrection of the righteous and of the wicked is to be contemporaneous. At least, that is the mode in which the subject is always presented. The element of time (i. e. the chronological succession of the events) may indeed in these representations be omitted, as is so often the case in the prophecies of the Old Testament. But unless it can be proved from other sources, that events which are foretold as contemporaneous, or as following the one the other in immediate succession, are in fact separated by indefinite periods of time, no such separation can properly be assumed. In the evangelists and epistles the resurrection of the righteous and that of the wicked are spoken of as contemporaneous, and since their separation in time is nowhere else revealed, the only proper inference is that they are to occur together. In Matt. 24, 3, the coming of Christ and the end of the world are coupled together as contemporaneous. And throughout that chapter our Lord foretells what is to happen before that event, and adds, "Then shall appear the sign of the Son of Man in heaven . . . and he shall send his angels with the sound of a great trumpet, and they shall gather together the elect from the four winds, from one end of heaven to the other," vs. 30. 31. In John 5, 28. 29 it is said, "The hour is coming when all (good and bad) who are in their graves shall hear the voice of the Son of Man, and shall come forth, they that have done good unto the resurrection of life, and they that have done evil unto the resurrection of damnation." In 2 Thess. 1, 7–10, Christ is said to come to take vengeance on those who obey not the gospel, and to be glorified in the saints. These events go together. Besides, our Lord repeatedly says that he will raise up his people "at the last day," John 6, 39. 40. 11, 24, and therefore not an indefinitely long period before the last day. According to the uniform representations of the Scriptures, when Christ comes he is to raise all the dead and separate the wicked from among the just as a shepherd divides his sheep from the goats. Or, according to another figure, he is to send forth his angels and separate the tares from the wheat. It has therefore been the constant faith of the church that the second advent of Christ, the resurrection of the just and of the unjust, the final judgment and end of the world—are parts of one great transaction, and not events which are to succeed each other at long intervals of time. All this, however, is said with diffidence and submission. It may prove to be otherwise. The predictions of the Old Testament produced the universal impression that the first coming of Christ was to be attended at once by events which we learn from the New Testament require ages to bring about. Still, we are bound to take the Scriptures as they stand, and events which are described as contemporaneous are to be assumed to be so, until the event proves the contrary. We may be perfectly sure that the Scriptures will prove infallibly true. The predictions of the Old Testament, although in some points misinterpreted, or rather interpreted too far, by the ancient church, were fully vindicated and explained by the event.

The second question to be considered is, When is the end of the world to take place? According to some, at Christ's coming; according to others, at an indefinite period after his second coming. It may be admitted that this verse is not decisive on this point. It marks the succession of certain events, but determines nothing as to the interval between them. First, Christ's resurrection; then the resurrection of his people; then the end of the world. But as it is said that those who are Christ's shall rise at his coming, and then cometh the end; the natural impression is that nothing remains to be done after the resurrection before the end comes. This view is confirmed by the numerous passages of the New Testament, several of which have already been quoted, which connect the general judgment and end of the world as intimately with the coming of Christ as the resurrection of his people. Some of those who assume that an indefinite period is to elapse between the coming of Christ and the end of the world, suppose that the intervening period is to be occupied not in the work of conversion, but in the subjugation of the enemies of Christ spoken of in the following verses. The common opinion among those who adopt this interpretation is, that the interval in question is to be occupied by the personal reign of Christ on earth. This is the doctrine of the ancient Chiliasts, and of modern Millenarians. The form which this doctrine has commonly assumed in ancient and modern times is only a modified Judaism, entirely at variance with the spirituality of the gospel and with the teachings of the apostle in this chapter. He tells us that flesh and blood, i. e. bodies organized as our present bodies are, i. e. natural bodies, cannot inherit the kingdom of God. The whole design of the latter portion of this chapter is to show that after the resurrection, the bodies of believers will be like the glorious body of the Son of God, adapted to a heavenly, and not to an earthly condition.

A third question which this verse presents is, In what sense is Christ to deliver up the kingdom to the Father? In the common text the words are ὅταν παραδῷ, *when he shall have delivered up;* most of the modern editors read παραδιδῷ, *when he delivers up.* That is, when the end comes, Christ is to deliver up the kingdom to his Father. What does this mean? The Scriptures constantly teach that Christ's kingdom is an everlasting kingdom, and of his dominion there is no end. In what sense, then, can he be said to deliver up his kingdom? It must be remembered, that the Scriptures speak of a threefold kingdom as belonging to Christ. 1. That which necessarily belongs to him as a divine person, extending over all creatures, and of which he can never divest himself. 2. That which belongs to him as the incarnate Son of God, extending over his own people. This also is everlasting. He will for ever remain the head and sovereign of the redeemed. 3. That dominion to which he was exalted after his resurrection, when all power in heaven and earth was committed to his hands. This kingdom, which he exercises as the Theanthropos, and which extends over all principalities and powers, he is to deliver up when the work of redemption is accomplished. He was invested with this dominion in his mediatorial character for the purpose of carrying on his work to its consummation. When that is done, i. e. when he has subdued all his enemies, then he will no longer reign over the universe as Mediator, but only as God; while his headship over his people is to continue for ever. *To God even the Father*, i. e. to him who is at once his God and Father. This is the Scriptural designation of the first person of the Trinity. He is the God of the Lord Jesus Christ, inasmuch as he is the God whom Christ came to reveal, and whose work he performs. He is his Father in virtue of the eternal relation subsisting between the first and second persons in the Godhead.

The fourth question which this pregnant verse suggests is presented in the last clause. *When he shall have put down all rule, and authority and power.* Calvin and others understand this to mean, 'When he shall have abrogated all other dominion than his own.' Whatever authority is now exercised by one man over others is at last to be abolished, and merged in the all-pervading authority of God. Most commentators, in obedience to the context, understand the passage to refer to all hostile powers, whether demoniacal or human. These are *to be put down*, i. e. effectually subdued; not annihilated, and not converted; but simply deprived of all power to disturb the harmony of his kingdom.

25. For he must reign, till he hath put all enemies under his feet.

This verse assigns the reason why Christ cannot relinquish his dominion over the universe as mediator until the end comes, and why he will then deliver it up. He must reign until the purpose for which he was invested with this universal dominion is accomplished. As in Ps. 110 it is said to the Messiah, "Sit thou on my right hand until I make thy enemies thy footstool," many assume that *God* is the subject of the verb *has put*. The meaning would then be, 'He must reign until *God* has put all his enemies under his feet.' But this is inconsistent with the context. Christ is to put down all rule, authority and power, v. 24, and he reigns until he has accomplished that work. The two modes of representation are perfectly consistent. The Father created the world, though he did it through the Son, Heb. 1, 3. The work, therefore, is sometimes ascribed to the one and sometimes to the other. In like manner the Father subdues the powers of darkness, but it is through Christ to whom all power in heaven and earth has been committed. It is therefore equally proper to say that God makes the enemies of Christ his footstool, and that Christ himself puts his enemies under his feet. The enemies who are to be thus subdued are not only intelligent beings hostile to Christ, but all the forms of evil, physical and moral, because death is specially included. By subduing, however, is not meant destroying or banishing out of existence. The passage does not teach that Christ is to reign until all evil is banished from the universe. Satan is said to be subdued, when deprived of his power to injure the people of God. And evil in like manner is subdued when it is restrained within the limits of the kingdom of darkness.

26. The last enemy (that) shall be destroyed (is) death.

Death shall reign until the resurrection. Then men shall never more be subject to his power. Then death shall be swallowed up in victory, Luke 20, 26. "Neither shall they die any more," 2 Tim. 1, 10. Rev. 20, 14.

27. For he hath put all things under his feet. But when he saith, All things are put under (him, it is) manifest that he is excepted, which did put all things under him.

The proof that death is finally to be destroyed is derived from the 8th Psalm, where the subjection of *all things* to the Messiah is predicted. There are two passages of the Old Testament frequently quoted in the New Testament as foretelling the absolutely universal dominion of the Messiah, Ps. 110 and Ps. 8. The former is quoted, or its language appropriated, in v. 25. Matt. 22, 44. Acts 2, 34. Eph. 1, 22. Heb. 1, 13. 10, 12. 13. 1 Pet. 3, 22. In this there is no difficulty, as that Psalm clearly refers to the Messiah and to none else. The 8th Psalm is quoted and applied to Christ in this passage, and in Eph. 1, 22. Heb. 2, 8, and 1 Pet. 3, 22. As this Psalm has no apparent reference to the Messiah, but is a thanksgiving to God for his goodness to man, the use made of it in the New Testament is to be understood as an inspired exposition of its hidden meaning. That is, when the Psalmist said, "Thou madest him to have dominion over the works of thy hands, thou hast put all things under his feet," we learn from the New Testament that the Spirit of God intended by these words far more than that man was invested with dominion over the beasts of the field. There is no limit to the *all things* here intended. Heb. 2, 8. Man is clothed with dominion over the whole universe, over all principalities and powers, and every name that is named, not only in this world but also in that which is to come. This is fulfilled in the man Christ Jesus, into whose hands all power in heaven and earth has been committed. This may be called the hidden meaning of the Psalm, because it never would have been discovered without a further revelation such as we find in the exposition given by the inspired apostles. *When he saith*, ὅταν εἴπῃ. This may mean either, when the Scripture saith, or *when God saith.* The latter is better on account of what follows. The verb is not to be translated as in the present tense, but, as the better commentators agree, in the past future, see v. 24. Heb. 1, 6. 'When God shall have said.' That is, when God shall have declared his purpose to subject all things to Christ accomplished, it will then be manifest that all things are subject to him, God only excepted.

28. And when all things shall be subdued unto him, then shall the Son also himself be subject unto him that put all things under him, that God may be all in all.

When the work of redemption has been accomplished, the dead raised, the judgment held, the enemies of Christ all subdued, then, and not till then, will the Son also himself be subject to him who put all things under him. This passage is evidently parallel with that in v. 24. The subjection of the Son to the Father here means precisely what is there meant by his delivering up the kingdom to God even the Father. The thing done, and the person who does it, are the same. The subjection here spoken of is not predicated of the eternal Logos, the second person of the Trinity, any more than the kingdom spoken of in v. 24 is the dominion which belongs essentially to Christ as God. As there the word *Christ* designates the Theanthropos, so does the word *Son* here designate, not the Logos as such, but the Logos as incarnate. And as the delivery of the kingdom or royal authority over the universe committed to Christ after his resurrection, is consistent at once with his continued dominion as God over all creatures, and with his continued headship over his people; so is the subjection here spoken of consistent with his eternal equality with the Father. It is not the subjection of the Son as Son, but of the Son as Theanthropos of which the apostle here speaks. The doctrine of the true and proper divinity of our Lord is so clearly revealed in Scripture, and is so inwrought into the faith of his people, that such passages as these, though adduced with so much confidence by the impugners of that doctrine, give believers no more trouble than the ascription of the limitations of our nature to God. When the Bible says that God repents, we know that it is consistent with his immutability; and when it says the Son is subject or inferior to the Father, we know that it is consistent with their equality, as certainly as we know that saying that man is immortal is consistent with saying he is mortal. We know that both of the last-mentioned propositions are true; because mortality is predicated of man in one aspect, and immortality in another aspect. In one sense he is mortal, in another sense he is immortal. In like manner we know that the verbally inconsistent propositions, the Son is subject to the Father, and, the Son is equal with the Father, are both true. In one sense he is subject, in another sense he is equal. The son of a king may be the equal of his father in every attribute of his nature, though officially inferior. So the eternal Son of God may be coëqual with the Father, though officially subordinate. What difficulty is there in this? What shade does it cast over the full Godhead of our adorable Redeemer? The subordination, however, here spoken of, is not that of the human nature of Christ separately considered, as when he is said to suffer, or to die, or to be ignorant; but it is the official subordination of the incarnate Son to God as God. The words αὐτὸς ὁ υἱός, *the Son himself*, here designate, as in so many other places, not the second person of the Trinity as such, but that person as clothed in our nature. And the subjection spoken of, is not of the former, but of the latter, i. e. not of the Son as Son, but of the Son as incarnate; and the subjection itself is official and therefore perfectly consistent with equality of nature.

There is another difficulty connected with this verse which it may be well to notice. According to the Scriptures and the creeds of all the great historical churches (Greek, Latin, Lutheran and Reformed), the term Son, as applied to Christ, designates his divine nature. It is a term of nature and not of office. He was from eternity the Son of God. Yet it is of the Son that subjection is here predicated. This is urged as an argument against his eternal sonship. The fact, however, is, that the person of Christ may be designated from one nature, when the predicate belongs either to the opposite nature or to the whole person. That is, he may be called God when what is said of him is true only of his human nature or of his complex person as God and man; and he may be called man, when what is said is true only of his divine nature. Thus he is called the Son of Man when omnipresence and omniscience are ascribed to him; and he is called God, the Son of God, the Lord of glory when he is said to die. These passages do not prove that the human nature of Christ is every where present; or that his divine nature suffered and died. Neither do such expressions as that in the text prove that the Son as such is inferior to the Father, nor that the term Son is not a scriptural designation of his divine nature. The principle here adverted to is so important, and serves to explain so many passages of Scripture, that it will bear to be often repeated.

That God may be all in all. Before the ascension of Christ, God reigned as God; after that event he reigned and still reigns through the Theanthropos; when the end comes, the Theanthropos will deliver up this administrative kingdom, and God again be all in all. Such is the representation of Scripture, and such seems to be the simple meaning of this passage. When our Lord ascended up on high all power in heaven and earth was given to him. It was given to him then, and therefore not possessed before. He is to retain this delegated power in his character of Mediator, God-man, until his enemies are put under his feet. Then he, the God-man, is to deliver it up. And God as God will reign supreme. The phrase here used, τὰ πάντα (or πάντα) ἐν πᾶσιν, *all in all*, depends (as is the case with all similar formulas), for its precise meaning on the connection. If words be taken by themselves, and made to mean any thing which their signification will admit, without regard to the context or to the analogy of Scripture, then the authority of the word of God is effectually subverted. No book, human or divine, can be interpreted on a principle so unreasonable. Some, however, regardless of this universally admitted rule of interpretation, say that these words teach that the whole universe is to be merged in God—he is to become all in all—he will be all, and all will be God. Others limit the last *all* to intelligent creatures, and the sense in which God is *all* is restricted to his gracious influence; so that while the continued personal existence of rational creatures is provided for, it is assumed that God is to reign supreme in all intelligent beings. All sin and evil will thus be banished from the whole universe. This interpretation is, in the first place, perfectly arbitrary. If the meaning of the words is to be pressed beyond the limits assigned by the context and the analogy of Scripture, why limit ἐν πᾶσι to intelligent creatures, and τὰ πάντα to mere gracious control? The passage teaches pantheism, if it teaches universalism. Secondly, this interpretation is contrary to the context. Paul is speaking simply of the continuance of the mediatorial dominion of Christ over the universe. That dominion was given to him for a specific purpose; when that purpose is accomplished, he will give it up, and God, instead of reigning through Christ, will be recognized as the immediate sovereign of the universe; his co-equal, co-eternal Son, clothed in our nature, being, as the everlasting head of the redeemed, officially subordinate to him. In other words, the whole question, so to speak, is whose hands are to hold the reins of universal dominion. They are now in the hands of Christ; hereafter they are to be in the hands of God as such. The passage does not teach us the design of redemption, but what is to happen when the redemption of God's people is accomplished. Then the Messianic reign is to cease, and God is to rule supreme over a universe reduced to order, the people of God being saved, and the finally impenitent shut up with Satan and his angels in the prison of despair. Thirdly, the interpretation which makes this passage teach the restoration of all intelligent creatures to holiness, is contrary to the express declarations of Scriptures and to the faith of the church universal. This the most accomplished of its advocates virtually admit. See for example Olshausen's commentary on this epistle. If the evidence in support of the doctrine of the everlasting perdition of the wicked were not overwhelming, it never could have become a part of the faith of the universal church. And that doctrine being once established on its own grounds, doubtful passages must be interpreted in accordance with it.

There is another orthodox interpretation of this passage. It is assumed to treat of the final result of the work of redemption. God will reign supreme in all. But the *all* is restricted to the subjects of redemption. The whole chapter treats of those who are in Christ. It is of their resurrection, and of the effect of redemption in their case, the apostle is assumed to speak. 'All who are in Christ shall be made alive, v. 22, and God shall reign in them all.' The sense is good, but this interpretation overlooks what intervenes between vs. 22 and 28 concerning the kingdom of Christ and its being given up.

29. Else what shall they do which are baptized for the dead, if the dead rise not at all? why are they then baptized for the dead?

The apostle, after the preceding digression, returns to his argument for the resurrection. 'The dead are certainly to be raised, *otherwise* (ἐπεί) what shall they do who are baptized for the dead?' This practice (whatever it was) of baptizing for the dead, takes for granted that the dead are to rise. *What shall they do*, i. e. What account will they give of themselves? what explanation of their conduct can they make? The most important of the numerous interpretations of this verse admit of being reduced to the following classes: 1. Those which turn on the sense given to the word *baptize*. 2. Those which depend on the explanation of the preposition ὑπέρ, *for*.

3. Those which assume an ellipsis in the verse. 4. Those which turn on the explanation of τῶν νεκρῶν, *the dead.* 1. The simplest and most natural interpretation takes the word baptize in its ordinary sense. 'What do they do who allow themselves to be baptized in the place of the dead?' This supposes that the custom of vicarious baptism, as afterwards practised by the Cerinthians and Marcionites, had already been introduced into Corinth. Among those heretical sects, if a catechumen died before baptism, some one was baptized in his name, in order that he might be enrolled among Christians and receive the benefit of the ordinance. The objections to this interpretation are, that the practice was superstitious, founded on wrong views of the nature and efficacy of baptism. 2. That there are no traces elsewhere of the prevalence of vicarious baptism before the second century. 3. That it was universally condemned by the churches as heretical. 4. That it cannot be supposed that the apostle would refer to such a superstitious custom without condemning it. These objections are in a measure met by the following considerations: 1. Paul, so far from intimating any approbation of the custom, distinctly separates himself from its abettors. He does not say, 'What shall we do'—'What shall *they* do.' It was something with which he had no fellowship. 2. That this method of arguing against others from their own concessions, is one which the apostle frequently employs. 3. That when his mind is full of a particular subject he does not leave it, to pronounce judgment on things incidentally introduced. Thus, in chap. 11, 5, when treating of women speaking in the church unveiled, he expresses no disapprobation of their speaking in public, although he afterwards condemned it. A still more striking example of the same thing is to be found 10, 8, where he speaks of the Corinthians "sitting at meat in an idol's temple," without any disapprobation of the thing itself, but only of its influence on the weaker brethren. Yet, in 10, 14–22, he proves that the thing itself was an act of idolatry. 4. That the entire disappearance of this custom in the orthodox church, although other superstitious observances not less objectionable soon prevailed, is probably to be referred to the practice having been forbidden by the apostle as soon as he reached Corinth. This may have been one of the things which he left "to be set in order when he came," 11, 34. 5. The state of the church in Corinth, as disclosed by this epistle, was not such as to render the adoption of such a custom by a portion of the people, incredi-

ble. Baptizing for the dead was not so bad as sitting at the table of devils, 10, 21. A second interpretation under this head gives the word *baptize* the figurative sense which it has in Matt. 20, 22. Luke 12, 50, "I have a baptism to be baptized with; and how am I straitened until it be accomplished!" According to this view, Paul here refers to the baptism of afflictions. 'Why do men suffer so for the hopelessly dead? if the dead are not to rise, what is the use of suffering so much for them? i. e. of labouring so much, and enduring so much for men who, when dead, are never to live again.' This, however, evidently puts a sense on the word *dead*, which it will not bear. It is assumed to designate not those actually dead, but men who when dead are not to rise again.

Of the second class of interpretations some propose to render ὑπέρ by *over*. 'Why do they baptize over the dead? i. e. over their graves.' Sometimes, for the sake of expressing their faith in the resurrection, Christians are said to have been baptized over the graves of the martyrs. Others say that ὑπέρ means in *the place of*. 'Why should men be baptized in place of the dead? i. e. to supply their places in the church, and thus keep up the ranks of believers.' A third class propose to take νεκρῶν for the singular, and to read, 'Why are they baptized for one dead?' Others say the meaning is, *for the dead*, i e. for bodies. What is the use of being baptized for a dead body? a body which is never to live again. He that is baptized receives the ordinance believing that his body is not to remain dead. Calvin and others understand the *dead* to mean here, those about to die. 'Why should baptism be administered for those on the verge of the grave—if there be no resurrection?' Finally, some suppose the passage is elliptical. Fully expressed it would be, 'What do they do who are baptized for the resurrection of the dead?' i. e. in hope of the resurrection which was professed by all who receive baptism. The darkness which rests on this passage can never be entirely cleared away, because the reference is to a custom of which no account is extant. *If the dead rise not at all* belongs tc the latter member of the verse. 'If the dead rise not at all, why are they baptized for them?' Instead of τῶν νεκρῶν, *the dead*, modern editors read αὐτῶν, *them*.

30. And why stand we in jeopardy every hour?

Here Paul speaks for himself. With baptizing for the

dead, he had nothing to do. 'Why do *they* allow themselves,' he asks, 'to be baptized for the dead?' That, as would appear, is what his opponents did. As an additional argument for the doctrine which he is defending, he urges, that its denial destroys at least one of the great motives to self-denial. 'If there be no resurrection, on which all our hopes as Christians depend, why should we voluntarily encounter perpetual danger?' It is to be remembered that, according to Paul's doctrine and previous argument, if there be no resurrection, then Christ is not risen, and if Christ be not risen, there is no atonement, no reconciliation with God. We are in a state of final and hopeless condemnation. What is the use of labouring to save men, if there be no salvation?

31. I protest by your rejoicing which I have in Christ Jesus our Lord, I die daily.

Paul solemnly assures his readers that he was constantly in jeopardy, for, says he, *I die daily*, i. e. I am constantly exposed to death, 2 Cor. 4, 10. *By your boasting which I have.* This is not the meaning, but, '*By my boasting concerning you.*' That is, 'as surely as I boast of you, and rejoice over you.' The pronoun ὑμετέραν, *your*, is to be taken objectively (as in Rom. 11, 31; comp. also 1 Cor. 9, 12) the boasting of which you are the object. *Which I have in Christ Jesus*, i. e. which I have in communion with Christ. It was a rejoicing which he, as a Christian minister, had over them as the seals of his ministry.

32. If after the manner of men I have fought with beasts at Ephesus, what advantageth it me, if the dead rise not? let us eat and drink; for to-morrow we die.

The apostle refers to one, and probably a recent instance of his exposure to death. *If after the manner of men*, i. e. with those views and interests which determine the conduct of ordinary men, i. e. without hope in the resurrection. *I have fought with beasts at Ephesus.* This may be understood either literally or figuratively. Against the literal interpretation is urged, 1. The improbability that, as a Roman citizen, he should have been subjected to that punishment. But his being a Roman citizen did not prevent his being thrice beaten with rods, by Roman magistrates, or at least, by others than

Jews, and contrary to law, 2 Cor. 11, 25. 2. The silence of The Acts on the subject. But we learn from 2 Cor. 11, 23–29, that scarcely a tithe of what Paul did and suffered is recorded in The Acts. 3. The omission of any reference to his exposure to wild beasts in the long enumeration of his sufferings in 2 Cor. 11, 23–29. This is a more serious objection. Considering, moreover, that Paul was at Ephesus exposed to the violent tumult of the people, and that this expression is often used by the ancients figuratively for contests with enraged men, the probability is, that it is to be so understood here. *What to me is the advantage?* 'If I have no other views or hopes than ordinary men, whose expectations are confined to this world, what is the use of incurring so many dangers?' *If the dead rise not.* This clause does not belong to the one preceding, as it is pointed in our version, but to what follows. 'If the dead rise not, let us eat and drink, for to-morrow we die.' The natural consequence of denying the doctrine of the resurrection, involving as it does the denial of the gospel, and the consequent rejection of all hope of salvation, is to make men reckless, and to lead them to abandon themselves to mere sensual enjoyments. If man has no glorious hereafter, he naturally sinks towards the level of the brutes, whose destiny he is to share.

33. Be not deceived: evil communications corrupt good manners.

This warning flows naturally from what had been said. If the tendency of the denial of the resurrection be to render men reckless and sensual, then the Corinthians should not be deceived by the plausible arguments or specious conduct of the errorists among them. They should avoid them, under the conviction that all evil is contagious. Evil *communications.* The word properly means *a being together*, *companionship.* It is contact, association with evil, that is declared to be corrupting. This is a fact of common experience, and therefore the apostle expresses it in a verse borrowed from the Greek poet, Menander, which had probably become a proverb. It is only when men associate with the wicked with the desire and purpose to do them good, that they can rely on the protection of God to preserve them from contamination.

34. Awake to righteousness, and sin not; for some have not the knowledge of God: I speak (this) to your shame.

Surrounded by evil teachers, the Corinthians had need not only of being on their guard against deception, but also of vigilance. *Awake.* The word properly means, *to become sober*, to arouse from a state of drunkenness or torpor. The call is to prompt exertion to shake off the delusion under which they were lying as to their security. *To righteousness*, literally, *righteously*, i. e. in a proper manner. 'Awake rightly,' or, as Luther renders it, *Wake right up*. *And sin not*, i. e. do not allow yourselves to be carried away into sin. This was the end to be answered by their vigilance. There was need of this exhortation, *for some have not the knowledge of God;* literally, *have ignorance of God.* They are ignorant of God; and therefore they deny the resurrection. Comp. Matt. 22, 29, where our Lord says to the Sadducees who denied the resurrection, "Ye do err, not knowing the Scriptures, nor the power of God." *I speak this to your shame.* It should make you ashamed that there are men among you capable of calling in question one of the great essential facts of the gospel—the resurrection of the dead.

Nature of the resurrection body, vs. 35–58.

Having proved the fact of the resurrection, the apostle comes to illustrate its nature, or to teach with what kind of bodies the dead are to rise. It seems that the great objection against the doctrine in the minds of his readers rested on the assumption that our future bodies are to be of the same nature with those which we now have; that is, natural bodies consisting of flesh and blood, and sustained by air, food and sleep. Paul says this is a foolish assumption. Our future bodies may be material and identical with our present bodies, and yet organized in a very different way. You plant a seed; it does not come up a seed, but a flower. Why then may not the future be to the present body what the flower is to the seed? vs. 35–37. Matter admits of indefinite varieties in organization. There is not only immense diversity in the vegetable productions of the earth, but even flesh is variously modified in the different orders of animals, vs. 38. 39. This is true not only as to the earth, for there are heavenly as well as earthly bodies. And even the sun, moon and stars differ from each other in glory; why then may not our future differ from our present bodies in glory? vs. 40. 41. Such not only may be, but will be the case. The body deposited in the grave is corruptible, mean, weak, and, in a word, natural; as raised from the grave, it will be incorruptible, glorious, powerful, and spiritual, vs. 42–44. This is according to Scripture. Adam was created with a natural body, adapted to an earthly state of existence; Christ, as a life-giving spirit, has a spiritual body. As Adam was before Christ, so our earthly tabernacles are before our heavenly ones. As we have borne the image of the earthly, we shall bear the image of the heavenly, vs. 45–49. It is freely admitted that flesh and blood, i. e. bodies organized as ours now are, are unfit for heaven. Corruption cannot inherit incorruption, v. 50. But our bodies are to be changed. This change shall be instantaneous and at the last day. It shall embrace both the living and the dead. Corruption shall put on incorruption, mortality shall put on immortality, vs. 51–53. When this is done, the original promise that death shall be swallowed up in victory, will be fully accomplished, v. 54. Death, therefore, to the believer, has lost its sting, and the grave is conquered. Death has no sting but sin; sin has no strength but from the law; the law has no power over those who are in Christ Jesus, therefore thanks be to God, who giveth us the victory through Christ Jesus our Lord! vs. 55–57. Seeing then that we have such a glorious hereafter, we should be steadfast, unmoveable, always abounding in the work of the Lord, v. 58.

35. But some (man) will say, How are the dead raised up? and with what body do they come?

The discussion of the fact of the resurrection being ended, the apostle comes to consider the manner of it. He supposes some objector to ask, *How are the dead raised up?* This may mean, How can a corrupted and disorganized body be restored to life? And the next question, *With what body do they come?* may refer to the result of the process. What is to be the nature of our future bodies? Or the latter question may be merely explanatory of the former, so that only one point is presented. *How*, i. e. with what kind of body are the dead raised? There are, however, two distinct questions, for although the two are not connected by καί, *and*, but by the particle δέ, which might be merely explanatory, yet the apostle really answers, in what follows, both questions, viz., How it is possible for life to come out of death, and, What is to be the nature of the body after the resurrection. The latter difficulty was the main one, and therefore to that the most of what follows refers. The great objection in the minds of the Corinthians to the doctrine of the resurrection was evidently the same as that of the Sadducees. Both supposed our future bodies are to be like our present ones. Our Lord's answer to the Sadducees, therefore, is the same as that which Paul gives to the Corinthian objectors. The future body is not to be like the present. To reject a plainly-revealed and most important doctrine on such grounds as these is wicked as well as foolish, and therefore the apostle says in the next verse—

36. (Thou) fool, that which thou sowest is not quickened, except it die.

It is not, *Thou* fool, but simply, Fool! an exclamation both of disapprobation and contempt. Luke 12, 20. Rom. 1, 22. Eph. 5, 15. It does not, however, necessarily express any bitterness of feeling; for our blessed Lord said to his doubting disciples, "O fools, and slow of heart to believe all that the prophets have spoken!" Luke 24, 25. It was the senselessness of the objection that roused the apostle's indignation. The body cannot live again because it dies. Fool! says Paul, a seed cannot live unless it does die. Disorganization is the necessary condition of reorganization. If the seed remain a seed there is an end of it. But if it die, it bringeth forth much fruit, John 12, 24. The seed is as much disorganized, it as really ceases to be a seed when sown in the ground, as the body when laid in the grave. If the one dies, the other dies. Death is not annihilation, but disorganization; the passing from one form or mode of existence to another. How then can the disorganization of the body in the grave be an objection to the doctrine of a resurrection? It may be said that the apostle does not pursue the objection; that the body is not only disorganized but dispersed; its elements scattered over the earth, and embraced in new combinations; whereas in the seed the germ remains, so that there is no interruption of the organic life of the plant. To those who make this objection our Saviour's answer is, that they err, "not knowing the power of God." Who knows where the principle of the organic life of the body is? It may be in the soul, which when the time comes may unfold itself into a new body, gathering or regathering its materials according to its own law; just as the principle of vegetable life in the seed unfolds itself into some gorgeous flower, gathering from surrounding nature the materials for its new organization. The identity between the present and future body is implied in the apostle's illustration. But it is his object neither to assert that identity, nor to explain its nature. The latter is a very subordinate point. The Bible clearly teaches that our bodies hereafter are to be the same as those which we now have; but it nowhere teaches us wherein that sameness consists. In what sense is a sprouting acorn the same with the full-grown oak? Not in substance, not in form, not in appearance. It is, however, the same individual organism. The same is true of the human body. It is the same in old age that it was in infancy. But in what sense? The materials of which the body is composed change many times in the course of an ordinary life, yet the body remains the same. We may rest assured that our future bodies will be the same with those which we now have in a high and satisfying sense, though until the time comes we may be as little able to explain the nature of that identity as we are to tell what constitutes the identity of the body in this life. The same body which is sown in tears, shall be reaped in joy. To doubt the fact of the resurrection, because we cannot understand the process, is, as the apostle says, a proof of folly.

37. And that which thou sowest, thou sowest not that body that shall be, but bare grain, it may chance of wheat, or of some other (grain):

The first clause of this verse stands, as it were, absolutely. And *as to* that which thou sowest—*thou sowest not the body that shall be.* That is, you do not sow the plant, but the *bare grain*, i. e. the simple, naked grain—*it may be of wheat, or of some other grain.* The point of the illustration is, that what comes up is very different from that which is deposited in the ground. You sow a seed, a plant appears. You sow a natural, corruptible body; a spiritual, incorruptible body appears. Nature itself therefore teaches that the objection that the future body must be like the present, is of no force.

38. But God giveth it a body as it hath pleased him, and to every seed his own body.

What is deposited in the earth is very different from that which springs from it. Every seed produces its own plant. The product depends on the will of God. It was determined at the creation, and therefore the apostle says that God, in the continual agency of his providence, gives to each seed its own appropriate product, *as he willed*, i. e. he originally purposed. The point of this is, if God thus gives to all the products of the earth each its own form, why may he not determine the form in which the body is to appear at the resurrection? You cannot infer from looking at a seed what the plant is to be; it is very foolish, therefore, to attempt to determine from our present bodies what is to be the nature of our bodies hereafter.

39. All flesh (is) not the same flesh: but (there is) one (kind of) flesh of men, another flesh of beasts, another of fishes, (and) another of birds.

If even here, where the general conditions of life are the same, we see such diversity in animal organizations, flesh and blood appearing in so many forms, why should it be assumed that the body hereafter must be the same cumbrous vehicle of the soul that it is now?

40. (There are) also celestial bodies, and bodies terrestrial: but the glory of the celestial (is) one, and the (glory) of the terrestrial (is) another.

There is no limit to be set to the possible or actual modifications of matter. We not only see it in all the diversified forms of animal and vegetable life, but in the still greater diversities of heavenly and earthly bodies. What Paul here means by *bodies celestial*, is doubtful. 1. Many suppose the reference is to angels, either on the assumption that they too have bodies, or that the apostle refers to the forms in which they appear to men. When they become visible they must assume some material vehicle, which was always luminous or glorious. Of the angel who appeared at the sepulchre of Christ it is said, "His countenance was like lightning, and his raiment white as snow," Matt. 28, 3. There is a great contrast between the bodies of these celestial beings and those of men. 2. Others suppose that the reference is to the bodies of the saints in heaven. There are many kinds of bodies here on earth, and there are also celestial as well as terrestrial bodies. The one differing from the other in glory. 3. The common opinion is that the apostle means what is now generally meant by "the heavenly bodies," viz., the sun, moon and stars. To this it is objected that it is to make the apostle use the language of modern astronomy. This, however, has little force; for whatever the ancients conceived the sun, moon and stars to be, they regarded them as bodies, and used the word σῶμα in reference to them or to the universe. Galen, who was born not more than sixty or seventy years after the date of this epistle, uses nearly the same language as the apostle does. He too contrasts τὰ ἄνω σώματα (meaning the sun, moon and stars,) with τὰ γήϊνα σώματα. See Wetstein. The common interpretation is also sustained by the context, for the sun, moon and stars mentioned in the next verse are evidently included in the heavenly bodies here intended.

41. (There is) one glory of the sun, and another glory of the moon, and another glory of the stars; for (one) star differeth from (another) star in glory.

Not only do the heavenly bodies differ from the earthly bodies in glory, but there is great diversity among the heavenly bodies themselves. How different is the sun from the moon, the moon from the stars, and even one star from another. Standing, therefore, as we do in the midst of this wonderful universe, in which we see matter in every conceivable modification, from a clod of earth to a sunbeam, from dust to the lustre of the human eye, how unutterably absurd is it to say that if we are to have bodies hereafter, they must be as gross, and heavy, and as corruptible as those which we have now.

42. So also (is) the resurrection of the dead. It is sown in corruption, it is raised in incorruption:

So also is the resurrection of the dead. That is, as the heavenly bodies differ from the earthly bodies, and as one star differs from another star, so the resurrection body will differ from our present body. The apostle does not mean that as one star differs from another star in glory, so one risen believer will differ from another. This, no doubt, is true; but it is not what Paul here says or intimates. His object is simply to show the absurdity of the objection founded on the assumption that the body hereafter must be what it is here. He shows that it may be a body and yet differ as much from what it is now as the light of the sun differs from a piece of clay. He therefore proceeds to show wherein this difference consists. The body *is sown in corruption; it is raised in incorruption.* The figure of the seed is again introduced. The bodies of the saints are as seed sown in the ground, not there to be lost or to remain; but at the appointed time, to rise in a state the very reverse of that in which they were committed to the dust. *It is sown in corruption,* i. e. it is now a corruptible body, constantly tending to decay, subject to disease and death, and destined to entire dissolution. *It is raised in incorruption.* Hereafter it will be imperishable; free from all impurity, and incapable of decay.

43. 44. It is sown in dishonour, it is raised in glory: it is sown in weakness, it is raised in power: it is sown a natural body, it is raised a spiritual body. There is a natural body, and there is a spiritual body.

The apostle contemplates the body as at the moment of interment, and therefore these predicates are to be understood with special reference to its condition at that time. It is the dead body that is sown in dishonour, despoiled of the short-lived attractiveness which it had while living. It is raised *in glory,* i. e. in that resplendent brightness which diffuses light and awakens admiration. It is to be fashioned like unto the glorious body of the Son of God, Phil. 3, 21. *It is sown in weakness.* Nothing is more absolutely powerless than a corpse —it can do nothing and it can resist nothing. The weakness which belonged to it in life, is perfected in death. *It is raised in power.* The future body will be instinct with energy, endowed, it may be, with faculties of which we have now no conception. *It is sown a natural body, it is raised a spiritual body.* This comprehends all that has been said. A natural body, σῶμα ψυχικόν, is a body of which the ψυχή, or animal life, is the animating principle; and a spiritual body, σῶμα πνευματικόν, is a body adapted to the πνεῦμα, the rational, immortal principle of our nature. We know from experience what a natural body is. It is a body which has essentially the same properties as those of brutes. A natural body consists of flesh and blood; is susceptible of pain and decay; and needs air, food, and rest. It is a mere animal body, adapted to the conditions of an earthly existence. What a spiritual body is, we know only from Paul's description, and from the manifestation of Christ in his glorified body. We know that it is incorruptible, glorious, and powerful, adapted to the higher state of existence in heaven, and therefore not adapted to an earthly condition. *Spiritual*, in this connection, does not mean ethereal, refined, much less *made of spirit*, which would be a contradiction. Nor does it mean animated by the Holy Spirit. But as σῶμα ψυχικόν is a body adapted to the ψυχή or principle of animal life, the σῶμα πνευματικόν is a body adapted to the πνεῦμα or principle of rational life. The Bible uses these terms just as we do, without intending to teach that the ψυχή or *life*, is a distinct substance or subject from the πνεῦμα or *rational spirit*, but only that as we have certain attributes, considered as living creatures, in common with irrational animals, so we have now a body suited to those attributes; and, on the other hand, as we have attributes unspeakably higher than those which belong to brutes, we shall hereafter possess bodies adapted to those higher attributes. The Bible recognizes in man only two subjects or distinct separable substances, the soul and body. And this has ever been a fundamental principle of Christian anthropology.

There is a natural body, and there is a spiritual body. This is a vindication of the apparently contradictory expression, *spiritual body*, which, according to the letter, is tantamount to *immaterial matter*. If, however, it is proper to speak of σῶμα ψυχικόν, *a natural body*, i. e. a body adapted to the principle of animal life; it is right to speak of a σῶμα πνευματικόν, *a spiritual body*, i. e. a body adapted to the spirit. Lachmann, Rückert, and Tischendorf, after the ancient MSS. and versions, adopt the reading εἰ ἔστι, κ.τ.λ. *If* there is a natural body, there is a spiritual body. Just as certainly as we have a body adapted to our lower nature, we shall have one adapted to our higher nature. If the one exists, so does the other.

45. And so it is written, The first man Adam was made a living soul; the last Adam (was made) a quickening spirit.

So it is written, i. e. the Scriptures are in accordance with the preceding representation. They represent Adam as having been created with an animal nature, and therefore as having an animal body. Whereas, the second Adam is a person of a far higher order. The proof with regard to the nature of Adam does not rest exclusively on the words quoted, but on the whole account of his creation, of which those words form a part. It is evident from the entire history, that Adam was formed for an existence on this earth, and therefore with a body adapted to the present state of being; in its essential attributes not differing from those which we have inherited from him. He was indeed created immortal. Had he not sinned, he would not have been subject to death. For death is the wages of sin. And as Paul elsewhere teaches, death is by sin. From what the apostle, however, here says of the contrast between Adam and Christ; of the earthly and perishable nature of the former as opposed to the immortal, spiritual nature of the latter, it is plain that Adam as originally created was not, as to his body, in that state which would fit him for his immortal existence. After his period of probation was passed, it is to be inferred, that a change in him would have taken place, analogous to that which is to take place in those believers who shall be alive when Christ comes. They shall not die, but they shall be changed. Of this change in the constitution of his body, the tree of life was probably constituted the sacrament. For when he sinned, he was excluded from the garden of Eden, "lest he put forth his hand and take of the tree of life, and eat, and live for ever," Gen. 3, 22. Some change, therefore, was to take place in his body, to adapt it to live for ever. *He was made a living soul*, *ψυχὴν ζῶσαν*. He had a *ψυχή*, and therefore a body adapted to it. Both the Greek word *ψυχή* and the corresponding Hebrew term are frequently used for the immortal principle of our nature—the rational soul—but they also, and perhaps most frequently, mean life in that form which we have in common with other animals. This idea is included in the passage quoted from Genesis. It is to be remembered that the quotations given in the New Testament from the Old Testament are not mere quotations, but authoritative expositions. Paul tells us what the Spirit of God meant, when he called Adam a *living soul*.

The last Adam, i. e. Christ. This was not an unusual designation for the Messiah among the Jews, though not found in Scripture elsewhere than here. The appropriateness of the designation is evident. Christ is the second great head and representative man, of whom Adam is declared to have been the type, Rom. 5, 14. Was made *a quickening spirit*. Adam was in his distinctive character, that is, as distinguished from Christ, an animal—a creature endowed with animal life, whereas Christ has life in himself, and can give life to as many as he will, John 5, 21. 26. This does not of course mean that Adam had nothing more than animal life. It does not deny that he had a rational and immortal soul. Neither does it imply that our Lord had not, while on earth, a ψυχή or principle of life in common with us. The apostle simply contrasts the first and second Adam as to their distinguishing characteristics. The one was a man; the other infinitely more.

There are two questions suggested by this passage. The first is, on what ground does the apostle assert that Christ was made a quickening spirit? When he says, at the beginning of the verse, "So it is written," does he intend to appeal to the support of Scripture not only for what he says of the nature of Adam, but also for what he says of the person of Christ? If so, the proof cannot rest on the passage quoted, for that relates exclusively to Adam. If the apostle intended to cite the Scriptures for both parts of the declaration in the preceding verse, "there is a natural body, and there is a spiritual body," he must mean the Scriptures in express terms declare Adam to have had a living soul, and they set forth Christ as a life-giving Spirit. It is more commonly assumed, however, that the quotation is limited to the first clause. 'The Scriptures say that the first Adam "was made a living soul;" the last Adam (we know) was made a life-giving Spirit.'

The second question is, When was Christ made a quickening spirit? The apostle does not refer to what Christ was before his incarnation, but to what he became. The subject of discourse is, *the last Adam*. When did he become a quickening spirit? Some say at his incarnation. This is undoubtedly true. As the incarnate Son of God he was life-giving. "It pleased the Father that he should have life in himself," John 5, 26. That is, that the divine and human nature should be united in his person. And in this constitution of his person it was already determined that, although while on earth he should have a body like our own, yet his whole person, including 'his true body and reasonable soul,' should be adapted to sit at the right hand of God. Adam was first formed for this earth, and had an earthly body; the person of Christ was constituted in reference to his reigning in heaven, and therefore he has a spiritual body. The apostle argues from the nature of Adam to the nature of his body; and from the nature of Christ to the nature of his body. This argument does not involve the assumption that the body of Christ was here a spiritual one—for we know that it was flesh and blood; but that such was the state to which, from the very constitution of his person, he was destined, a spiritual body alone could be suited to him. The last Adam, therefore, was made a quickening spirit, by the union of the divine with the human in the constitution of his person. Others say that it was at his resurrection; and others, at his ascension. As to the former opinion, it is enough to say, that no change took place at his resurrection in the nature of Christ's body. It was necessary in order to its satisfactory identification that it should remain the same that it was before. He therefore not only called upon his disciples to handle his risen body and to satisfy themselves of its identity by probing the wounds in his hands and feet, but he also repeatedly ate before them. He did not assume his permanent pneumatic state until his ascension. But this did not make him a quickening spirit. It only affected his body, which then assumed the state adapted to its condition in heaven.

46. Howbeit that (was) not first which is spiritual, but that which is natural; and afterward that which is spiritual.

This does not mean simply that the natural *body* precedes the spiritual *body*. But it announces, as it were, a general law. The lower precedes the higher; the imperfect the perfect. This is true in all the works of God, in which there is a development. Adam's earthly state was to be preparatory to a heavenly one. The present life is like a seed time, the harvest is hereafter. The natural comes before the spiritual; as Calvin says, we are born before we are regenerated, we live before we rise.

47. The first man (is) of the earth, earthy: the second man (is) the Lord from heaven.

The general principle stated in the preceding verse, that

the natural precedes the spiritual, is here illustrated by the fact that Adam came before Christ. *The first man was of the earth*, i. e. formed out of the earth, and therefore *earthy*. *The second man is the Lord from heaven.* Here the text is doubtful. The authorities are about equally divided for and against the reading ὁ κύριος, *the Lord*. The sentence is more simple if that word be omitted. 'The first man was from the earth; the second man was from heaven.' If the common text be retained, the word *Lord* is in apposition with the words *the second man*. 'The second man, the Lord, was from heaven.' This passage was used by the early heretics of the Gnostic school to sustain their doctrine that our Lord was not really born of the Virgin Mary, but was clothed in a body derived from heaven, in opposition to whom the early creeds declare that he was as to his human nature consubstantial with man, and as to his divine nature consubstantial with God. The text, however, simply asserts the heavenly origin of Christ. Adam was of the earth; Christ was from heaven; comp. John 3, 13. Adam, therefore, had a body suited to the earth; Christ has a body suited to heaven.

48. As (is) the earthy, such (are) they also that are earthy; and as (is) the heavenly, such (are) they also that are heavenly.

The earthy is of course Adam; *they that are earthy* are his descendants. *The heavenly* is Christ; *they that are heavenly* are his risen people. The descendants of Adam derive from him an earthly body like his. Those who are Christ's are to have a body fashioned like unto his glorious body, Phil. 3, 21.

49. And as we have borne the image of the earthy, we shall also bear the image of the heavenly.

In this passage, instead of the future φορέσομεν, *we shall bear*, the great majority of the oldest MSS. read the conjunctive φορέσωμεν, *let us bear*. The context, however, so evidently demands the future, that the common reading is preferred by almost all editors. An exhortation here would be entirely out of place. The apostle is evidently proceeding with his discussion. He is obviating the objection to the doctrine of the resurrection founded on the assumption that our bodies hereafter are to be of the same kind as those which we have here. This is not so. They are to be like the body of Christ. As we have borne the image of Adam as to his body, we shall bear the image of Christ as to his body. The idea that as we have derived a corrupt nature from Adam, we derive a holy nature from Christ, though true in itself, is altogether foreign to the connection.

50. Now this I say, brethren, that flesh and blood cannot inherit the kingdom of God; neither doth corruption inherit incorruption.

This I say. These words admit of three interpretations. 1. They may be understood concessively. 'This I concede, brethren. I admit that flesh and blood, our bodies as now organized, cannot inherit the kingdom of God. But that is not what I teach when I preach the doctrine of the resurrection. Our bodies are to be changed.' 2. The sense may be, 'This is what I say, the sum of what I have said is that flesh and blood,' &c. 3. The words may mean, 'This I assert, brethren. I assure you of this fact, that flesh and blood,' &c. In 7, 29 the expression is used in this sense. Comp. also Rom. 3, 8 and 1 Cor. 10, 19.

Flesh and blood means our body as now constituted, not sinful human nature. The phrase never has this latter sense. In Heb. 2, 14, it is said, "Inasmuch as the children are partakers of flesh and blood, he (Christ) also himself likewise took part of the same," Matt. 16, 17. Gal. 1, 16. Eph. 6, 12. It is indeed true, that our unsanctified nature, or unrenewed man, cannot inherit the kingdom of God. But that is not what the apostle is speaking about. He is speaking of the body and of its state after the resurrection. It is of the body as now constituted that he says, *it cannot inherit the kingdom of heaven*, i. e. the kingdom of Christ as it is to exist after the resurrection, Matt, 8, 11. Luke 13, 28. 1 Cor. 6, 9. Gal. 5, 21. 2 Tim. 4, 18. The same idea is repeated in abstract terms and as a general proposition in the next clause, *neither can corruption inherit incorruption.* The mortal cannot be immortal; the perishable imperishable. Incorruption cannot be an attribute of corruption. Our bodies, therefore, if they are to be immortal and imperishable must be changed. And this the apostle in the next verse announces on the authority of a direct revelation, is actually to occur.

51. Behold, I shew you a mystery; We shall not all sleep, but we shall all be changed,

A mystery; something revealed, and which could not otherwise be known, Matt. 13, 11. 1 Cor. 4, 1, and often elsewhere. What is here expressed by saying, *I show you a mystery*, is in 1 Thess. 4, 15 expressed by saying, 'This I say unto you *by the word of the Lord*,' i. e. by divine revelation. The revelation which Paul now declares, and to which he calls special attention by the word, Behold! is, that all are not to die, but all are to be changed, i. e. so changed that their corruptible body shall be rendered incorruptible. The common text is, πάντες μὲν οὐ κοιμηθησόμεθα, the negative being connected with the verb, so that the literal sense would be, *all are not to die.* This is said of *all* whom Paul addressed. The apostle tells them all that they are not to die. To avoid this impossible sense, for Paul certainly did not mean to assure the Corinthians that it had been revealed to him that none of them should die, most of the older commentators assume in common with our translators a not unusual trajection of the negative particle, πάντες οὐ standing for οὐ πάντες. Others explain the verse thus: 'We all — shall indeed not die (before the resurrection) — but we shall all be changed.' It is said this is contrary to the context, inasmuch as *being changed* is something peculiar to those who should be alive at the coming of Christ, and is not affirmed of the dead. This, however, is contrary to the fact. Paul had said, v. 50, that flesh and blood could not inherit the kingdom of God. All, therefore, who enter that kingdom, whether they die before the second advent or survive the coming of Christ, must be changed. And that is the fact which Paul says had been revealed to him. Those who died before the advent would not fail of the blessings of Christ's kingdom, and those who should be alive when he came, would not be left in their corruptible bodies. Both should be changed, and thus prepared for the heavenly state.*

* The difficulty, however, attending the common text, has given rise to a great variety of readings in the MSS. and versions. A. C. F. G. have πάντες μὲν κοιμηθησόμεθα, οὐ πάντες δὲ ἀλλαγησόμεθα, *we shall indeed all die, but we shall not all be changed.* D. and the Vulgate have: πάντες μὲν ἀναστησόμεθα, οὐ πάντες δὲ ἀλλαγησόμεθα, *we shall all rise, but we shall not all be changed.* There are several less important variations. These are all explained as attempts on the part of transcribers to escape making the apostle say that the Christians of that generation were not to die. But as the common text does not make him say that, there is no necessity for departing from it.

Comp. 1 Thess. 4, 15–17. The modern commentators, both German and English, understand the apostle as expressing the confident expectation that he and others of that generation should survive the coming of Christ. 'Though we (who are now alive) shall not all die, we shall all be changed.' But 1. This is altogether unnecessary. The *we all* includes all believers who had lived, were living, or ever should live. There is nothing either in the form of expression or in the context to limit it to the men of that generation. In the same way Paul says in 1 Thess. 4, 15, "We that are alive at the coming of the Lord shall not prevent them that are asleep." This does not imply that he expected to be alive when Christ came. In his second Epistle to the Thessalonians he warns them against the expectation of the speedy advent of Christ, telling them that a great apostasy and the revelation of the Man of Sin were to occur before that event. 2. The plenary inspiration of the sacred writers rendered them infallible in all they taught; but it did not render them omniscient. They could not err in what they communicated, but they might err, and doubtless did err, as to things not included in the communications of the Spirit. The time of the second advent was not revealed to them. They profess their ignorance on that point. They were, therefore, as to that matter, on a level with other men, and may have differed in regard to their private conjectures on the subject just as others differ. It would not, in the least, therefore, encroach on their authority as infallible teachers, if it should be apparent that they cherished erroneous expectations with regard to that about which they professed to know nothing. Knowing that Christ was to come, and not knowing when he was to come, it was perfectly natural that they should look on his advent as constantly imminent, until it was revealed that certain events not yet accomplished, were to occur before Christ came. But all this is very different from any didactic statement that he was to come within a certain period. Paul might exhort Christians to wait and long for the coming of the Lord; but he could not tell them *by the word of the Lord* that he and others then living would be alive when he came. This would not only be teaching error, but it would be claiming divine authority, or a special revelation, for that error. It is, therefore, only at the expense of all confidence in the inspiration of the apostle that the exposition above mentioned can be adopted.

52. In a moment, in the twinkling of an eye, at the last trump: for the trumpet shall sound, and the dead shall be raised incorruptible, and we shall be changed.

The change in question is to be instantaneous; *in a moment*, literally, *an atom*, i. e. in a portion of time so short as to be incapable of further division. It is to take place *at the last trump*, i. e. on the last day. As the trumpet was used for assembling the people or marshalling a host, it became the symbol for expressing the idea of the gathering of a multitude. So, in Matt. 24, 31, Christ says, "He will send his angels with a great sound of a trumpet; and they shall gather his elect from the four winds, from one end of heaven to another." Comp. Is. 27, 13. 1 Thess. 4, 16. This trumpet is called the *last*, not because several trumpets (the Jews say seven) are to sound in succession, but because it is the last that ever is to sound. In other words, the resurrection is to take place on the last day. *For the trumpet shall sound.* This is a confirmation of the preceding. That day shall surely come—the voice of the archangel, the trump of God, shall certainly resound as it did from Sinai, Ex. 19, 16. *And*, i. e. and then, in consequence of the summons of God, *the dead shall be raised* in the manner described in vs. 42. 43, incorruptible, glorious and powerful. *And we shall be changed.* This is in exact accordance with 1 Thess. 4, 15. Those who are alive when Christ comes "shall not prevent them which are asleep." The dead in Christ shall rise first, and then the living shall undergo their instantaneous change. As remarked on the preceding verse, it is not necessary to understand the apostle as including himself and fellow believers in Corinth, when he says *We* shall be changed. The connection indeed is different here from what it is there. There he says, "*We* shall not all die." If that means that the men of that generation should not all die, it is a positive assertion of what the event has proved to be false. But here he simply says, all who are alive when Christ comes shall be changed. If he hoped that he might be of the number there would be nothing in that expectation inconsistent with his inspiration. Calvin, therefore, so understands the passage.* Considering, however, his ex-

* Quum autem dicit, *Nos immutabimur* in eorum numero se comprehendit qui victuri sunt ad Christi adventum; quoniam jam erant postrema tempora, expectandus fuit dies ille in singulas horas.

press teaching in 2 Thess. 2, 2–12 on the subject, it is far more natural to understand him as contemplating the vast company of believers as a whole, and saying 'Those of us who are dead shall rise, and all who are alive shall be changed.'

53. For this corruptible must put on incorruption, and this mortal (must) put on immortality.

This is the reason why we must be changed. 'We must all be changed, for this corruptible must put on incorruption.' It is impossible that corruption should inherit incorruption. This reason applies equally to the quick and to the dead. With regard to both classes it is true that these vile bodies must be fashioned like unto Christ's glorious body.

54. So when this corruptible shall have put on incorruption, and this mortal shall have put on immortality, then shall be brought to pass the saying that is written, Death is swallowed up in victory.

When the change above described has been accomplished, when once the resurrection has taken place, then, according to the language of Scripture, death shall be completely conquered. Not only shall those over whom he had triumphed, and whom he had so long detained in the prison of the grave, be delivered from his power, but there shall be no more death. The passage quoted is Isaiah 25, 8, "He will swallow up death in victory." In Hebrew the last words mean literally *for ever.* They are, however, frequently translated by the LXX. as they are here rendered by the apostle. The sense is the same. The victory over death is to be complete and final.

55. O death, where (is) thy sting? O grave, where (is) thy victory?

The apostle places himself and his readers in presence of the Saviour and of the risen dead arrayed in immortality; and in view of that majestic scene he breaks out in these words of triumph: 'Christ has conquered. His people are redeemed. Death is disarmed. Hades is no more.' Death is addressed under the figure of an animal armed with a poisonous sting which pierces even to the soul; for that sting is sin. *The grave*, or the Greek word Hades, means, *what is un-*

seen, the invisible world, the abode of the dead in the widest sense. It depends on the context whether the immediate reference be to the grave, the place of departed spirits, or hell, in the modern sense of that word. Here where the special reference is to the bodies of men and to the delivery of them from the power of death, it is properly rendered the grave. The only sense in which the body can be in Hades is that it is in the grave. The apostle is not speaking of the delivery of the souls of men from any intermediate state, but of the redemption of the body. In Hosea 13, 14 God says, "O death, I will be thy plagues; O grave, I will be thy destruction." This is a literal version of the Hebrew. The Vulgate comes near to it, Ero mors tua, O mors! Morsus tuus ero, inferne! The LXX. depart from the figure, "Where is thy judgment (or vengeance), O death? where is thy sting, O grave?" These are all different forms of expressing the idea that death and the grave are completely conquered. The apostle does not quote the prophet. He expresses an analogous idea in analogous terms. In speaking of death as furnished with a sting, the most natural figure is that of a scorpion. Others say that κέντρον· here means *a goad*, and that death is compared to a man driving animals before him with such an instrument. The power of a goad is as nothing to that of the sting of a scorpion, Rev. 9, 5. 6. 10, and the figure is therefore far more forcible as commonly understood.*

56. The sting of death (is) sin; and the strength of sin (is) the law.

The sting of death is sin; that is, death would have no power to injure us if it were not for sin. This is true for two reasons. 1. Because if there were no sin there would be no death. Death is by sin, Rom. 5, 12. 2. Because sin gives death, when it has been introduced, all its terrors. If sin be pardoned, death is harmless. It can inflict no evil. It becomes a mere transition from a lower to a higher state. *The strength of sin is the law.* This must be the law of God in its widest sense; not the Mosaic law, which would make the declaration amount to nothing. The law is the strength of

* The MSS. B. D. E. F. G., and most of the versions, read, ποῦ σοῦ, θάνατε, τὸ κέντρον; ποῦ σοῦ, θάνατε, τὸ νῖκος; *where, O death, is thy sting? where, O death, thy victory?* A reading which Tischendorf and other modern editors have adopted.

sin for two reasons. 1. Because without law there would be no sin, Rom. 4, 15. The very idea of sin is want of conformity on the part of moral creatures to the law of God. If there be no standard to which we are bound to be conformed, there can be no such thing as want of conformity. Sin is the correlative, not of reason, nor of expediency, but of law. If you take away law, men may act unreasonably, or in a way injurious to themselves or others, but they cannot sin. 2. Because if there be no law there can be no condemnation. Sin is not imputed where there is no law, Rom. 5, 13. There is still another reason, which, though presented elsewhere by the apostle, is foreign to this connection, and that is, that the law not only reveals and condemns sin, but it exasperates and excites it, and thus gives it strength, Rom. 7, 8–12.

57. But thanks (be) to God, which giveth us the victory through our Lord Jesus Christ.

The victory here meant is, of course, the victory over death and the grave. Thanks be to God, who delivers us from the power of death, redeeming even our bodies from the grave, and making us partakers of everlasting life. This is done through Jesus Christ our Lord, i. e. our divine possessor and absolute ruler. It is through him, and through him alone. 1. Because he has satisfied the demands of the law. It has no power to condemn those who are clothed in his righteousness. There is no condemnation to those who are in Christ Jesus, Rom. 8, 1. Who shall lay any thing to the charge of God's elect? It is God that justifieth, who is he that condemneth? Rom. 8, 33. 34. Christ by his death hath destroyed him that had the power of death, that is, the devil, and delivered them who through fear of death were all their lifetime subject to bondage, Heb. 2, 14. 15. That is, in virtue of the death of Christ, by which the demands of justice are satisfied, Satan, the great executioner of divine justice, has no longer the right or power to detain the people of Christ under the power of death. If, therefore, it be the law which gives sin its reality and strength, and if sin gives death its sting, he who satisfies the law destroys the strength of sin, and consequently the sting of death. It is thus that Christ deprives death of all power to injure his people. It is for them disarmed and rendered as harmless as an infant. 2. But Christ not only gives us this victory through his justifying righteousness, but by his almighty power, he new creates the soul after the image of God, and, what is here principally intended, he repairs all the evils which death had inflicted. He restores us to that state, and even to more than that state, from which sin had cast us down. He rescues our bodies from the grave, and fashions them like unto his glorious body, even by that power whereby he is able to subdue all things unto himself, Phil. 3, 21. Had it not been for Christ, death would have reigned for ever over our fallen race; but thanks be to God, Christ hath given us the victory; so that the believer may even now say, O death, where is thy sting? O grave, where is thy victory?

58. Therefore, my beloved brethren, be ye steadfast, unmoveable, always abounding in the work of the Lord, forasmuch as ye know that your labour is not in vain in the Lord.

Such being the truth and importance of the doctrine of the resurrection, Christians should be firm in their adherence to it, not suffering themselves to be moved by the specious objections of philosophy falsely so called. They should remember that if the dead rise not, then is Christ not risen; and if Christ be not risen, their faith is vain, and they are yet in the power of sin. But as Christ has risen, and as his resurrection illustrates and renders certain that of his people, what more natural and proper than that they should abound in the work of the Lord. *The work of the Lord* is either that work in which the Lord is engaged, the destruction of death by destroying sin; or, it is the work which the Lord has given us to do, as parents and children, as husbands and wives, as ministers and Christians. In this work we should abound, i. e. be abundant. As Paul says, 2 Cor. 11, 23, "In labours more abundant." *Forasmuch as ye know that your labour is not in vain in the Lord.* This with Paul was more than faith; it was knowledge. He knew that labour in the work of the Lord would not be in vain. The reward secured for it by the grace of God and merit of Christ is participation of the glories of a blessed resurrection.

CHAPTER XVI.

Treats, 1. Of the collection to be made for the saints in Jerusalem, vs. 1–9. 2. Of Timothy and Apollos, whom the apostle commends to the confidence of the Corinthians, vs. 10–14. 3. The third paragraph contains exhortations and greetings, vs. 15–20. 4. The last paragraph is the salutation written with Paul's own hand, vs. 21–24.

Concerning the Collection for the Saints at Jerusalem.

FOR some reason not now to be certainly ascertained, poverty prevailed in Jerusalem among the believers more than in any other part of the church. Almost all the special exhortations to provide for the poor, in Paul's epistles, have primary reference to the poor in Jerusalem. He had exhorted the churches of Galatia to make a collection for their relief; and then those of Macedonia, and he now addresses the Corinthians on the subject. It is a very common opinion that the poverty of the Christians in Jerusalem arose from the community of goods introduced among them at the beginning; an error which arose from an excess of love over knowledge. In thirty years that mistake may have produced its legitimate effects. Perfection in one thing requires perfection in all. Perfect equality in goods requires perfect freedom from selfishness and indolence. The collection made by the Syrian churches, as recorded in Acts 11, 29, was in consequence of the dearth the Christian prophet Agabus warned his brethren was to come on all the world. Whatever may have been the cause, the fact is certain that the saints in Jerusalem stood in special need of the assistance of their richer brethren. Paul, therefore, undervalued and suspected as he was by the Jewish Christians, laboured assiduously in their behalf. He exhorts the Corinthians to adopt the same arrangements in reference to this matter, which he had established in the churches of Galatia. A contribution was to be made on the Lord's day every week, proportioned to their resources, so that the collection might be ready when he came, vs. 1. 2. He would either send it by persons whom they might approve to Jerusalem, or if the sum were of sufficient magnitude to make it worth while, he would himself accompany their messengers, vs. 3. 4. He announces his purpose to visit the Corinthians after having passed over Macedonia, and perhaps to pass the winter with them. His prospects of usefulness in Ephesus would detain him in that city until Pentecost, vs. 5–9.

As *to Timothy and Apollos* he exhorts them to treat the former in such a manner that he might be free from fear among them, for he was worthy of their confidence, vs. 10. 11. Of the latter he says he had urged him to go to Corinth with the other brethren, but that he was unwilling to do so then, but would go when a suitable occasion offered, vs. 12–14. He exhorts them to submission to the household of Stephanas, and to every one who was labouring in the good cause, vs. 15. 16. He expresses his gratification in seeing the brethren from Corinth, and sends salutations from those around him to the Christians in Achaia, vs. 17–20. The conclusion of the epistle was written with his own hand as an authentification of the whole, vs. 21–24.

1. Now concerning the collection for the saints, as I have given order to the churches of Galatia, even so do ye.

But concerning the collection which is for the saints. What saints were intended was already known to the Corinthians. Instead of *for the saints*, in Rom. 15, 26 we have the more definite expression, "for the poor of the saints who are in Jerusalem," in whose behalf, he tells the Romans, Macedonia and Achaia had made a contribution. The Greek word λογία, in the sense of συλλογή, *collection*, is only found in this passage. *As I have given orders*, i. e. as I arranged or ordered. This is the language of authority. For although these contributions were voluntary, and were required to be made cheerfully, 2 Cor. 9, 7, yet they were a duty, and therefore both the collection itself, and the mode in which it should be accomplished, were proper subjects for apostolic direction. In the epistle to the Galatians there is no mention of this collection. It was probably ordered when Paul visited those churches. *So do ye*, i. e. adopt the same plan as to the mode of making the collection. What that was, is stated in the following verse.

2. Upon the first (day) of the week let every one of you lay by him in store, as (God) hath prospered him, that there be no gatherings when I come.

The collection was to be made every Lord's day; every one was to contribute; and the contributions were to be in proportion to the means of the giver. These are the three principles which the apostle had established among the churches of Galatia, and which he urged the Corinthians to adopt. *Upon the first day of the week*, literally, *upon one of the Sabbath*, according to the Jewish method of designating the days of the week. The Hebrew word, sabbath (*rest*), is used not only in the singular, but also in the plural form, both for the seventh day, and for the whole week, Luke 18, 12. That the first day of the week was, by divine appointment, made the sacred day for Christians, may be inferred, 1. From the distinction put upon that day by our Lord himself, John 20, 19. 26. 2. From the greatness of the event which its observance was intended to commemorate. The sanctification of the seventh day of the week was intended to keep in mind the great truth of the creation of the world, on which the whole system of revealed religion was founded; and as Christianity is founded on the resurrection of Christ, the day on which Christ rose became for that reason the Christian Sabbath. 3. From its being called by the apostle John the Lord's day, i. e. the day set apart for the service of the Lord, Rev. 1, 10. 4. From the evidence that it was from the beginning the day on which Christians assembled for worship, Acts 20, 7. 5. From the uniform practice of the whole church, which practice, having the clear evidence of apostolic sanction, is authoritative.

Let every one of you. It was an important feature of these apostolic arrangements, that the contributions were not to be confined to any one class of the people. The same amount might perhaps have been raised from the rich few. But this would not have answered one important end which the apostle had in view. It was the religious effect which these gifts were to produce in promoting Christian fellowship, in evincing the truth and power of the gospel, and in calling forth gratitude and praise to God, even more than the relief of the temporal necessities of the poor, that Paul desired to see accomplished, 2 Cor. 9, 12–14. Every one was to *lay by himself*, i. e. most modern commentators say, *at home*, παρ' ἑαυτῷ. Compare πρὸς ἑαυτόν, in Luke 24, 12; see also John 20, 10. The direction then is that every one should, on the first day of the week, lay aside at home whatever he was able to give, thus *treasuring up* his contribution. To this interpretation it may be objected that the whole expression is thus obscure and awkward. 'Let every one at home place, treasuring up what he has to give.' The words do not mean *to lay by at home*, but *to lay by himself*. The direction is nothing more definite than, *let him place by himself*, i. e. let him take to himself what he means to give. What he was to do with it, or where he was to deposit it, is not expressed. The word θησαυρίζων means *putting into the treasury*, or *hoarding up*, and is perfectly consistent with the assumption that the place of deposit was some common treasury, and not every man's own house. 2. If Paul directed this money to be laid up *at home*, why was the first day of the week selected? It is evident that the first day must have offered some special facility for doing what is here enjoined. The only reason that can be assigned for requiring the thing to be done on the first day of the week, is, that on that day the Christians were accustomed to meet, and what each one had laid aside from his weekly gains could be treasured up, i. e. put into the common treasury of the church. 3. The end which the apostle desired to accomplish could not otherwise have been effected. He wished that *there might be no collections when he came.* But if every man had his money laid by at home, the collection would be still to be made. The probability is, therefore, Paul intended to direct the Corinthians to make a collection every Lord's day for the poor, when they met for worship. *As God hath prospered him;* literally, *whatever has gone well with him.* He was to lay aside what by his success in business he was able to give. This is another principle which the apostle would have Christians to act upon. Their contribution should be in proportion to their means.

3. And when I come, whomsoever ye shall approve by (your) letters, them will I send to bring your liberality unto Jerusalem.

Paul was not to receive the money himself. It was to be given to men selected and approved by the Corinthians, whom Paul promised to send, furnished with letters from himself, to Jerusalem. The words δι' ἐπιστολῶν, *with letters*, are not to be connected with what precedes, "approved by *your* letters," but with what follows, "I will send with letters." Otherwise there would have been no need of Paul's sending them, i. e. the persons approved by the Corinthians. The people were to collect the money; it was to be committed to men of their own selection; but Paul, as the author of the collection, was to send it to Jerusalem. If the apostle deemed it wise to place himself above suspicion, and to avoid giving even the most malicious the opportunity of calling his integrity in question, as is intimated here, and expressly stated in 2 Cor. 8, 19. 20, it must be wise for other men and ministers to act with equal caution. If called to disburse the money of others or of the church, let that money, if possible, be in some other custody than their own, that others may know what is done with it. Thus at least Paul acted.

4. And if it be meet that I go also, they shall go with me.

And if it is deserving of my going; that is, if the collection be of an amount to make it proper for me also to go with it to Jerusalem, your messengers shall go with me. According to Acts 19, 21, Paul purposed, after visiting Macedonia and Achaia, to go to Jerusalem. But whether he would go at the time the contribution of the Corinthians was sent, depended on its amount. He would not modify his plans for the sake of having charge of the distribution of an inconsiderable sum.

5. Now I will come unto you, when I shall pass through Macedonia: for I do pass through Macedonia.

It appears from 2 Cor. 1, 15. 16, that Paul's original plan was to go directly from Ephesus to Corinth, and from there into Macedonia, and then back again to Corinth, and thence to Jerusalem. He now informs them that he would go to Macedonia before going to Corinth. So eager were the false teachers in Corinth to find grounds of complaint against him, that they made this change of plan a grievous offence, and a proof that he was not to be depended upon either as to his purposes or his doctrine. This is apparent from the vindication of himself in the second Epistle. *For I do pass through Macedonia;* not, *I am passing;* the present tense expresses the purpose of the apostle as settled. The mistake as to the force of the tense here, probably led transcribers to date this epistle from Philippi; whereas, it is clear from v. 8, that it was written from Ephesus.

6. And it may be that I will abide, yea, and winter with you, that ye may bring me on my journey whithersoever I go.

'I pass through Macedonia, but I will abide with you.' His visit to the former was to be transient, to the latter prolonged. In the second Epistle he speaks of himself as in Macedonia, and in Acts 20, 2. 3, we find that he left Ephesus after the uproar in that city and went to Macedonia, and thence to Greece, where he abode three months. The plan here sketched was therefore executed. He would remain with them for the winter, he says, *in order that* they might help him forward on his journey, i. e. attend him on his way, which was the customary mark of respect. Paul wished to receive this courtesy from the Corinthians rather than from others, as his affection for them, notwithstanding the trouble and anxiety they occasioned him was, as is evident from his second Epistle, peculiarly strong.

7. For I will not see you now by the way; but I trust to tarry a while with you, if the Lord permit.

By some ἄρτι, *now*, is connected with ϑέλω, *I will.* 'I do not now wish, as I formerly intended.' Its natural connection is with ἰδεῖν, *to see.* 'I do not wish to see you now in passing.' "*But* I hope;" instead of δέ, *but*, the older MSS. read γάρ; "*for* I hope to tarry with you." It seems that the intelligence which Paul received in Ephesus concerning the disorders in Corinth, determined him to write them this letter, instead of making them a passing visit, and to defer his visit for some months in order that his letter might have time to produce its effect. The same reason determined him, when he did go to Corinth, to remain there some time, that he might correct the abuses which had sprung up in his absence. The second Epistle shows how anxious he was about the effect of this letter, and how overjoyed he was when Titus brought him the intelligence that it had brought the people to repentance. *If the Lord permit*, (ἐπιτρέπῃ), or, 'If the Lord shall have permitted' (ἐπιτρέψῃ). The latter reading is adopted by the later editors. *The Lord* is Christ, whom Paul recognized as order ing all events, and whose guidance he sought and always sub mitted to.

8. 9. But I will tarry at Ephesus until Pentecost. For a great door and effectual is opened unto me, and (there are) many adversaries.

There were two reasons, therefore, for his remaining at Ephesus, his abundant opportunities of usefulness, and the necessity of withstanding the adversaries of the gospel. Paul's plan was to spend the spring at Ephesus, the summer in Macedonia, and the winter in Corinth. The Pentecost of the following year he spent in Jerusalem. He could not leave Ephesus soon, *for*, he says, *a great and effectual door is opened to me. A door* is a way of entrance, and figuratively an opportunity of entering into the possession of the convictions and hearts of men. A great door was opened to the apostle, he had a wide field of usefulness. The epithet *effectual* does not agree with the figure, but the meaning is plain—the opportunities were such as could be turned to good effect. *And there are many adversaries.* The opponents of the gospel varied very much in character in different places. Those in Ephesus were principally men interested in the worship of Diana. The pressure of the heathen seems to have driven the Jews and Christians to make common cause, Acts 19, 22. Whereas, in Corinth, Paul's most bitter opponents were Judaizers. The presence of such violent adversaries rendered the personal support of the apostle more necessary to the church.

10. Now if Timotheus come, see that he may be with you without fear: for he worketh the work of the Lord, as I also (do.)

In Acts 19, 22, we read that Paul "sent into Macedonia two of those who ministered to him, Timotheus and Erastus; but he himself stayed in Asia for a season." Timothy, therefore, at this time, was travelling through Macedonia, and expected to reach Corinth, whither the apostle had sent him; see 4, 17. Besides this mission of Timothy, there was another some time later, consisting of Titus and other brethren, who were sent to learn the effect produced by this letter; and whose return the apostle so anxiously awaited, 2 Cor. 2, 12. 13. Paul requests the Corinthians so to receive Timothy that he might be there *without fear.* It was not fear of personal violence, but the fear of not being regarded with respect and confidence. The reason by which he enforces his request shows the nature of the evil which he apprehended, *for he worketh the work of the Lord.* If they would recognize this, Timothy would be satisfied. *The work of the Lord*, as in 15, 58, may mean either that work in which the Lord himself is engaged; or that which he has prescribed. *As I also do.* A comprehensive commendation. Timothy preached the same gospel that Paul preached; and with like assiduity and fidelity.

11. Let no man therefore despise him: but conduct him forth in peace, that he may come unto me: for I look for him with the brethren.

Therefore, i. e. because he works the work of the Lord, he is entitled to respect, and ought not to be despised. Perhaps it was Timothy's youth that made the apostle specially solicitous on this account, 1 Tim. 4, 12. *But conduct him forth in peace;* i. e. attend him on his journey in a friendly manner. *That he may come to me.* It was not Paul's wish that Timothy should remain in Corinth; but after having executed his commission, 4, 17, he was to return to the apostle. He did thus return, and was with Paul when he wrote the second Epistle, 2 Cor. 1, 1. *I expect him with the brethren*, i. e. the brethren whom Paul had appointed as Timothy's travelling companions. It is rare in the New Testament that we read of any one going on a missionary tour alone.

12. As touching (our) brother Apollos, I greatly desired him to come unto you with the brethren: but his will was not at all to come at this time; but he will come when he shall have convenient time.

Either the Corinthians, among whom Apollos had already laboured, had requested Paul to send him to them again; or for some other reason, the apostle earnestly wished that he would accompany the brethren from Corinth, who were to carry this epistle back with them; see v. 17. It appears from this verse that Apollos was not under Paul's authority. No reason is given for his declining to go to Corinth but that he was not willing. Why he was not willing is matter of conjecture. Many suppose it was because his name had been mixed up with the party strifes which disturbed the church there,

1, 12. *I greatly desired him ;* or, *I often exhorted him, that he would come,* &c. ἵνα does not here mean, *in order that,* but indicates the purport of the request.

13. 14. Watch ye, stand fast in the faith, quit you like men, be strong. Let all your things be done with charity.

These concise exhortations form a fitting close to the epistle; each being adapted to the peculiar circumstances of the Corinthians, though of course applicable to all Christians in their conflicts with the world. 1. He exhorts *them to watch,* i. e. to be wakeful, constantly on the alert, that their spiritual enemies might not gain advantage over them before they were aware of their danger. 2. Beset as they were with false teachers, who handled deceitfully the word of God, 2 Cor. 4, 2, he exhorts them to *stand fast in the faith.* Do not consider every point of doctrine an open question. Matters of faith, doctrines for which you have a clear revelation of God, such for example as the doctrine of the resurrection, are to be considered settled, and, as among Christians, no longer matters of dispute. There are doctrines embraced in the creeds of all orthodox churches, so clearly taught in Scripture, that it is not only useless, but hurtful, to be always calling them into question. 3. *Quit you like men.* The circumstances of the Corinthians called for great courage. They had to withstand the contempt of the learned, and the persecutions of the powerful. 4. *Be strong.* Not only courage, but strength, was needed to withstand their enemies, and to bear up under the trials which were to come upon them. 5. *Let all your affairs be conducted in love,* i. e. let love prevail, in your hearts, in your families, in your assemblies. The preceding parts of the epistle show how much need there was for this exhortation; as the church was rent with factions, and even the Lord's supper, every where else a feast of love, had become in Corinth a fountain of bitterness.

15. 16. I beseech you, brethren, [ye know the house of Stephanas, that it is the first-fruits of Achaia, and (that) they have addicted themselves to the ministry of the saints,] that ye submit yourselves unto such, and to every one that helpeth with (us,) and laboureth.

The family of Stephanas was the first family in Achaia that embraced the gospel. In Rom. 16, 5, Epenetus, according to the common text, is said to have been the first fruits of *Achaia;* but there the true reading is *Asia;* so that there is no conflict between the two passages. Of the family of Stephanas it is said, that *they addicted themselves to the ministering of the saints*, i. e. devoted themselves to the service of believers. The expression does not necessarily involve the idea of any official service. The exhortation is, *that ye also submit yourselves to such.* 'As they serve you, do you serve them.' Nothing is more natural than submission to the good. *And to every one that helpeth with* (such), *and laboureth.* This may mean, submit yourselves to every one who co-operates with such persons; i. e. to all who in like manner are addicted to the service of believers. Those who serve, should be served.

17. I am glad of the coming of Stephanas and Fortunatus and Achaicus: for that which was lacking on your part they have supplied.

These were members of the church in Corinth, who visited Ephesus probably for the express purpose of seeing the apostle, and of consulting him on the condition of the church. They were probably the bearers of the letter from the Corinthians to Paul, to which he alludes in 7, 1. The reason why he rejoiced in their presence was, that they *supplied what was lacking on the part of the Corinthians;* or rather, *the want of you* (τὸ ὑμέτερον ὑστέρημα; ὑμέτερον being objective, as in 15, 31.) The presence of these brethren made up to the apostle, in a measure, the absence of the Corinthians. Another explanation is, 'they have done what you failed to do,' i. e. informed me of the true state of things in Corinth. The former view of the meaning is the common one, and is more in keeping with the tone of the passage, which is affectionate and conciliatory. This too is confirmed by what follows.

18. For they have refreshed my spirit and yours: therefore acknowledge ye them that are such.

For, i. e. They have supplied your place, for their presence has had the same effect as would have followed from our being together. It has refreshed me, and it has had a corresponding effect on you. 'To them,' as Meyer and others explain it, 'you owe whatever in my letter serves to refresh you.' Others think that the apostle refers to the effect of the return of these brethren to Corinth, and the assurances they would carry with them of the apostle's love. Or, Paul may mean, that what refreshed him, must also gratify them. They would rejoice in his joy. However understood, it is one of the examples of urbanity with which this apostle's writings abound. *Therefore acknowledge them that are such*, i. e. recognize and appreciate them properly.

19. The churches of Asia salute you. Aquila and Priscilla salute you much in the Lord, with the church that is in their house.

Asia here means proconsular Asia, of which Ephesus was the capital, and which included the seven apocalyptic churches. *To salute*, in a general sense, is to wish safety to; in a Christian sense, it is to wish salvation to any one. This was included in the Hebrew formula of salutation, "Peace be with you," which passed into the service of Christians. To salute any one *in the Lord*, is to salute him as a Christian and in a Christian manner. It is to salute him because he is in the Lord, and in a way acceptable to the Lord. Aquila and Priscilla, when driven from Rome, as mentioned in Acts 18, 2, settled in Corinth. They accompanied the apostle to Ephesus, and remained there, Acts 18, 18. *The church which is in their house*, i. e. the company of Christians which meet in their house. As the same expression is used Rom. 16, 5, in connection with their names, it is probable that both at Rome and Ephesus, they opened their house as a regular place of meeting for Christians. Their occupation as tent-makers probably required spacious apartments, suited for the purpose of such assemblies.

20. All the brethren greet you. Greet ye one another with a holy kiss.

As *all the brethren* in this verse are distinguished from the church in the house of Aquila and Priscilla, mentioned in v. 19, it may be inferred that only a portion, and probably a small portion of the Christians of Ephesus were accustomed to meet in that place. The apostle exhorts them to *greet one another with a holy kiss*, Rom. 16, 16. 2 Cor. 13, 12. 1 Thess. 5, 26.

This was the conventional token of Christian affection. In the East the kiss was a sign either of friendship among equals, or of reverence and submission on the part of an inferior. The people kissed the images of their gods, and the hands of princes. In the early church, the custom was for Christians when they met to kiss; and in their assemblies, especially after the Lord's supper, this token of Christian brotherhood was interchanged. Paul seems here to request, that when his letter was publicly read, the members of the church would give to each other this pledge of mutual forgiveness and love.

21. The salutation of (me) Paul with mine own hand.

As Paul commonly wrote by an amanuensis, he was accustomed to write with his own hand the concluding sentences of his epistle as an authentication of them, Col. 4, 18. 2 Thess. 3, 17. He remarks in Gal. 6, 11, on his having written that epistle with his own hand as something unusual, and as indicating a peculiar stress of feeling.

22. If any man love not the Lord Jesus Christ, let him be Anathema. Maran atha.

This and what follows is what Paul himself wrote. They are words which need no explanation. They carry with them their awful import to every heart. *If any man love not our Lord Jesus Christ.* If our Lord be "God over all and blessed for ever," want of love to him is the violation of our whole duty. If he be not only truly God, but God manifested in the flesh for our salvation; if he unites in himself all divine and all human excellence; if he has so loved us as to unite our nature to his own, and to humble himself and become obedient unto death, even the death of the cross, that we might not perish, but have everlasting life; then our own hearts must assent to the justness of the malediction pronounced even against ourselves, if we do not love him. We must feel that in that case we deserve to be *anathema.* Nay, we thereby are a thing accursed; we are an object of execration and loathing to all holy beings by the same necessity that holiness is opposed to sin. *Maran atha* are two Aramæan words signifying "The Lord," or "our Lord comes." It is a solemn warning. The Lord, whom men refuse to recognize and love, is about to come in the glory of his Father and with all his holy angels, to take vengeance on those who know not God, and who obey not the gospel. So deeply were the apostles impressed with the divinity of Christ, so fully were they convinced that Jesus was God manifest in the flesh, that the refusal or inability to recognize him as such, seemed to them a mark of reprobation. If this truth be hid, they say, it is hid to them that are lost, 2 Cor. 4, 3–6.

23. The grace of our Lord Jesus Christ (be) with you.

As to be anathema from Christ, to be the subject of his curse, is everlasting perdition; so his favour is eternal life. "May his love be with you," is a prayer for all good.

24. My love (be) with you all in Christ Jesus. Amen.

"My love in Christ" is my Christian love. Paul in conclusion assures them all, all the believers in Corinth, even those whom he had been called upon to reprove, of his sincere love.

THE END.